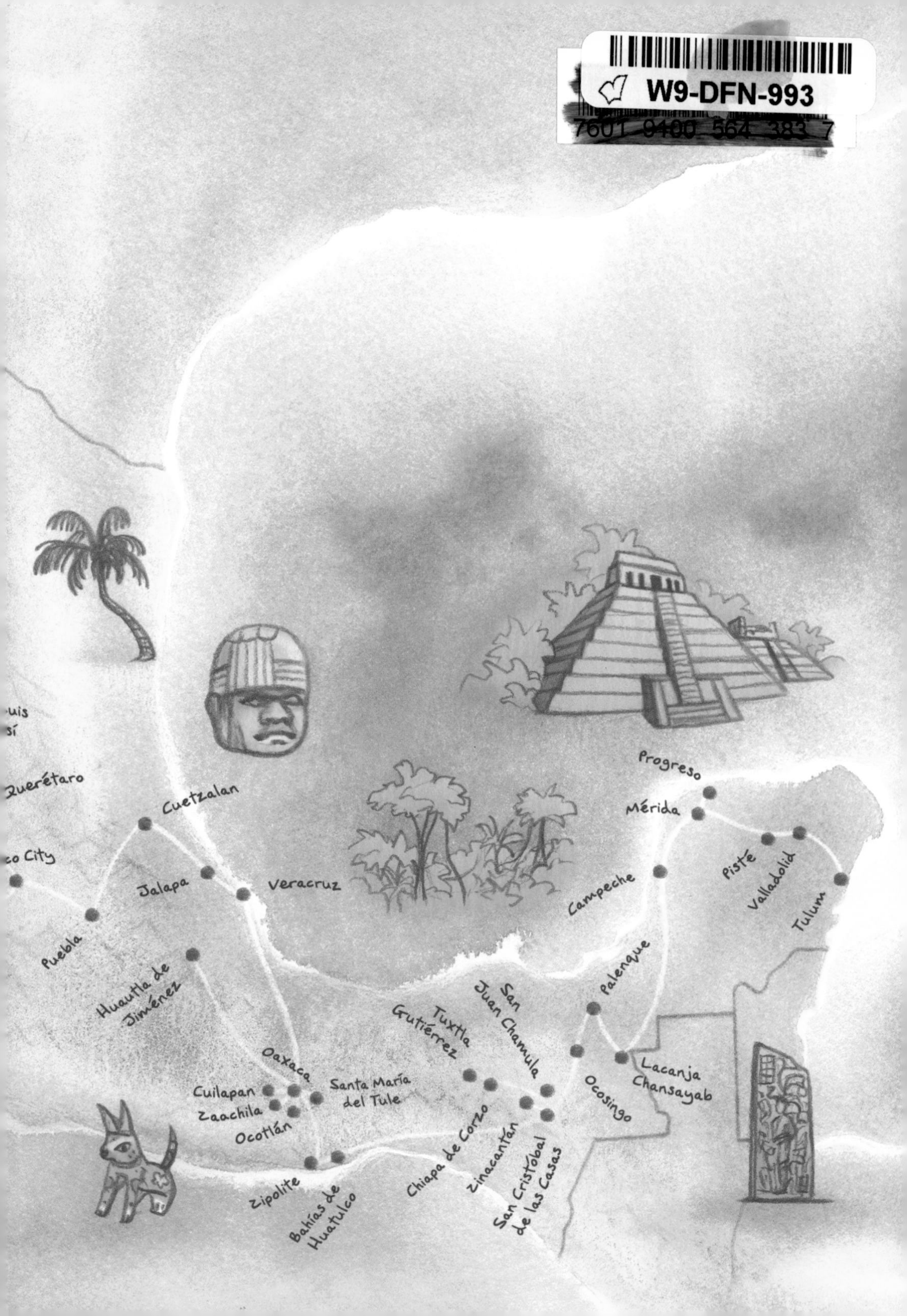

uis
sí
Querétaro
Cuetzalan
co City
Jalapa
Veracruz
Puebla
Huautla de Jiménez
Oaxaca
Cuilapan
Zaachila
Ocotlán
Santa María del Tule
Zipolite
Bahías de Huatulco
Chiapa de Corzo
Tuxtla Gutiérrez
San Juan Chamula
Zinacantán
San Cristóbal de las Casas
Ocosingo
Palenque
Lacanja Chansayab
Campeche
Progreso
Mérida
Pisté
Valladolid
Tulum

follow me in

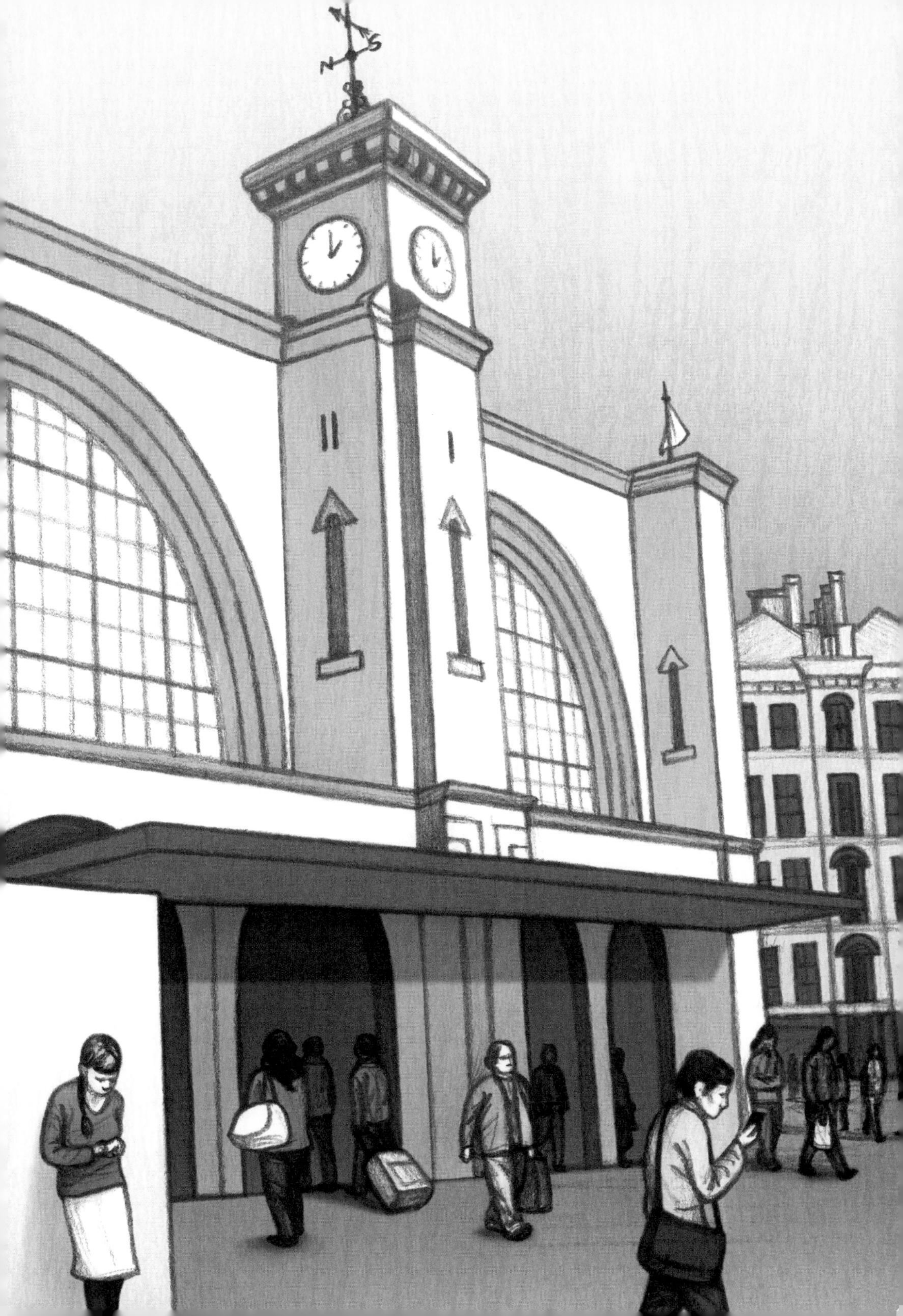

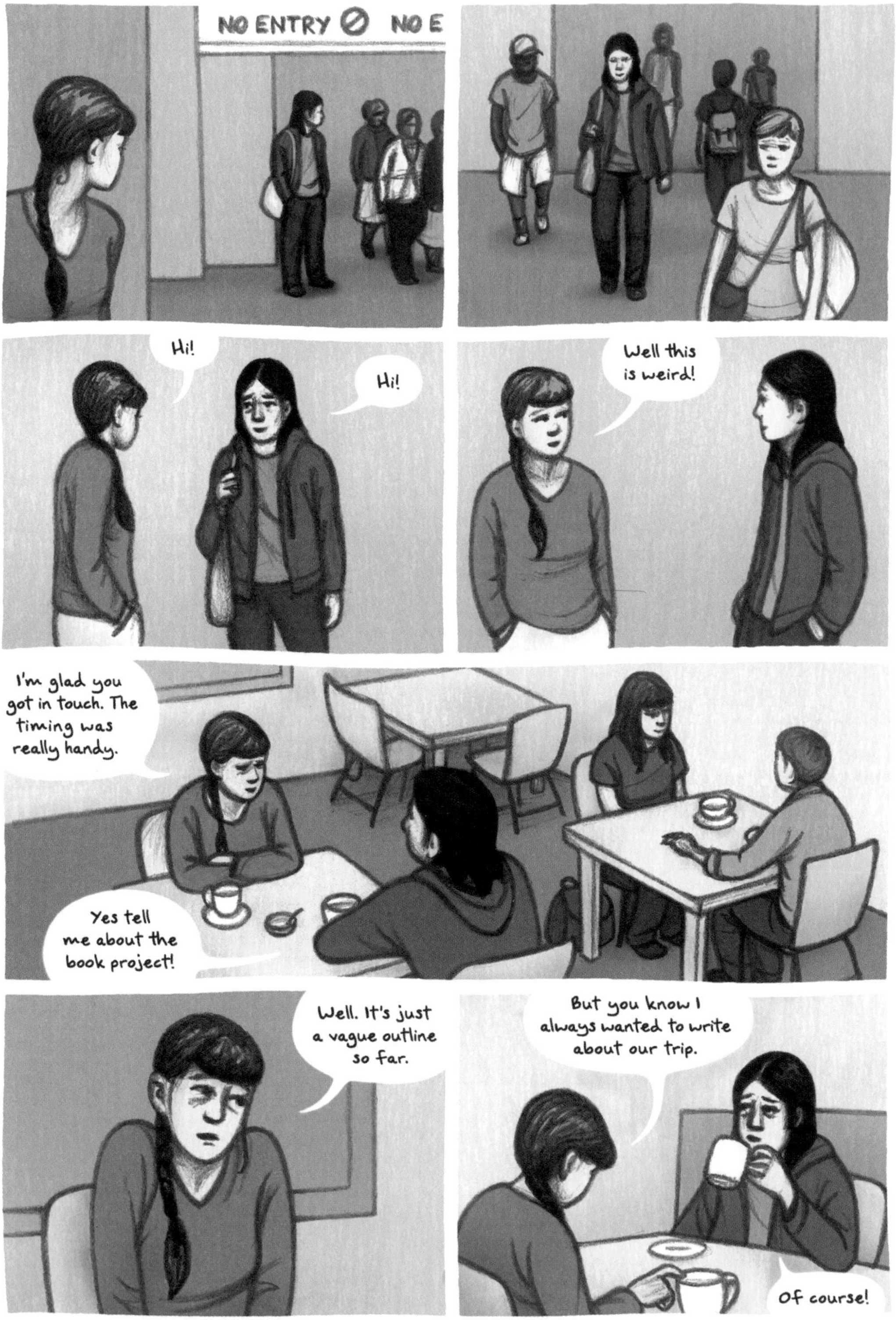
NO ENTRY NO E
Hi!
Hi!
Well this is weird!
I'm glad you got in touch. The timing was really handy.
Yes tell me about the book project!
Well. It's just a vague outline so far.
But you know I always wanted to write about our trip.
Of course!

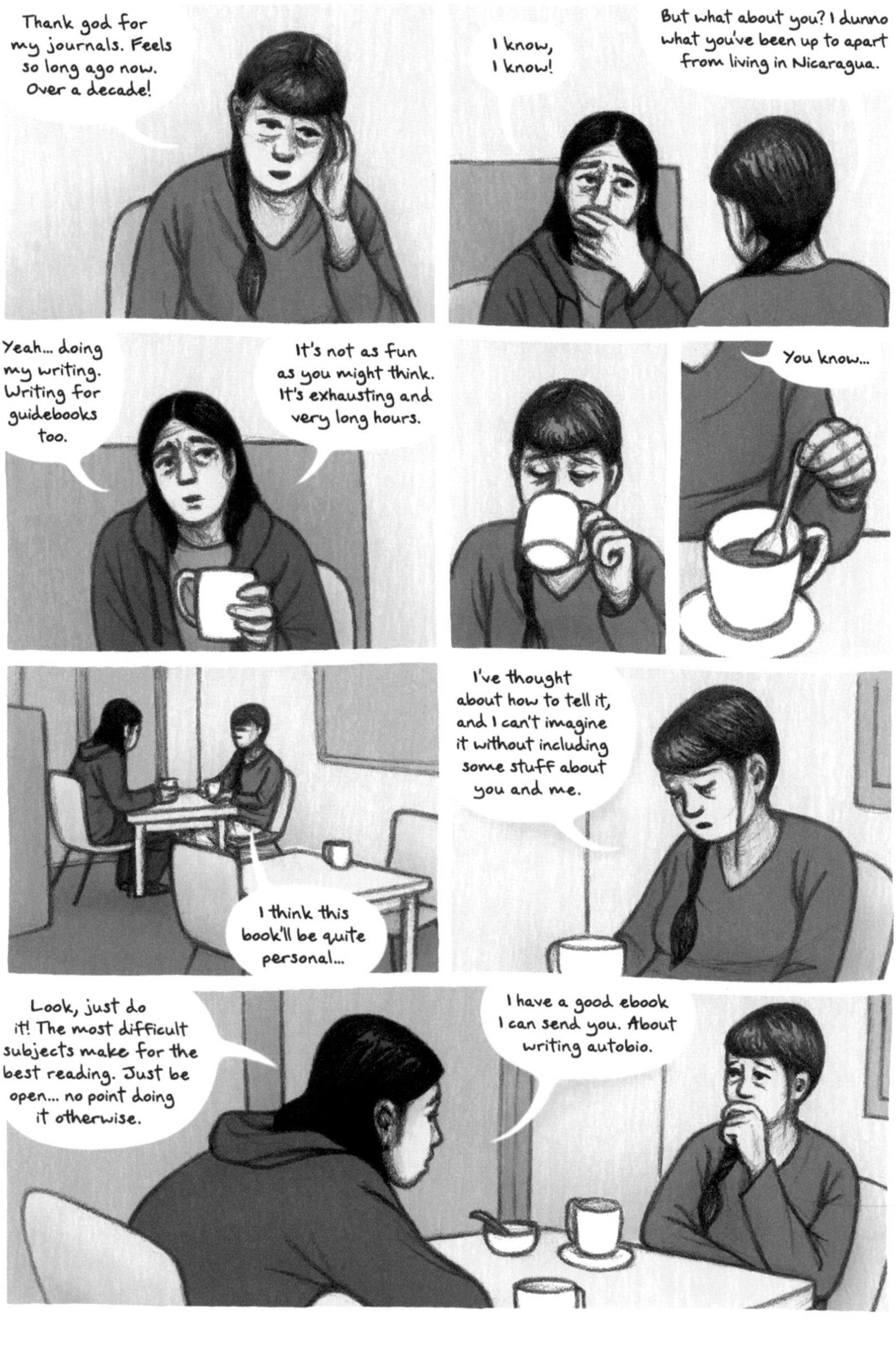
Thank god for my journals. Feels so long ago now. Over a decade!
I know, I know!
But what about you? I dunno what you've been up to apart from living in Nicaragua.
Yeah... doing my writing. Writing for guidebooks too.
It's not as fun as you might think. It's exhausting and very long hours.
You know...
I think this book'll be quite personal...
I've thought about how to tell it, and I can't imagine it without including some stuff about you and me.
Look, just do it! The most difficult subjects make for the best reading. Just be open... no point doing it otherwise.
I have a good ebook I can send you. About writing autobio.

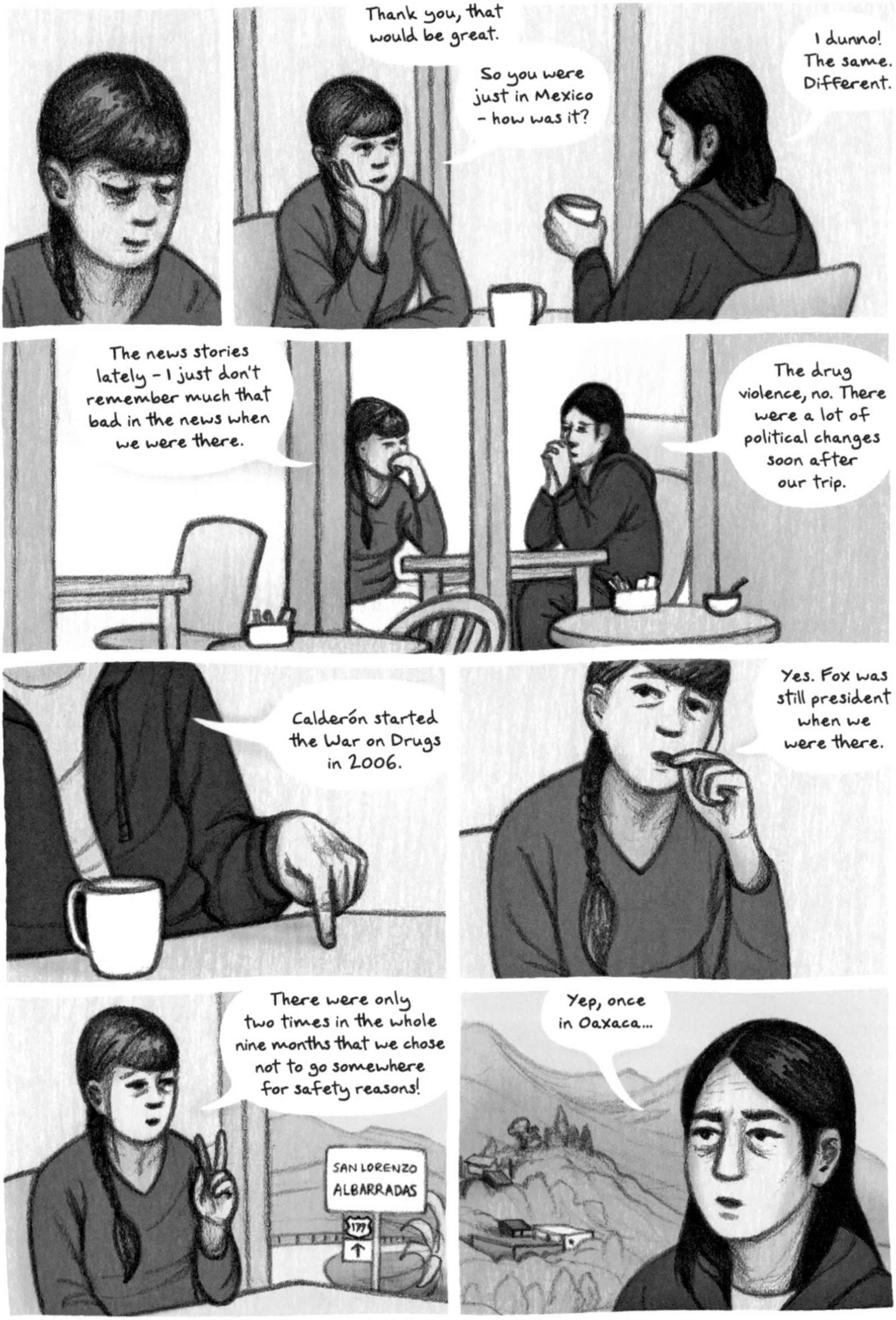
Thank you, that would be great.
So you were just in Mexico - how was it?
I dunno! The same. Different.
The news stories lately - I just don't remember much that bad in the news when we were there.
The drug violence, no. There were a lot of political changes soon after our trip.
Calderón started the War on Drugs in 2006.
Yes. Fox was still president when we were there.
There were only two times in the whole nine months that we chose not to go somewhere for safety reasons!
SAN LORENZO
ALBARRADAS
179
Yep, once in Oaxaca...

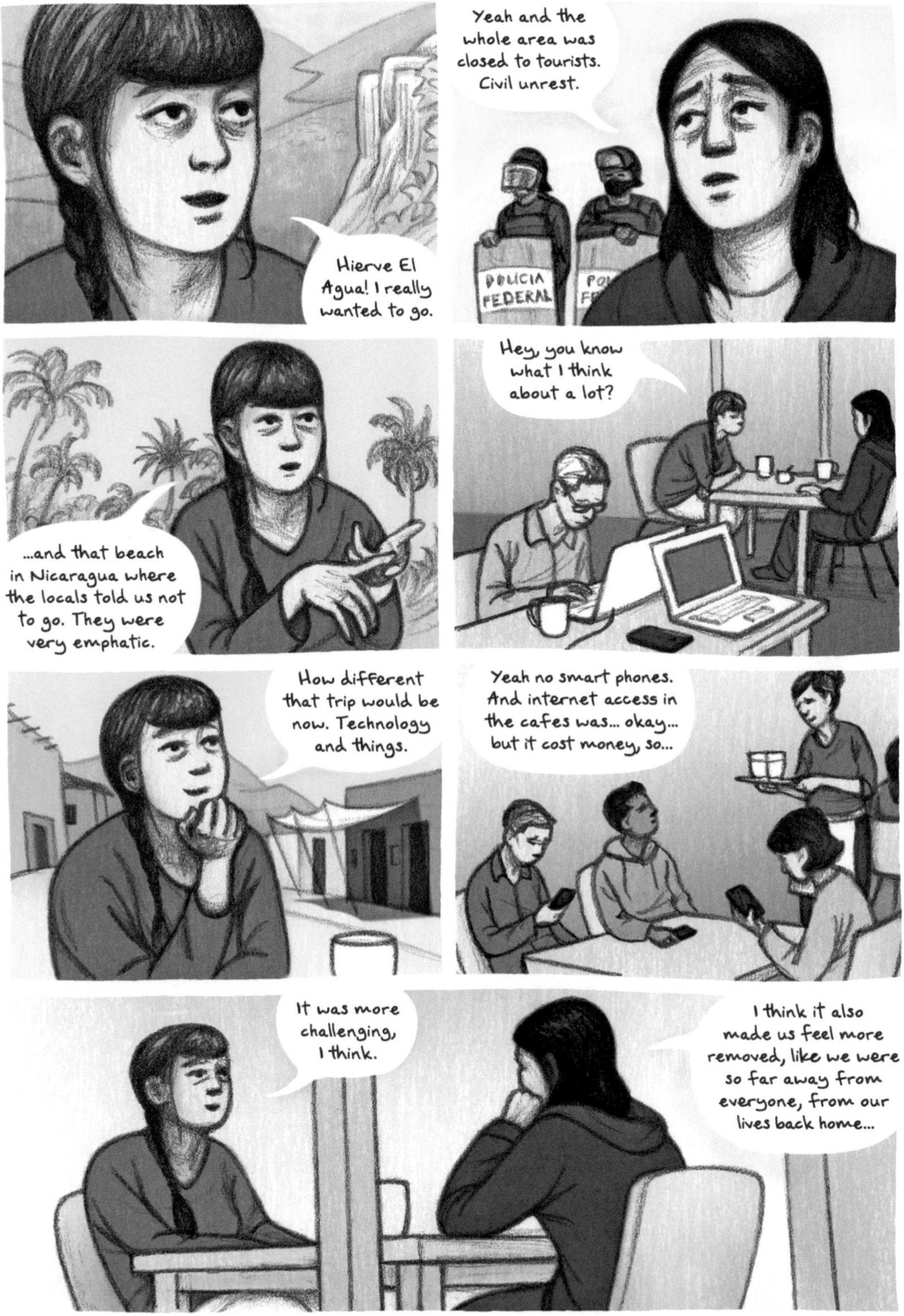
Hierve El Agua! I really wanted to go.
Yeah and the whole area was closed to tourists. Civil unrest.
POLICIA FEDERAL
...and that beach in Nicaragua where the locals told us not to go. They were very emphatic.
Hey, you know what I think about a lot?
How different that trip would be now. Technology and things.
Yeah no smart phones. And internet access in the cafes was... okay... but it cost money, so...
It was more challenging, I think.
I think it also made us feel more removed, like we were so far away from everyone, from our lives back home...

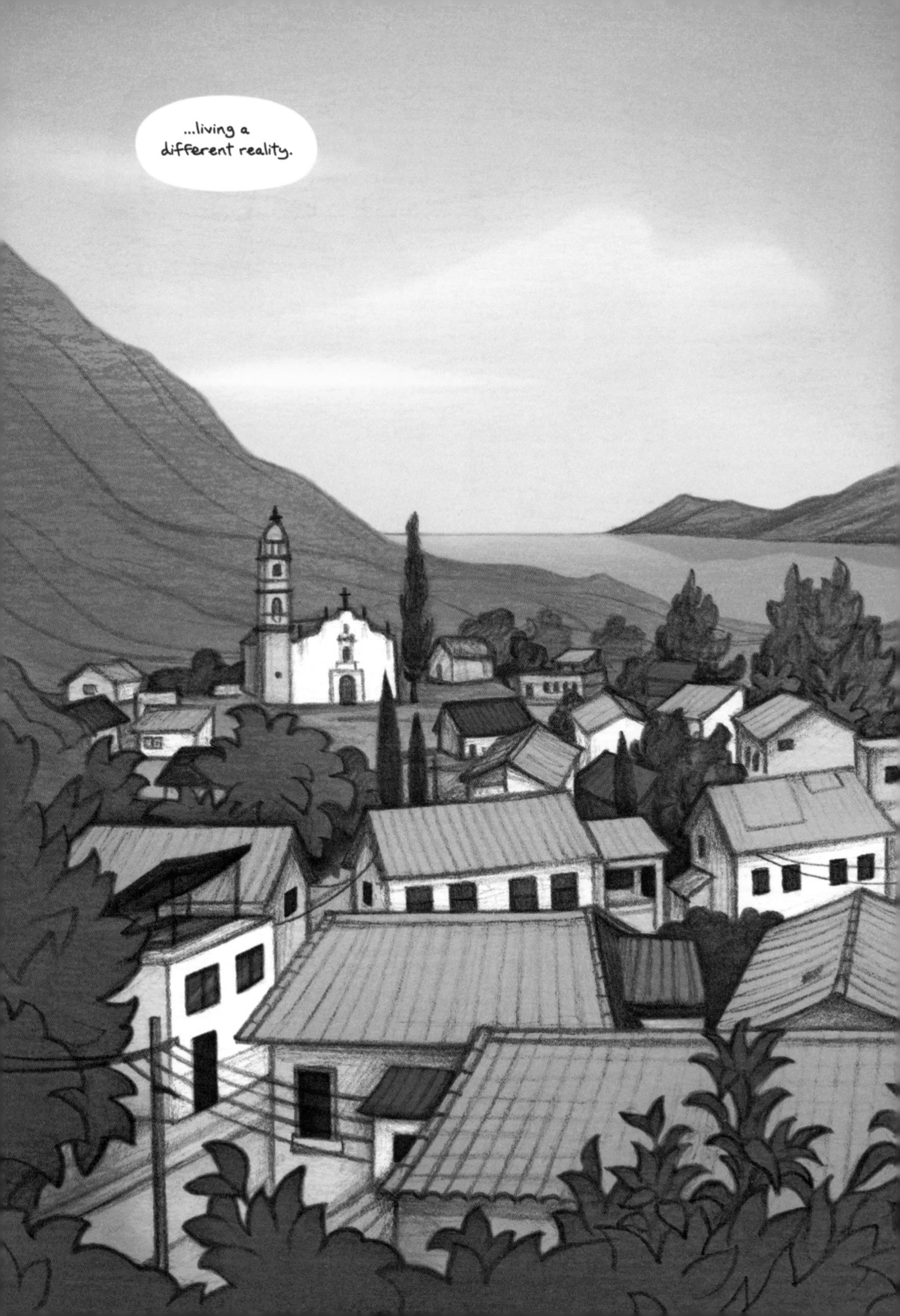
...living a different reality.

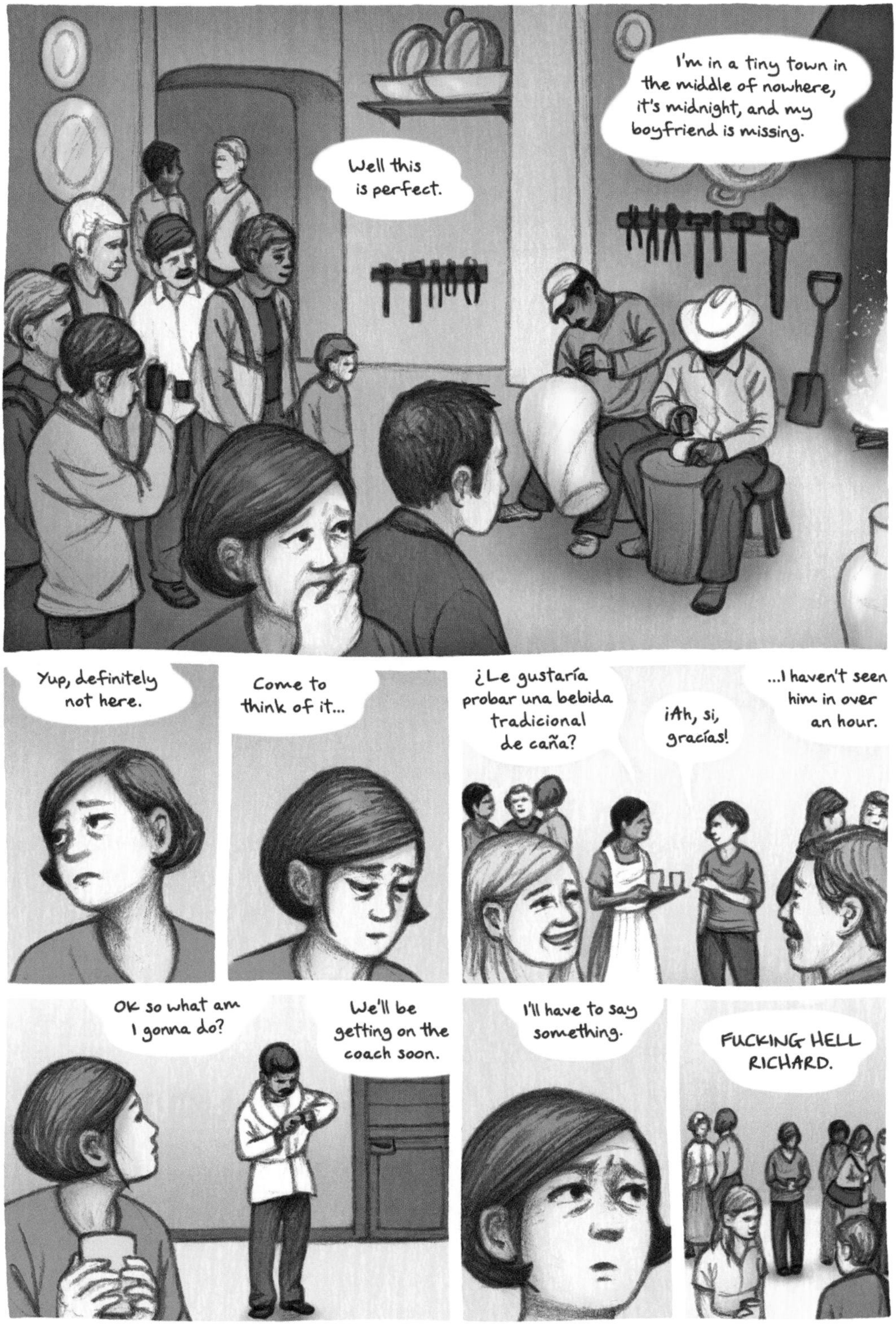
Well this is perfect.
I'm in a tiny town in the middle of nowhere, it's midnight, and my boyfriend is missing.
Yup, definitely not here.
Come to think of it...
¿Le gustaría probar una bebida tradicional de caña?
¡Ah, si, gracías!
...I haven't seen him in over an hour.
OK so what am I gonna do?
We'll be getting on the coach soon.
I'll have to say something.
FUCKING HELL RICHARD.

DIA DE LOS MUERTOS

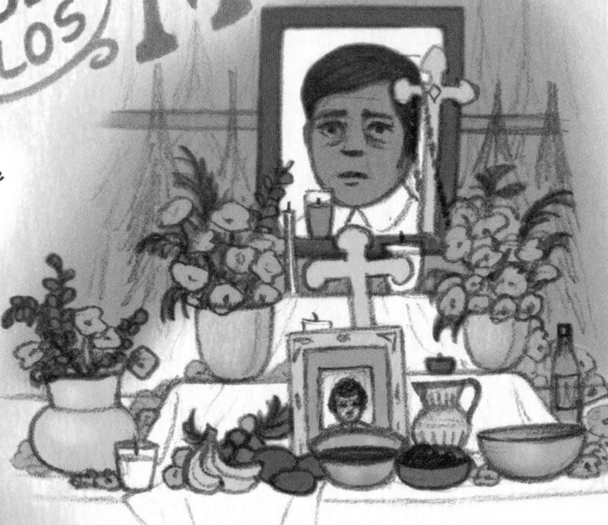

The Day of the Dead is a tradition where people gather to remember the dead, and help support their spiritual journey. Death is thought to be a continuation of life, and during the festival the souls of the dead return to visit the land of the living.

Like many pre-Hispanic traditions it became merged with western Christian customs, and came to be associated with Halloween.

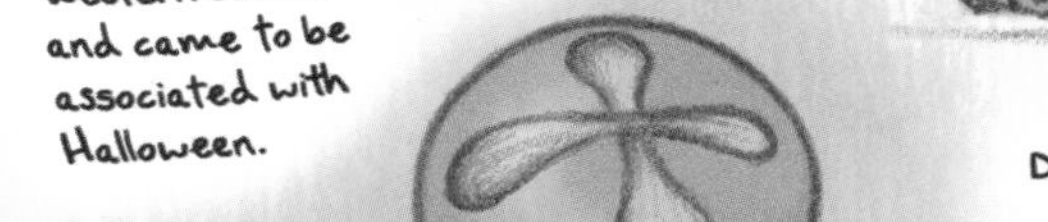

Day of the Dead practises vary from place to place. In the South there's an emphasis on street parades, whereas across central Mexico the focus is on the creation of altars in homes and the decoration of churchyards.

Offerings include photos, mementos and favourite foods and drinks. Toys for children, pan de muerto (bread of the dead) and sugar skulls. Marigolds are believed to attract the souls of the dead.

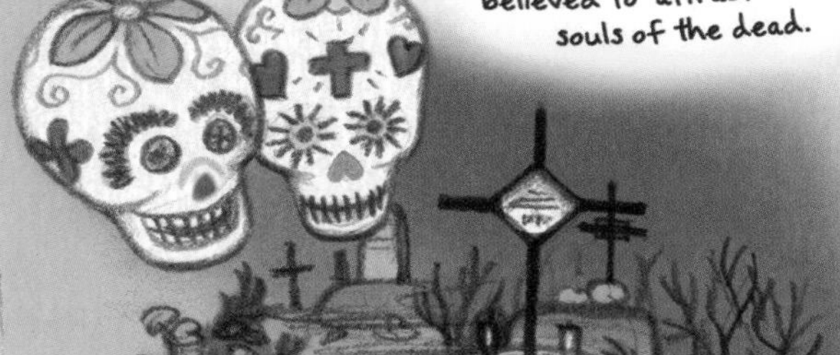

Valley of Mexico towns like Mixquic, Pátzcuaro and Janitzio are famous for all-night graveyard vigils. It's difficult for tourists to see the festivities – there's no public transport at night, so various companies offer all-night tours.

We had reservations about joining one of these... about how instrusive they might be. But we didn't find any other option. We ended up booking a tour that the organisers promised would be sensitive and discrete.

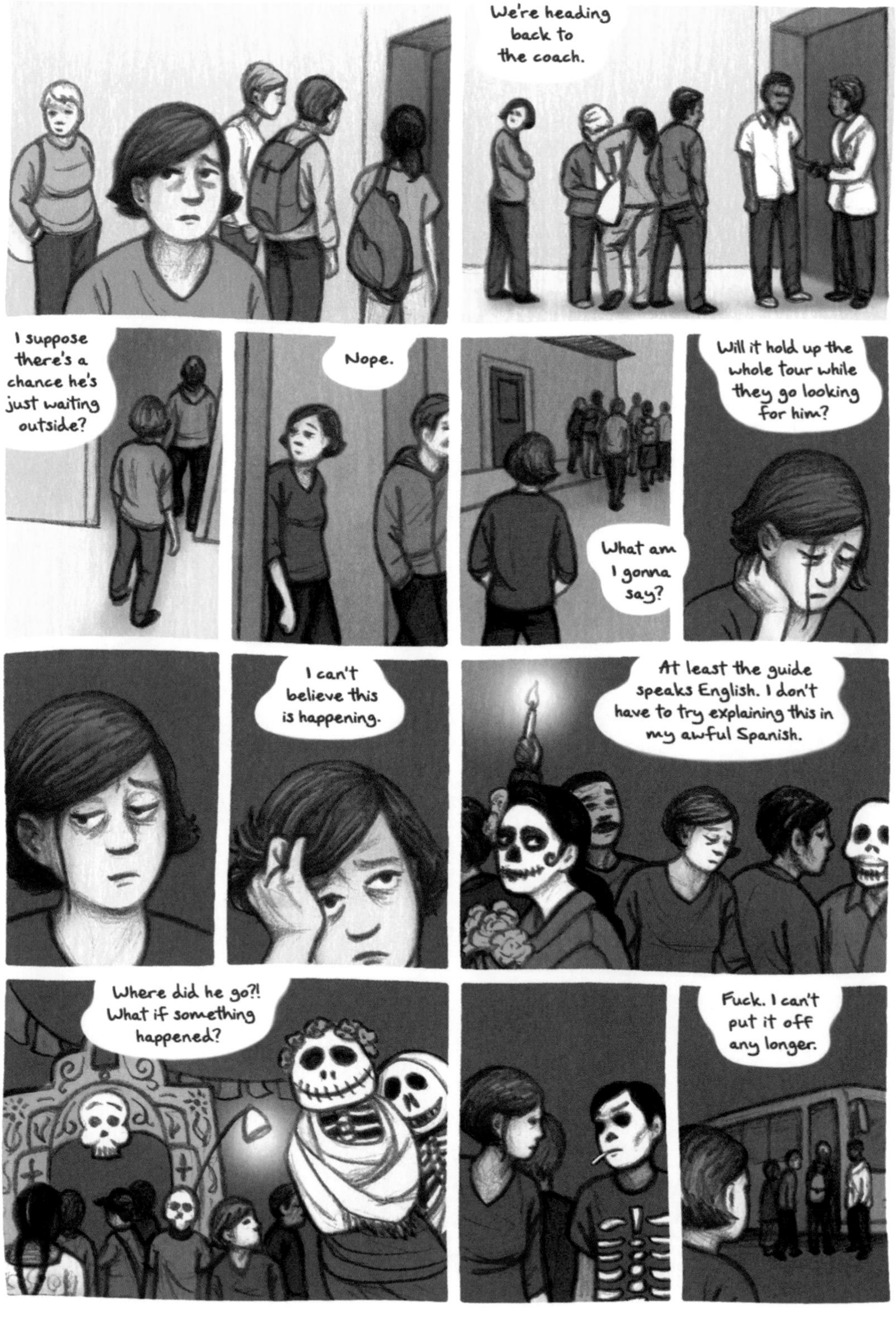
We're heading back to the coach.
I suppose there's a chance he's just waiting outside?
Nope.
What am I gonna say?
Will it hold up the whole tour while they go looking for him?
I can't believe this is happening.
At least the guide speaks English. I don't have to try explaining this in my awful Spanish.
Where did he go?! What if something happened?
Fuck. I can't put it off any longer.

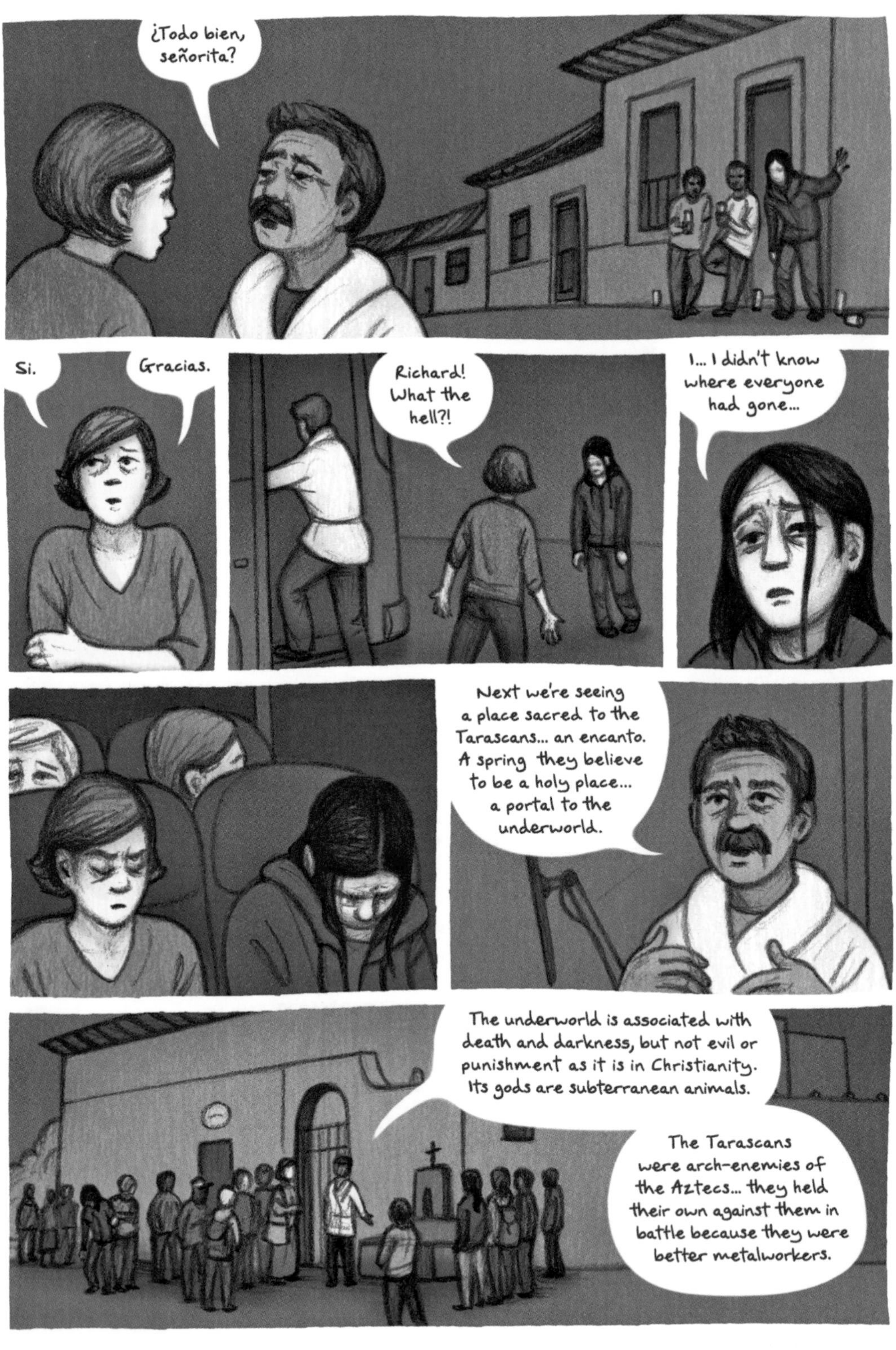
¿Todo bien, señorita?
Si.
Gracias.
Richard! What the hell?!
I... I didn't know where everyone had gone...
Next we're seeing a place sacred to the Tarascans... an encanto. A spring they believe to be a holy place... a portal to the underworld.
The underworld is associated with death and darkness, but not evil or punishment as it is in Christianity. Its gods are subterranean animals.
The Tarascans were arch-enemies of the Aztecs... they held their own against them in battle because they were better metalworkers.

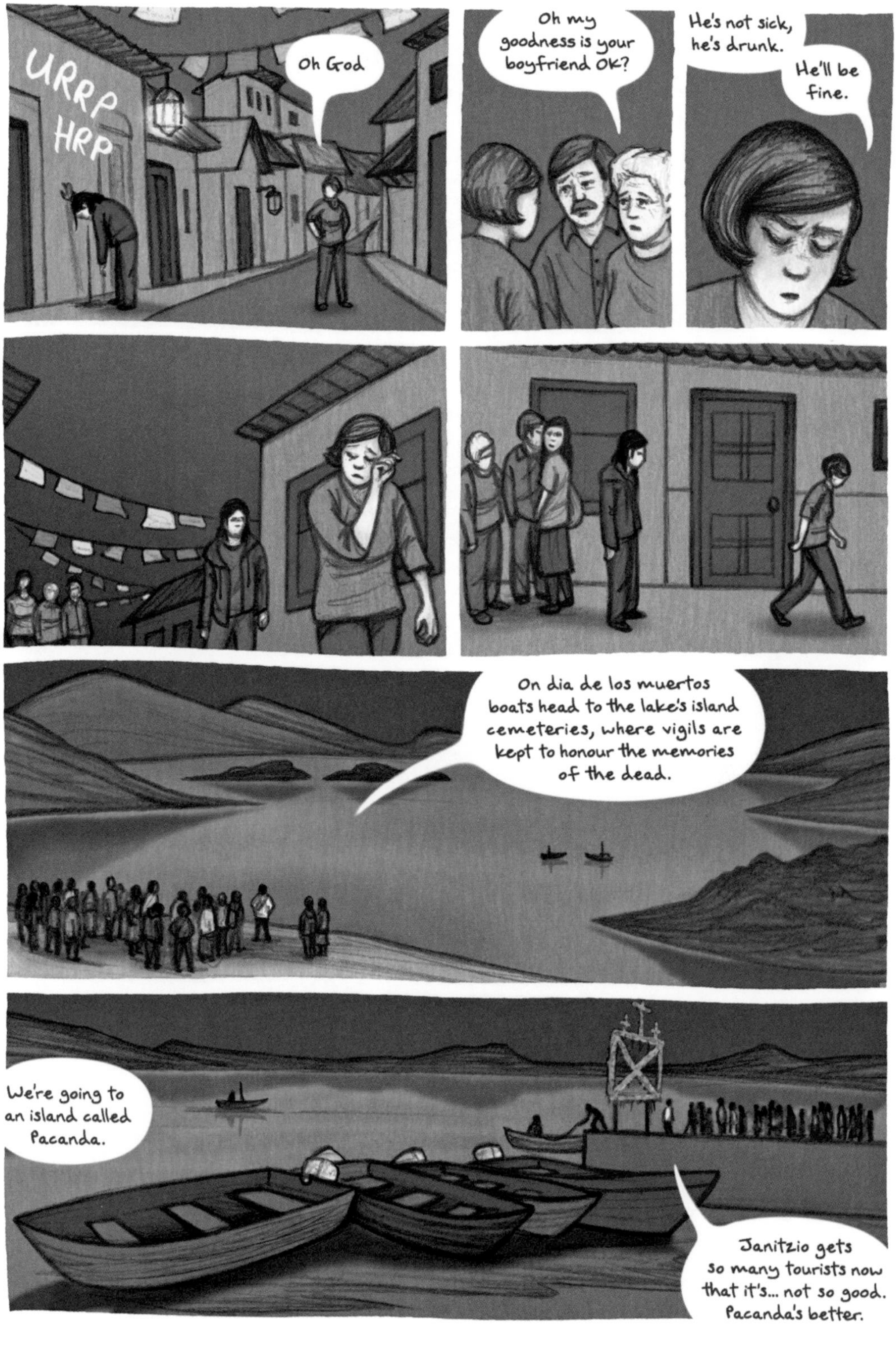
URRP HRP
Oh God
Oh my goodness is your boyfriend OK?
He's not sick, he's drunk.
He'll be fine.
On dia de los muertos boats head to the lake's island cemeteries, where vigils are kept to honour the memories of the dead.
We're going to an island called Pacanda.
Janitzio gets so many tourists now that it's... not so good. Pacanda's better.

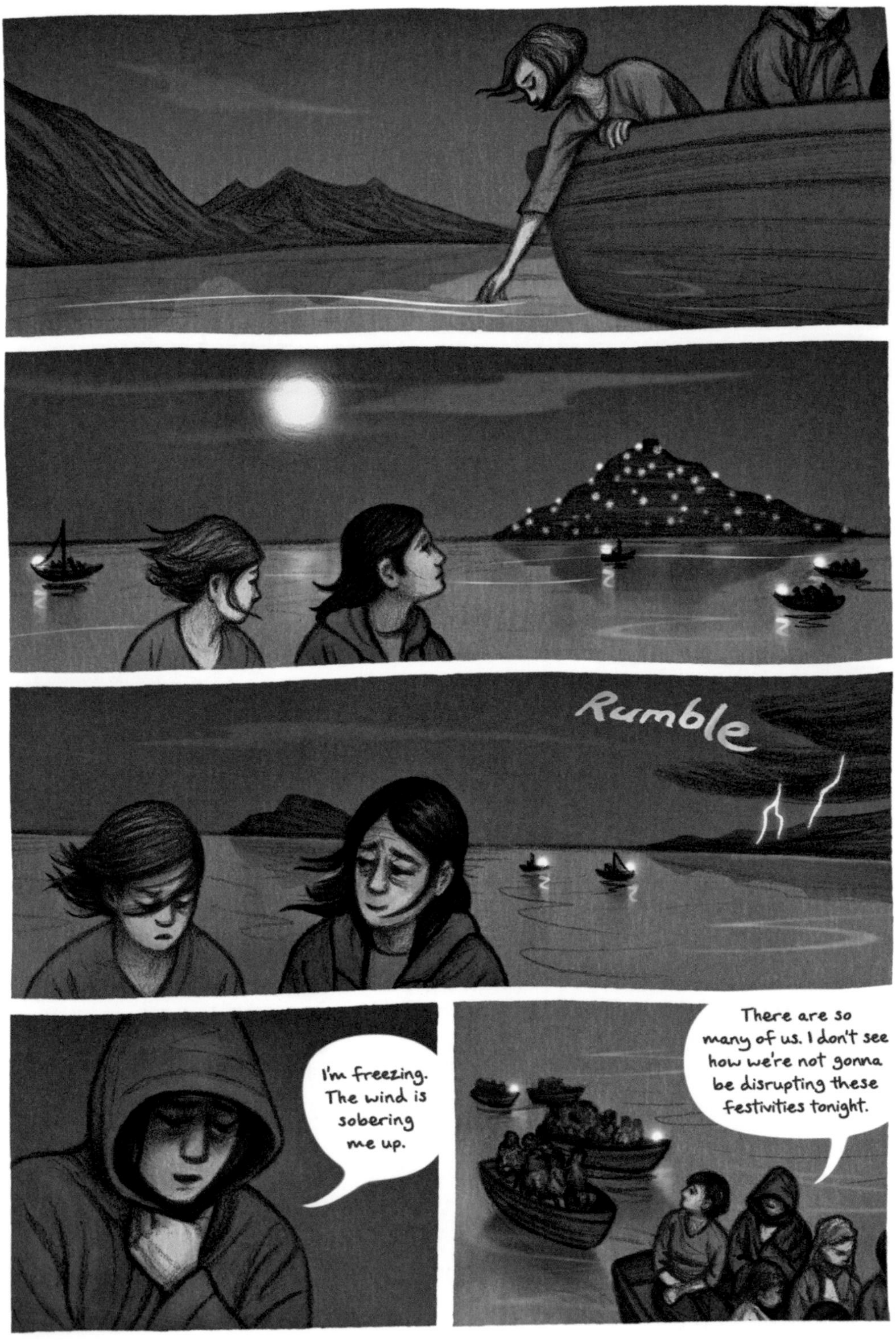
Rumble
I'm freezing. The wind is sobering me up.
There are so many of us. I don't see how we're not gonna be disrupting these festivities tonight.

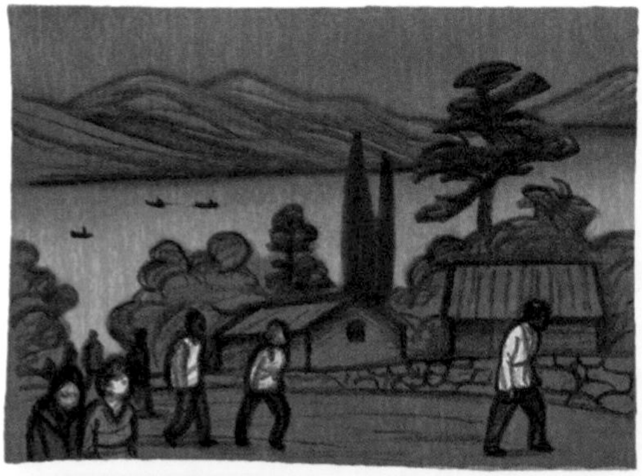

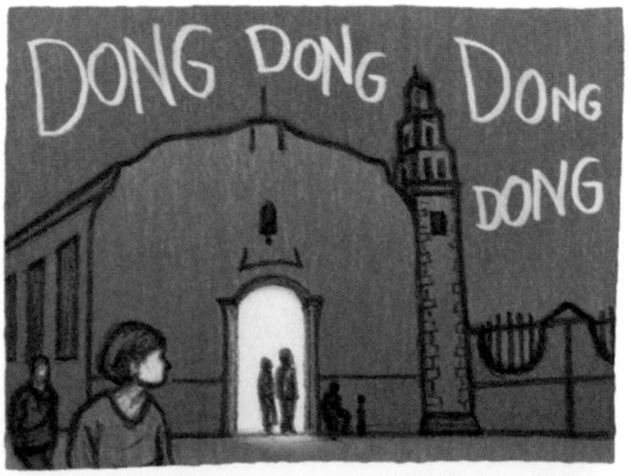
DONG DONG DONG
DONG

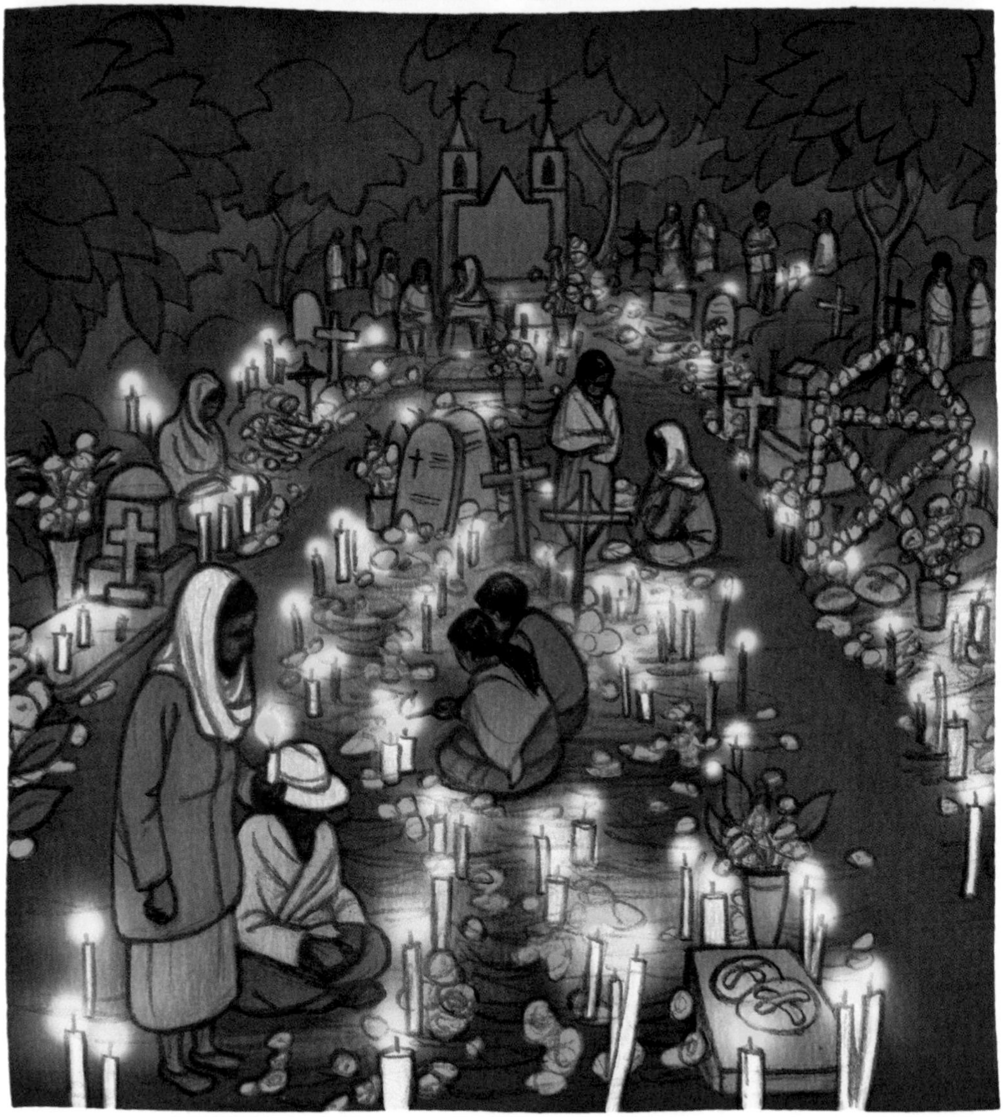

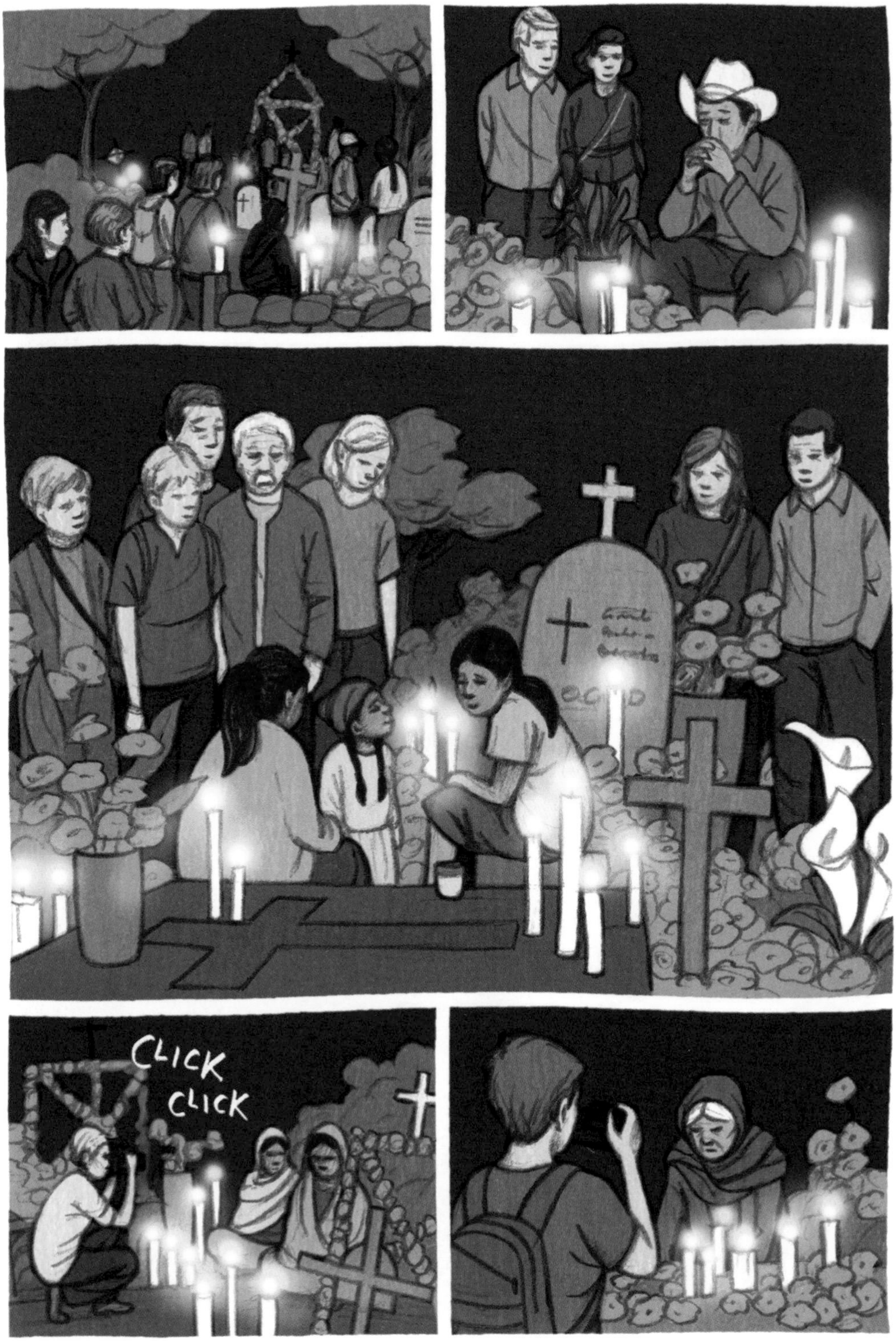
CLICK
CLICK

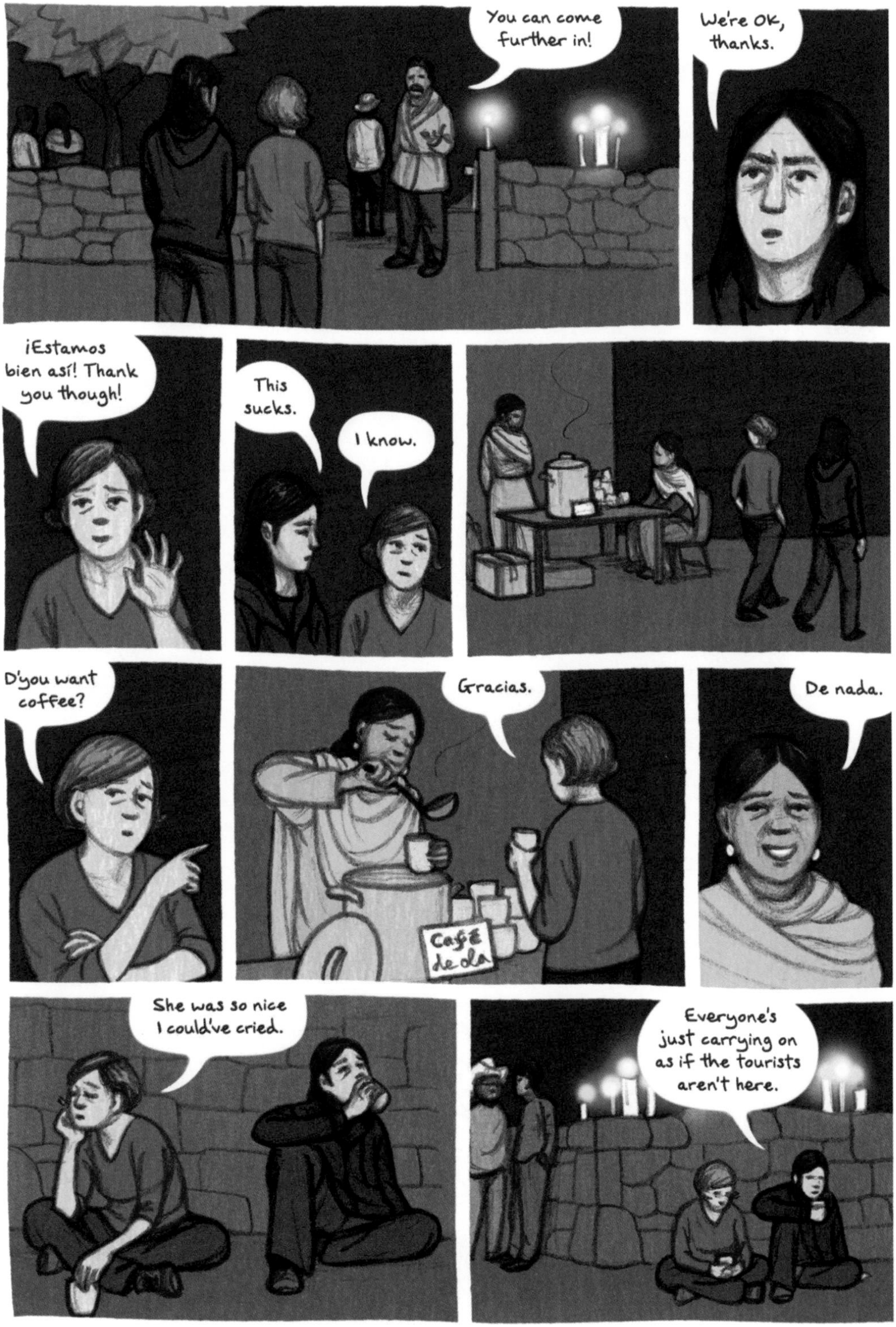
You can come further in!
We're OK, thanks.
¡Estamos bien así! Thank you though!
This sucks.
I know.
D'you want coffee?
Gracias.
Café de olla
De nada.
She was so nice I could've cried.
Everyone's just carrying on as if the tourists aren't here.

I can't wait around for him to sleep it off.

Need some time to myself.

So I guess this is my first time out alone in Mexico.

Cuidado muchacha, éste es muy picante.

That was the thing he was most looking forward to... one of his main reasons for coming here.

He won't even remember most of it. Mind you it was pretty bad.

If I was better at Spanish I'd go off on my own for a while. Take a break.

A week'd do it.

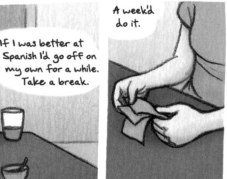

Who am I kidding, I can't travel here alone.

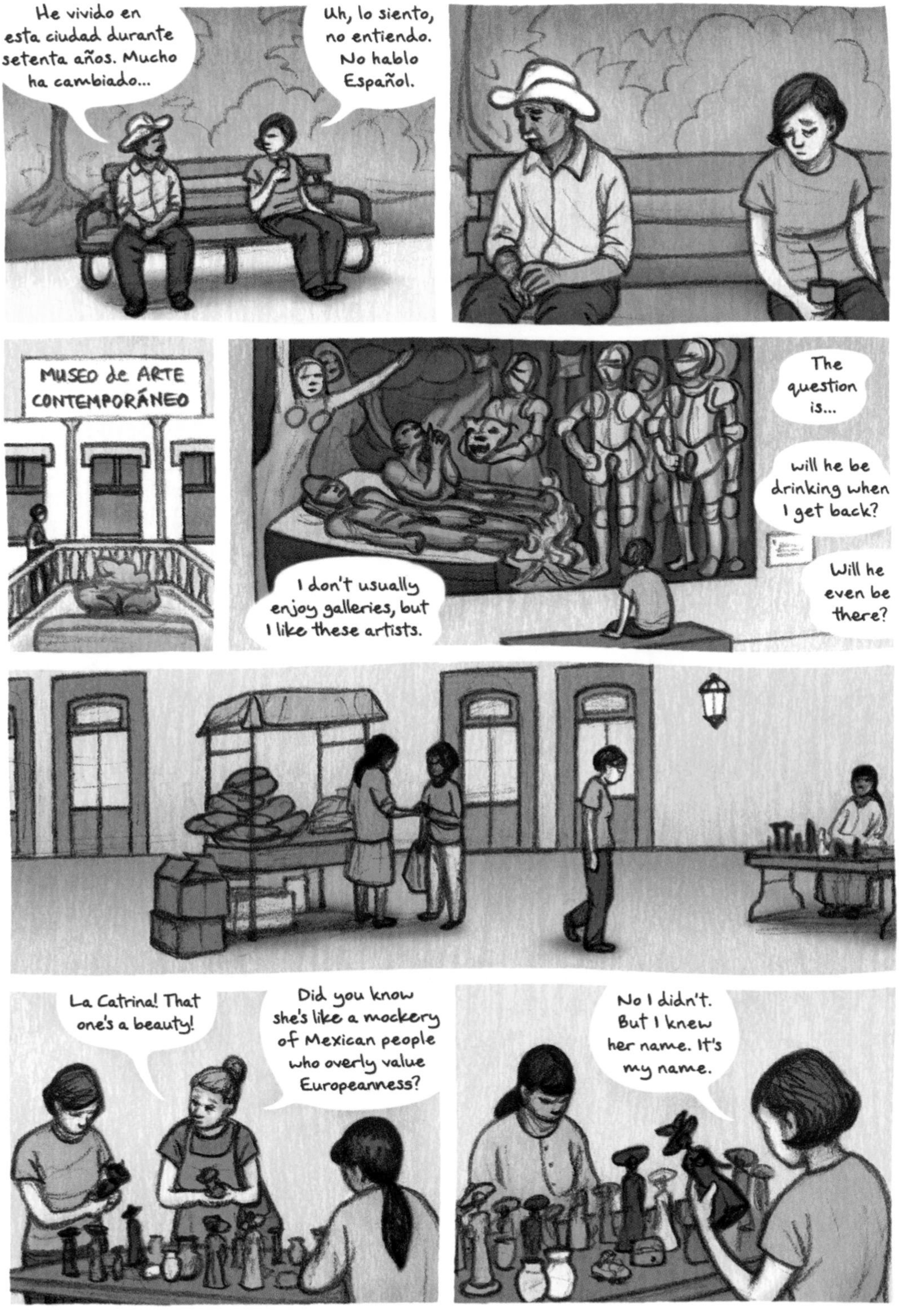
He vivido en esta ciudad durante setenta años. Mucho ha cambiado...
Uh, lo siento, no entiendo. No hablo Español.
MUSEO de ARTE CONTEMPORÁNEO
I don't usually enjoy galleries, but I like these artists.
The question is...
will he be drinking when I get back?
Will he even be there?
La Catrina! That one's a beauty!
Did you know she's like a mockery of Mexican people who overly value Europeanness?
No I didn't. But I knew her name. It's my name.

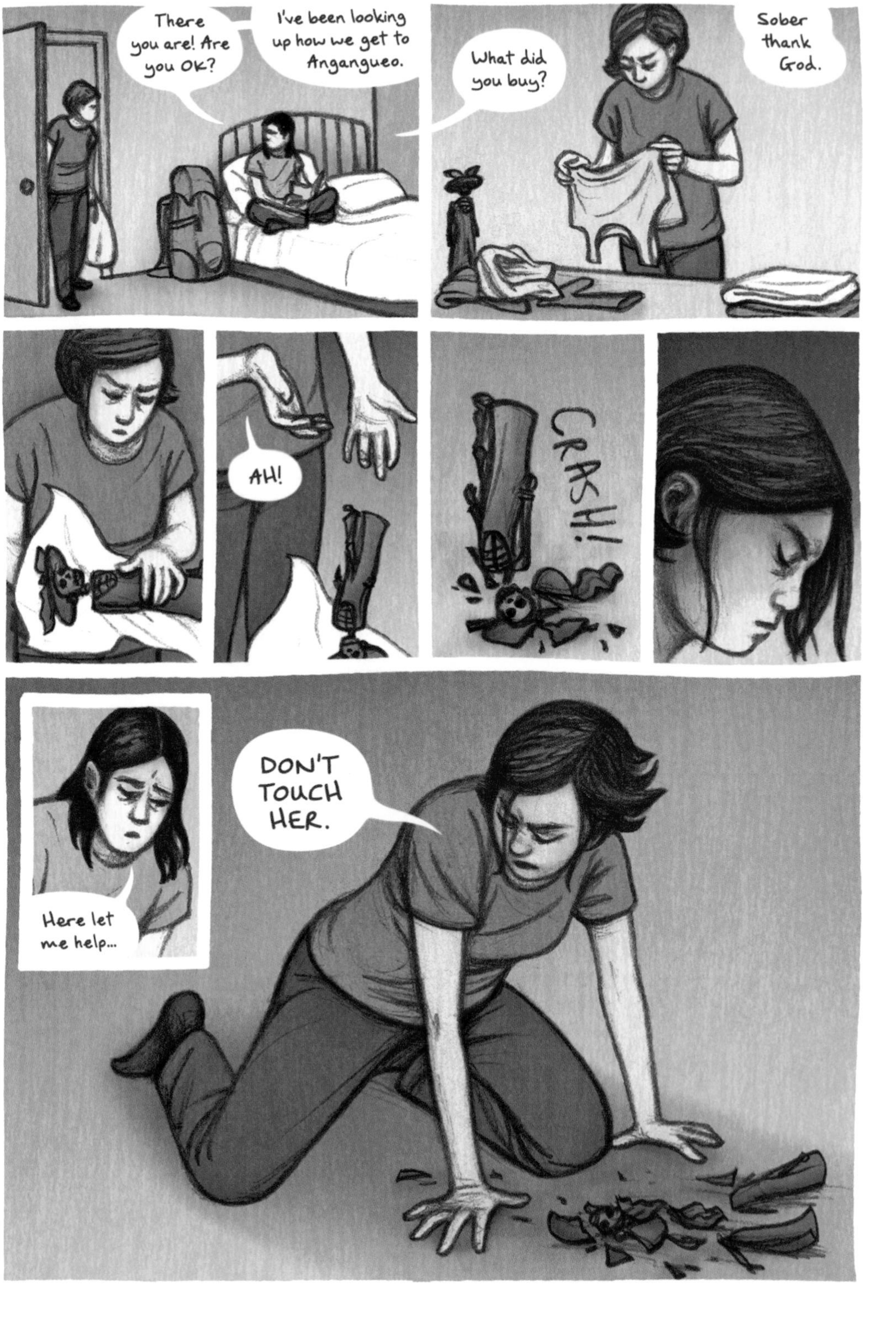

There you are! Are you OK?
I've been looking up how we get to Angangueo.
What did you buy?
Sober thank God.
AH!
CRASH!
Here let me help...
DON'T TOUCH HER.

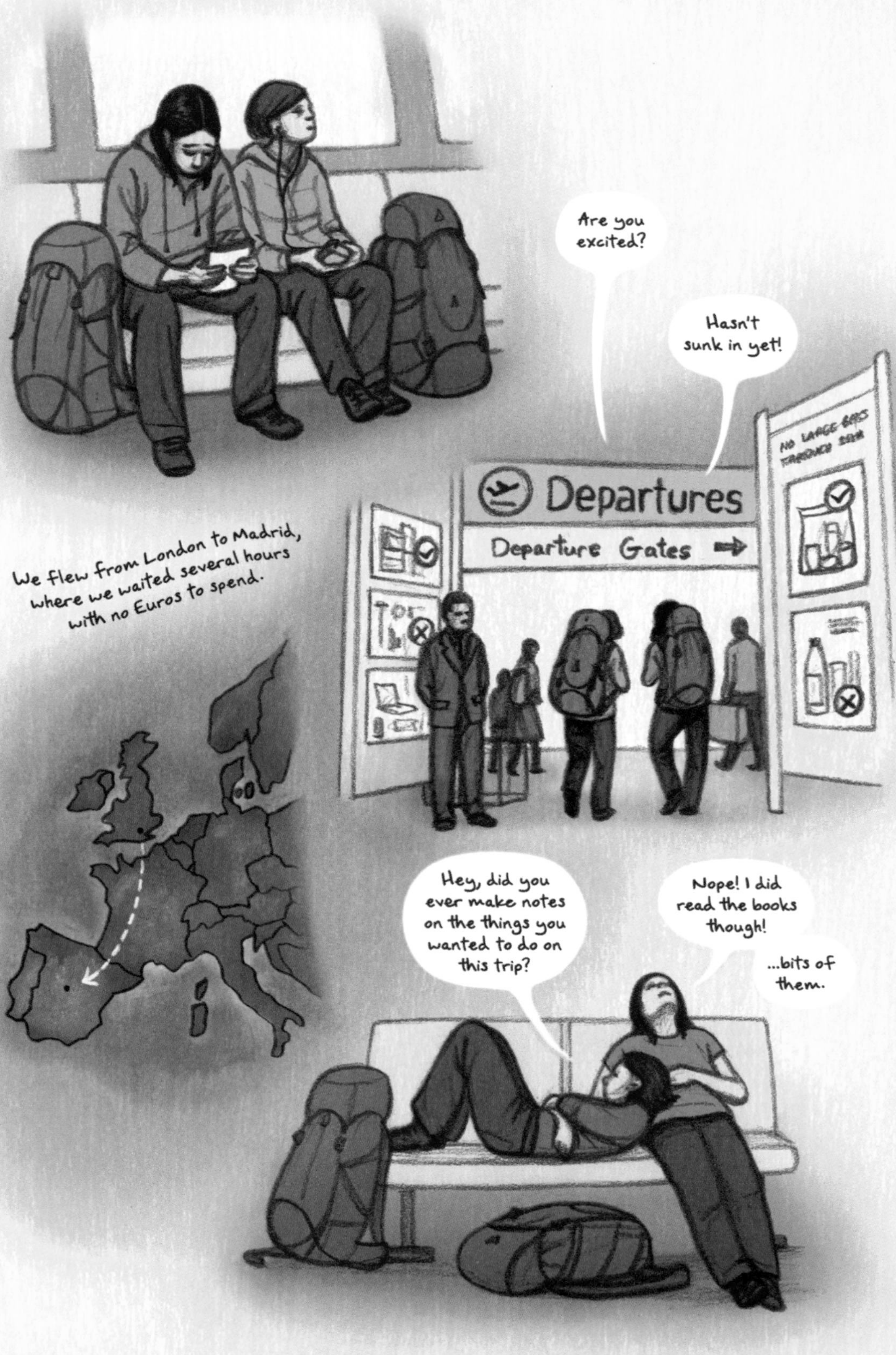
Are you excited?
Hasn't sunk in yet!
Departures
Departure Gates
We flew from London to Madrid, where we waited several hours with no Euros to spend.
Hey, did you ever make notes on the things you wanted to do on this trip?
Nope! I did read the books though!
...bits of them.

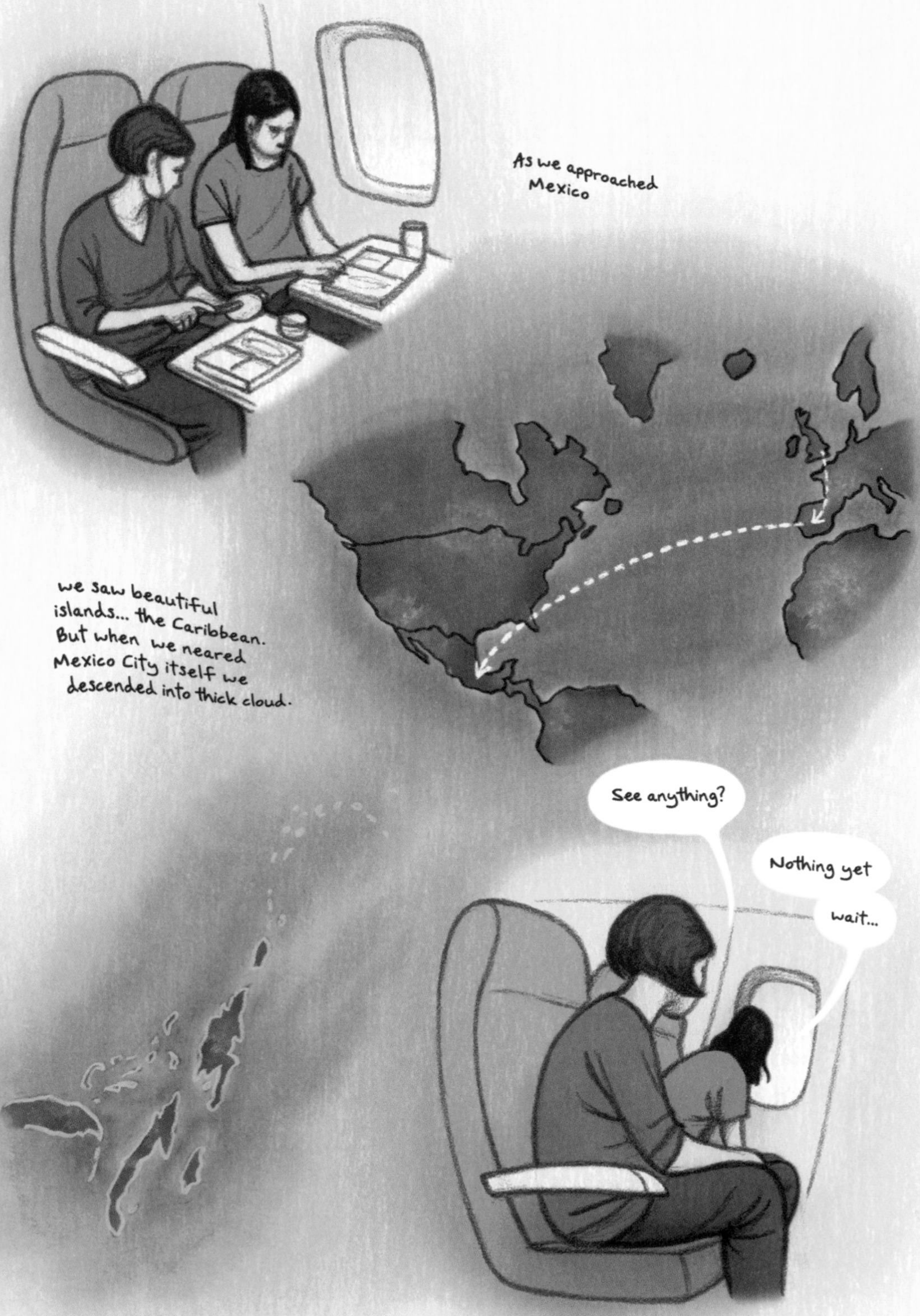
As we approached Mexico
we saw beautiful islands... the Caribbean.
But when we neared Mexico City itself we descended into thick cloud.
See anything?
Nothing yet
wait...

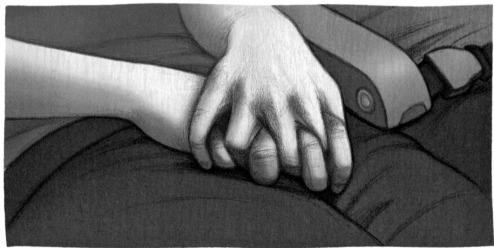

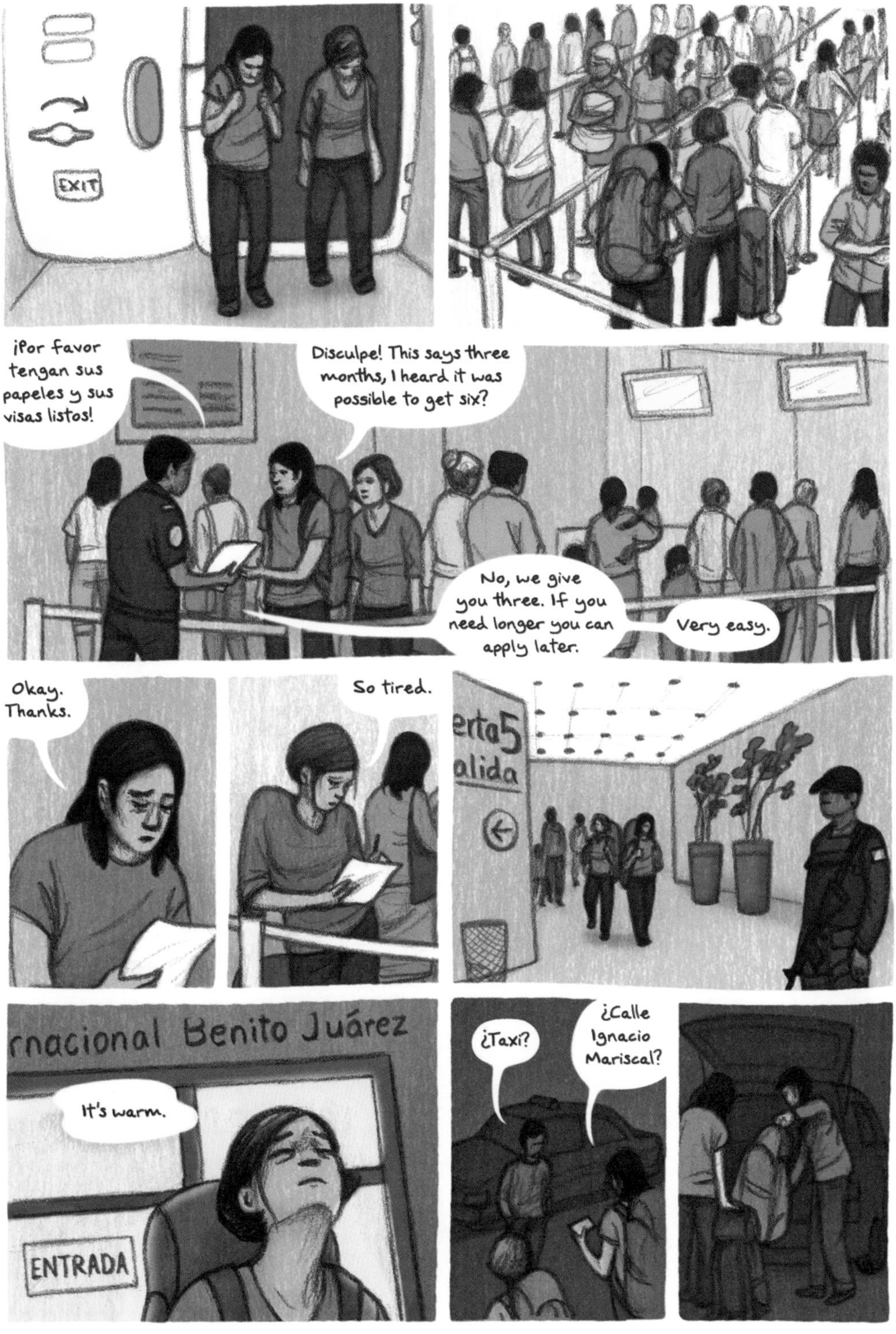
EXIT
¡Por favor tengan sus papeles y sus visas listos!
Disculpe! This says three months, I heard it was possible to get six?
No, we give you three. If you need longer you can apply later.
Very easy.
Okay. Thanks.
So tired.
erta5
alida
rnacional Benito Juárez
It's warm.
ENTRADA
¿Taxi?
¿Calle Ignacio Mariscal?

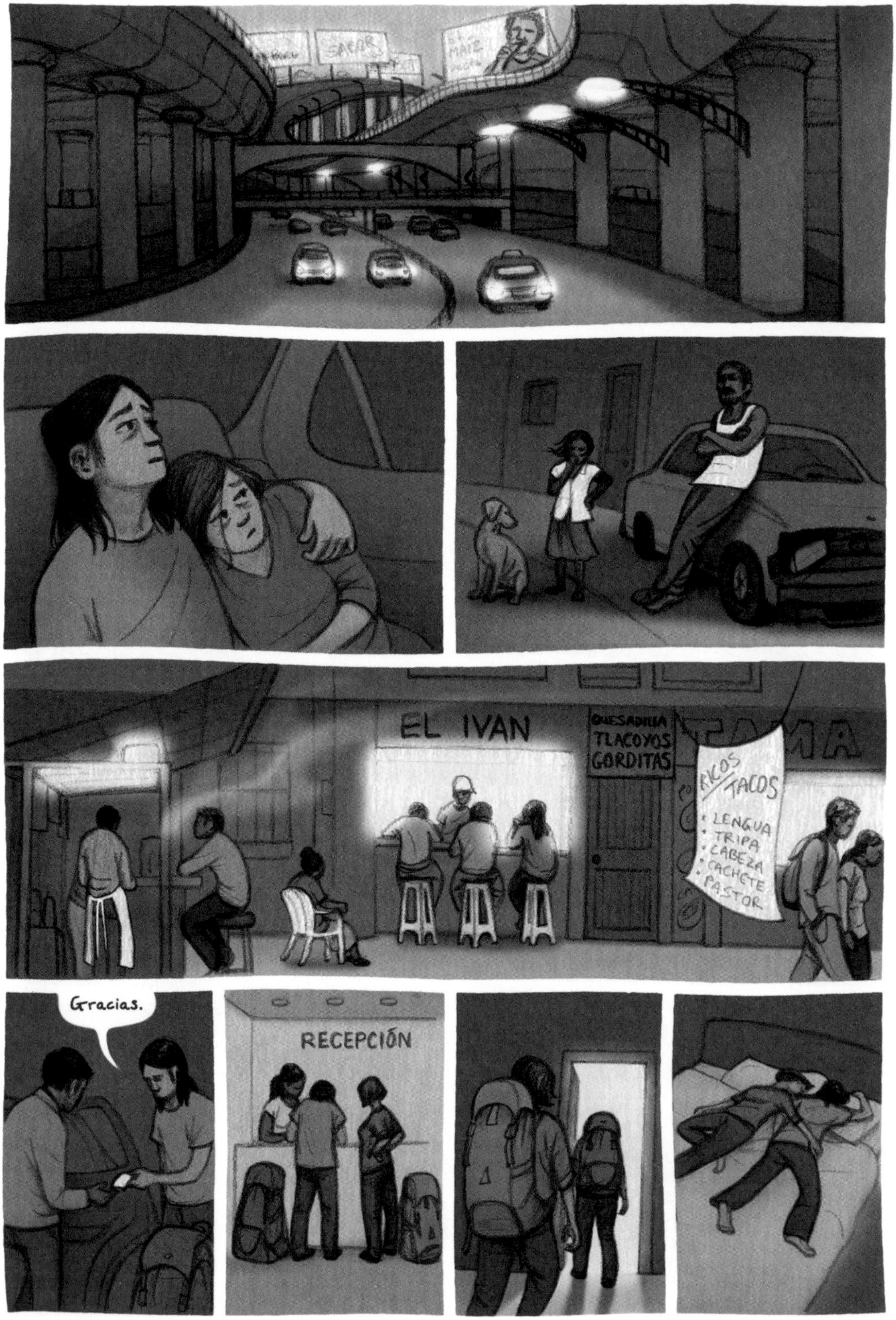
EL IVAN
QUESADILLA
TLACOYOS
GORDITAS
RICOS TACOS
• LENGUA
• TRIPA
• CABEZA
• CACHETE
• PASTOR
Gracias.
RECEPCIÓN

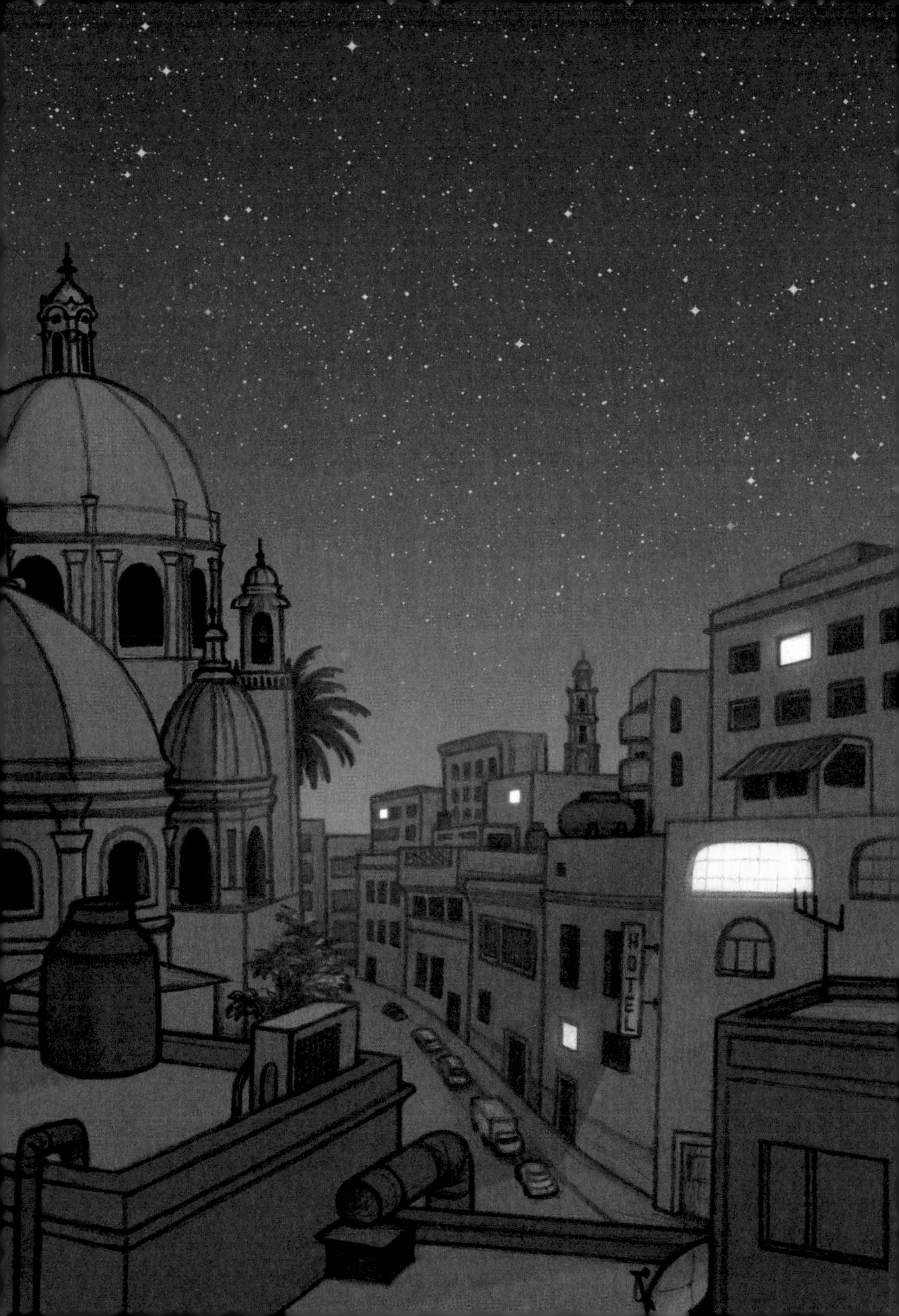
HOTEL

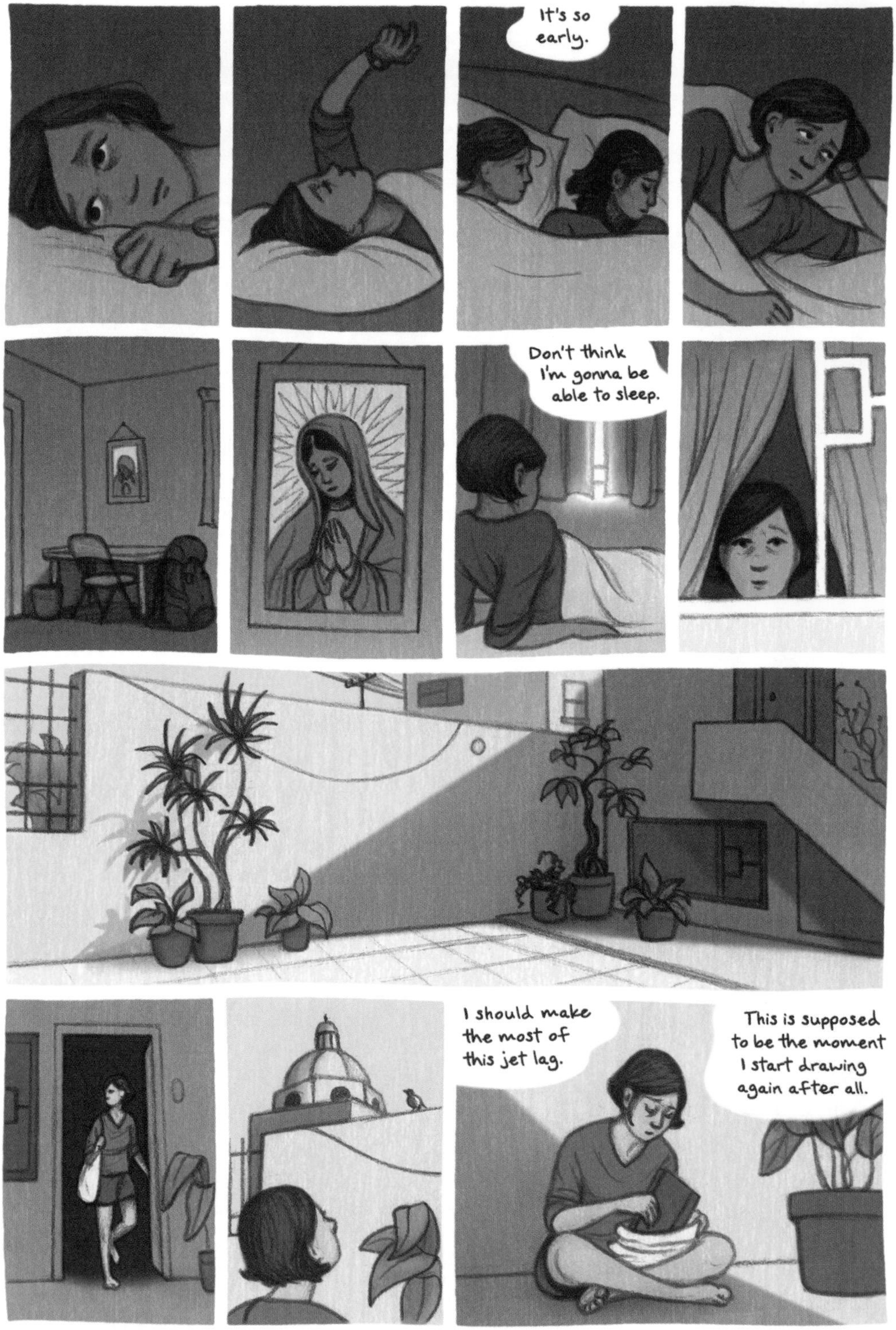
It's so early.
Don't think I'm gonna be able to sleep.
I should make the most of this jet lag.
This is supposed to be the moment I start drawing again after all.

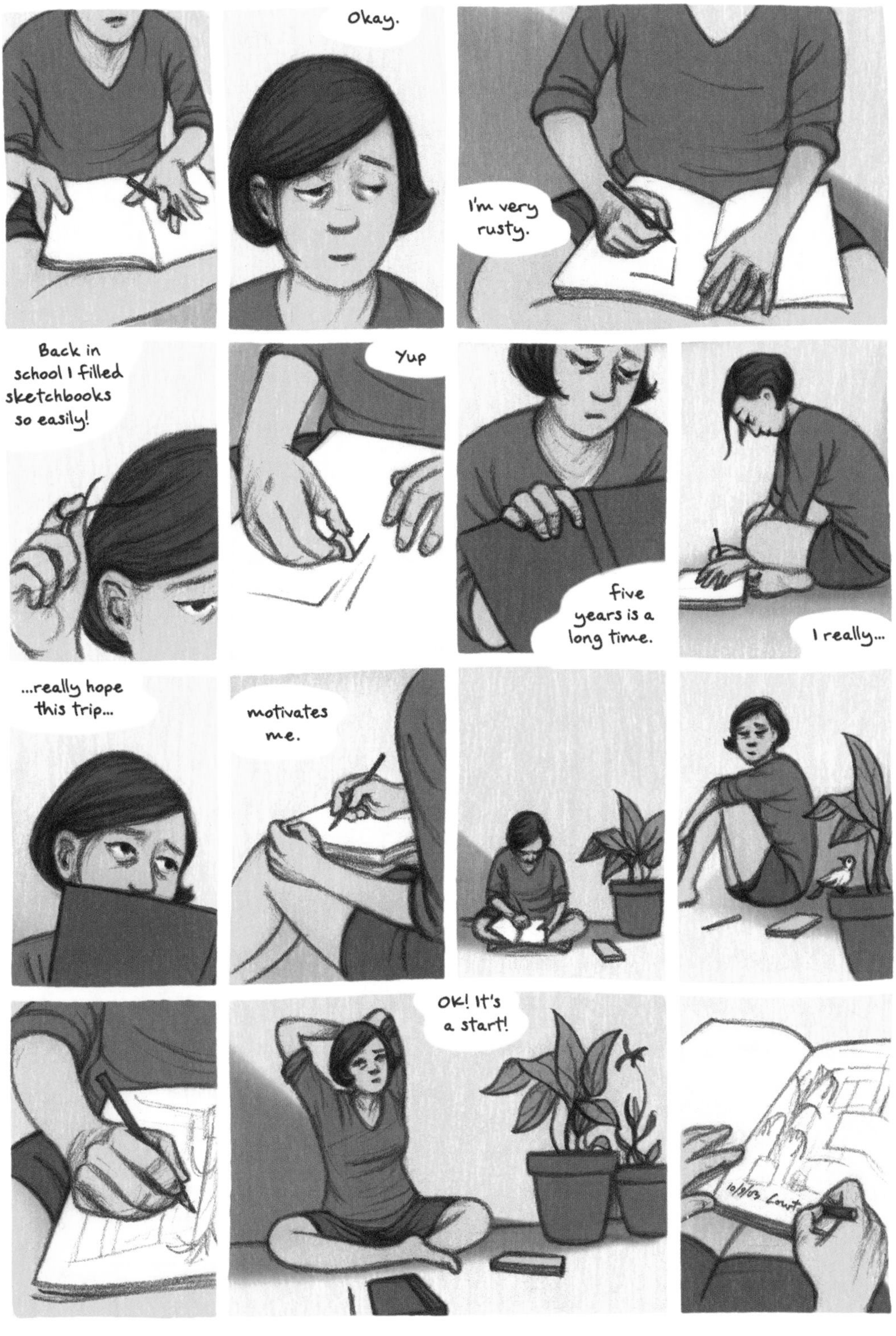
Okay.
I'm very rusty.
Back in school I filled sketchbooks so easily!
Yup
five years is a long time.
I really...
...really hope this trip...
motivates me.
OK! It's a start!
10/9/03 Court

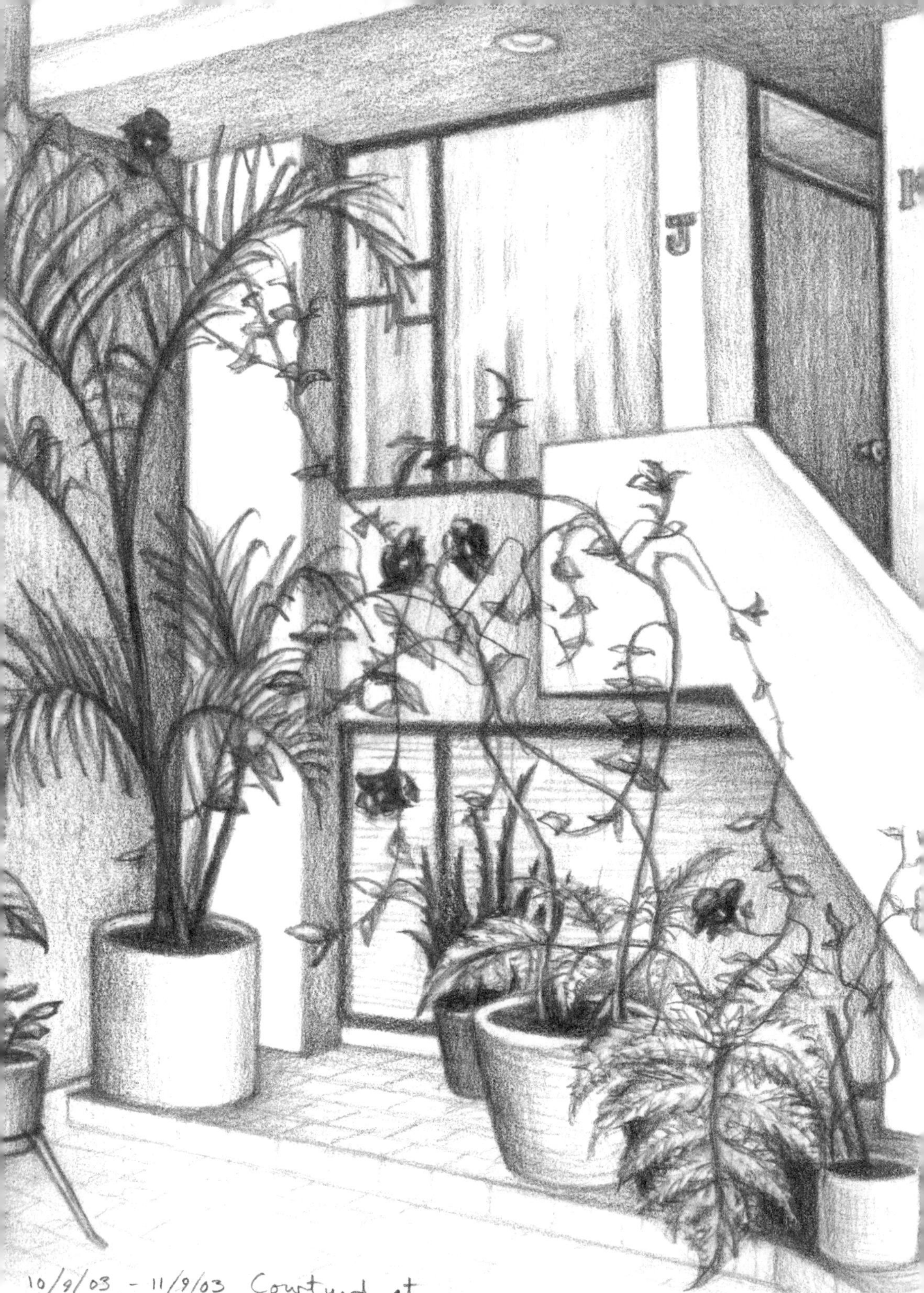
J

10/9/03 – 11/9/03 Courtyard at 'Casa de los Amigos. Our room 'K'.

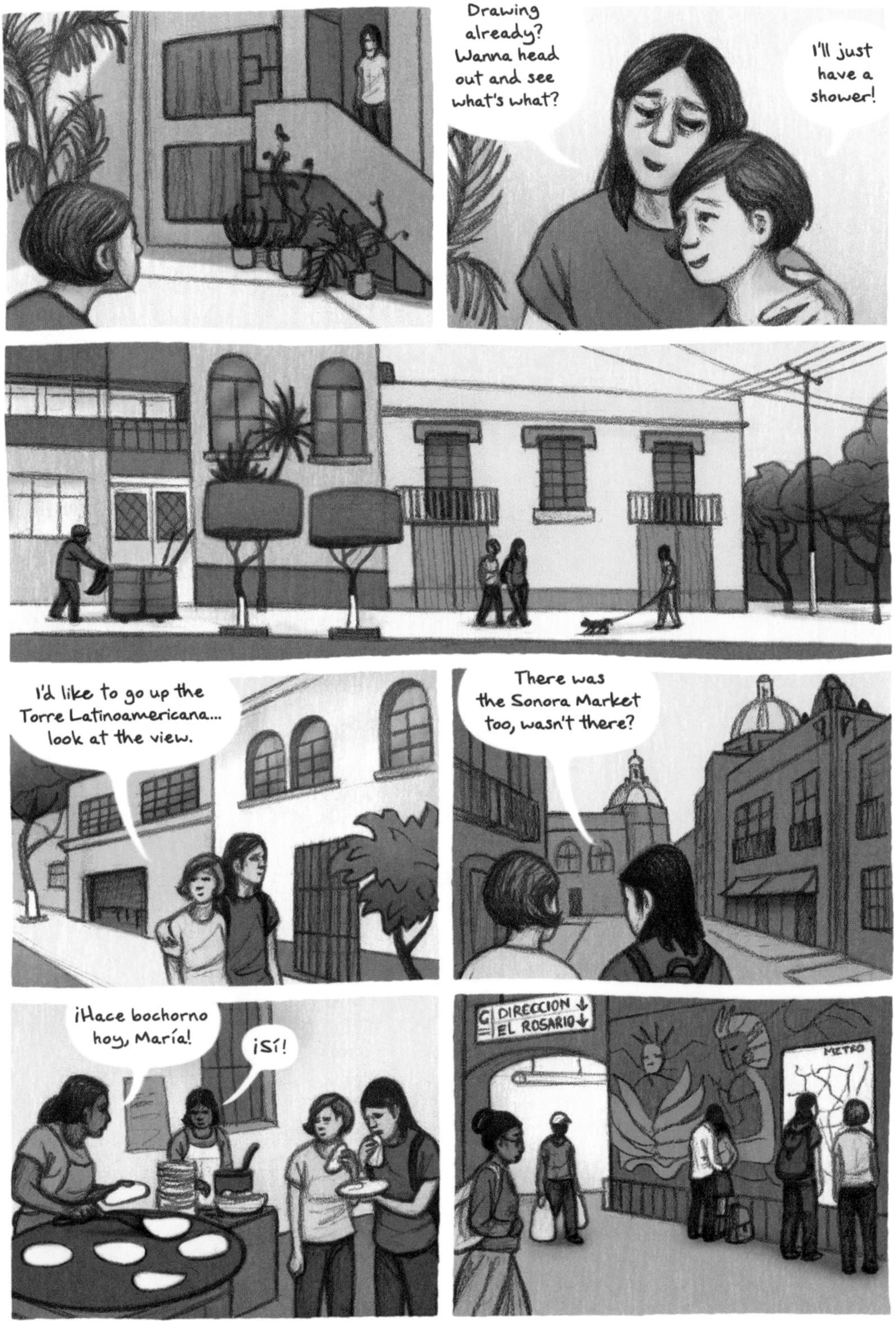
Drawing already? Wanna head out and see what's what?
I'll just have a shower!
I'd like to go up the Torre Latinoamericana... look at the view.
There was the Sonora Market too, wasn't there?
¡Hace bochorno hoy, María!
¡Sí!
DIRECCION
EL ROSARIO
METRO

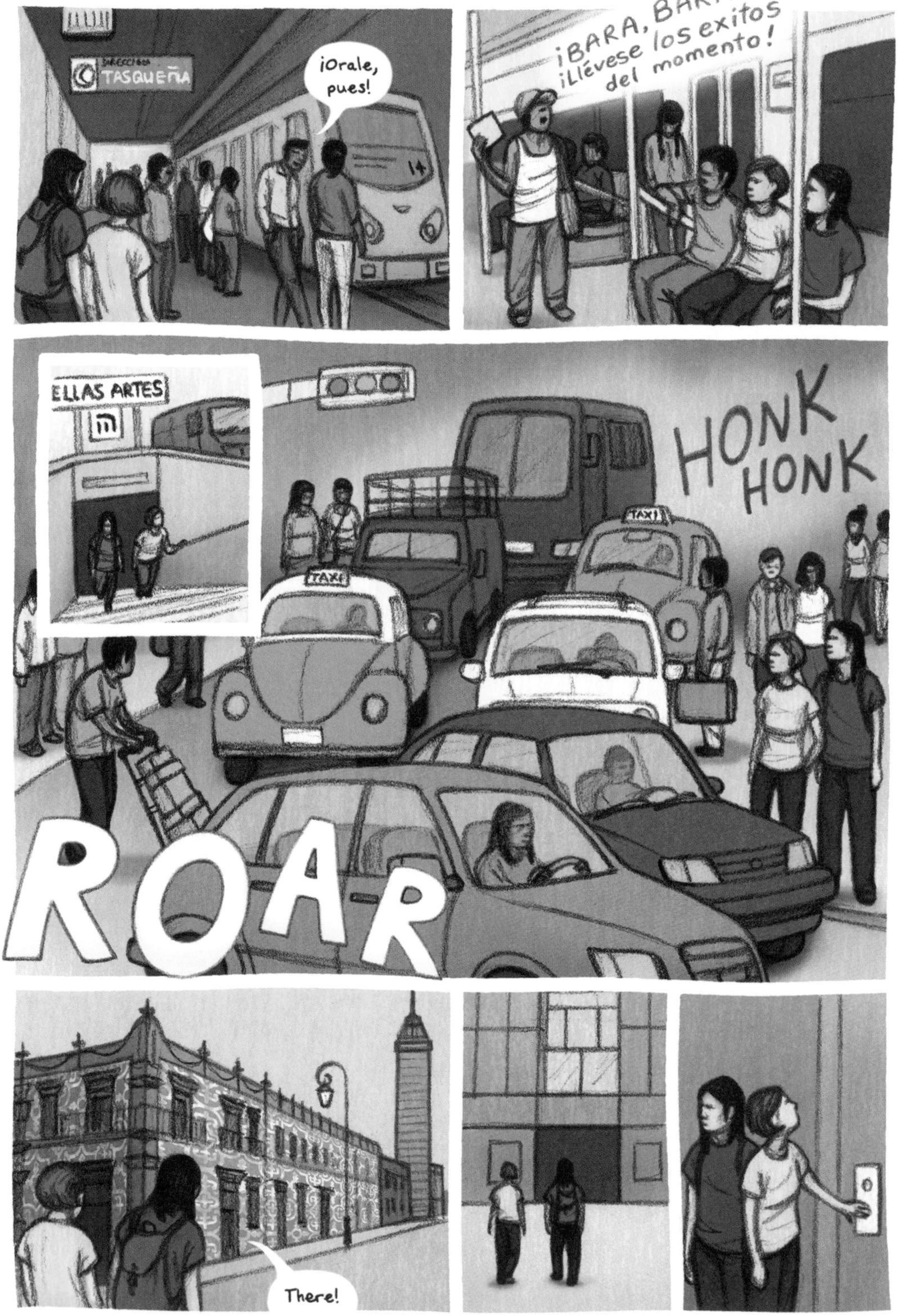
TASQUEÑA
¡Orale, pues!
¡BARA, BARA! ¡Llévese los exitos del momento!
ELLAS ARTES
TAXI
TAXI
HONK HONK
ROAR
There!

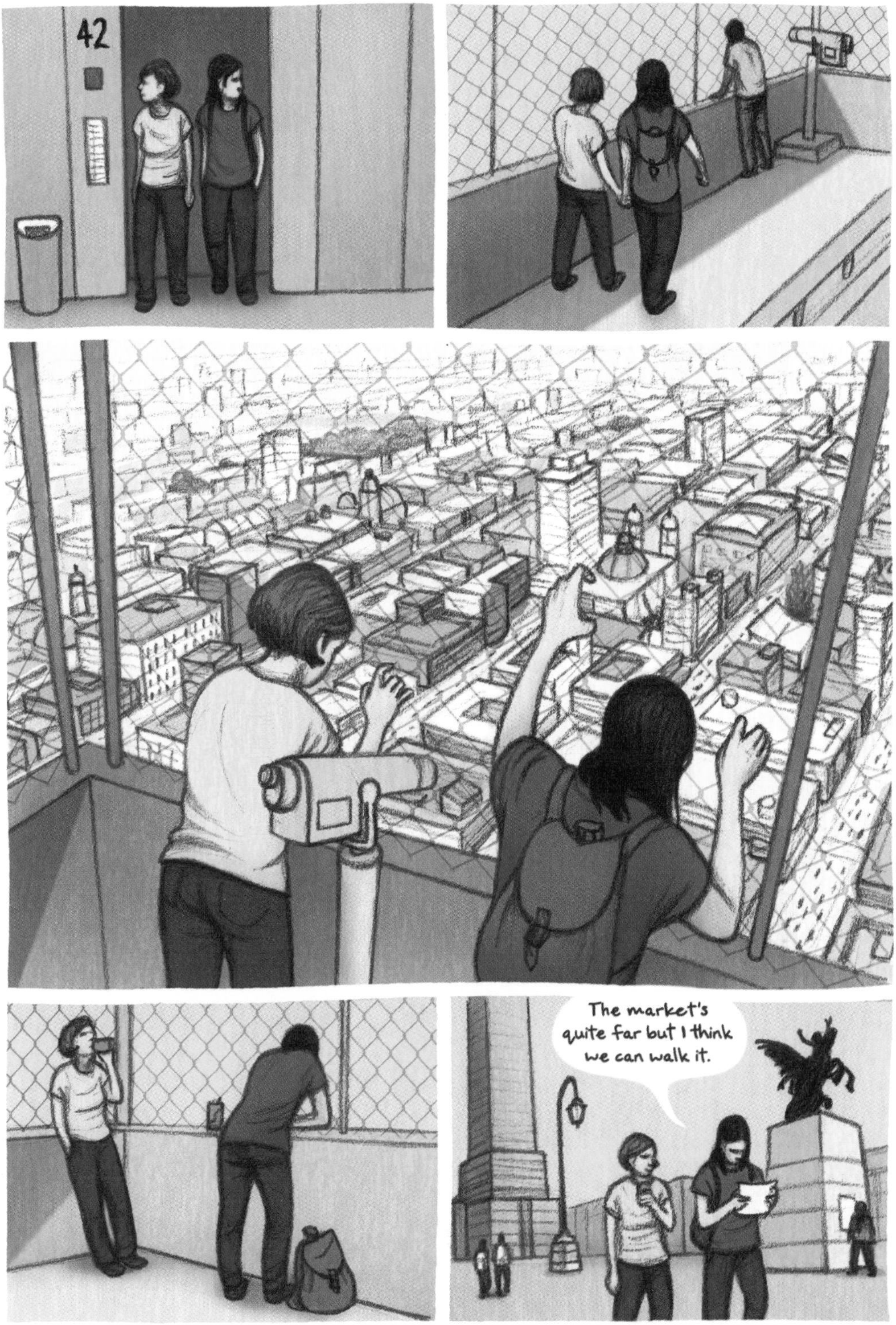
42
The market's quite far but I think we can walk it.

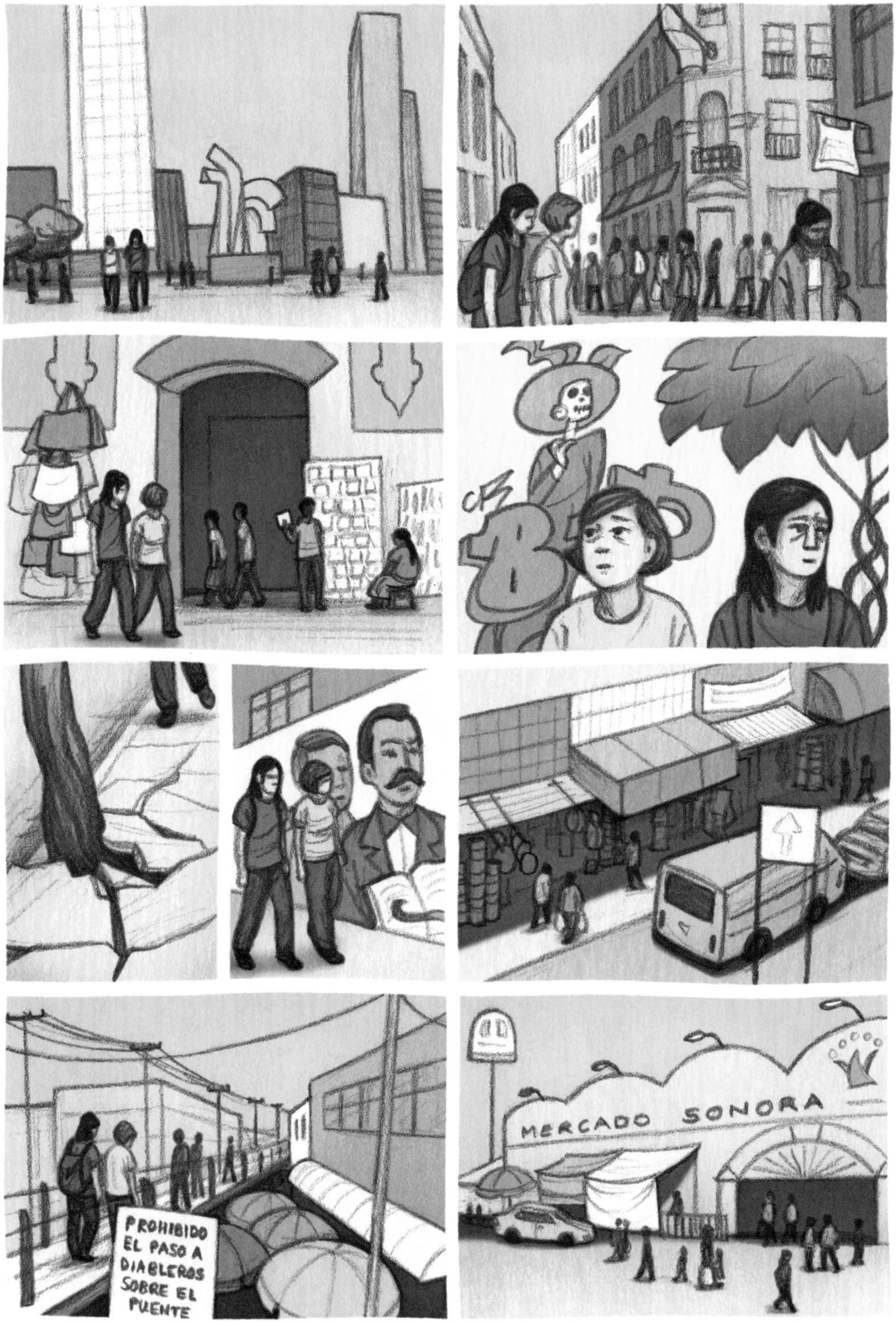
PROHIBIDO EL PASO A DIABLEROS SOBRE EL PUENTE
MERCADO SONORA

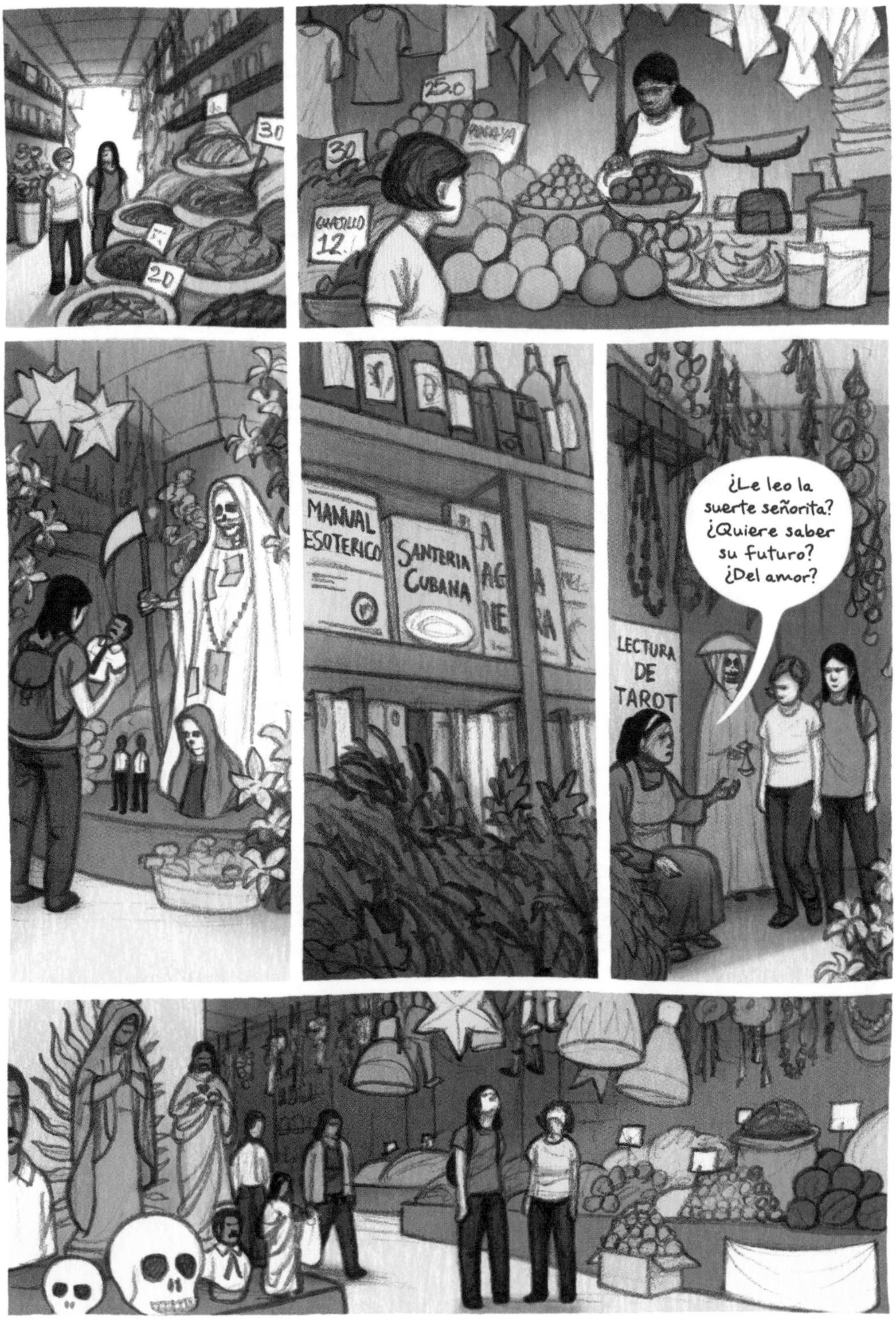
30
20
25.0
30
12
MANUAL
ESOTERICO
SANTERIA
CUBANA
LECTURA
DE
TAROT
¿Le leo la suerte señorita? ¿Quiere saber su futuro? ¿Del amor?

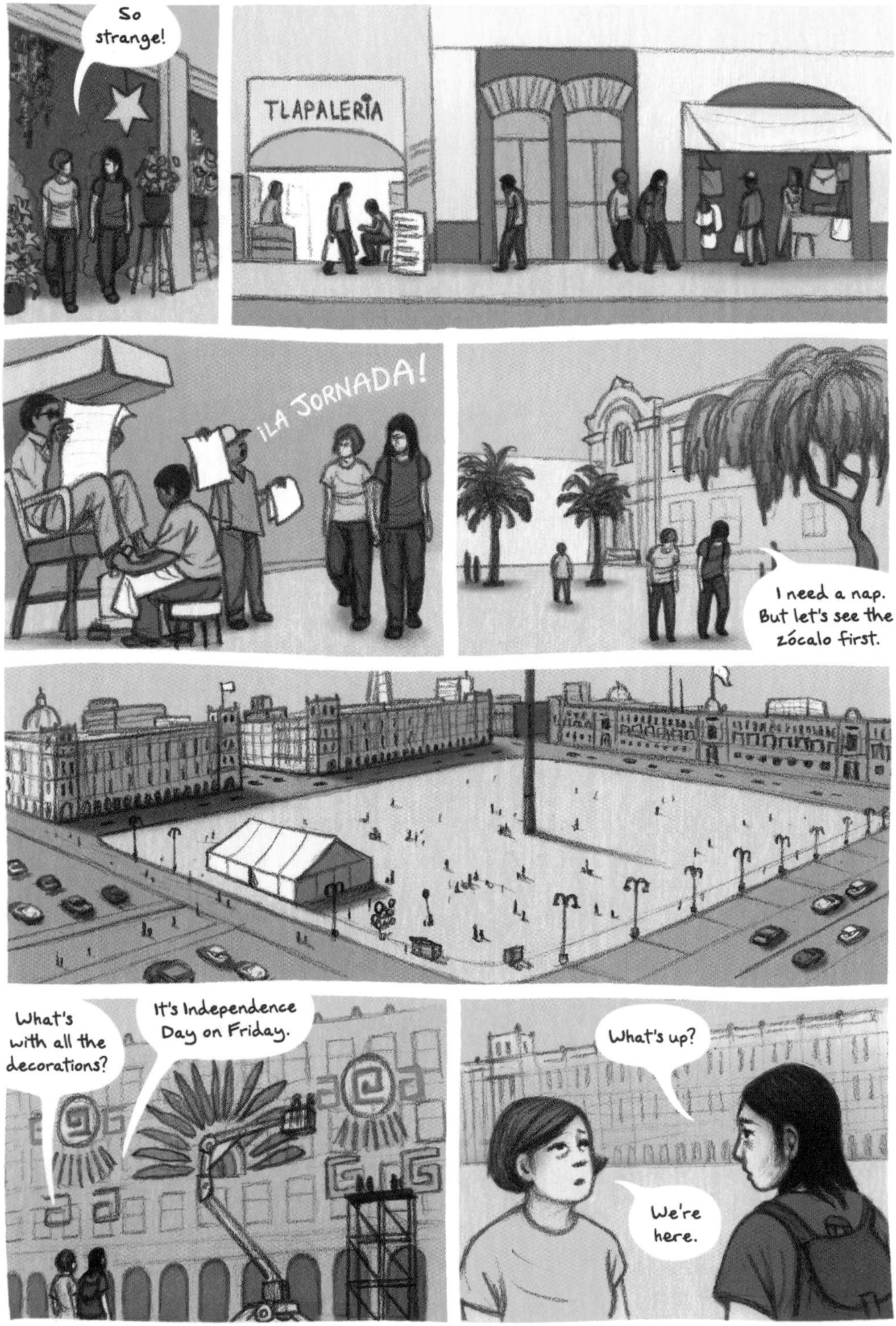

So strange!
TLAPALERIA
¡LA JORNADA!
I need a nap. But let's see the zócalo first.
What's with all the decorations?
It's Independence Day on Friday.
What's up?
We're here.

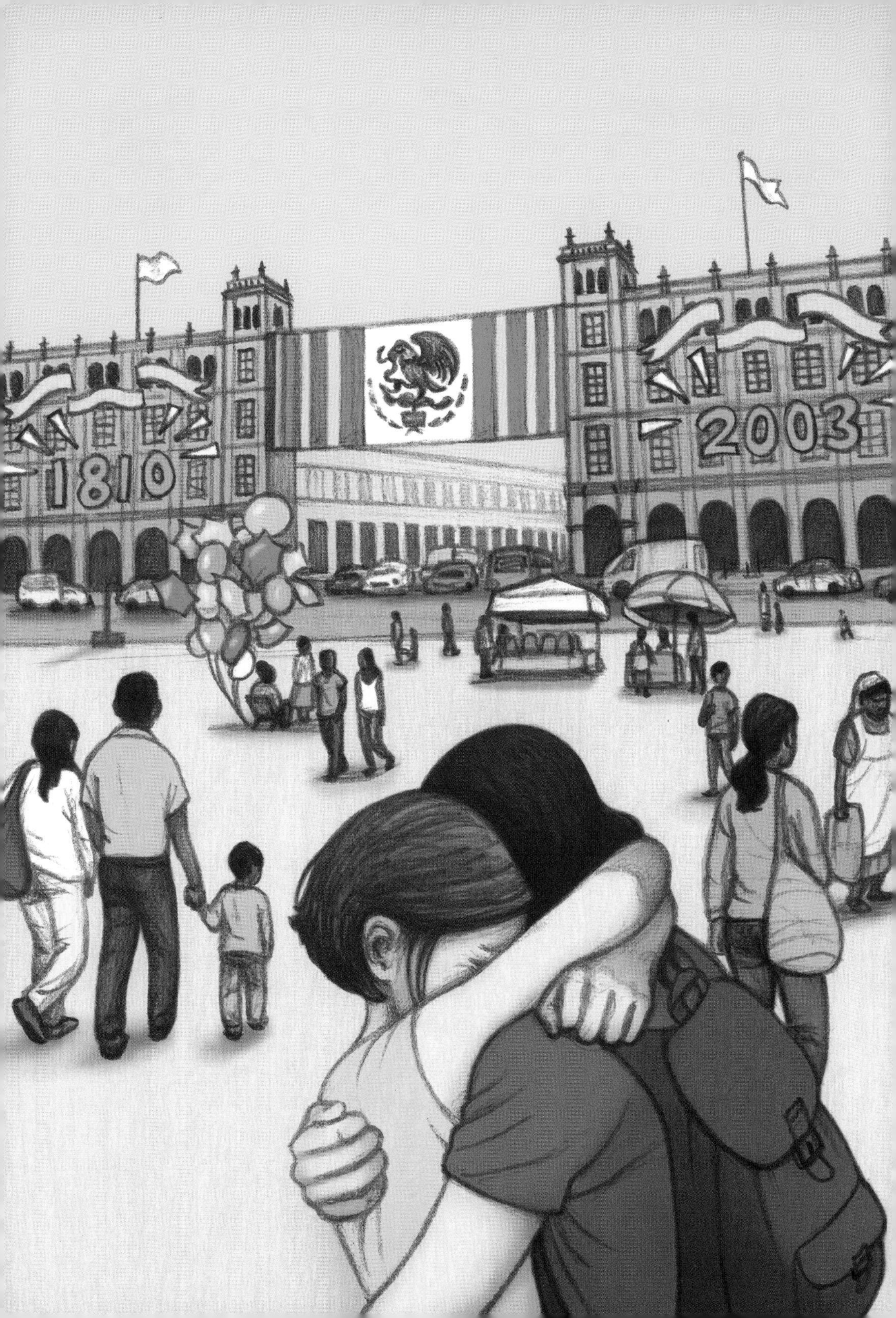
1810
2003

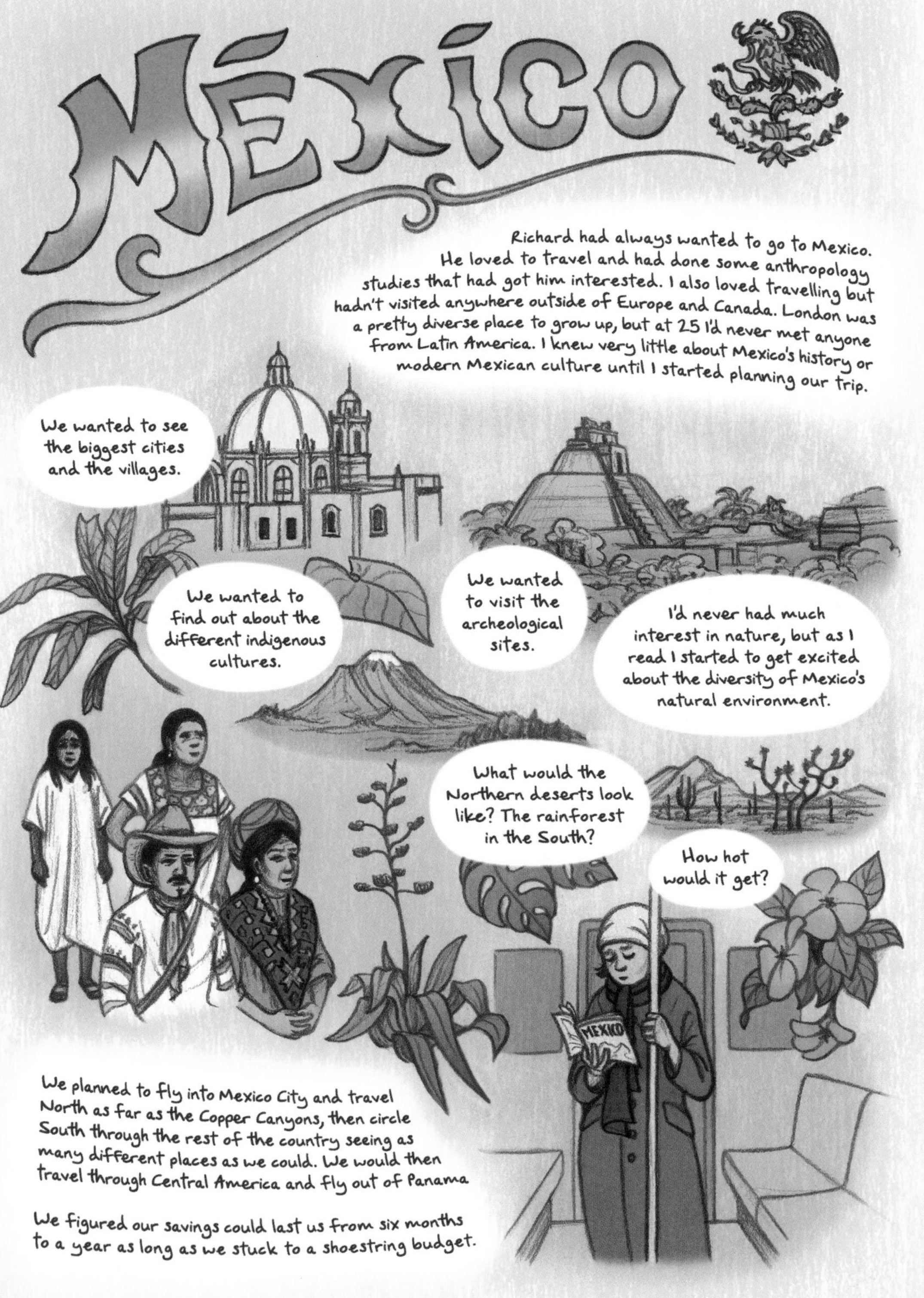
MÉXICO
Richard had always wanted to go to Mexico. He loved to travel and had done some anthropology studies that had got him interested. I also loved travelling but hadn't visited anywhere outside of Europe and Canada. London was a pretty diverse place to grow up, but at 25 I'd never met anyone from Latin America. I knew very little about Mexico's history or modern Mexican culture until I started planning our trip.
We wanted to see the biggest cities and the villages.
We wanted to find out about the different indigenous cultures.
We wanted to visit the archeological sites.
I'd never had much interest in nature, but as I read I started to get excited about the diversity of Mexico's natural environment.
What would the Northern deserts look like? The rainforest in the South?
How hot would it get?
MEXICO
We planned to fly into Mexico City and travel North as far as the Copper Canyons, then circle South through the rest of the country seeing as many different places as we could. We would then travel through Central America and fly out of Panama
We figured our savings could last us from six months to a year as long as we stuck to a shoestring budget.

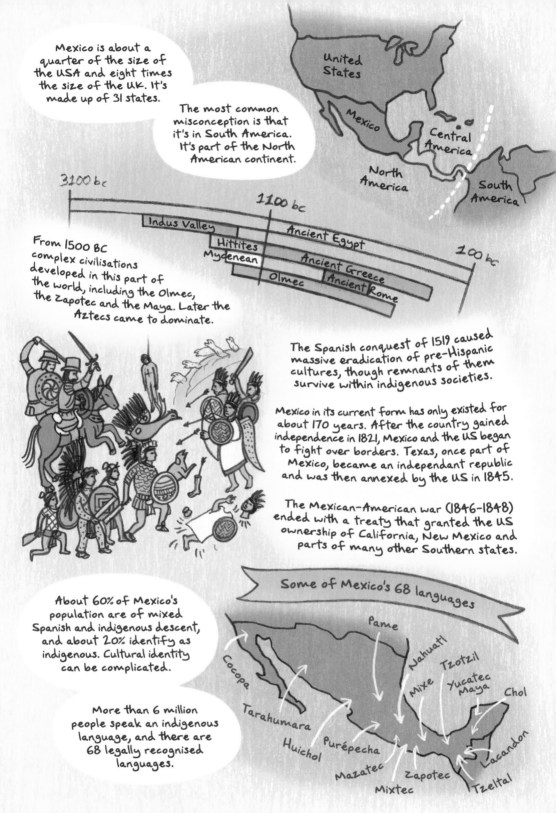

Mexico is about a quarter of the size of the USA and eight times the size of the UK. It's made up of 31 states.

The most common misconception is that it's in South America. It's part of the North American continent.

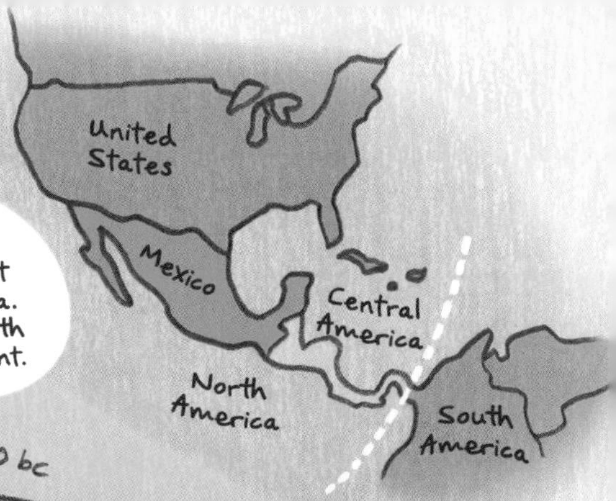
United States
Mexico
Central America
North America
South America

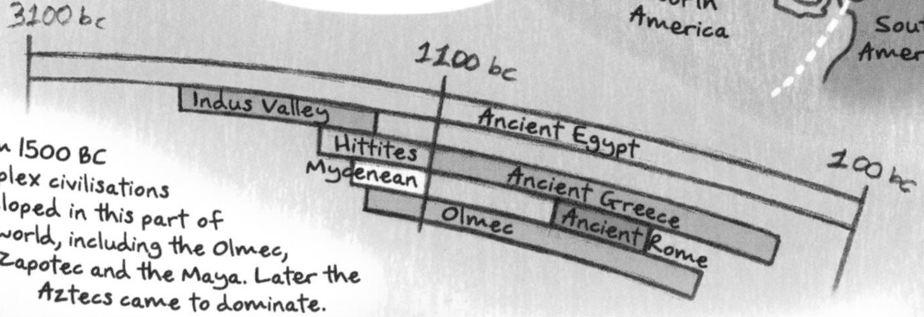
3100 bc
1100 bc
100 bc
Indus Valley
Ancient Egypt
Hittites
Mycenean
Ancient Greece
Olmec
Ancient Rome

From 1500 BC complex civilisations developed in this part of the world, including the Olmec, the Zapotec and the Maya. Later the Aztecs came to dominate.

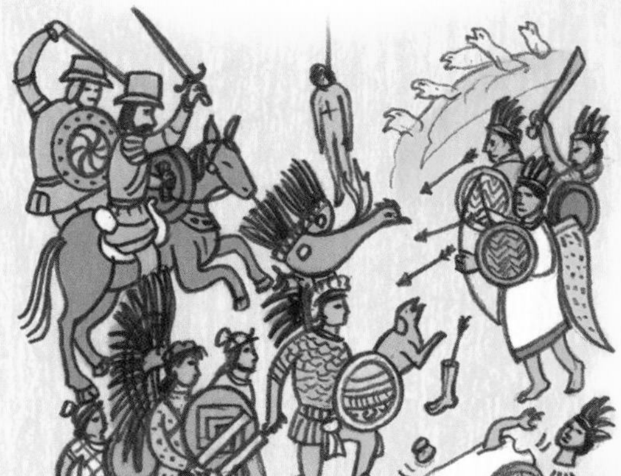

The Spanish conquest of 1519 caused massive eradication of pre-Hispanic cultures, though remnants of them survive within indigenous societies.

Mexico in its current form has only existed for about 170 years. After the country gained independence in 1821, Mexico and the US began to fight over borders. Texas, once part of Mexico, became an independant republic and was then annexed by the US in 1845.

The Mexican-American war (1846-1848) ended with a treaty that granted the US ownership of California, New Mexico and parts of many other Southern states.

About 60% of Mexico's population are of mixed Spanish and indigenous descent, and about 20% identify as indigenous. Cultural identity can be complicated.

More than 6 million people speak an indigenous language, and there are 68 legally recognised languages.

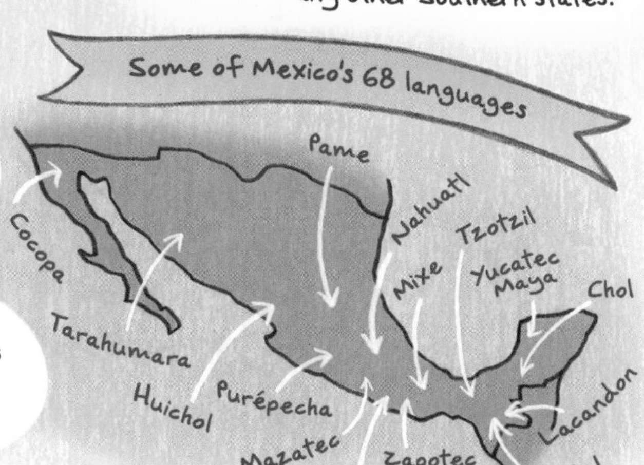
Some of Mexico's 68 languages
Cocopa
Tarahumara
Huichol
Purépecha
Mazatec
Mixtec
Zapotec
Pame
Nahuatl
Mixe
Tzotzil
Yucatec Maya
Chol
Lacandon
Tzeltal

The Bajío

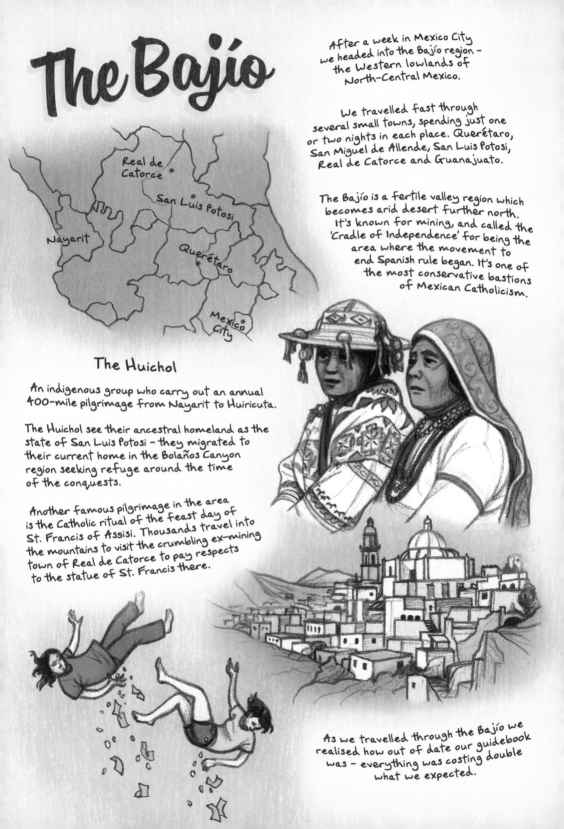

After a week in Mexico City we headed into the Bajío region – the Western lowlands of North-Central Mexico.

We travelled fast through several small towns, spending just one or two nights in each place. Querétaro, San Miguel de Allende, San Luis Potosi, Real de Catorce and Guanajuato.

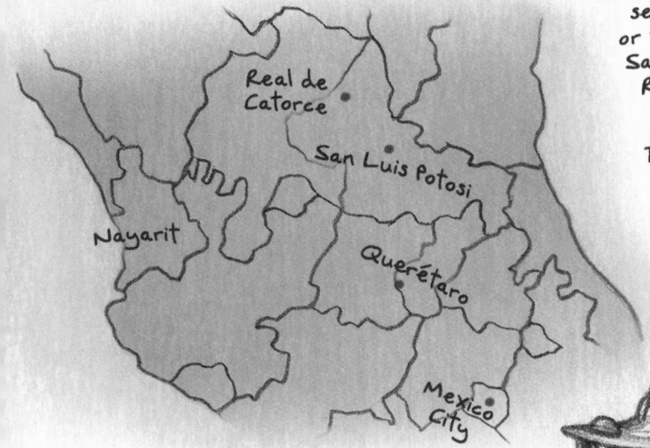
Real de Catorce
San Luis Potosi
Nayarit
Querétaro
Mexico City

The Bajío is a fertile valley region which becomes arid desert further north. It's known for mining, and called the 'Cradle of Independence' for being the area where the movement to end Spanish rule began. It's one of the most conservative bastions of Mexican Catholicism.

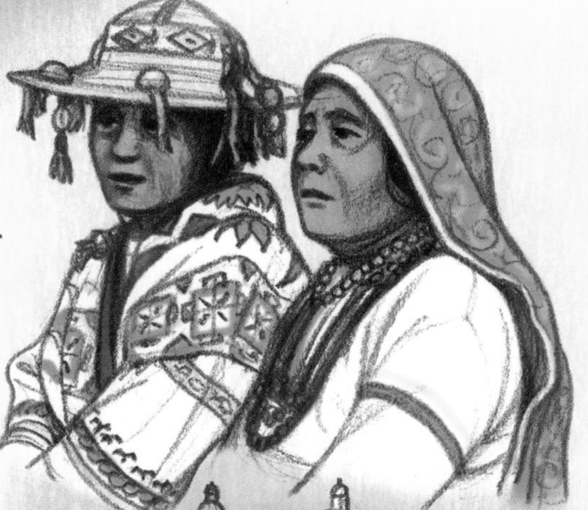

The Huichol

An indigenous group who carry out an annual 400-mile pilgrimage from Nayarit to Huiricuta.

The Huichol see their ancestral homeland as the state of San Luis Potosi – they migrated to their current home in the Bolaños Canyon region seeking refuge around the time of the conquests.

Another famous pilgrimage in the area is the Catholic ritual of the feast day of St. Francis of Assisi. Thousands travel into the mountains to visit the crumbling ex-mining town of Real de Catorce to pay respects to the statue of St. Francis there.

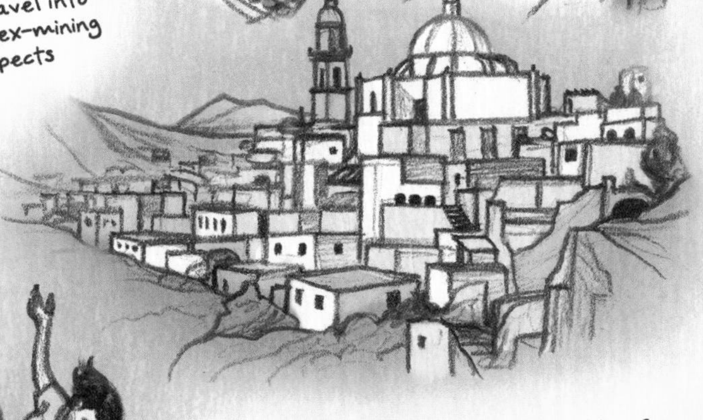

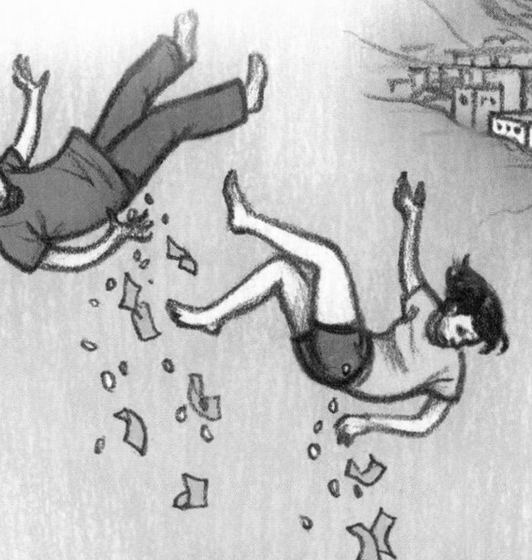

As we travelled through the Bajío we realised how out of date our guidebook was – everything was costing double what we expected.

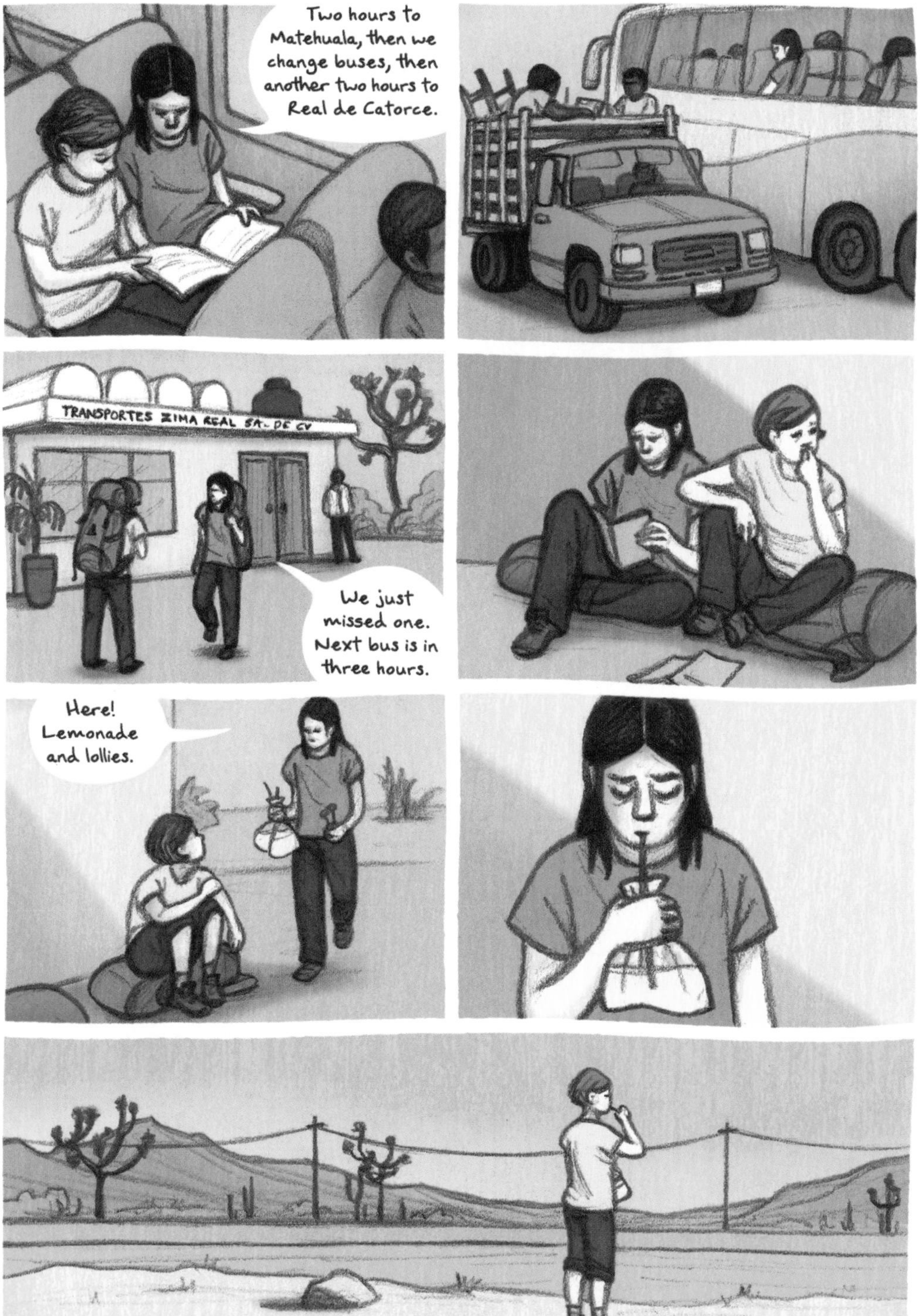
Two hours to Matehuala, then we change buses, then another two hours to Real de Catorce.
TRANSPORTES ZIMA REAL SA. DE CV
We just missed one. Next bus is in three hours.
Here! Lemonade and lollies.

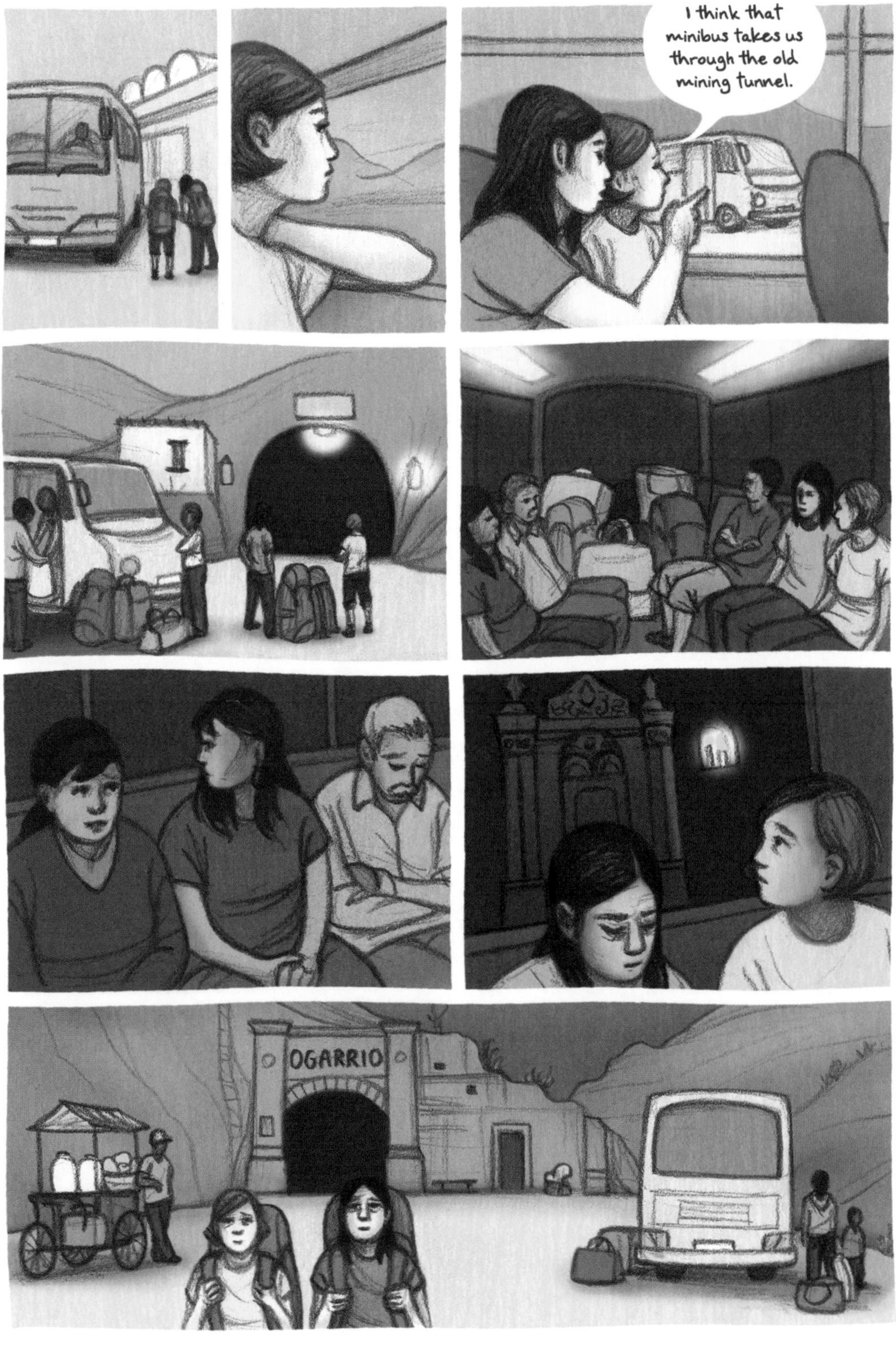
I think that minibus takes us through the old mining tunnel.
OGARRIO

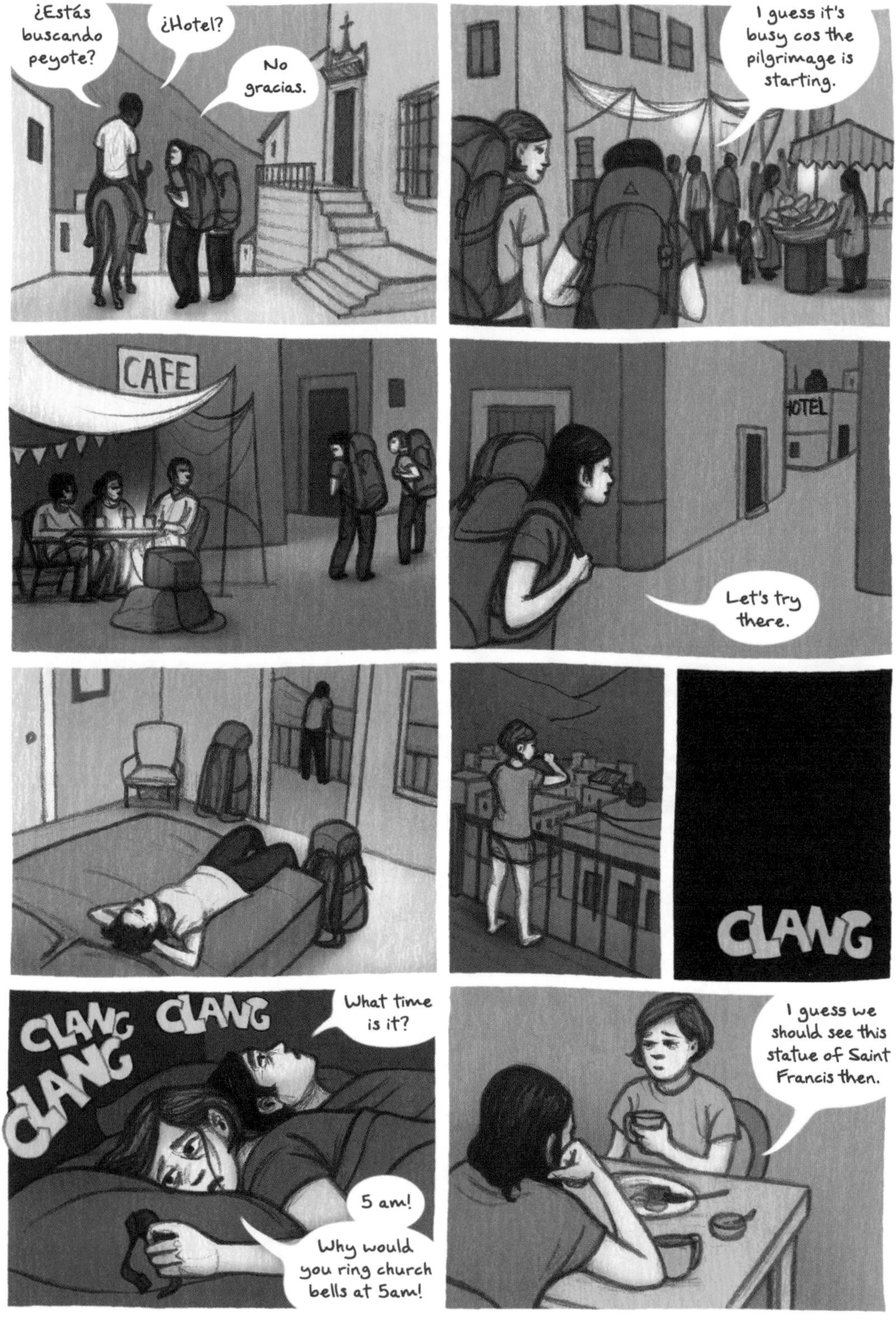
¿Estás buscando peyote?
¿Hotel?
No gracias.
I guess it's busy cos the pilgrimage is starting.
CAFE
HOTEL
Let's try there.
CLANG
CLANG CLANG CLANG
What time is it?
5 am!
Why would you ring church bells at 5am!
I guess we should see this statue of Saint Francis then.

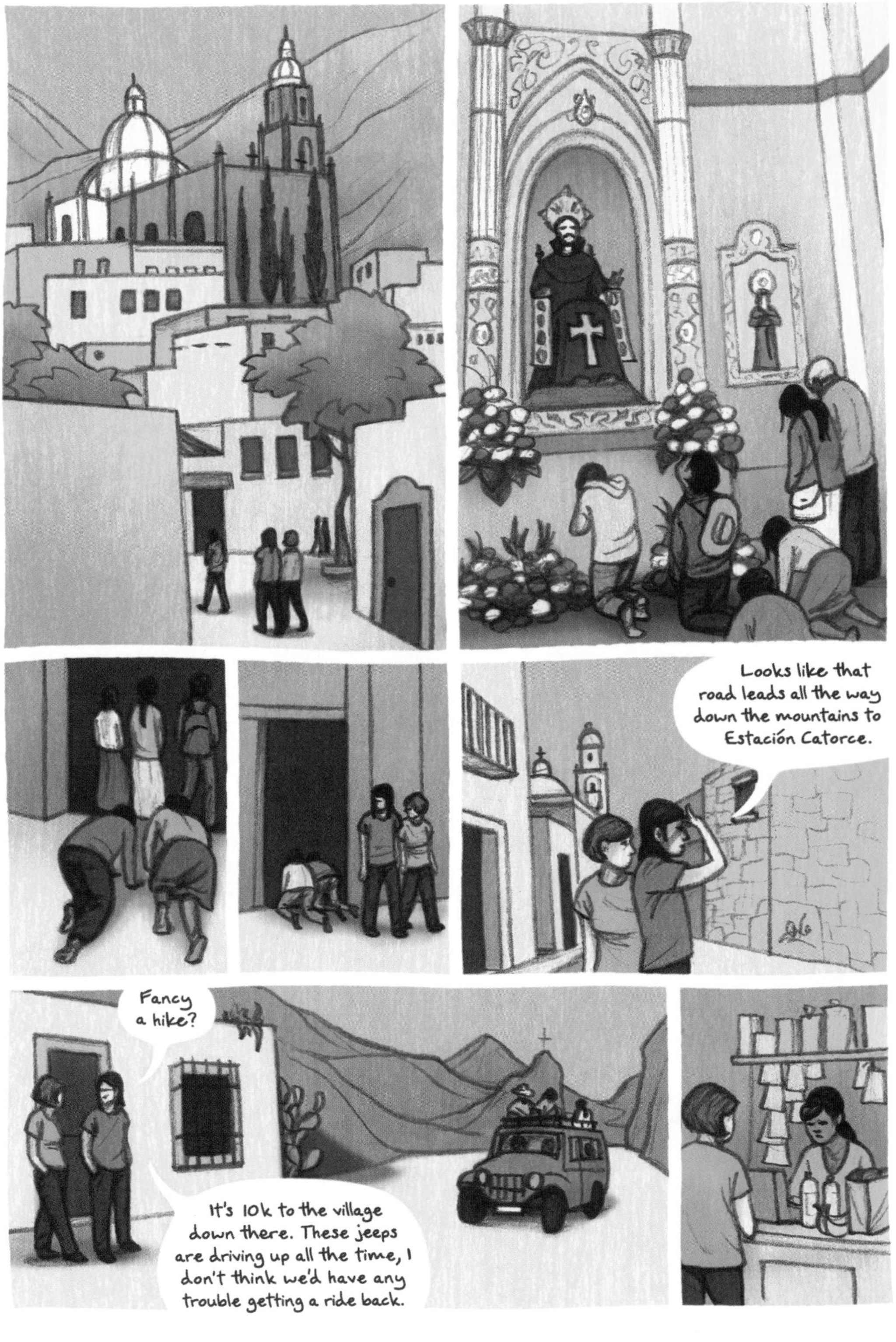
Looks like that road leads all the way down the mountains to Estación Catorce.
Fancy a hike?
It's 10k to the village down there. These jeeps are driving up all the time, I don't think we'd have any trouble getting a ride back.

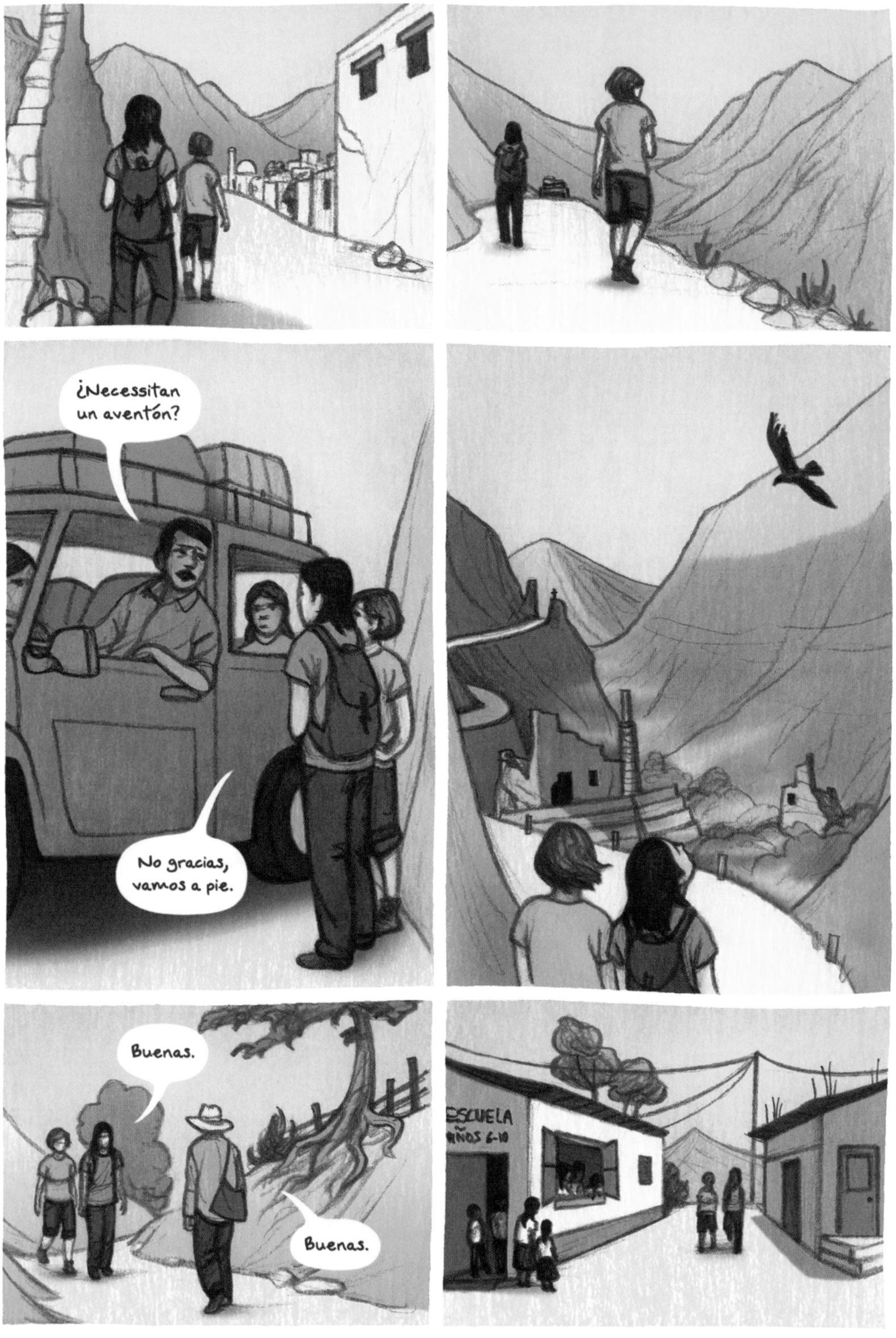
¿Necessitan un aventón?
No gracias, vamos a pie.
Buenas.
Buenas.
ESCUELA

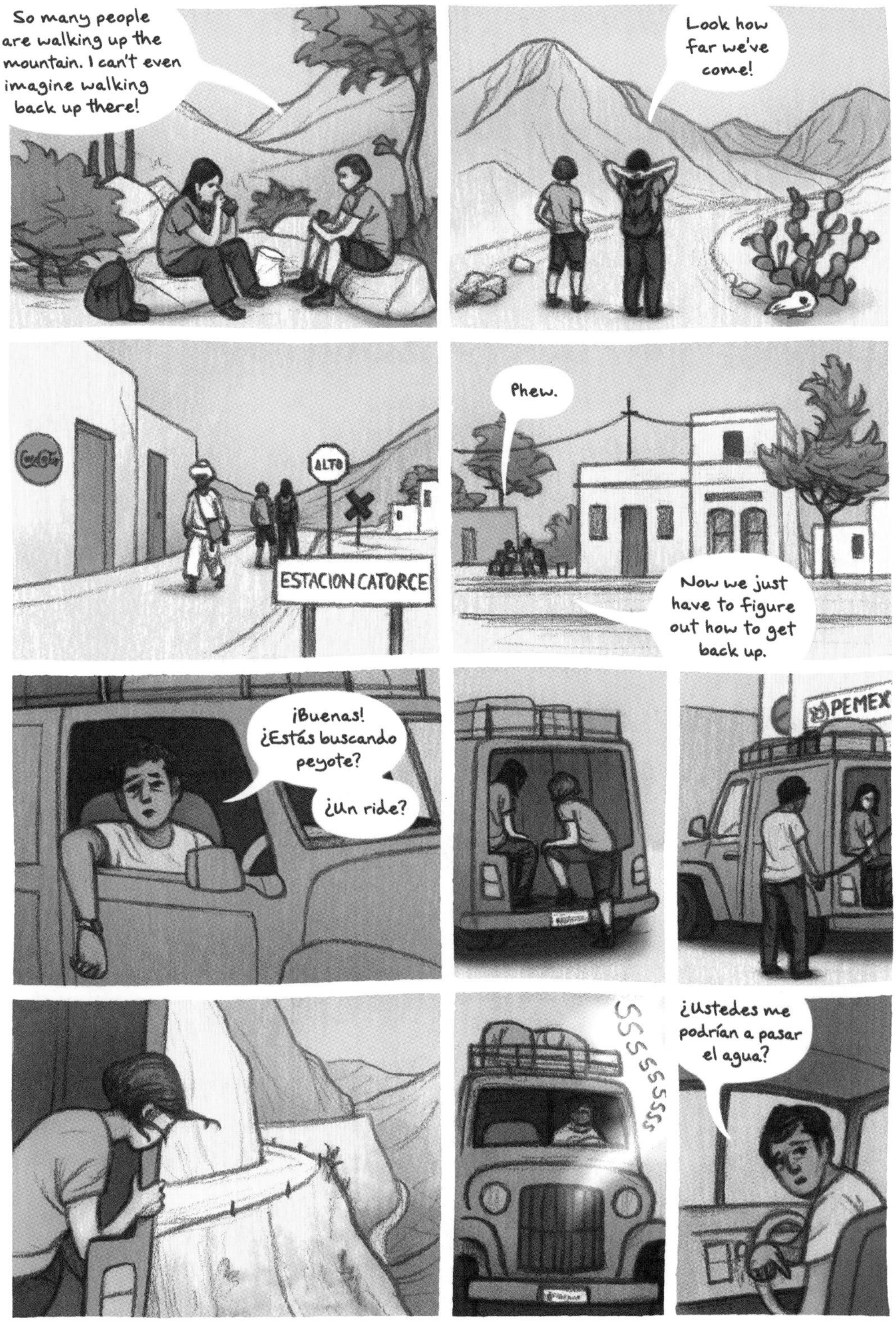
So many people are walking up the mountain. I can't even imagine walking back up there!
Look how far we've come!
ALTO
ESTACION CATORCE
Phew.
Now we just have to figure out how to get back up.
¡Buenas! ¿Estás buscando peyote?
¿Un ride?
PEMEX
SSSSSSSS
¿Ustedes me podrían a pasar el agua?

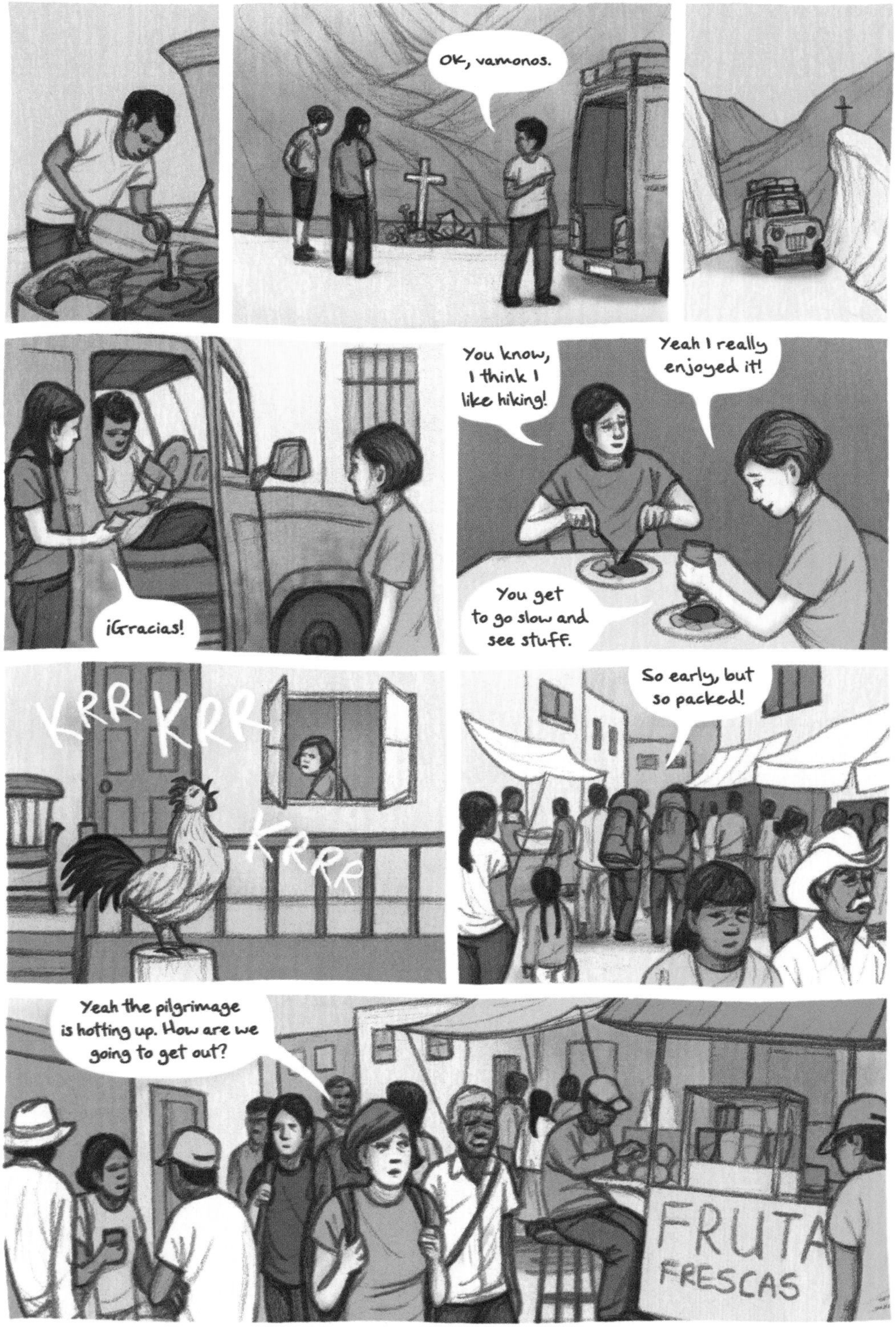
Ok, vamonos.
¡Gracias!
You know, I think I like hiking!
Yeah I really enjoyed it!
You get to go slow and see stuff.
KRR KRR
KRRR
So early, but so packed!
Yeah the pilgrimage is hotting up. How are we going to get out?
FRUTA FRESCAS

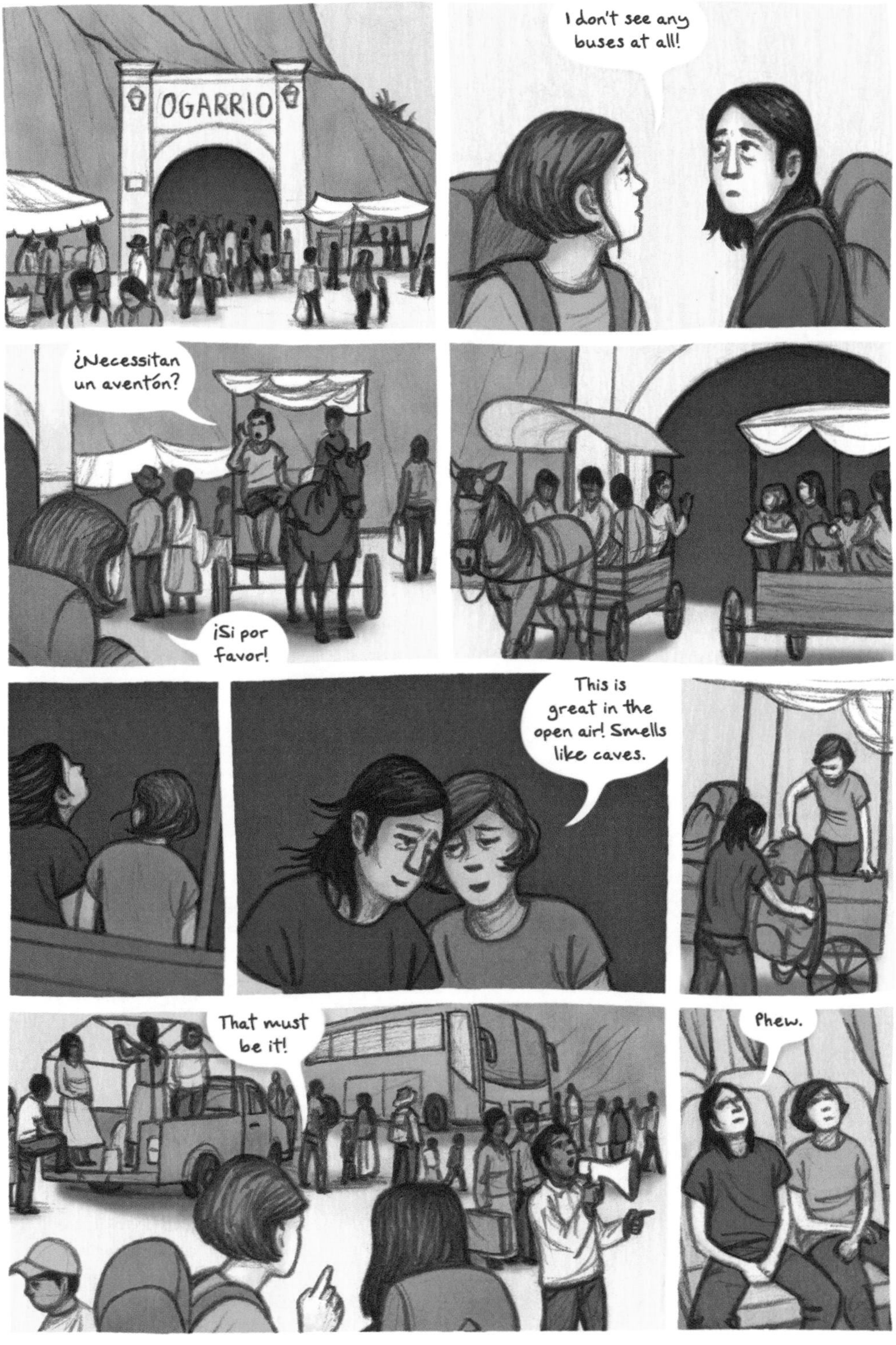
OGARRIO
I don't see any buses at all!
¿Necessitan un aventón?
¡Si por favor!
This is great in the open air! Smells like caves.
That must be it!
Phew.

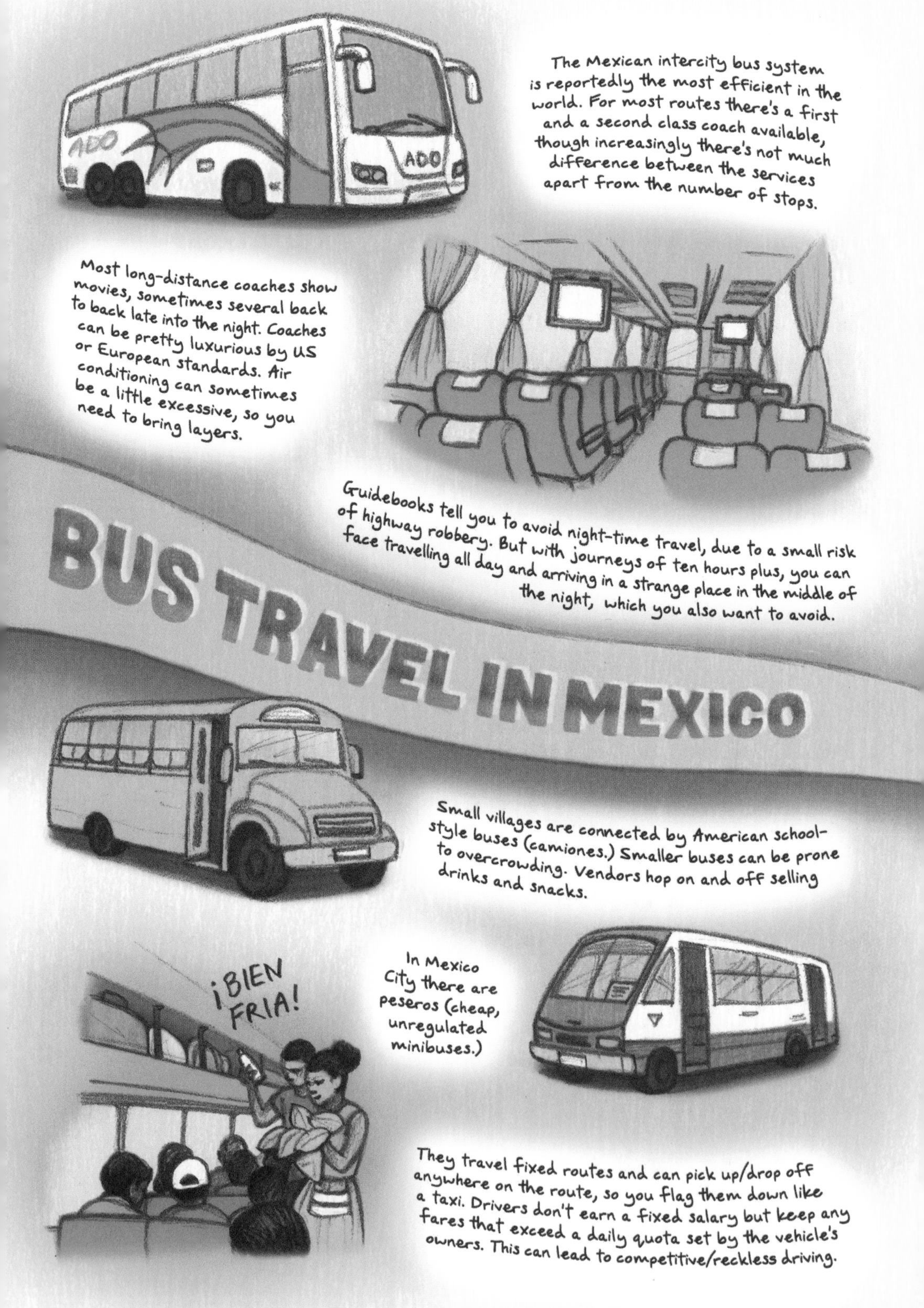
BUS TRAVEL IN MEXICO
ADO
ADO
The Mexican intercity bus system is reportedly the most efficient in the world. For most routes there's a first and a second class coach available, though increasingly there's not much difference between the services apart from the number of stops.
Most long-distance coaches show movies, sometimes several back to back late into the night. Coaches can be pretty luxurious by US or European standards. Air conditioning can sometimes be a little excessive, so you need to bring layers.
Guidebooks tell you to avoid night-time travel, due to a small risk of highway robbery. But with journeys of ten hours plus, you can face travelling all day and arriving in a strange place in the middle of the night, which you also want to avoid.
Small villages are connected by American school-style buses (camiones.) Smaller buses can be prone to overcrowding. Vendors hop on and off selling drinks and snacks.
In Mexico City there are peseros (cheap, unregulated minibuses.)
¡BIEN FRIA!
They travel fixed routes and can pick up/drop off anywhere on the route, so you flag them down like a taxi. Drivers don't earn a fixed salary but keep any fares that exceed a daily quota set by the vehicle's owners. This can lead to competitive/reckless driving.

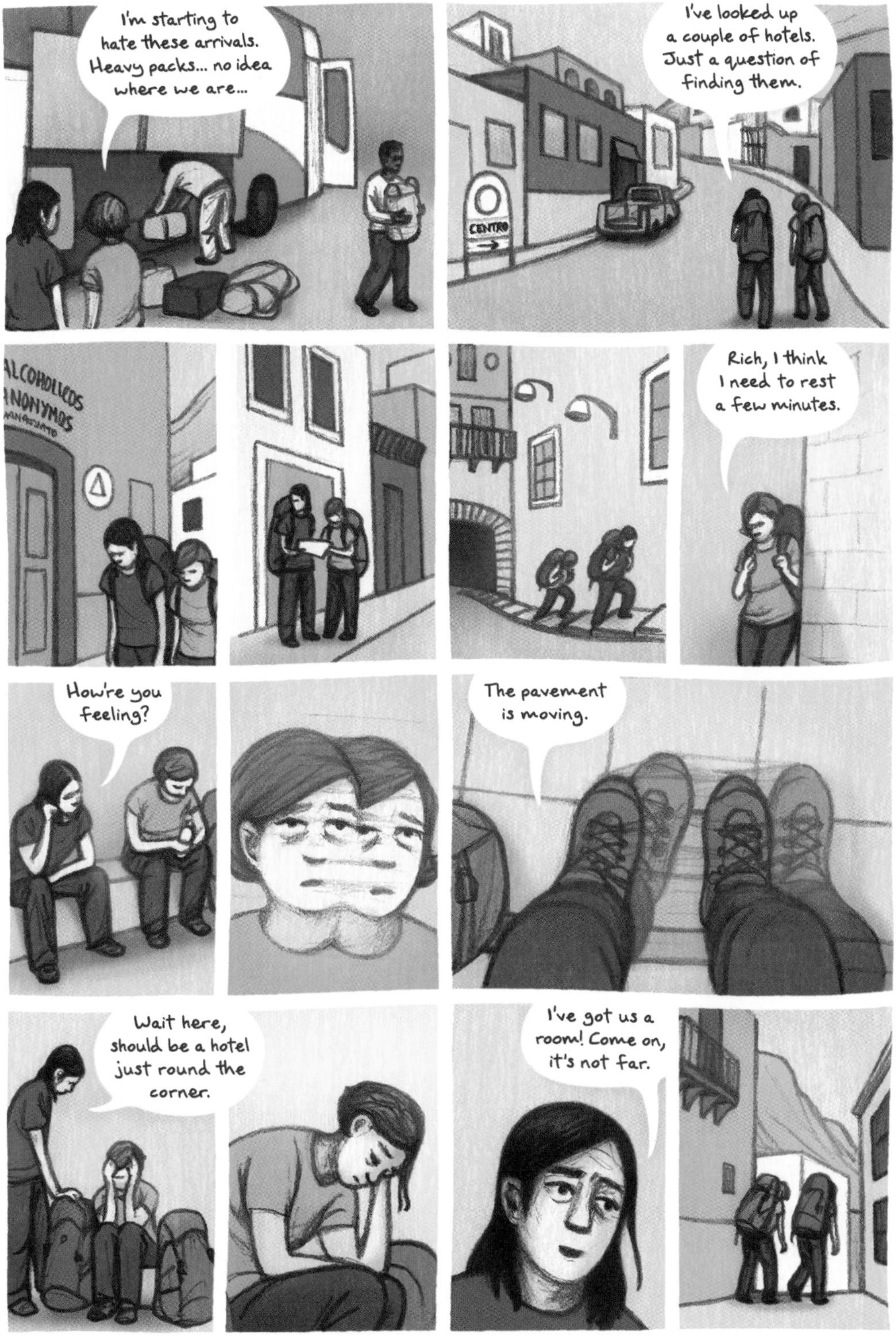
I'm starting to hate these arrivals. Heavy packs... no idea where we are...
I've looked up a couple of hotels. Just a question of finding them.
CENTRO
Rich, I think I need to rest a few minutes.
How're you feeling?
The pavement is moving.
Wait here, should be a hotel just round the corner.
I've got us a room! Come on, it's not far.

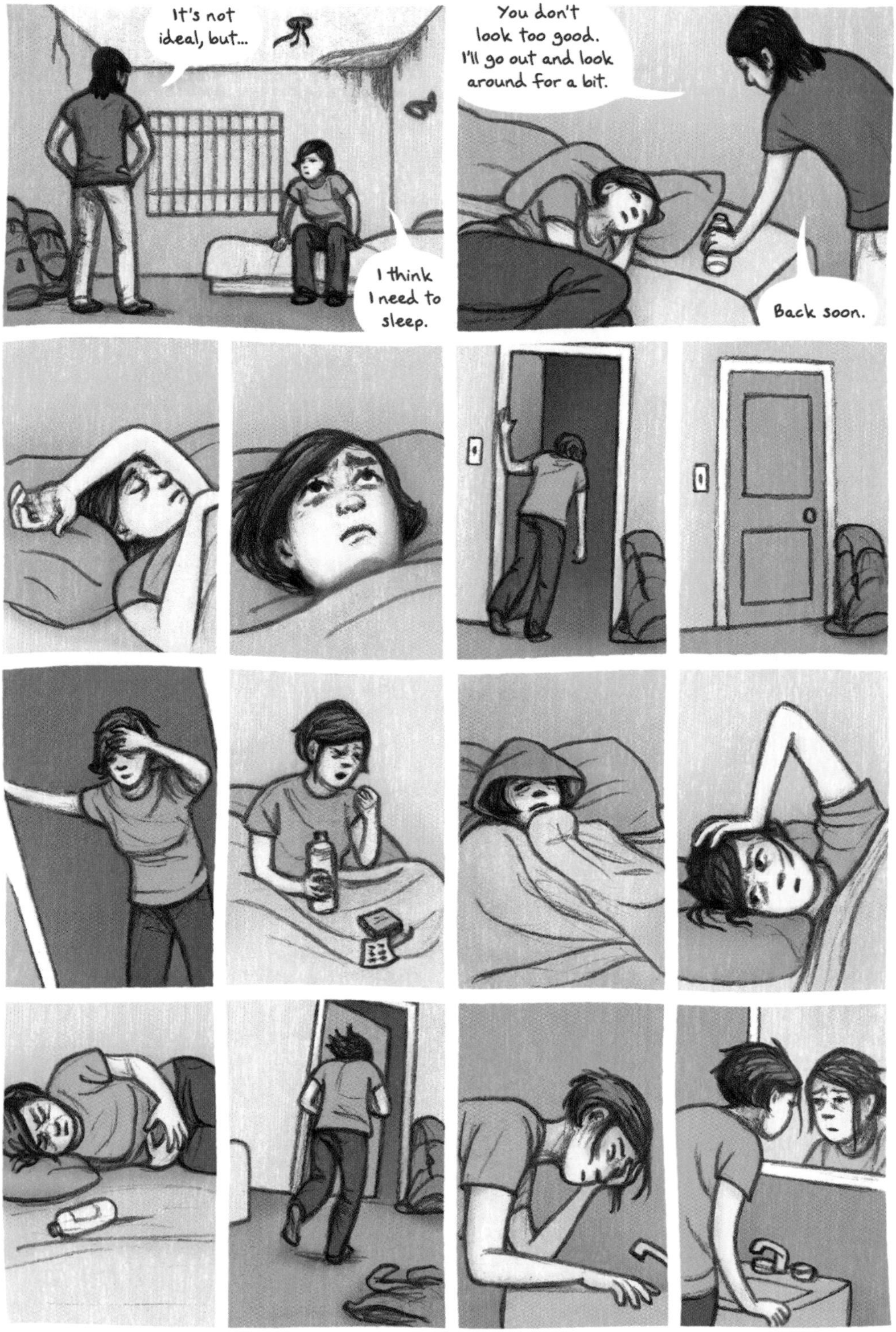
It's not ideal, but...
I think I need to sleep.
You don't look too good. I'll go out and look around for a bit.
Back soon.

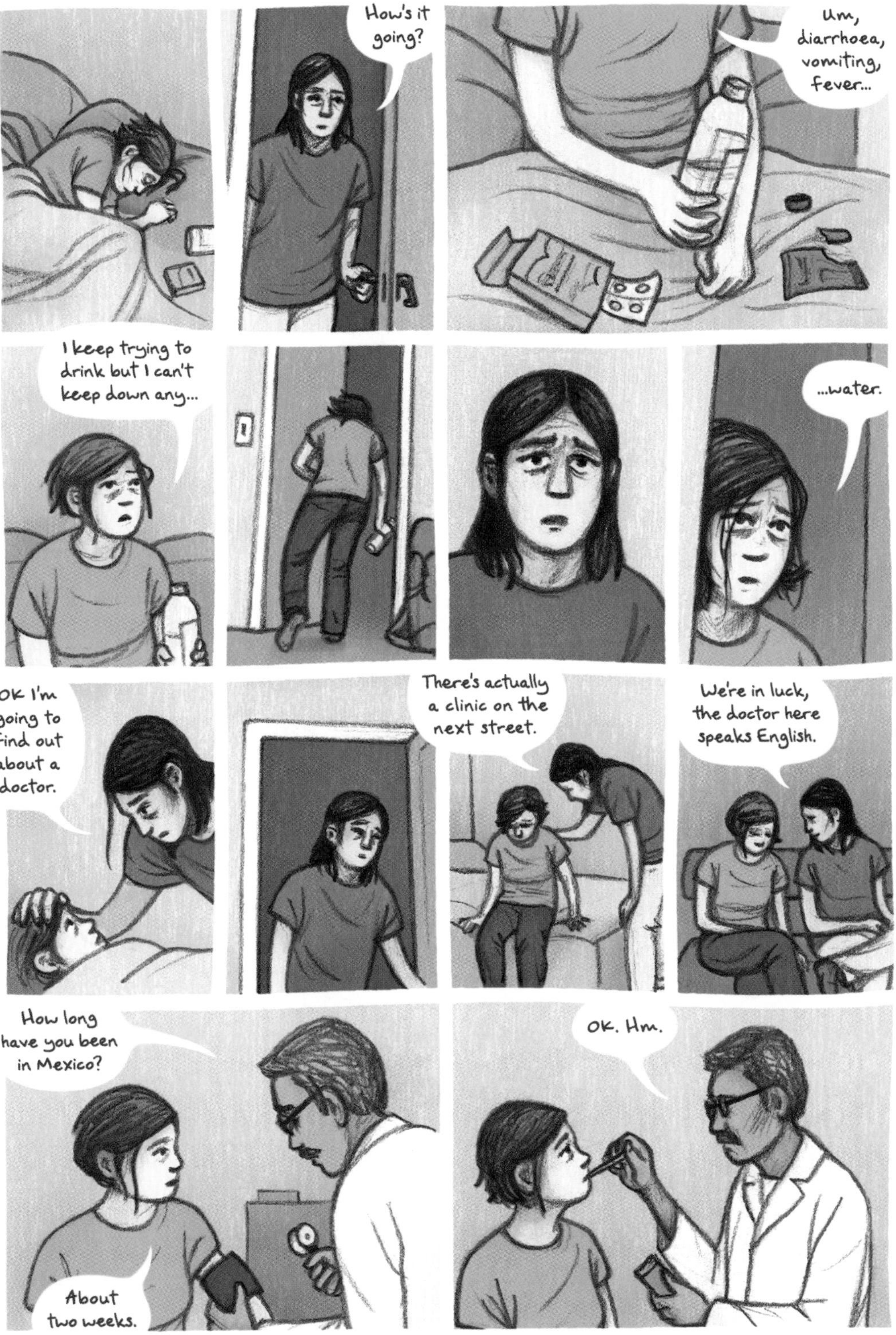
How's it going?
Um, diarrhoea, vomiting, fever...
I keep trying to drink but I can't keep down any...
...water.
OK I'm going to find out about a doctor.
There's actually a clinic on the next street.
We're in luck, the doctor here speaks English.
How long have you been in Mexico?
About two weeks.
OK. Hm.

Do you have insurance?

Yes.

Good. I think you need to stay overnight, we need to rehydrate you.

Have you been able to drink much water?

No.

This is the problem. Dehydration is very dangerous.

But if we put you on a drip, with antibiotics and saline, you should be up and about in 24 hours.

You'll be fine.

I've just never been to hospital before.

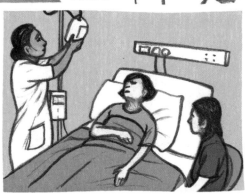

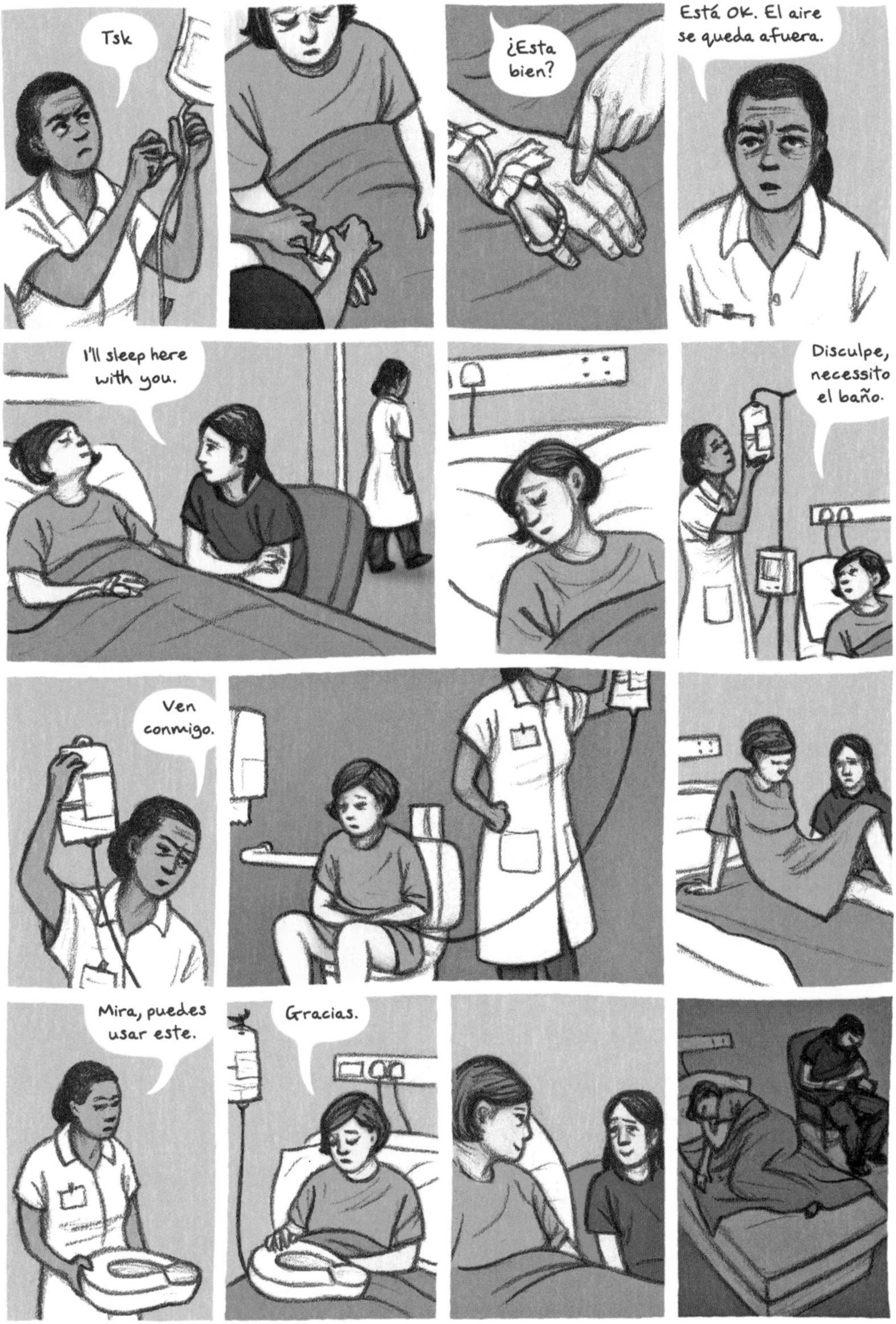
Tsk
¿Esta bien?
Está OK. El aire se queda afuera.
I'll sleep here with you.
Disculpe, necessito el baño.
Ven conmigo.
Mira, puedes usar este.
Gracias.

¡Buenas días! Morning!

¿Ingles, no?

Si.

Uh, cuantas veces... aqui...

Como... cuatro veces.

Muy bien.

Y...

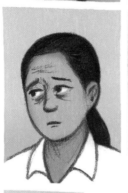

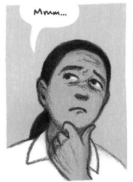

Mmm...

SHIT?

Uh, no.

Bien.

Y...

Ha experimentado algun...

'Throwing out?'

No. Siento mucho mejor.

Muy muy bien.

El doctor la atenderá pronto.

AGUA en MEXICO

Drinking tap water in Mexico is risky. Even aside from bacteria like ecoli and salmonella, tourists often get sick from pathogens that are just new to their systems. In different parts of the country water will come from different sources – sometimes mains water and sometimes not.

Tap water in Mexico City has a reputation for impurity. The famous 1985 earthquake broke mains pipelines and sewers all over the city, leading to an increase in waterborne diseases and the spread of cholera in the 1990s.

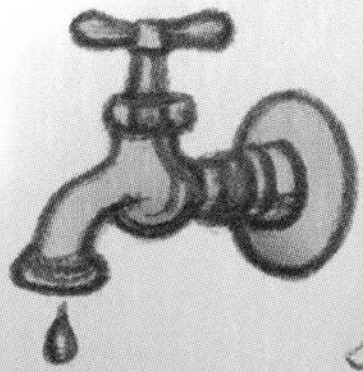

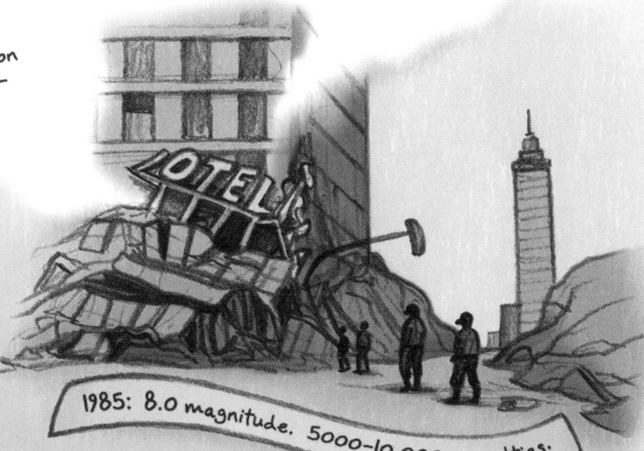

HOTEL

1985: 8.0 magnitude. 5000–10,000 casualties.

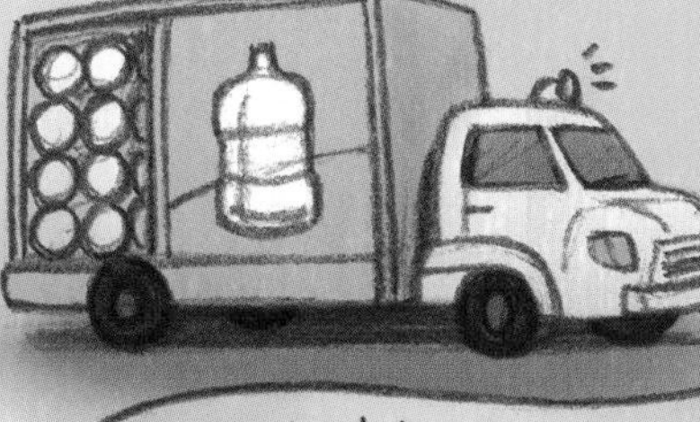

Companies deliver 20-litre bottles to homes and businesses.

Our guidebook told us that to be extra safe we should brush our teeth with bottled water and keep our mouths closed in the shower. It also suggested not buying pre-cut fruit from street vendors (washed in tap water) and to never have ice in our drinks. It was very hard to stick to the last one in the hottest parts of the country.

As we were hoping to travel for up to a year, we decided that some of this was impractical. We brushed our teeth with tap water, thinking that it'd be impossible to avoid it forever. We hoped we'd adjust to it with time.

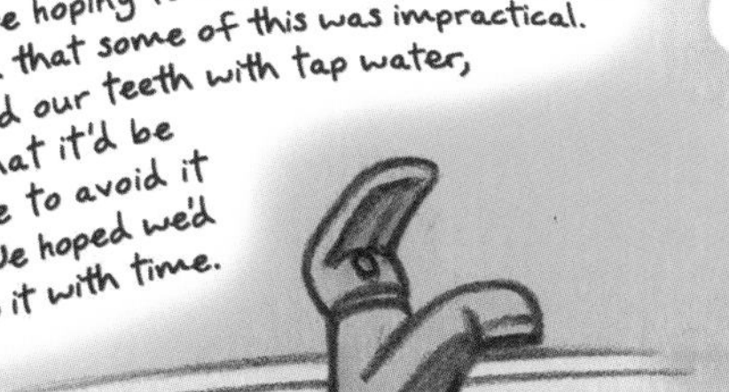

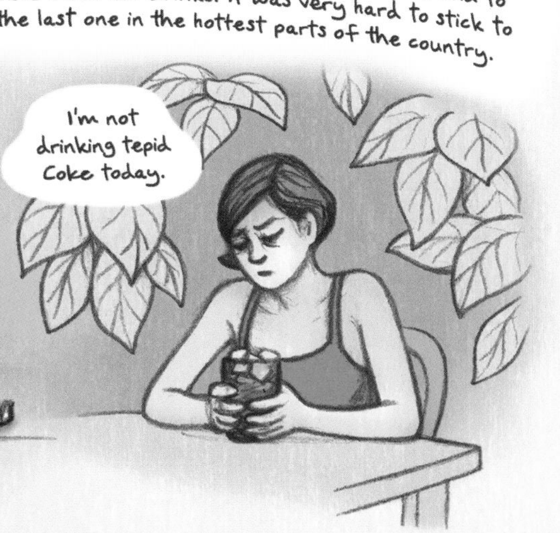

I'm not drinking tepid Coke today.

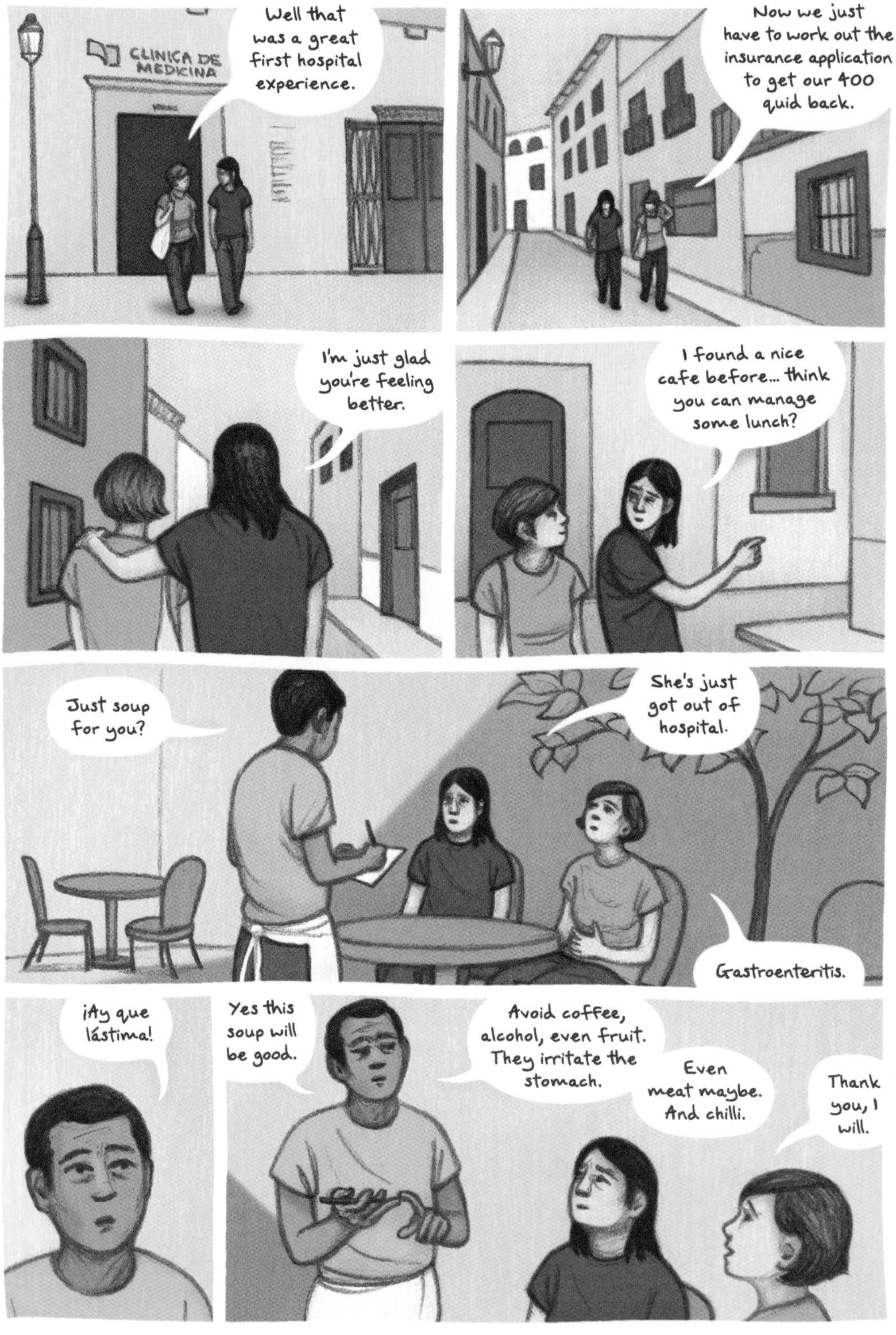
CLINICA DE MEDICINA
Well that was a great first hospital experience.
Now we just have to work out the insurance application to get our 400 quid back.
I'm just glad you're feeling better.
I found a nice cafe before... think you can manage some lunch?
Just soup for you?
She's just got out of hospital.
Gastroenteritis.
¡Ay que lástima!
Yes this soup will be good.
Avoid coffee, alcohol, even fruit. They irritate the stomach.
Even meat maybe. And chilli.
Thank you, I will.

Hospital, 19-20th Sept. Guanajuato
Drawing - 24th -26th.

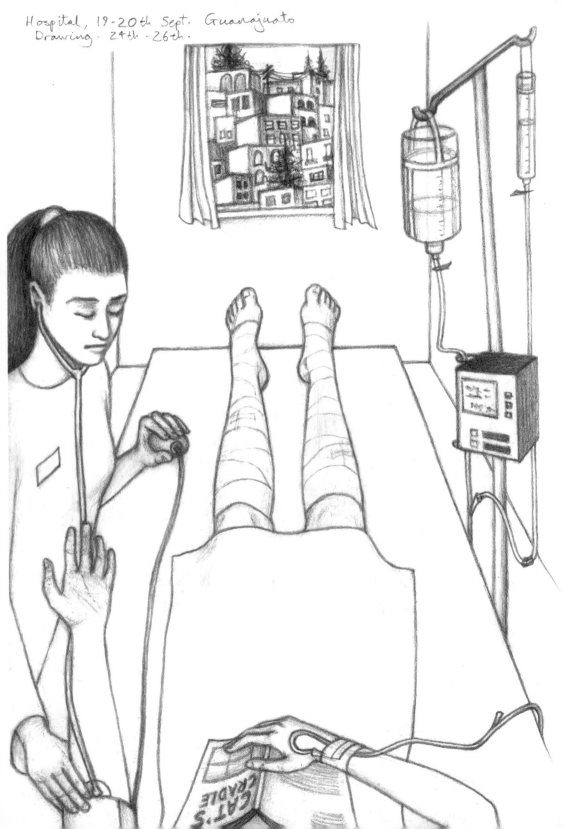

Zacatecas

From Guanajuato we headed north-west to Zacatecas, a mining city built from pink sandstone, and then on to Durango and Chupaderos. There we visited the ghost town Villa del Oeste where remnants of old Western film sets remain in the desert.

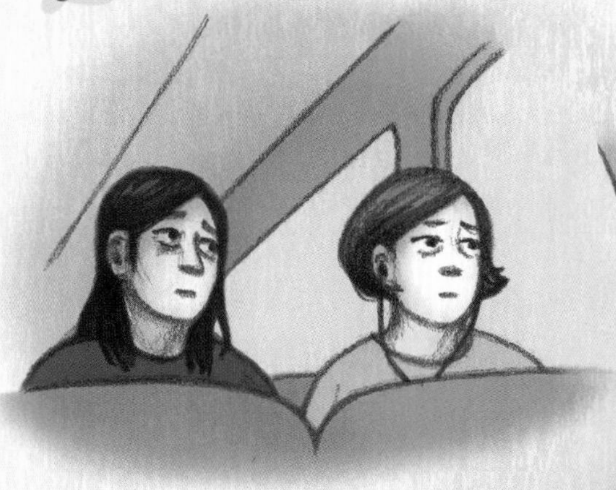

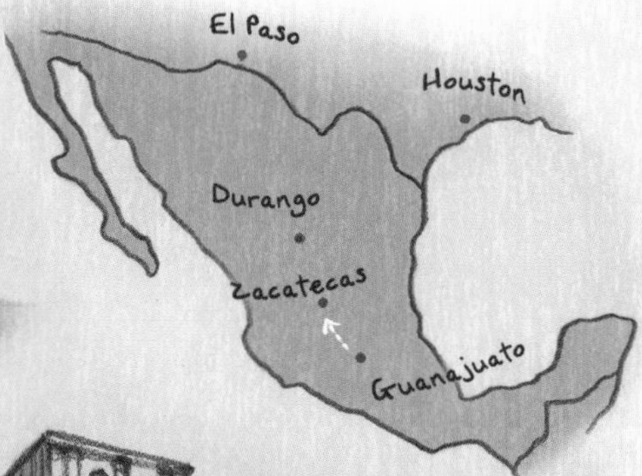
El Paso
Houston
Durango
Zacatecas
Guanajuato

Zacatecas is home to the Museo Rafael Coronal, a museum built in the partially restored ruins of a Franciscan monastery. It contains all kinds of art and artefacts; pre-Hispanic, indigenous, votive... pottery and paintings and handicrafts. It also has a collection of more than 4000 masks.

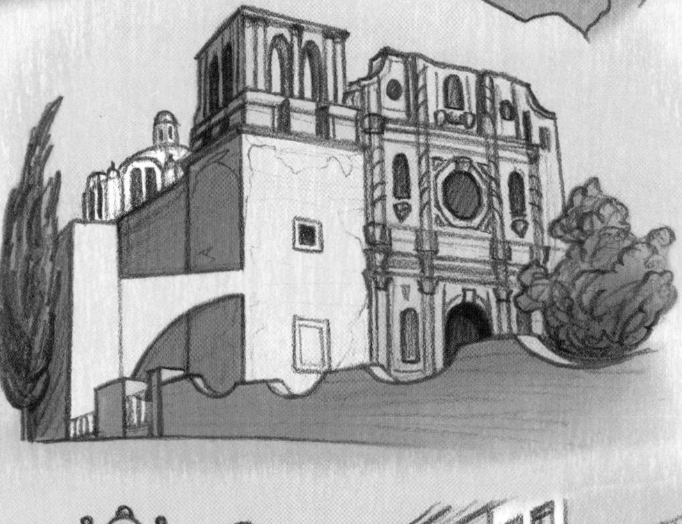

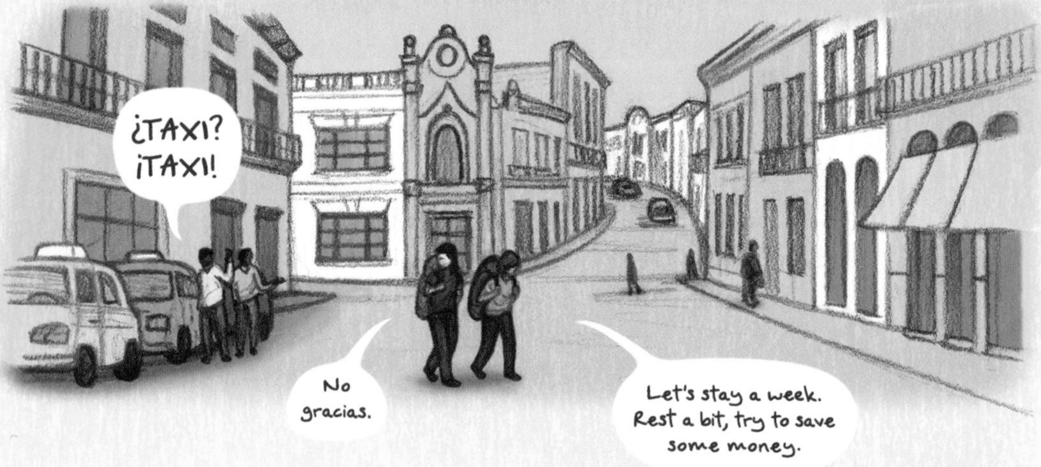
¿TAXI? ¡TAXI!
No gracias.
Let's stay a week. Rest a bit, try to save some money.

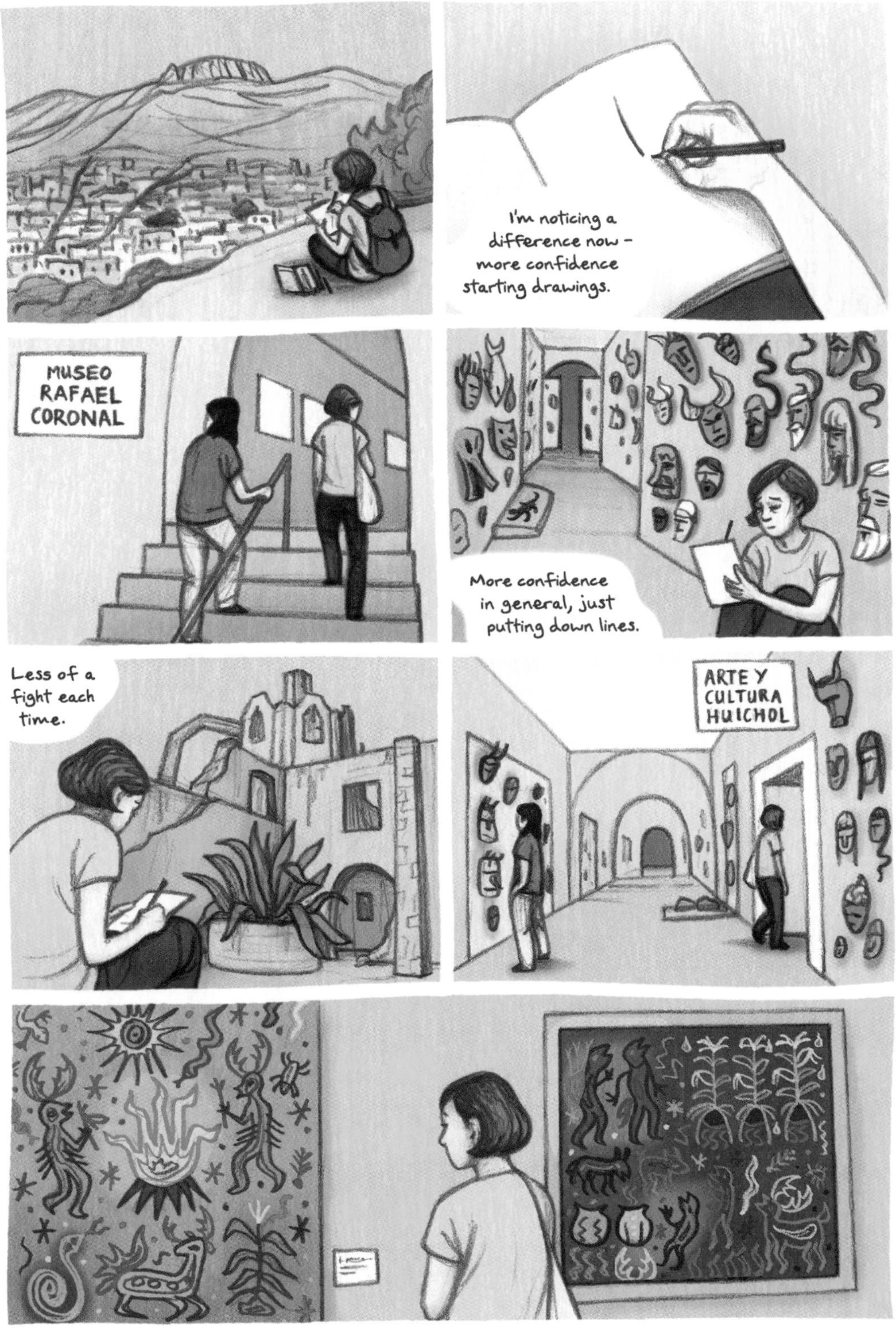
I'm noticing a difference now - more confidence starting drawings.
MUSEO RAFAEL CORONAL
More confidence in general, just putting down lines.
Less of a fight each time.
ARTE Y CULTURA HUICHOL

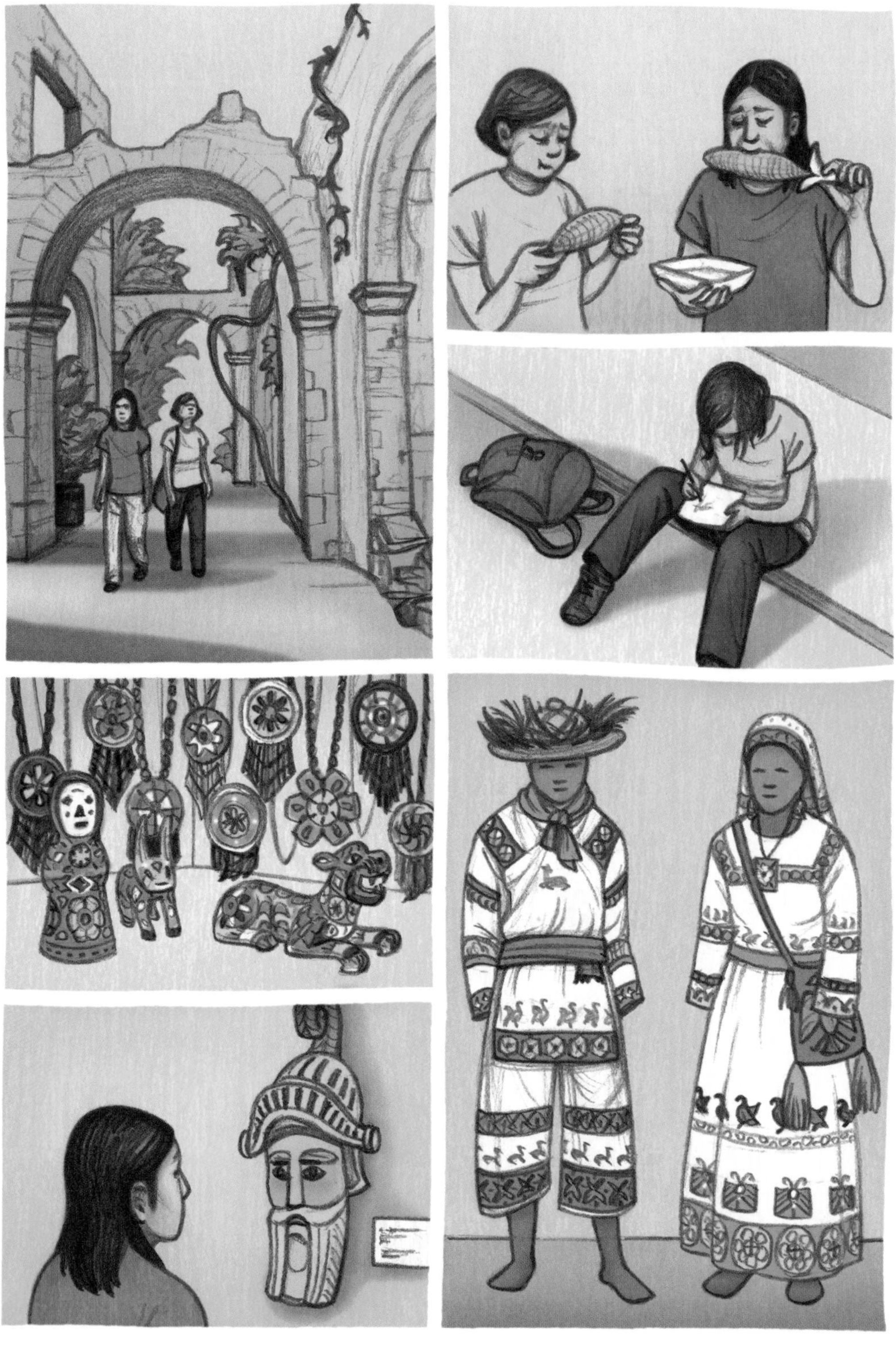

'La Bufa'
overlooking Zacatecas.

From the balcony of
the Hotel Rio Grande,
1 - 2/10/03

Barrancas del Cobre (the Copper Canyons)

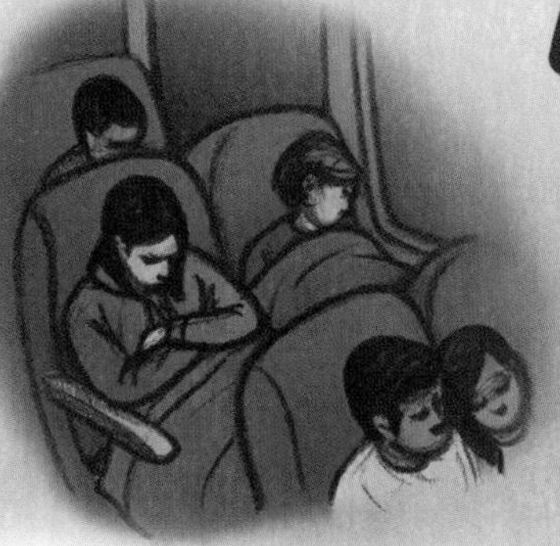

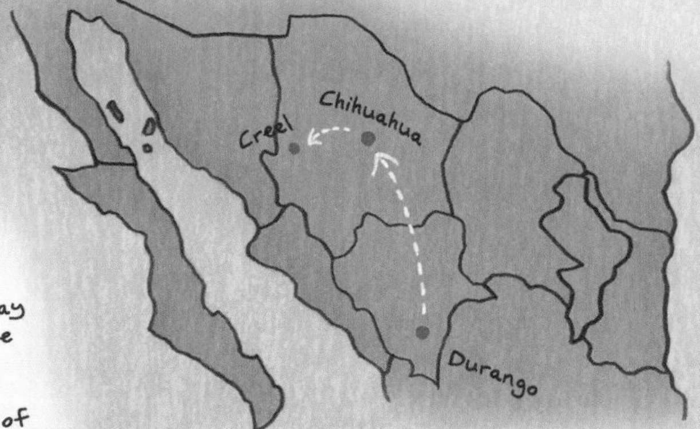

Chihuahua
Creel
Durango

Despite both of us being ill with stomach problems, we decided to tackle the twelve-hour journey from Durango to Creel - a small highland town in the Copper Canyons. My birthday was a day away, and we wanted to be somewhere beautiful to celebrate. We had to travel overnight - eight hours to Chihuahua then a change of bus and another four hours to Creel.

The Copper Canyons are a network of six canyons in the Sierra Madre Occidental mountain range. They reach 2000 meters deep.

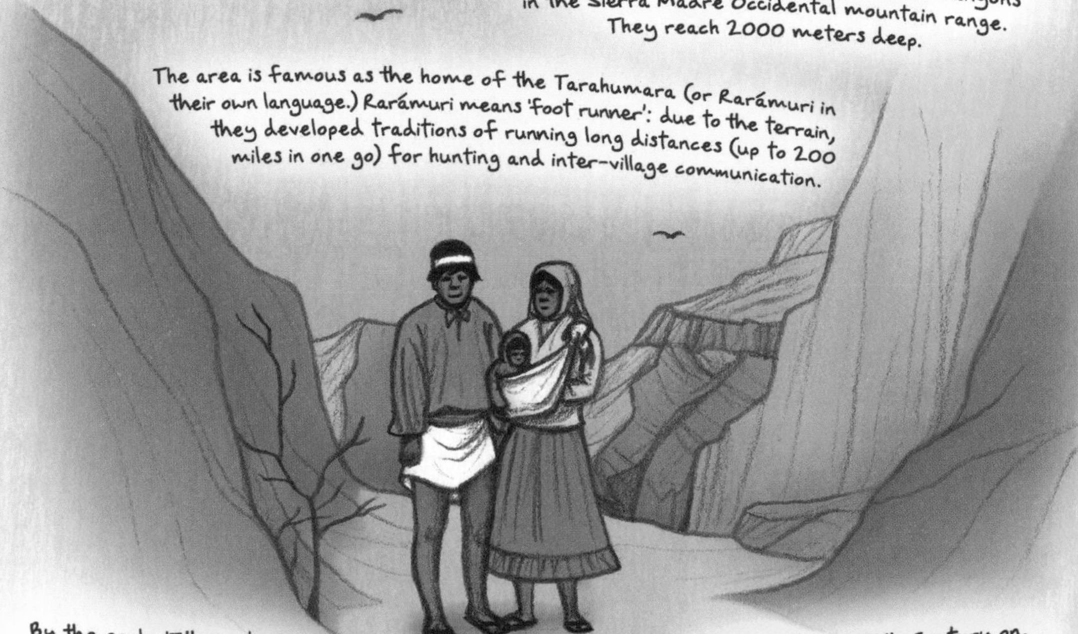

The area is famous as the home of the Tarahumara (or Rarámuri in their own language.) Rarámuri means 'foot runner': due to the terrain, they developed traditions of running long distances (up to 200 miles in one go) for hunting and inter-village communication.

By the early 17th century the Spanish began mining and establishing missions on Rarámuri land. Between 1648 and 1698 the Rarámuri waged sporadic war on them, suffering some defeats but also at times succeeding in driving them out.

From the mid 18th Century on, they were left free to modify and integrate Catholic beliefs into their own religion. Most still practise a traditional lifestyle, living in small cabins which sometimes make use of natural structures like caves in their construction.

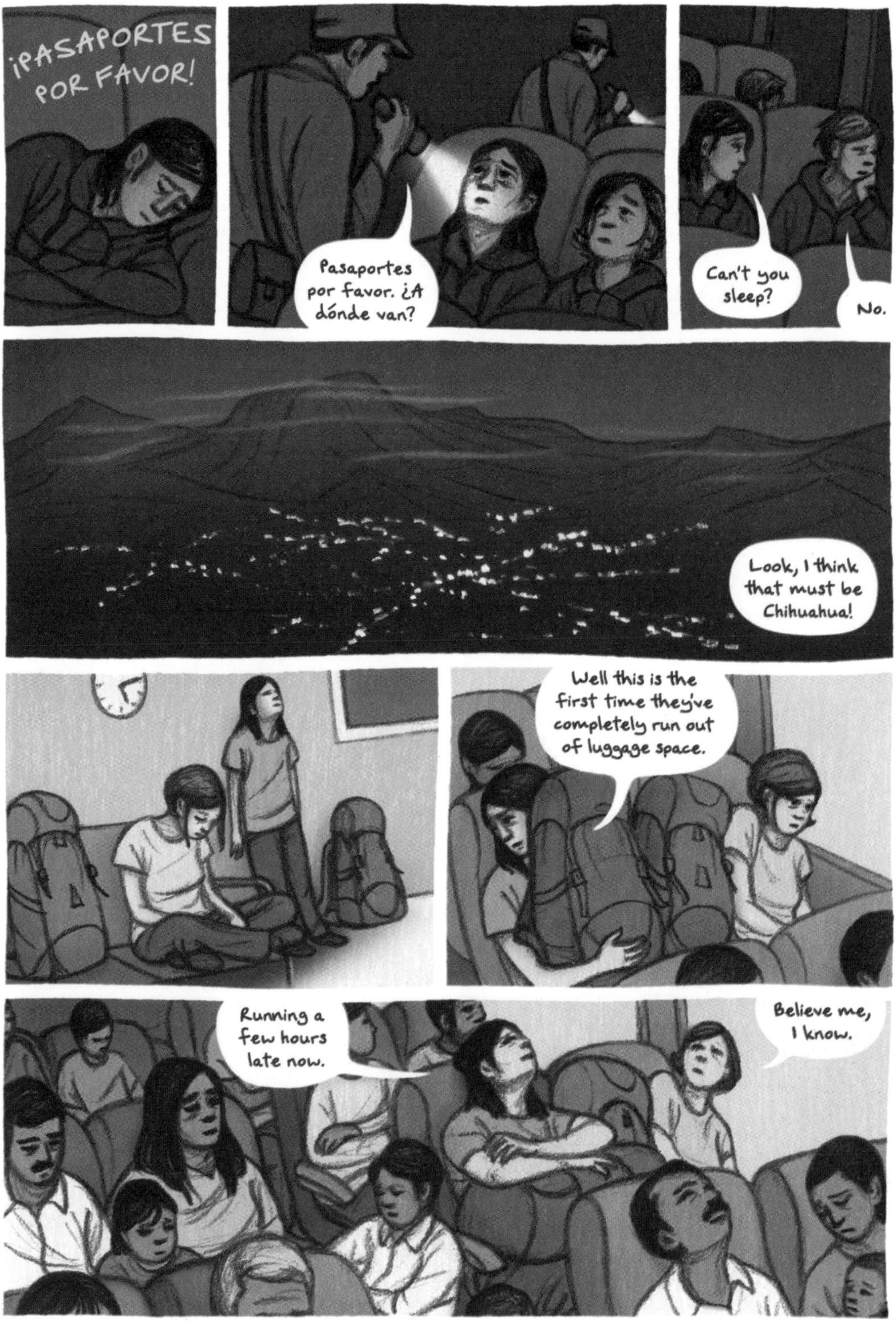
¡PASAPORTES POR FAVOR!
Pasaportes por favor. ¿A dónde van?
Can't you sleep?
No.
Look, I think that must be Chihuahua!
Well this is the first time they've completely run out of luggage space.
Running a few hours late now.
Believe me, I know.

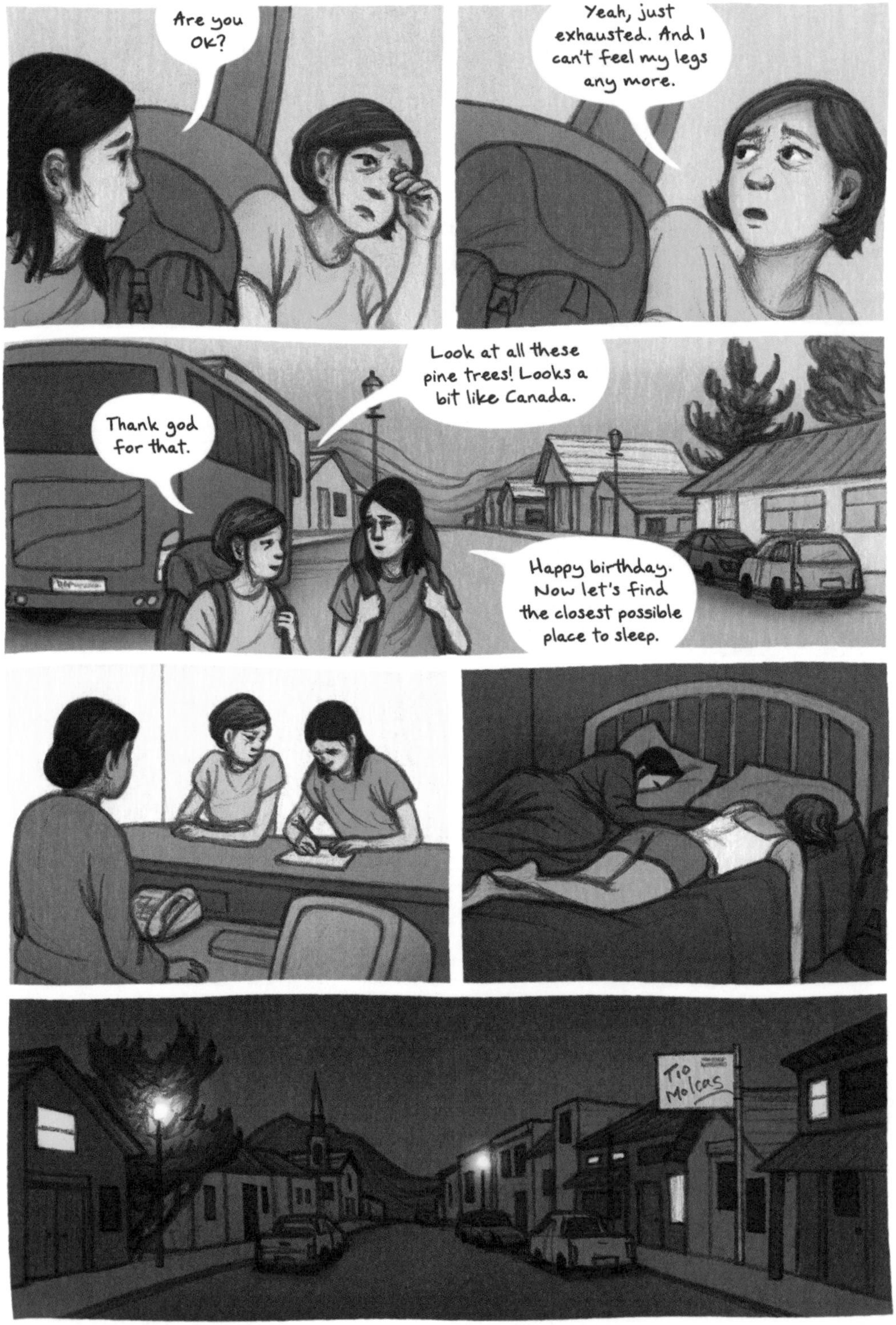

Are you OK?
Yeah, just exhausted. And I can't feel my legs any more.
Look at all these pine trees! Looks a bit like Canada.
Thank god for that.
Happy birthday. Now let's find the closest possible place to sleep.
Tio Molcas

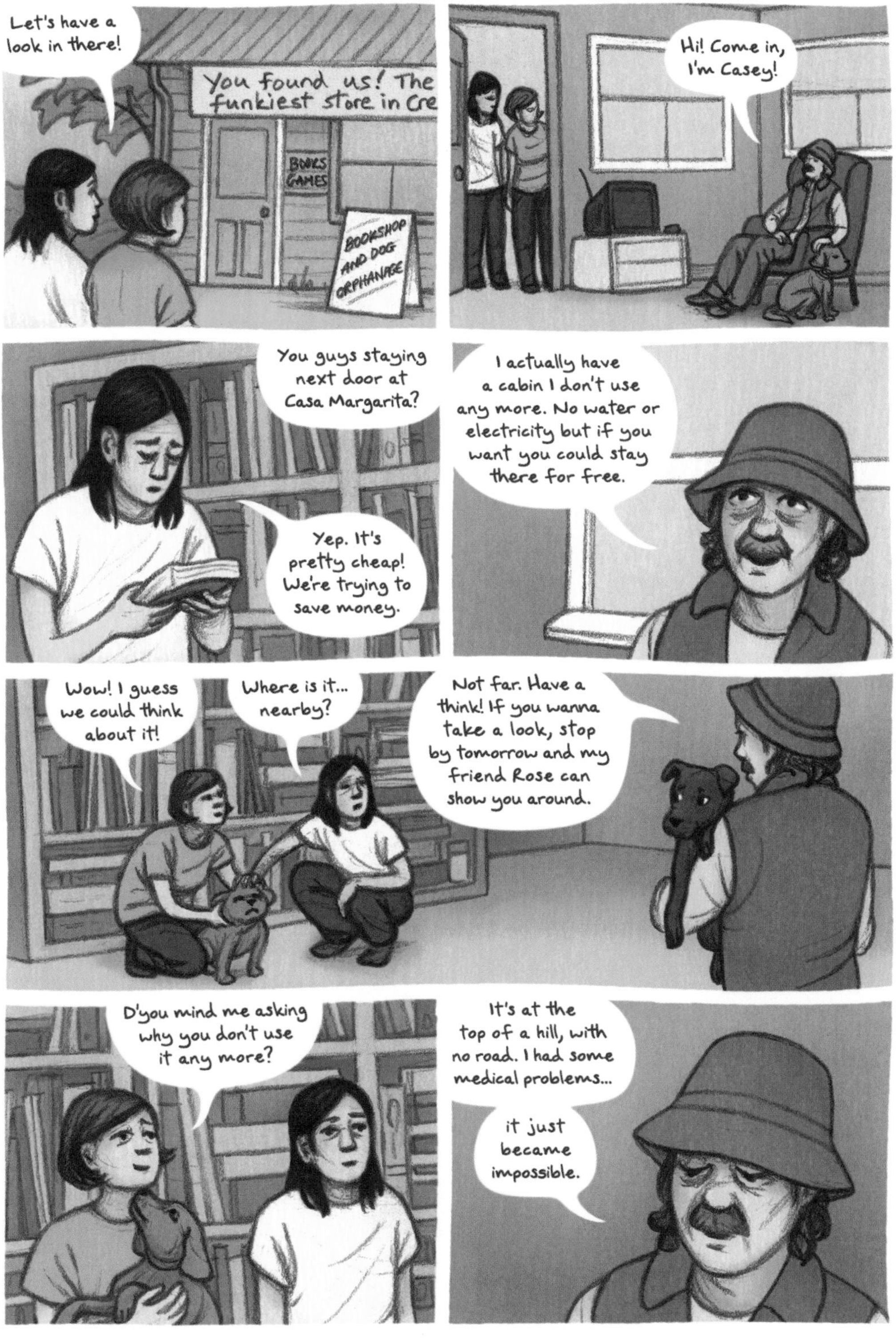
Let's have a look in there!
You found us! The funkiest store in Cre
BOOKS GAMES
BOOKSHOP AND DOG ORPHANAGE
Hi! Come in, I'm Casey!
You guys staying next door at Casa Margarita?
Yep. It's pretty cheap! We're trying to save money.
I actually have a cabin I don't use any more. No water or electricity but if you want you could stay there for free.
Wow! I guess we could think about it!
Where is it... nearby?
Not far. Have a think! If you wanna take a look, stop by tomorrow and my friend Rose can show you around.
D'you mind me asking why you don't use it any more?
It's at the top of a hill, with no road. I had some medical problems...
it just became impossible.

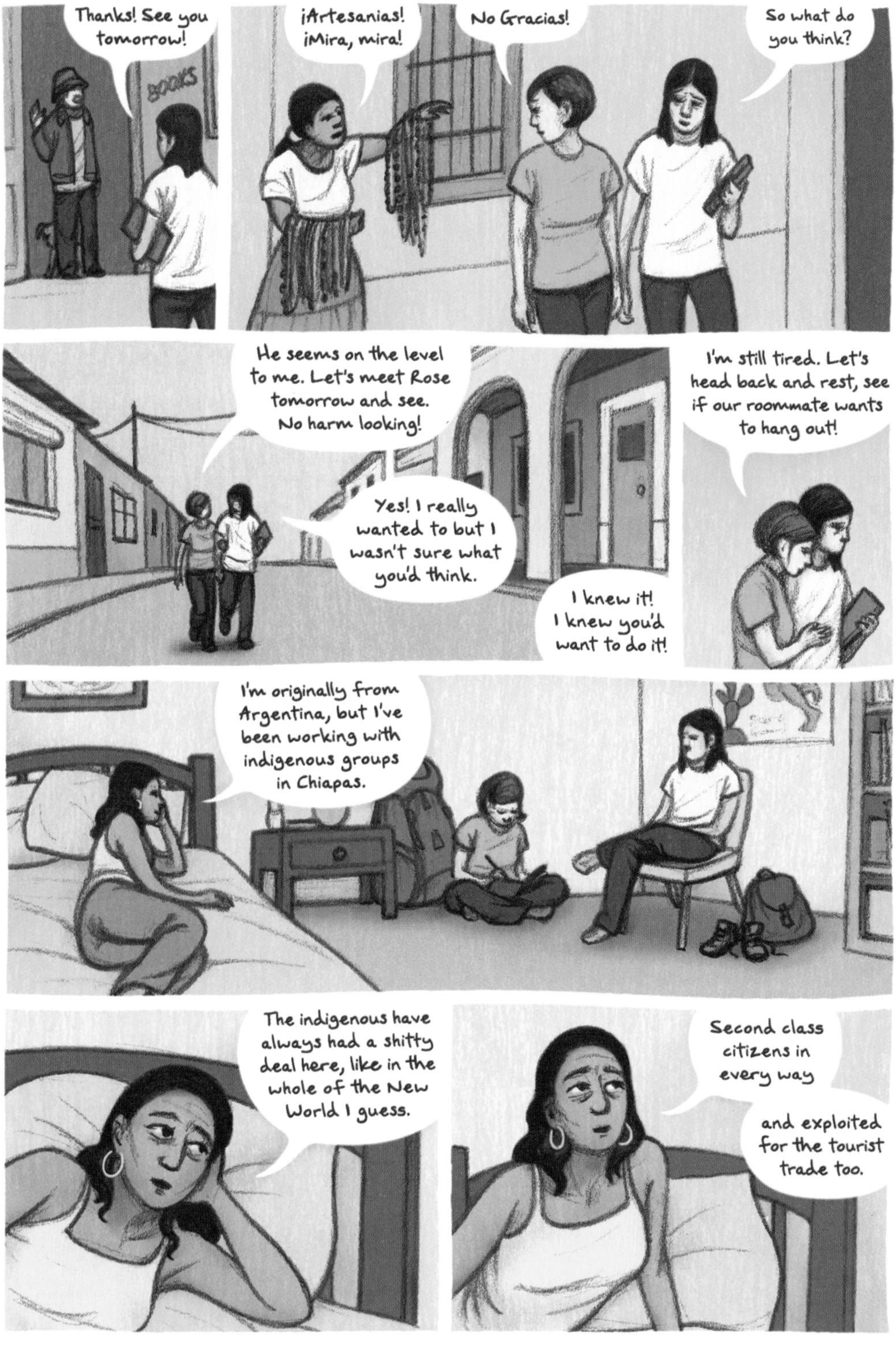
Thanks! See you tomorrow!
BOOKS
¡Artesanias! ¡Mira, mira!
No Gracias!
So what do you think?
He seems on the level to me. Let's meet Rose tomorrow and see. No harm looking!
Yes! I really wanted to but I wasn't sure what you'd think.
I knew it! I knew you'd want to do it!
I'm still tired. Let's head back and rest, see if our roommate wants to hang out!
I'm originally from Argentina, but I've been working with indigenous groups in Chiapas.
The indigenous have always had a shitty deal here, like in the whole of the New World I guess.
Second class citizens in every way
and exploited for the tourist trade too.

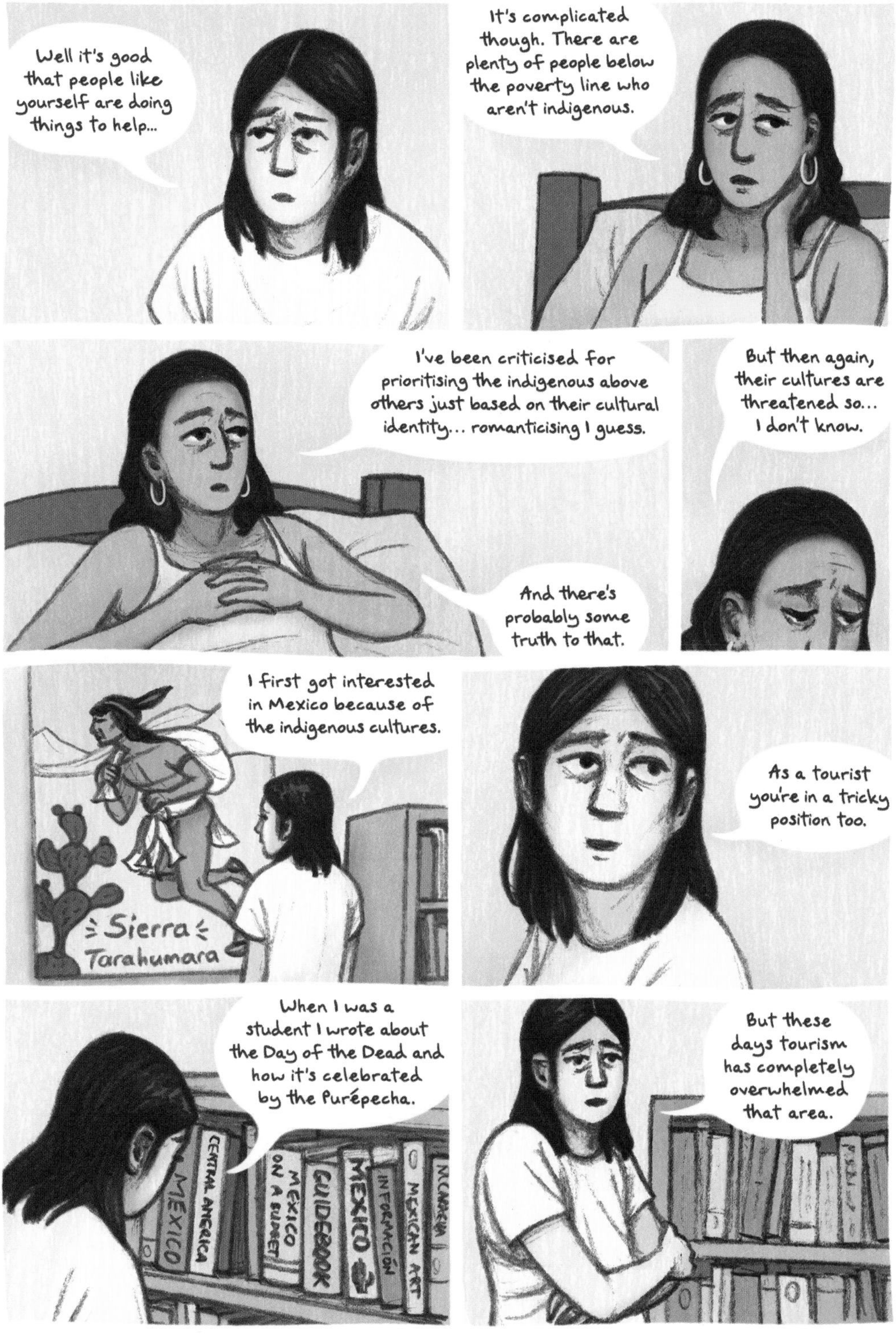
Well it's good that people like yourself are doing things to help...
It's complicated though. There are plenty of people below the poverty line who aren't indigenous.
I've been criticised for prioritising the indigenous above others just based on their cultural identity... romanticising I guess.
And there's probably some truth to that.
But then again, their cultures are threatened so... I don't know.
I first got interested in Mexico because of the indigenous cultures.
Sierra
Tarahumara
As a tourist you're in a tricky position too.
When I was a student I wrote about the Day of the Dead and how it's celebrated by the Purépecha.
MEXICO
CENTRAL AMERICA
MEXICO ON A BUDGET
GUIDEBOOK
MEXICO
INFORMACIÓN
MEXICAN ART
But these days tourism has completely overwhelmed that area.

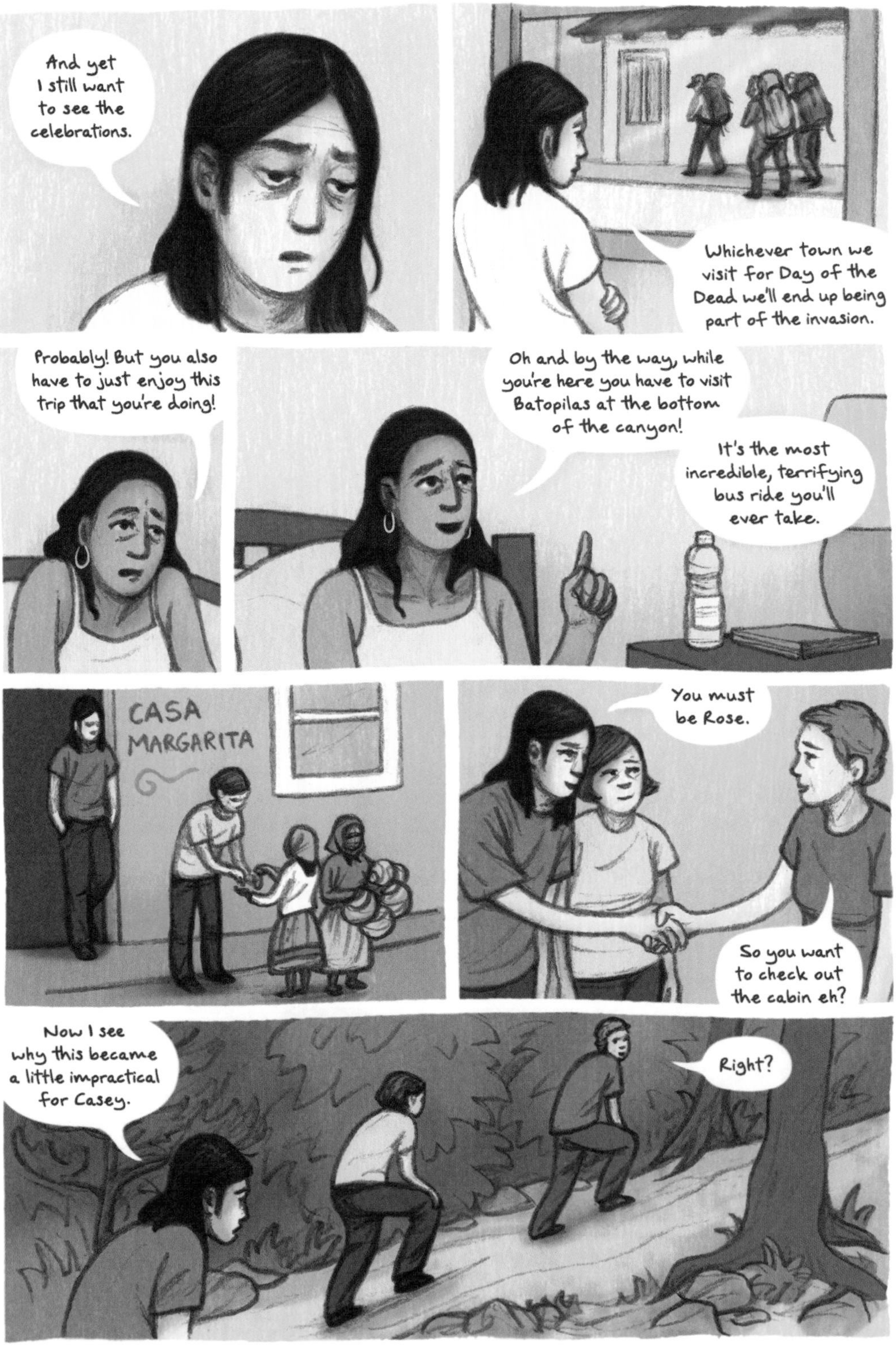

And yet I still want to see the celebrations.
Whichever town we visit for Day of the Dead we'll end up being part of the invasion.
Probably! But you also have to just enjoy this trip that you're doing!
Oh and by the way, while you're here you have to visit Batopilas at the bottom of the canyon!
It's the most incredible, terrifying bus ride you'll ever take.
CASA MARGARITA
You must be Rose.
So you want to check out the cabin eh?
Now I see why this became a little impractical for Casey.
Right?

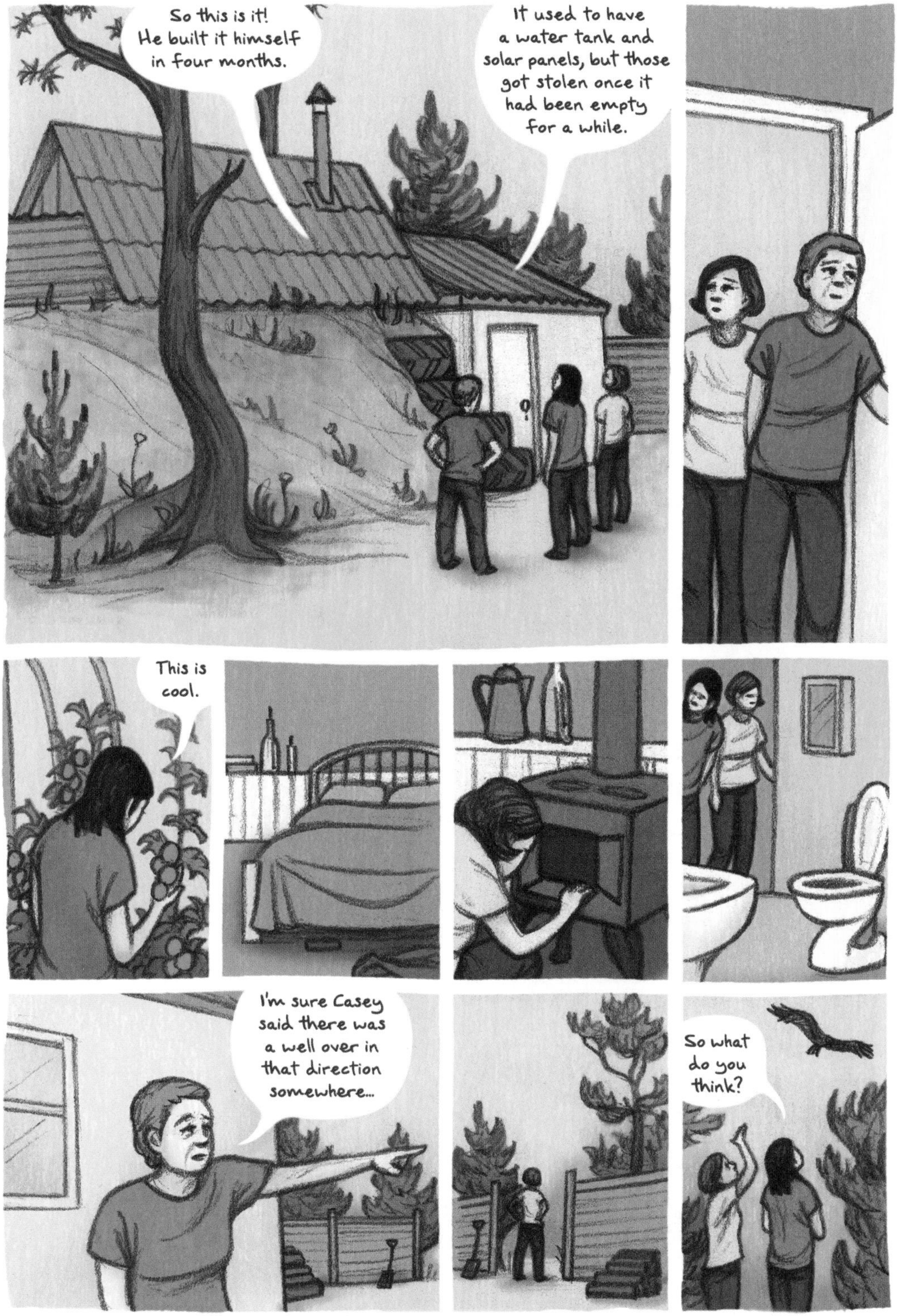
So this is it! He built it himself in four months.
It used to have a water tank and solar panels, but those got stolen once it had been empty for a while.
This is cool.
I'm sure Casey said there was a well over in that direction somewhere...
So what do you think?

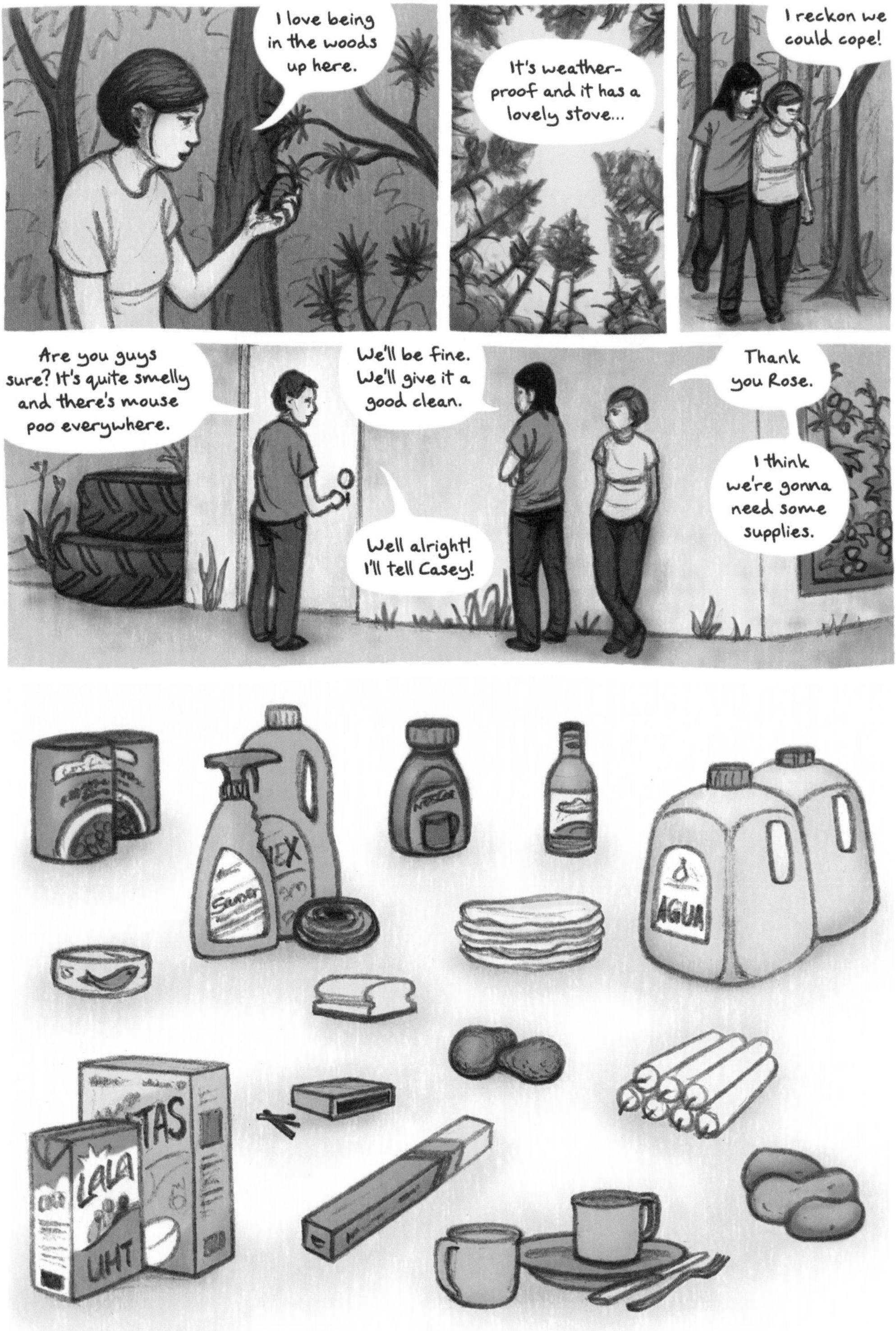
I love being in the woods up here.
It's weather-proof and it has a lovely stove...
I reckon we could cope!
Are you guys sure? It's quite smelly and there's mouse poo everywhere.
We'll be fine. We'll give it a good clean.
Well alright! I'll tell Casey!
Thank you Rose.
I think we're gonna need some supplies.
LALA
UHT
AGUA

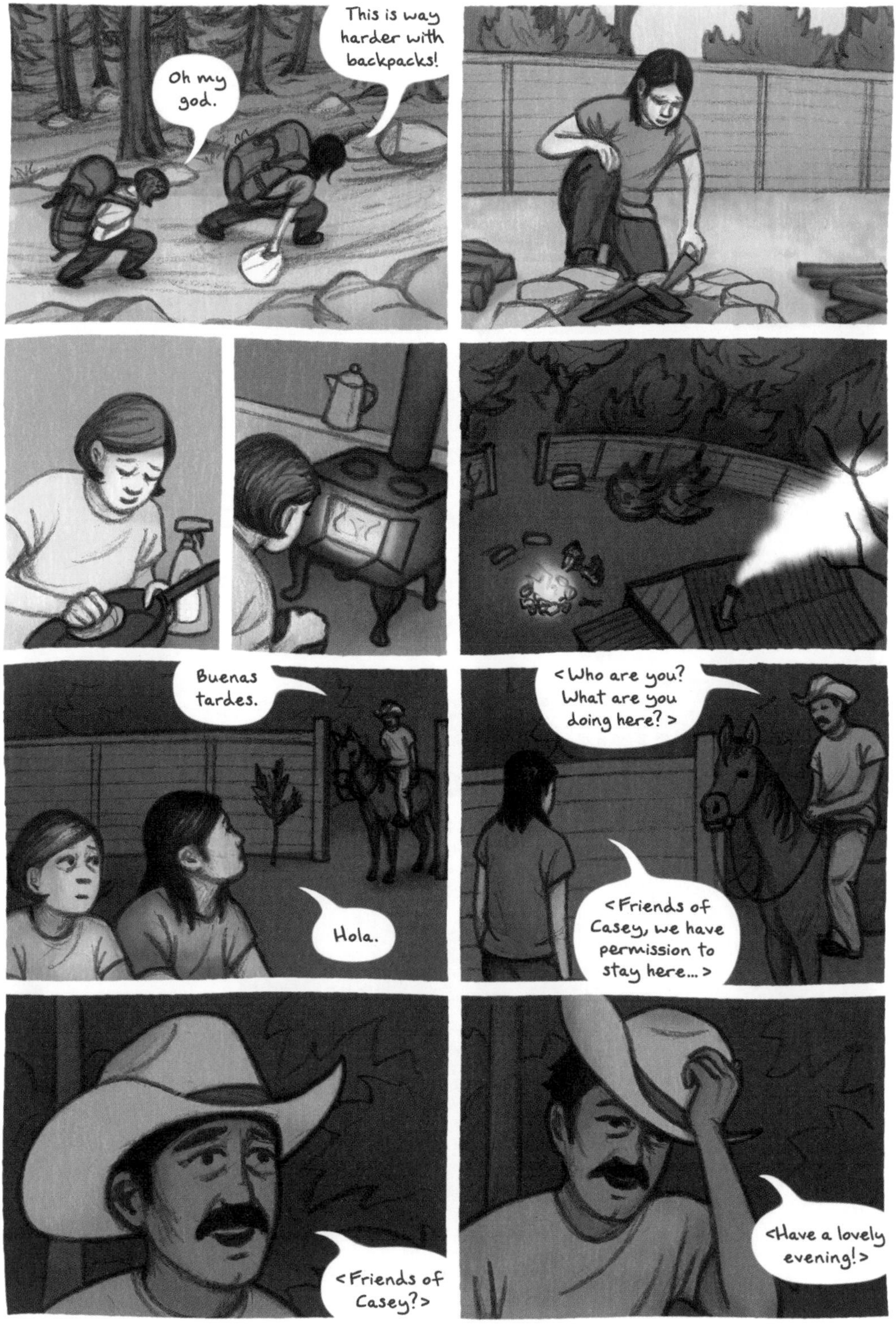
Oh my god.
This is way harder with backpacks!
Buenas tardes.
Hola.
<Who are you? What are you doing here?>
<Friends of Casey, we have permission to stay here...>
<Friends of Casey?>
<Have a lovely evening!>

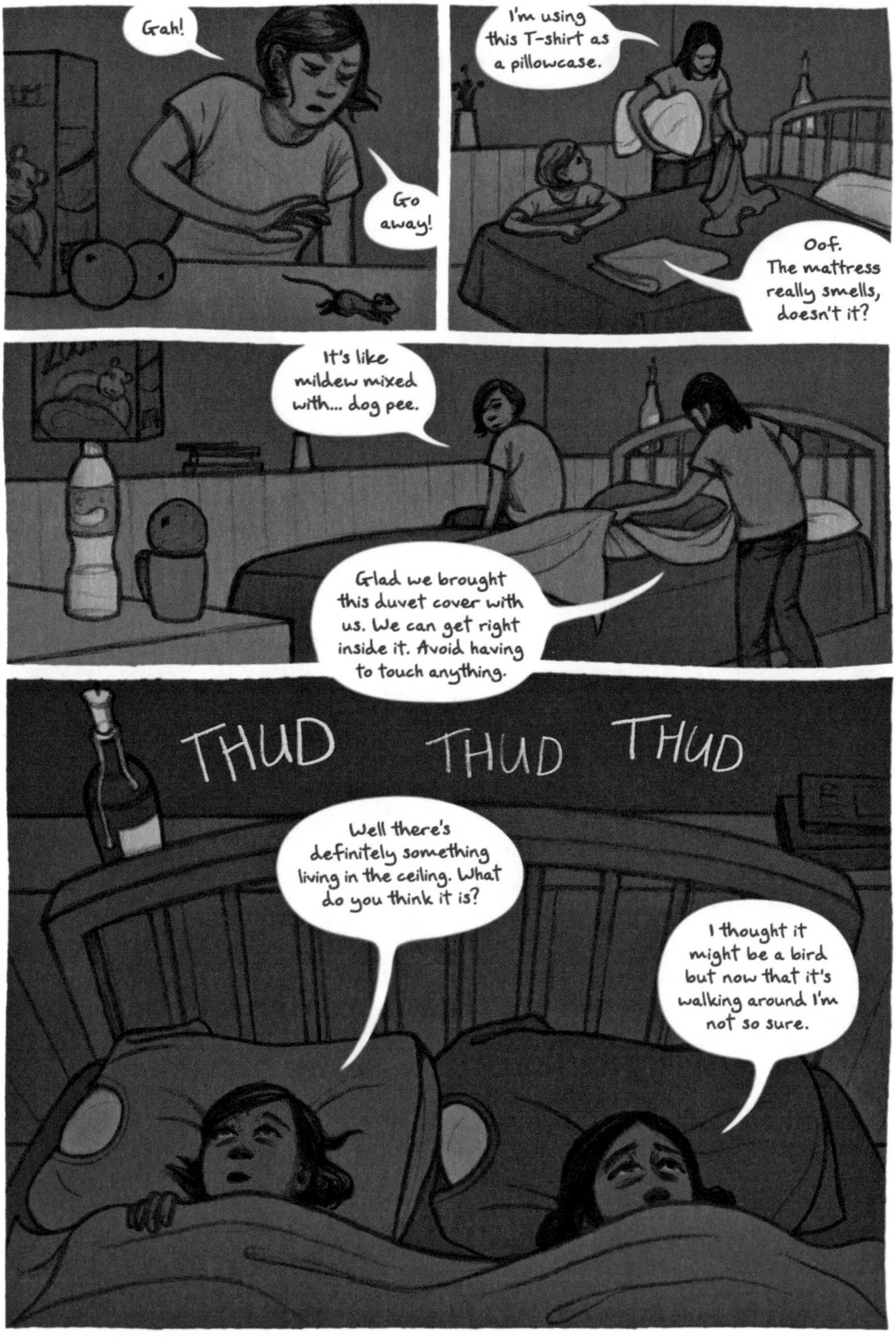
Gah!
Go away!
I'm using this T-shirt as a pillowcase.
Oof. The mattress really smells, doesn't it?
It's like mildew mixed with... dog pee.
Glad we brought this duvet cover with us. We can get right inside it. Avoid having to touch anything.
THUD THUD THUD
Well there's definitely something living in the ceiling. What do you think it is?
I thought it might be a bird but now that it's walking around I'm not so sure.

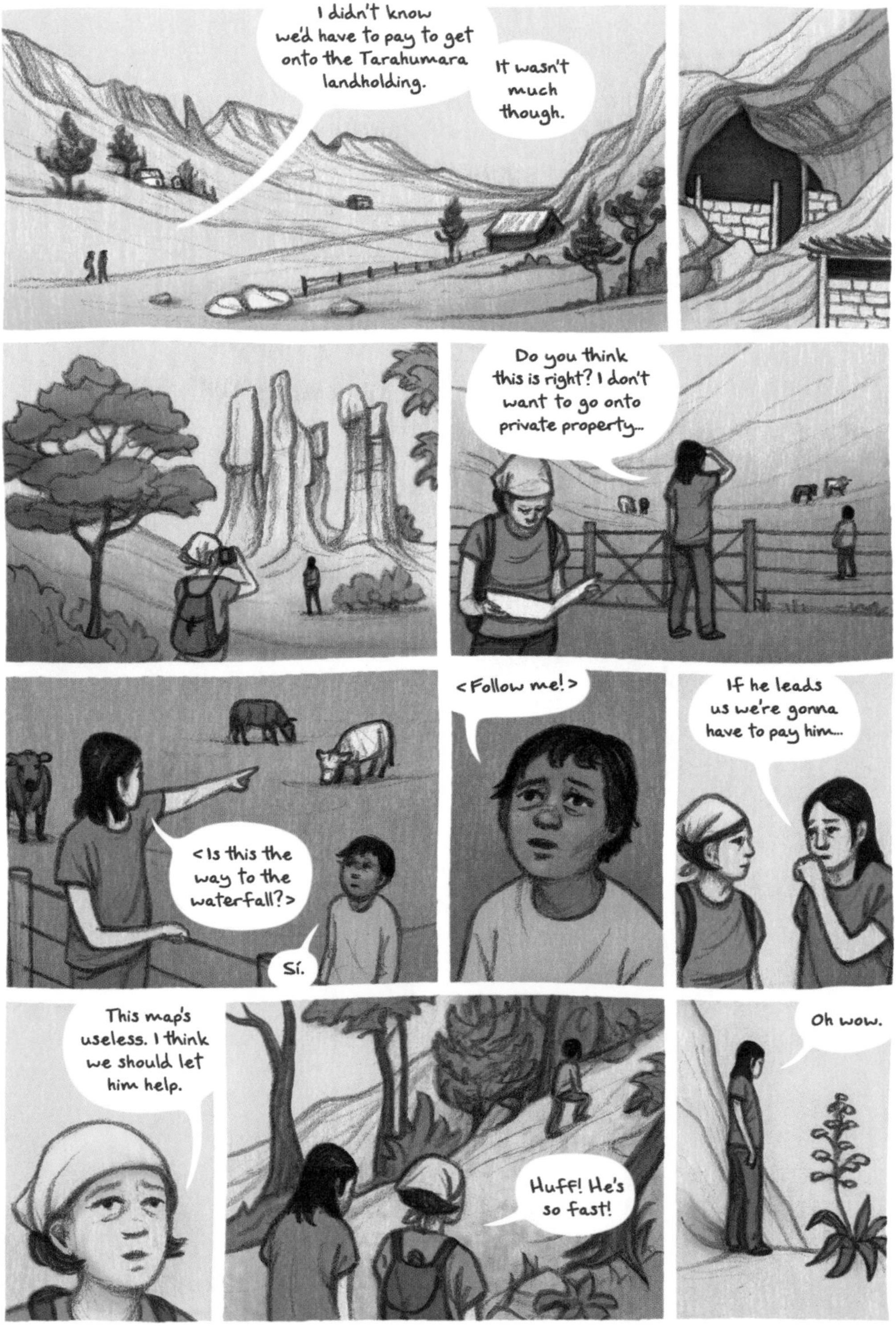
I didn't know we'd have to pay to get onto the Tarahumara landholding.
It wasn't much though.
Do you think this is right? I don't want to go onto private property...
<Is this the way to the waterfall?>
Sí.
<Follow me!>
If he leads us we're gonna have to pay him...
This map's useless. I think we should let him help.
Huff! He's so fast!
Oh wow.

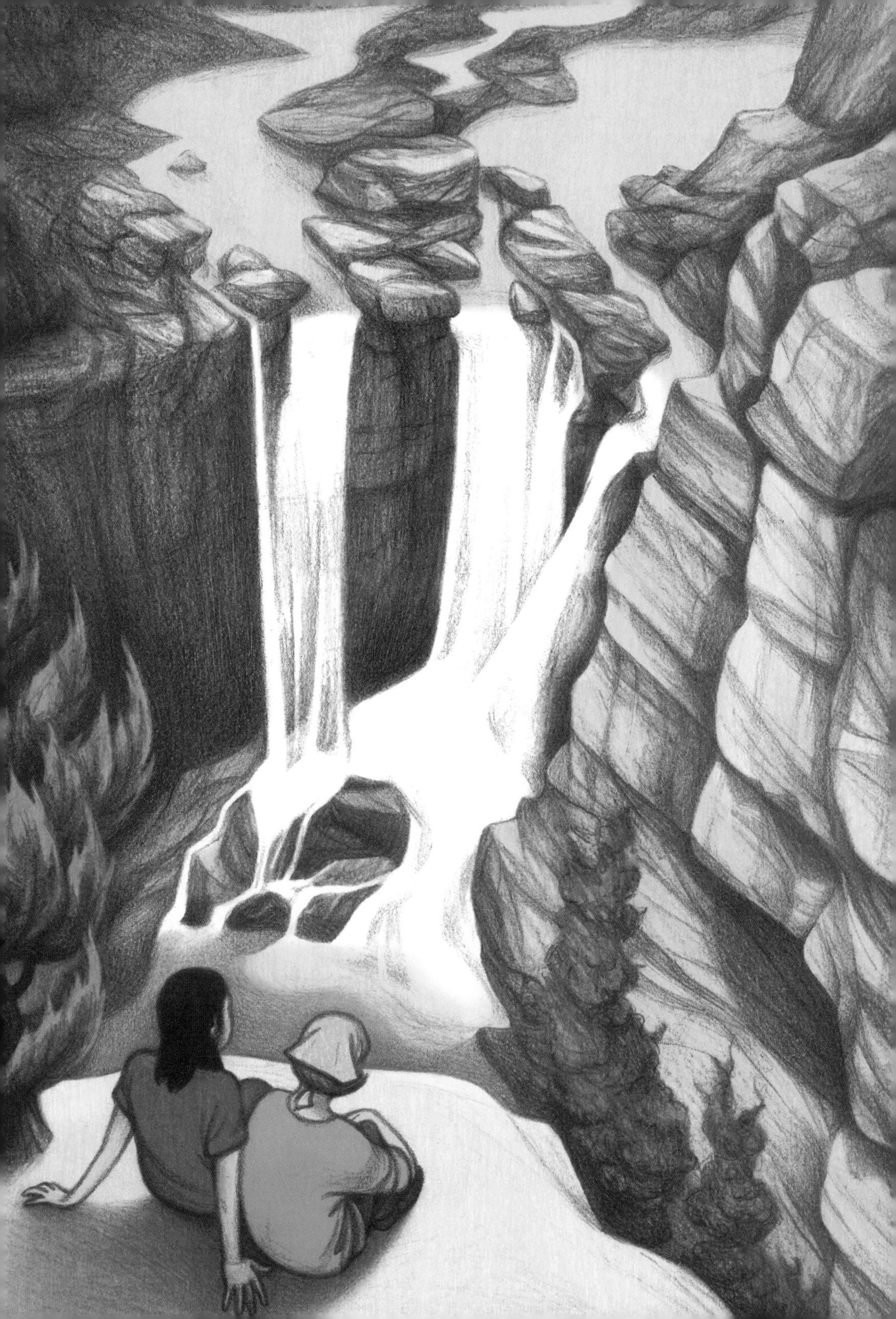

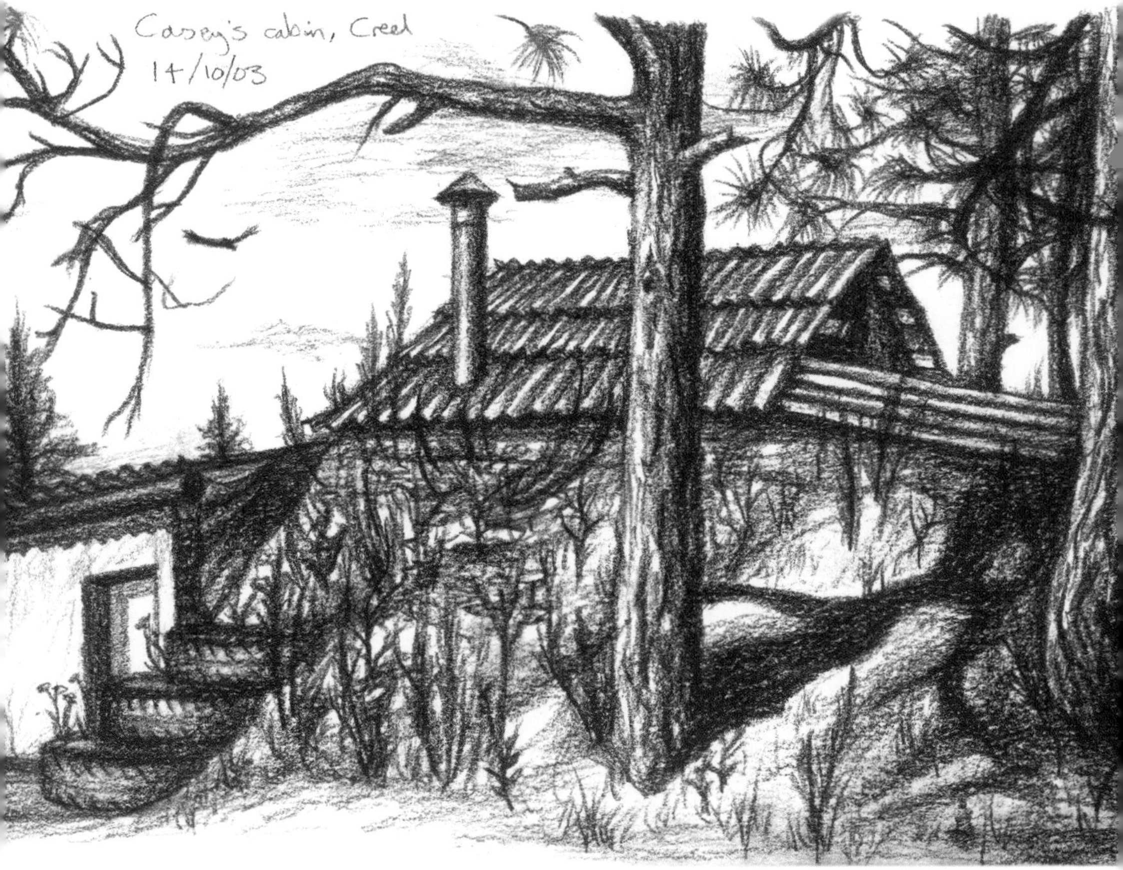
Casey's cabin, Creel
14/10/03

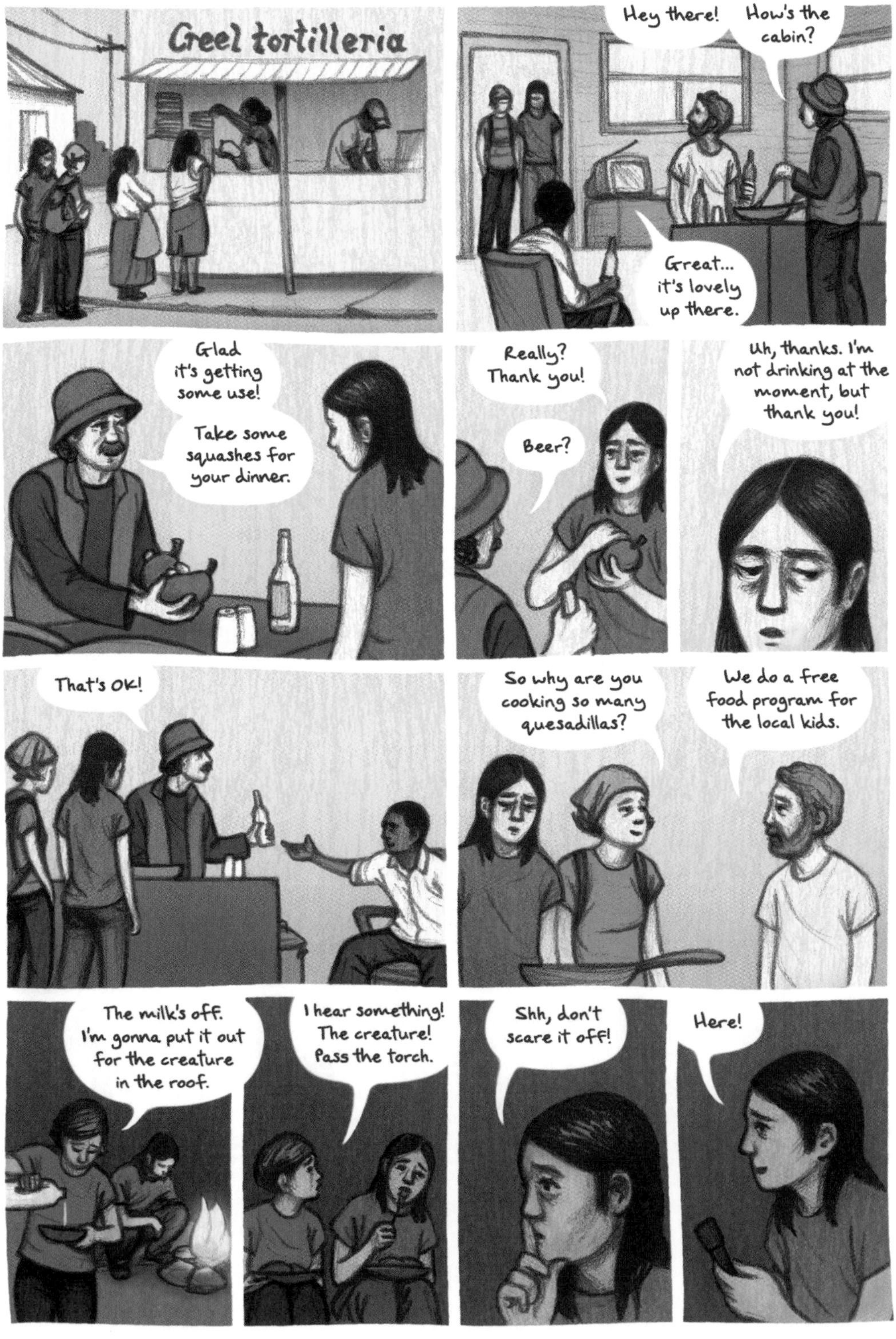
Creel tortilleria
Hey there!
How's the cabin?
Great... it's lovely up there.
Glad it's getting some use!
Take some squashes for your dinner.
Really? Thank you!
Beer?
Uh, thanks. I'm not drinking at the moment, but thank you!
That's OK!
So why are you cooking so many quesadillas?
We do a free food program for the local kids.
The milk's off. I'm gonna put it out for the creature in the roof.
I hear something! The creature! Pass the torch.
Shh, don't scare it off!
Here!

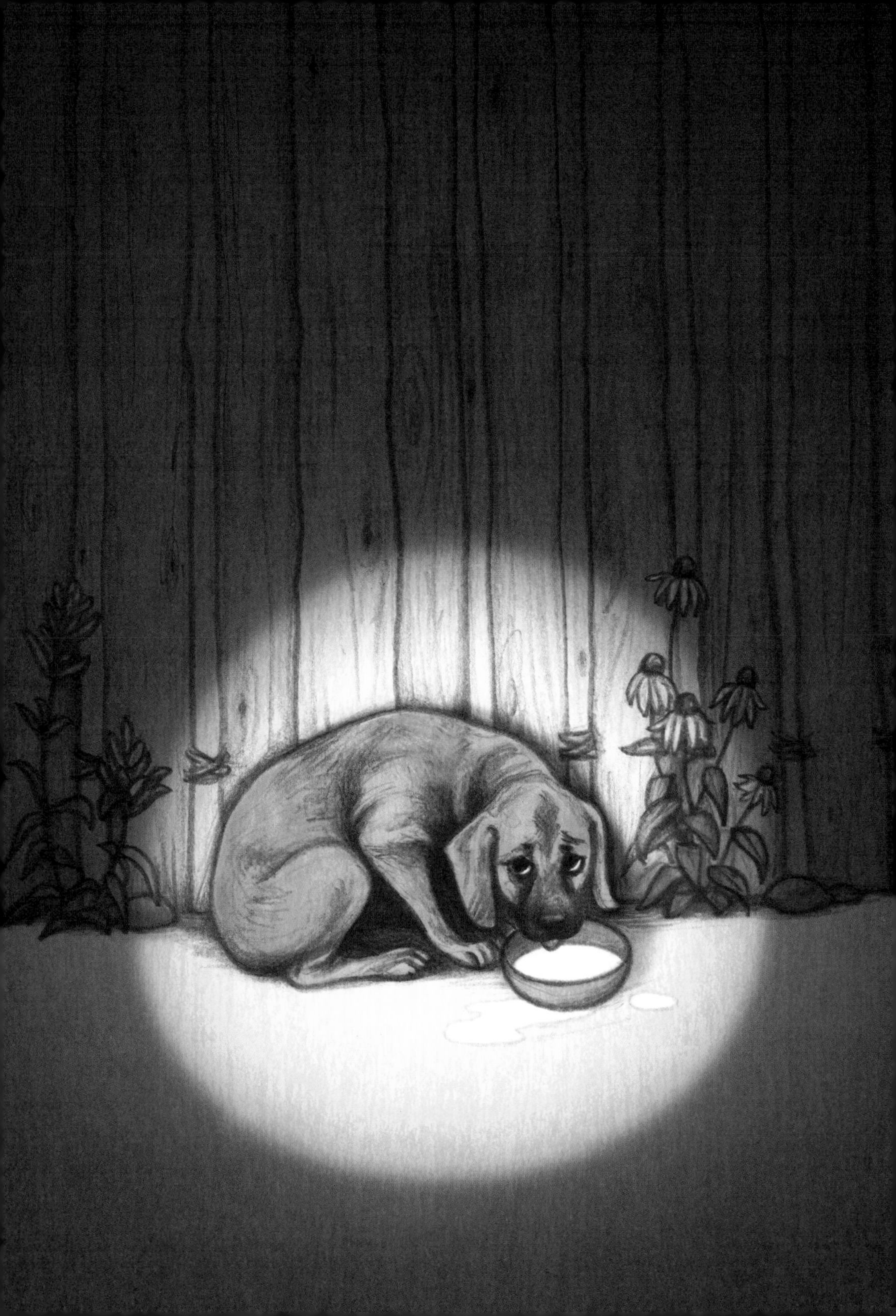

I was very unadventurous with food when I first got to Mexico, which was a shame as I missed out on a lot! The Mexican food you find outside of Mexico is almost always nothing like the real thing. It's usually more Tex-Mex than Mexican.

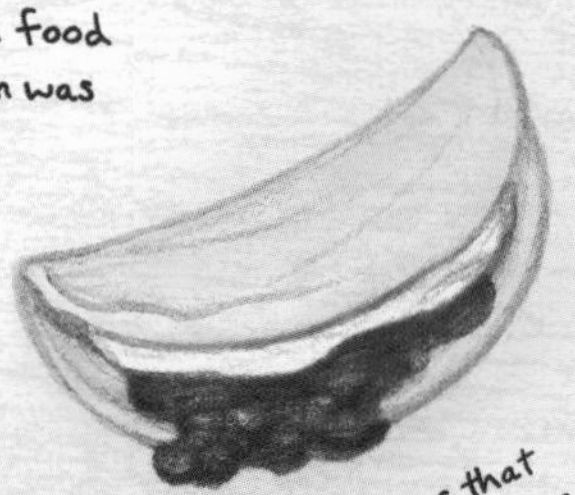

Huitlacoche: a fungus that grows on corn. Often used as a filling for tortilla-based dishes

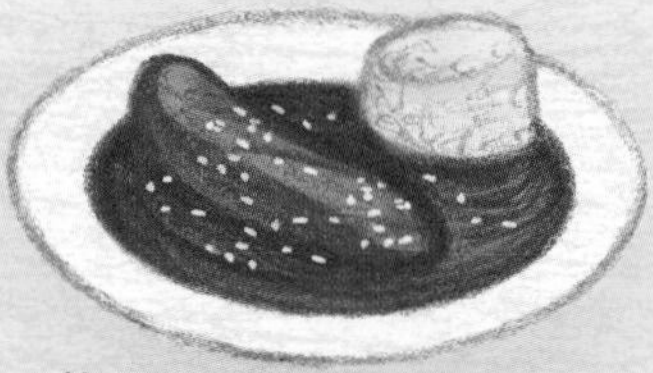

Mole negro: From Oaxaca. Dark rich sauce for meat made with many ingredients including chocolate and the herb hoja santa

A selection of Mexican foods

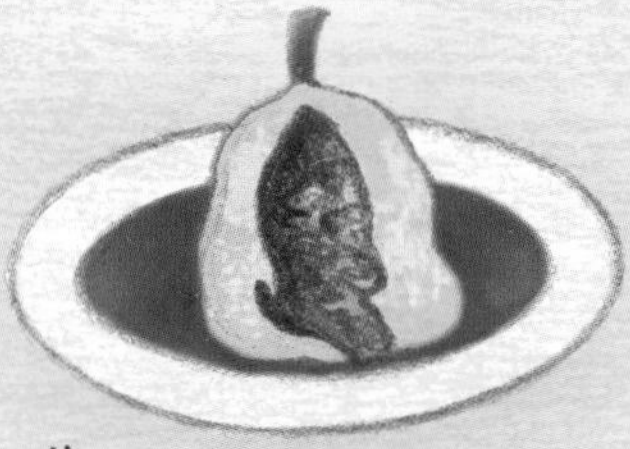

Huazontles: a broccoli-like vegetable, battered and deep-fried then served in tomato sauce

Vuelve a la vida: chilled seafood cocktail with tomato, onion and coriander. Known as a hangover cure

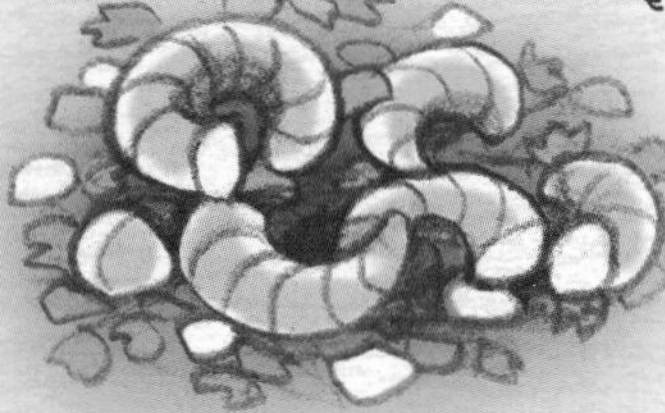

Coyotas

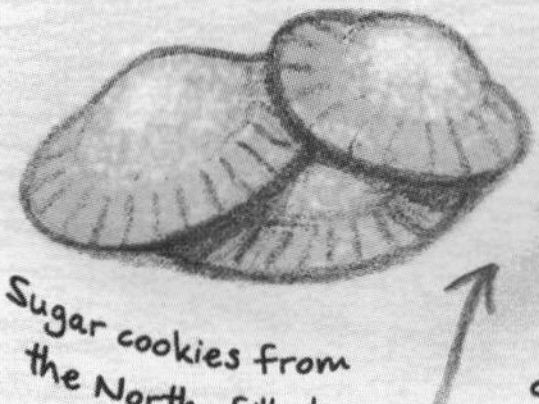

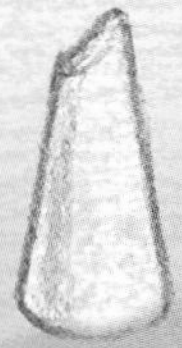

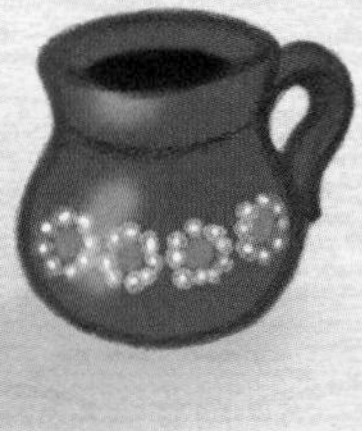

Sugar cookies from the North, filled with piloncillo

Piloncillo: unrefined cane sugar. Also used in...

Cafe de olla: coffee brewed in clay pots with cinnamon

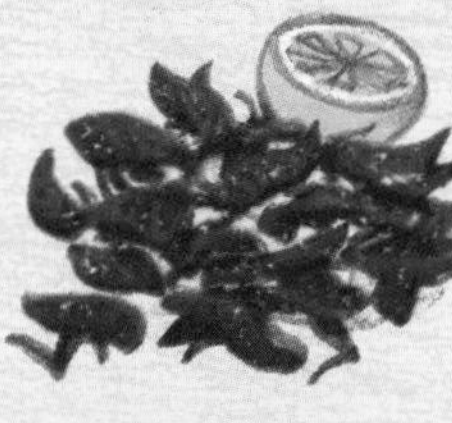

Chapulines: grasshoppers toasted with garlic, lime and salt

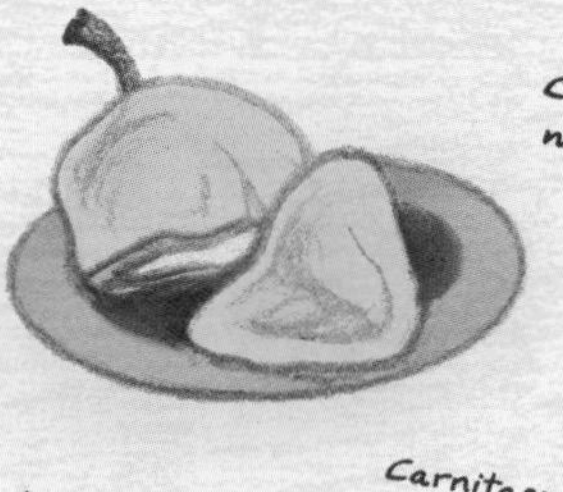

Chiles rellenos: mild Poblano peppers stuffed with various fillings

Gusanos de maguey: seasoned caterpillars

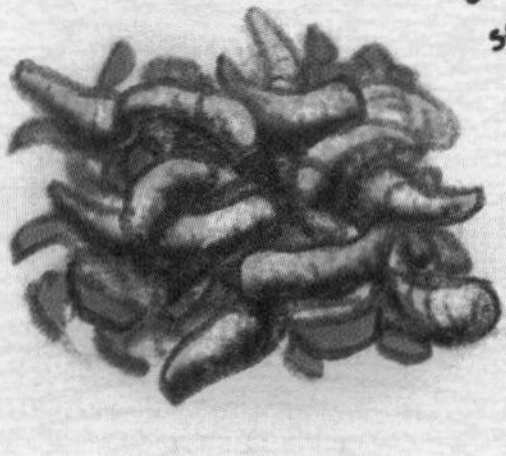

Escamoles: pre-Hispanic dish. Ant larvae cooked in butter and garlic

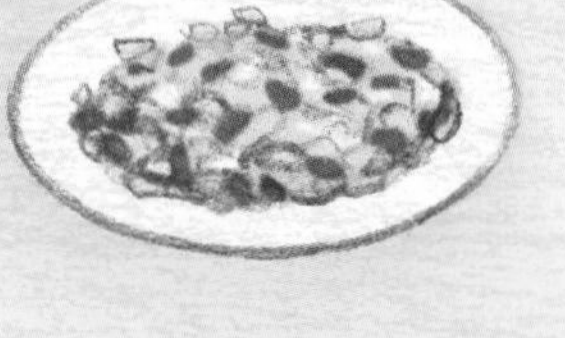

Carnitas: tender pork with onion and coriander

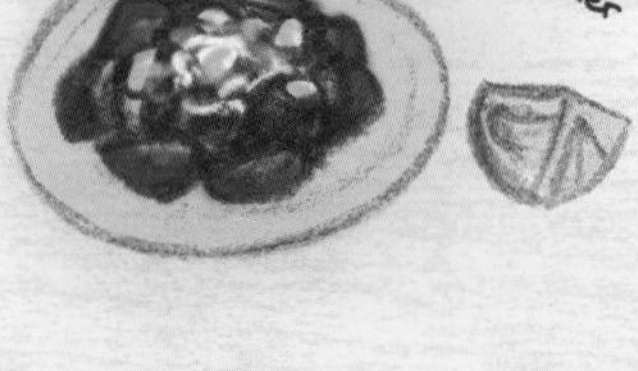

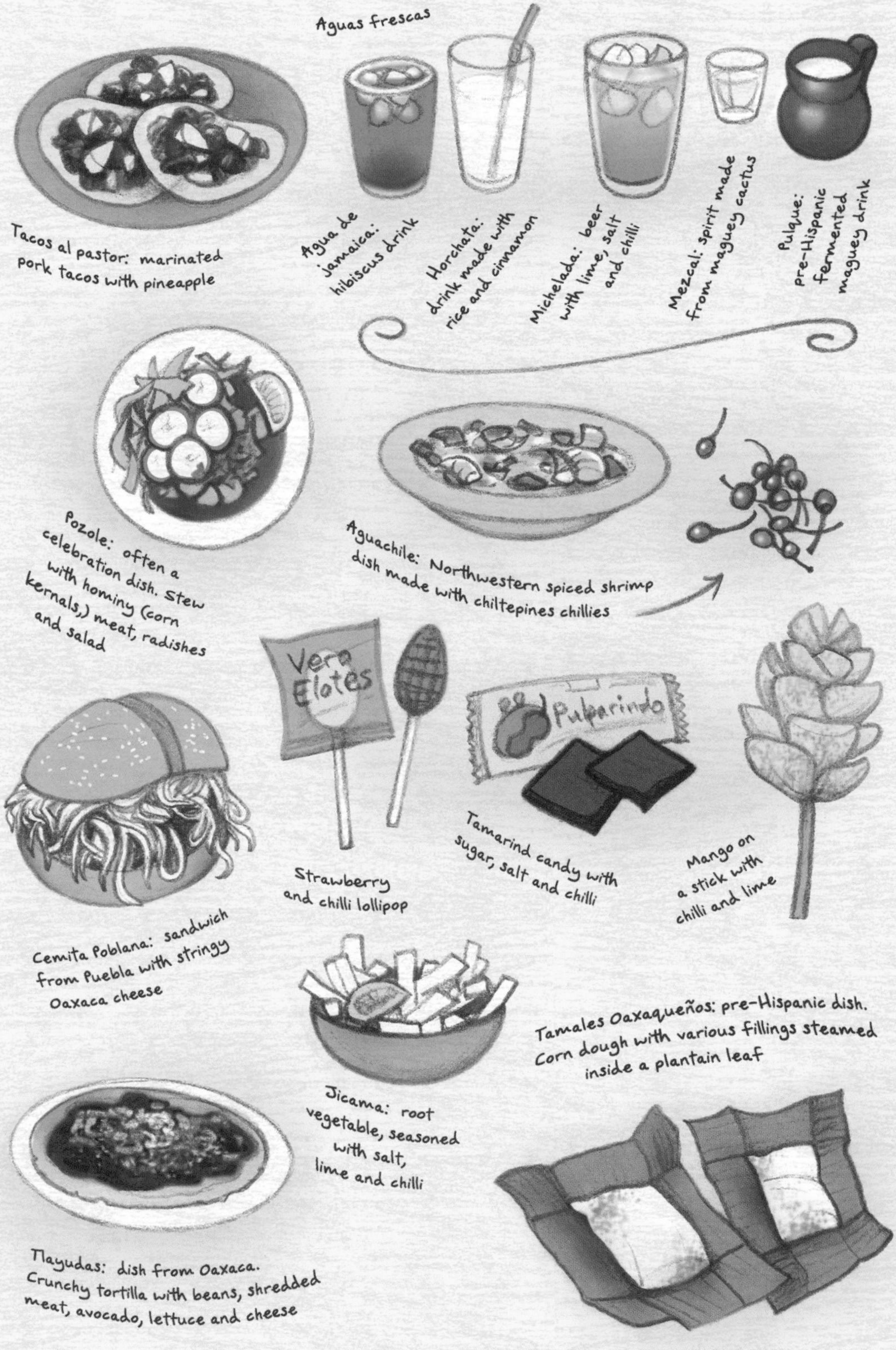
Aguas frescas
Tacos al pastor: marinated pork tacos with pineapple
Agua de jamaica: hibiscus drink
Horchata: drink made with rice and cinnamon
Michelada: beer with lime, salt and chilli
Mezcal: spirit made from maguey cactus
Pulque: pre-Hispanic fermented maguey drink
Pozole: often a celebration dish. Stew with hominy (corn kernals,) meat, radishes and salad
Aguachile: Northwestern spiced shrimp dish made with chiltepines chillies
Vero Elotes
Pulparindo
Strawberry and chilli lollipop
Tamarind candy with sugar, salt and chilli
Mango on a stick with chilli and lime
Cemita Poblana: sandwich from Puebla with stringy Oaxaca cheese
Tamales Oaxaqueños: pre-Hispanic dish. Corn dough with various fillings steamed inside a plantain leaf
Jicama: root vegetable, seasoned with salt, lime and chilli
Tlayudas: dish from Oaxaca. Crunchy tortilla with beans, shredded meat, avocado, lettuce and cheese

Five days without running water... that was kinda enough.

Can't wait for a hotel room in Batopilas. Can't believe it takes six hours to get down there.

Whoa.

This is so stunning it almost makes you forget that you're scared for your life.

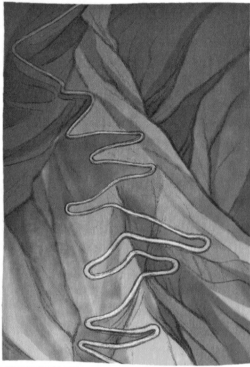

¿Que padre, no?

Órale.

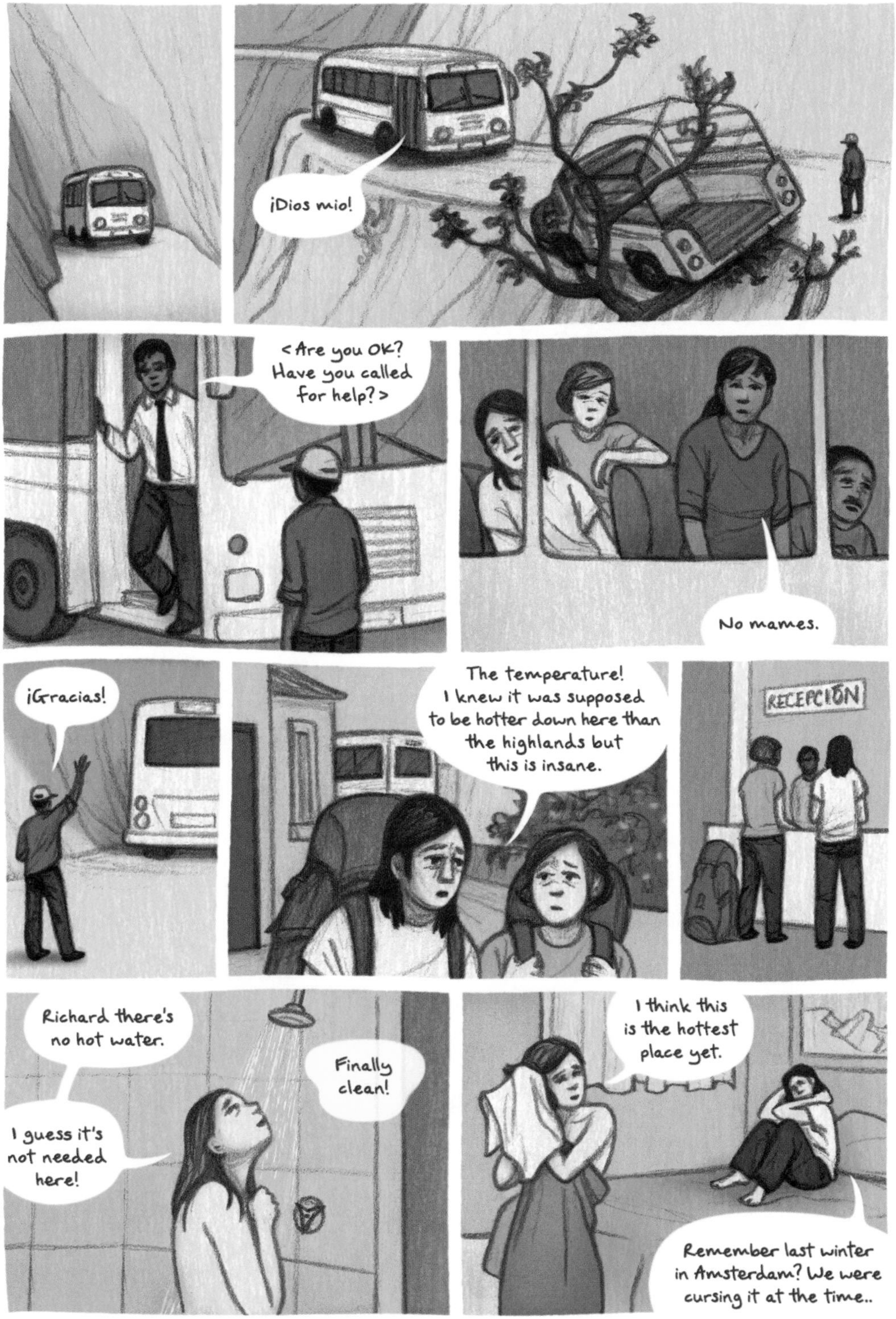
¡Dios mio!
<Are you OK? Have you called for help?>
No mames.
¡Gracias!
The temperature! I knew it was supposed to be hotter down here than the highlands but this is insane.
RECEPCIÓN
Richard there's no hot water.
I guess it's not needed here!
Finally clean!
I think this is the hottest place yet.
Remember last winter in Amsterdam? We were cursing it at the time..

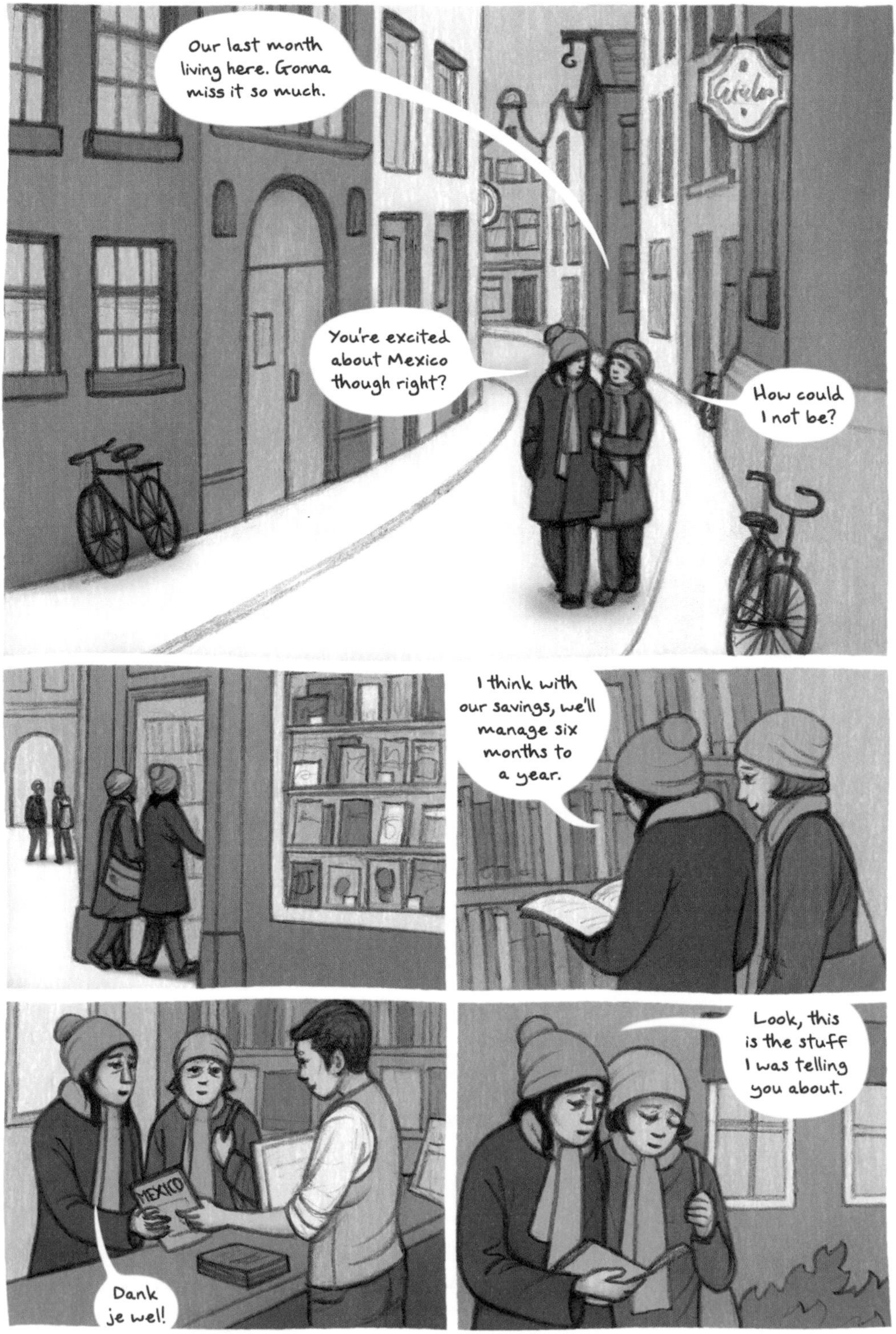
Our last month living here. Gonna miss it so much.
You're excited about Mexico though right?
How could I not be?
I think with our savings, we'll manage six months to a year.
MEXICO
Dank je wel!
Look, this is the stuff I was telling you about.

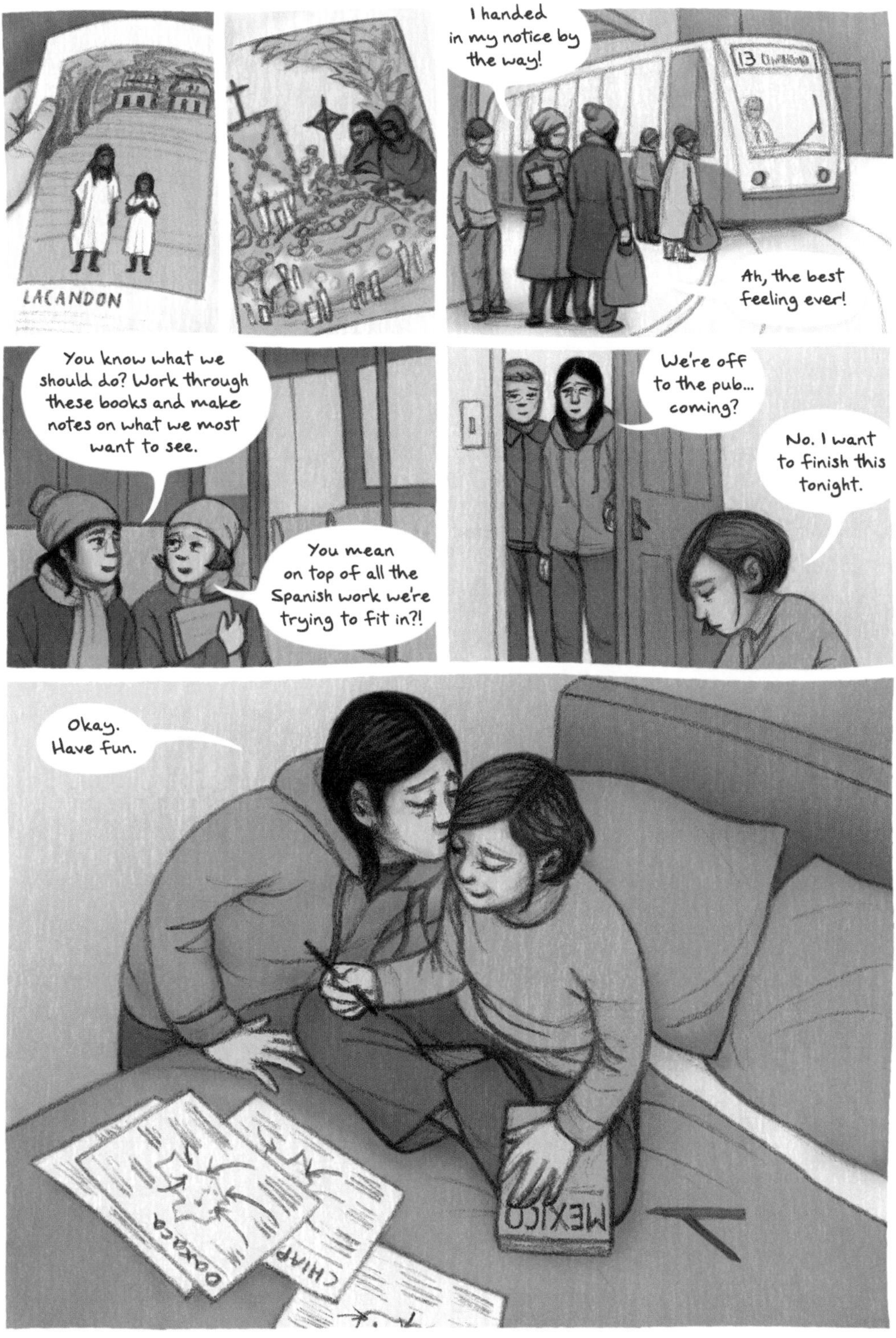
LACANDON
I handed in my notice by the way!
Ah, the best feeling ever!
You know what we should do? Work through these books and make notes on what we most want to see.
You mean on top of all the Spanish work we're trying to fit in?!
We're off to the pub... coming?
No. I want to finish this tonight.
Okay. Have fun.
MEXICO
Oaxaca
CHIAP

So. Two flights to Mexico City, with open-ended return flights out of Panama.

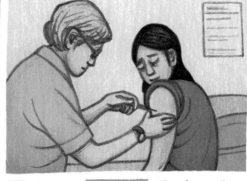

Yes, withdraw everything and close the account.

It's been a pleasure, take care!

So you're all set?

Yup!

There's something worrying me. It's kinda hard to say.

What is it?

We're worried Richard's drinking might put you at risk.

You'll be careful with that, right?

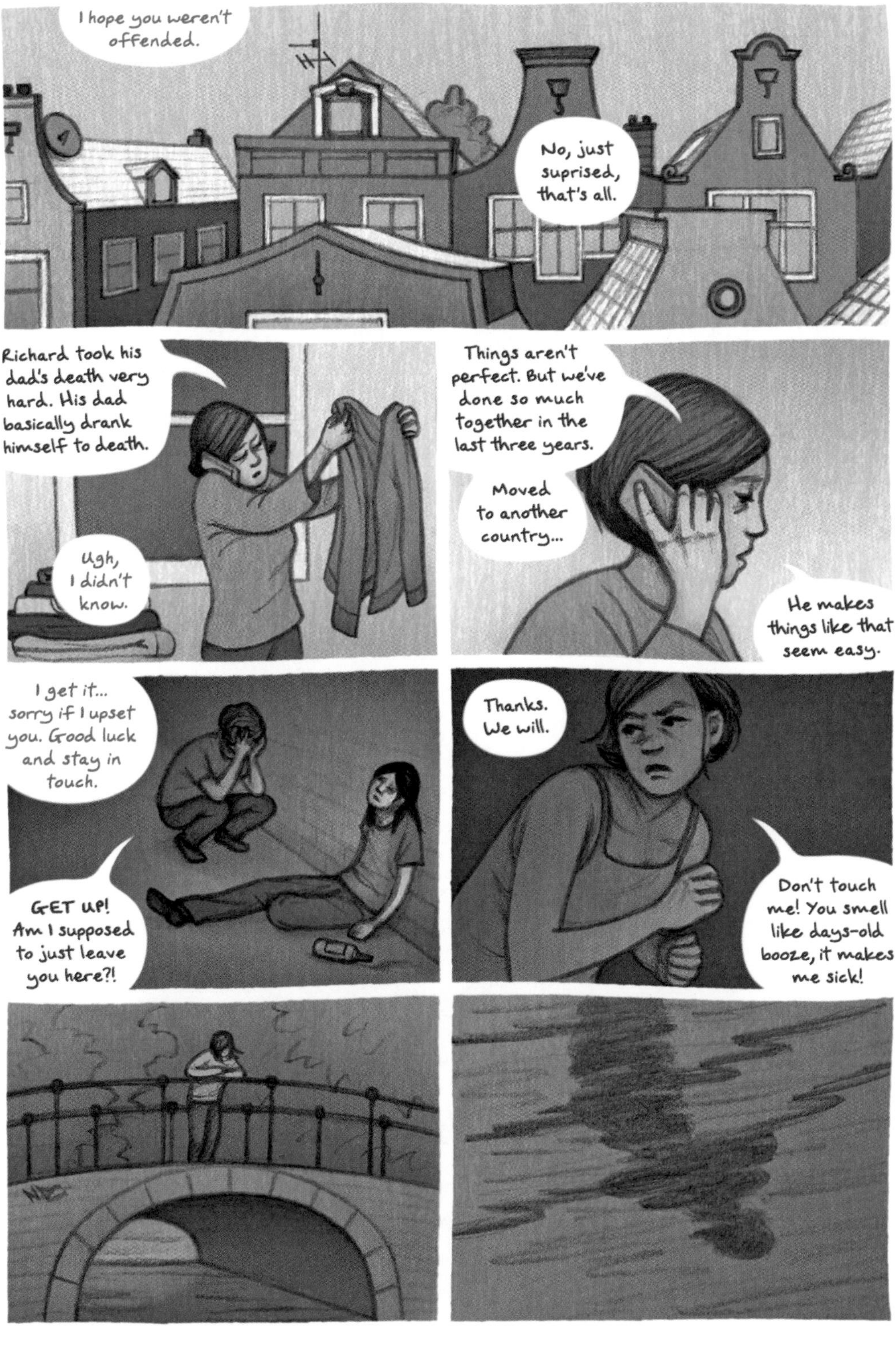
I hope you weren't offended.
No, just suprised, that's all.
Richard took his dad's death very hard. His dad basically drank himself to death.
Ugh, I didn't know.
Things aren't perfect. But we've done so much together in the last three years.
Moved to another country...
He makes things like that seem easy.
I get it... sorry if I upset you. Good luck and stay in touch.
GET UP! Am I supposed to just leave you here?!
Thanks. We will.
Don't touch me! You smell like days-old booze, it makes me sick!

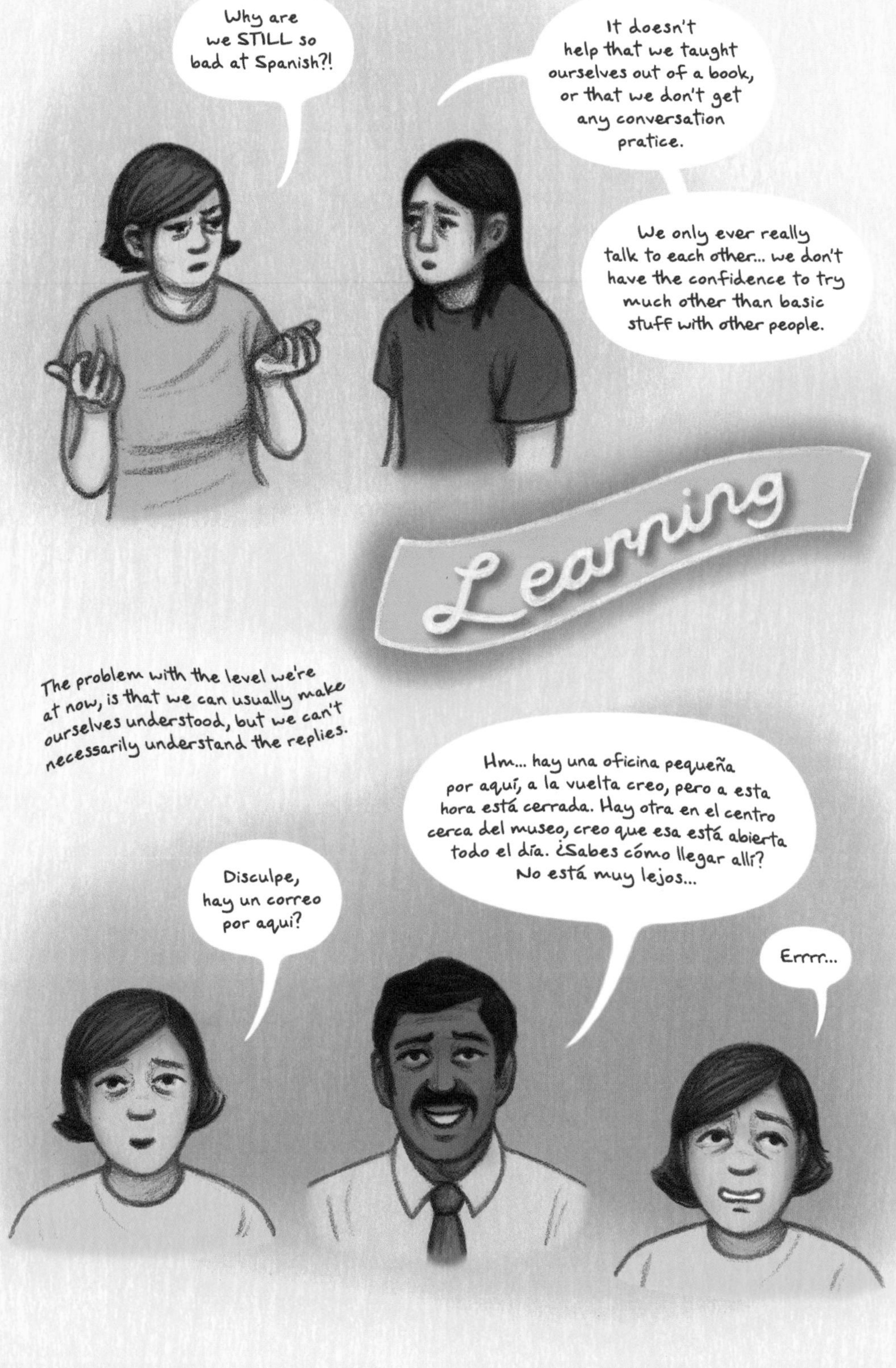
Why are we STILL so bad at Spanish?!
It doesn't help that we taught ourselves out of a book, or that we don't get any conversation pratice.
We only ever really talk to each other... we don't have the confidence to try much other than basic stuff with other people.
Learning
The problem with the level we're at now, is that we can usually make ourselves understood, but we can't necessarily understand the replies.
Disculpe, hay un correo por aqui?
Hm... hay una oficina pequeña por aquí, a la vuelta creo, pero a esta hora está cerrada. Hay otra en el centro cerca del museo, creo que esa está abierta todo el día. ¿Sabes cómo llegar allí? No está muy lejos...
Errrr...

Viajar   Conocer   Escribir

viajaré   conocere   escribiré

viajarás   conocerás   escribirás

viajará   conocerá   escribirá

viajaremos   conoceremos   escribiremos

viajarán   conocerán

I'm always excited to learn new vocabulary, but get very overwhelmed and lazy when I get into the grammar side of things.

Spanish

Mexican Spanish can be quite different to Spanish from Spain. There are also a LOT of idiomatic expressions which make no sense if you do a literal translation...

- Planning ahead: Le mide el agua a los camotes.
  "Measuring the water for the sweet potatoes"

- Killing time: Está picándose los ojos.
  "Poking one's eyes"

- Taking advantage: Te come el mandado.
  "Eating your groceries"

There were also non-verbal gestures that it took time to get used to...

I think that probably means 'just a moment,' but I'm not really sure...

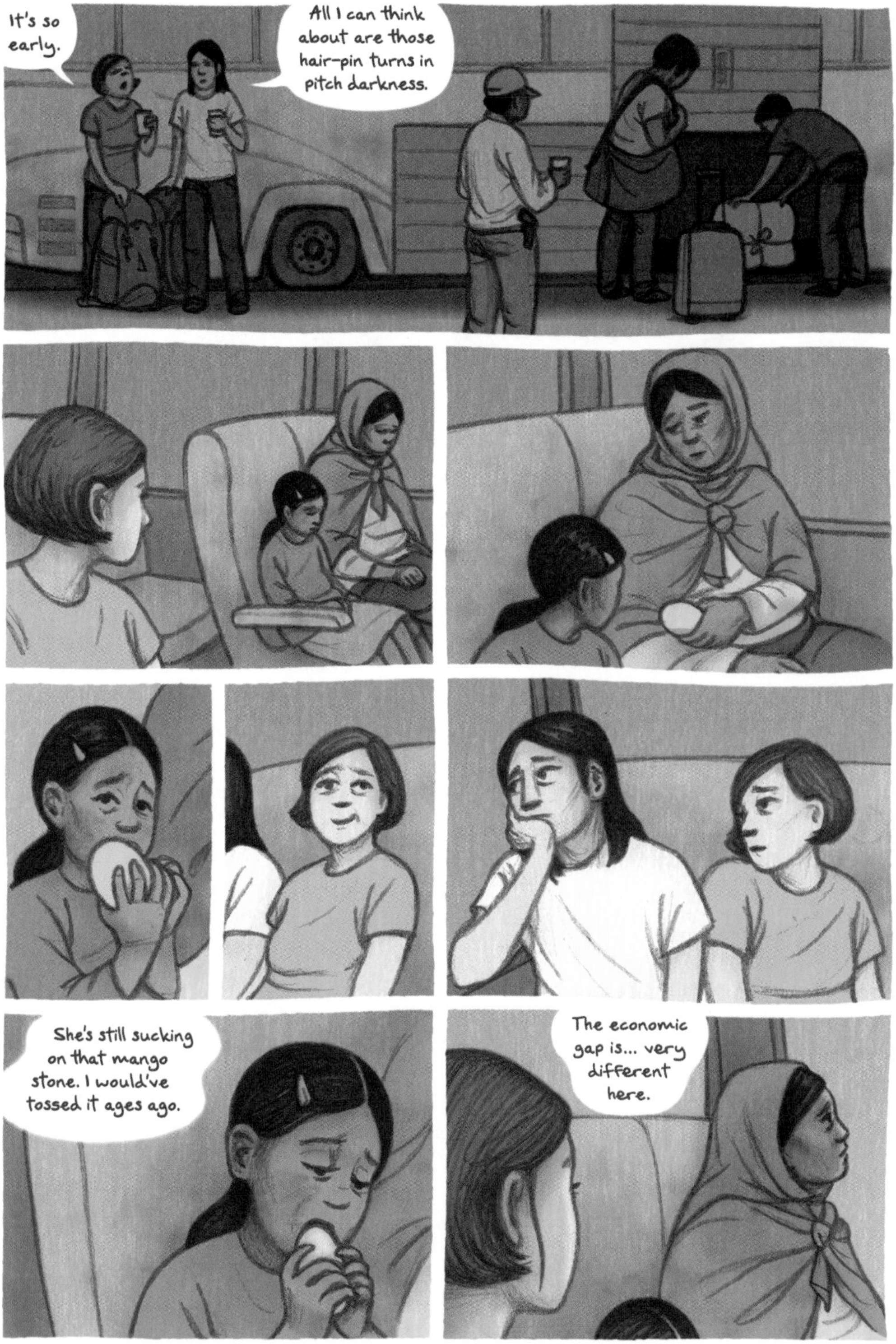
It's so early.
All I can think about are those hair-pin turns in pitch darkness.
She's still sucking on that mango stone. I would've tossed it ages ago.
The economic gap is... very different here.

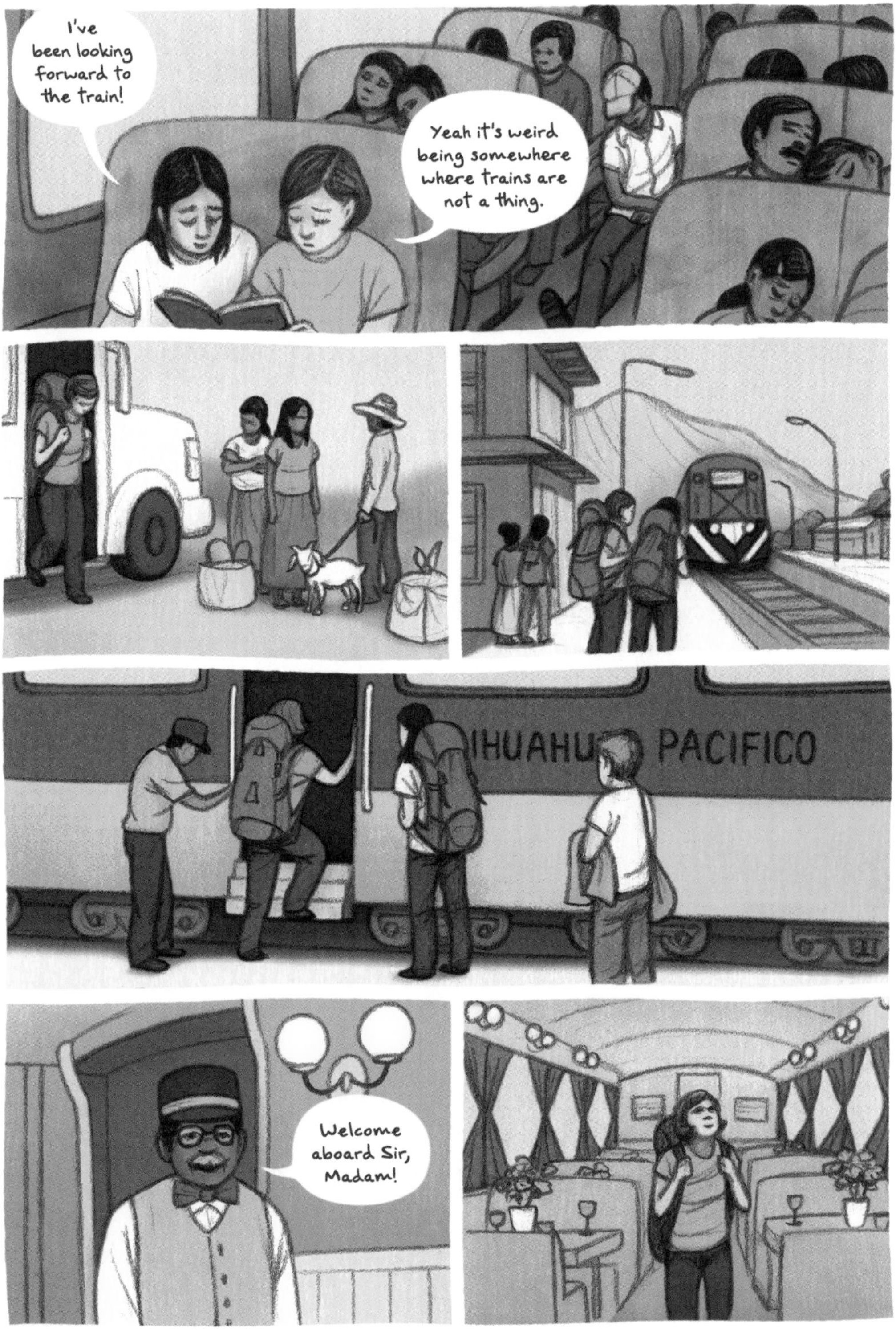
I've been looking forward to the train!
Yeah it's weird being somewhere where trains are not a thing.
IHUAHU PACIFICO
Welcome aboard Sir, Madam!

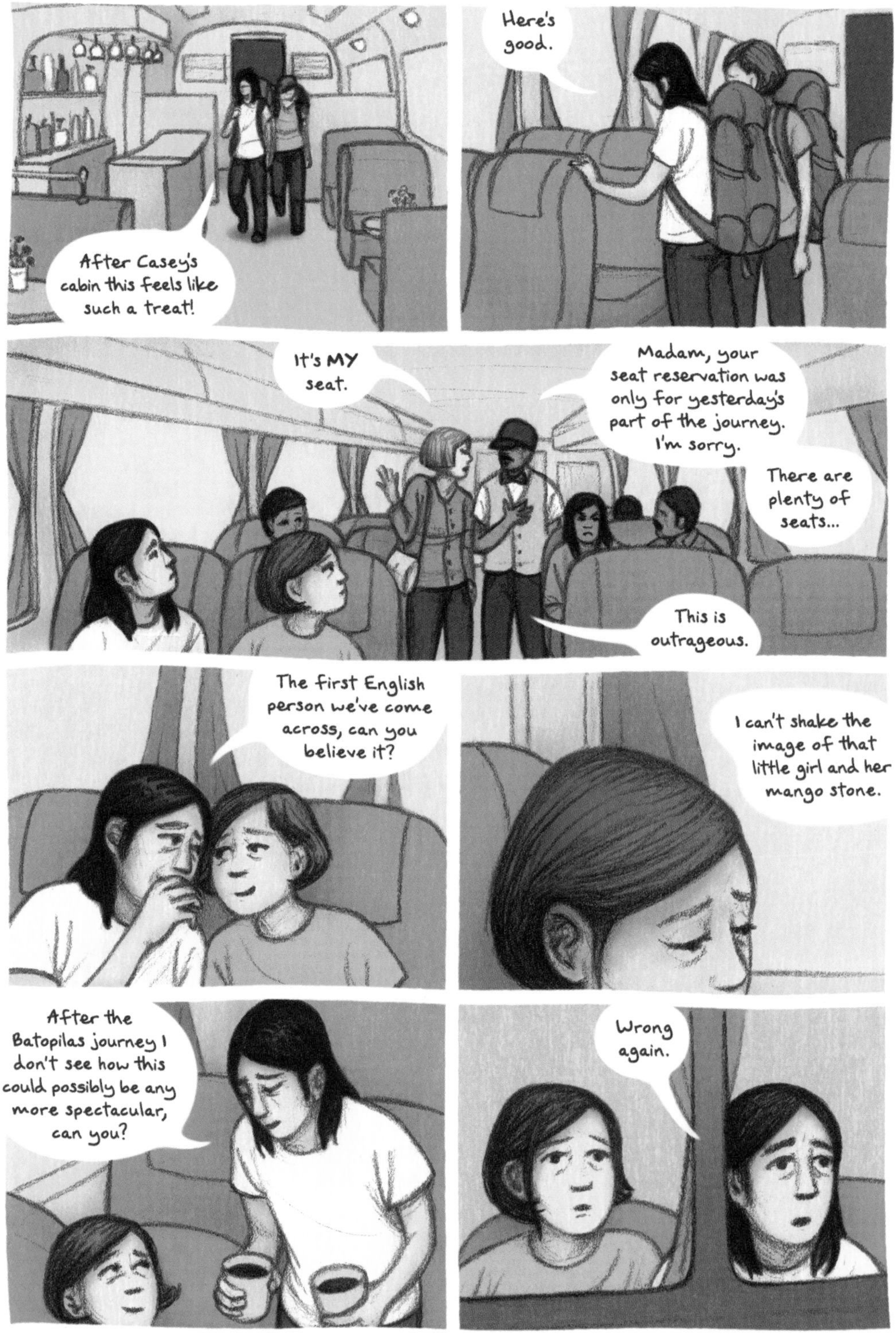
After Casey's cabin this feels like such a treat!
Here's good.
It's MY seat.
Madam, your seat reservation was only for yesterday's part of the journey. I'm sorry.
There are plenty of seats...
This is outrageous.
The first English person we've come across, can you believe it?
I can't shake the image of that little girl and her mango stone.
After the Batopilas journey I don't see how this could possibly be any more spectacular, can you?
Wrong again.

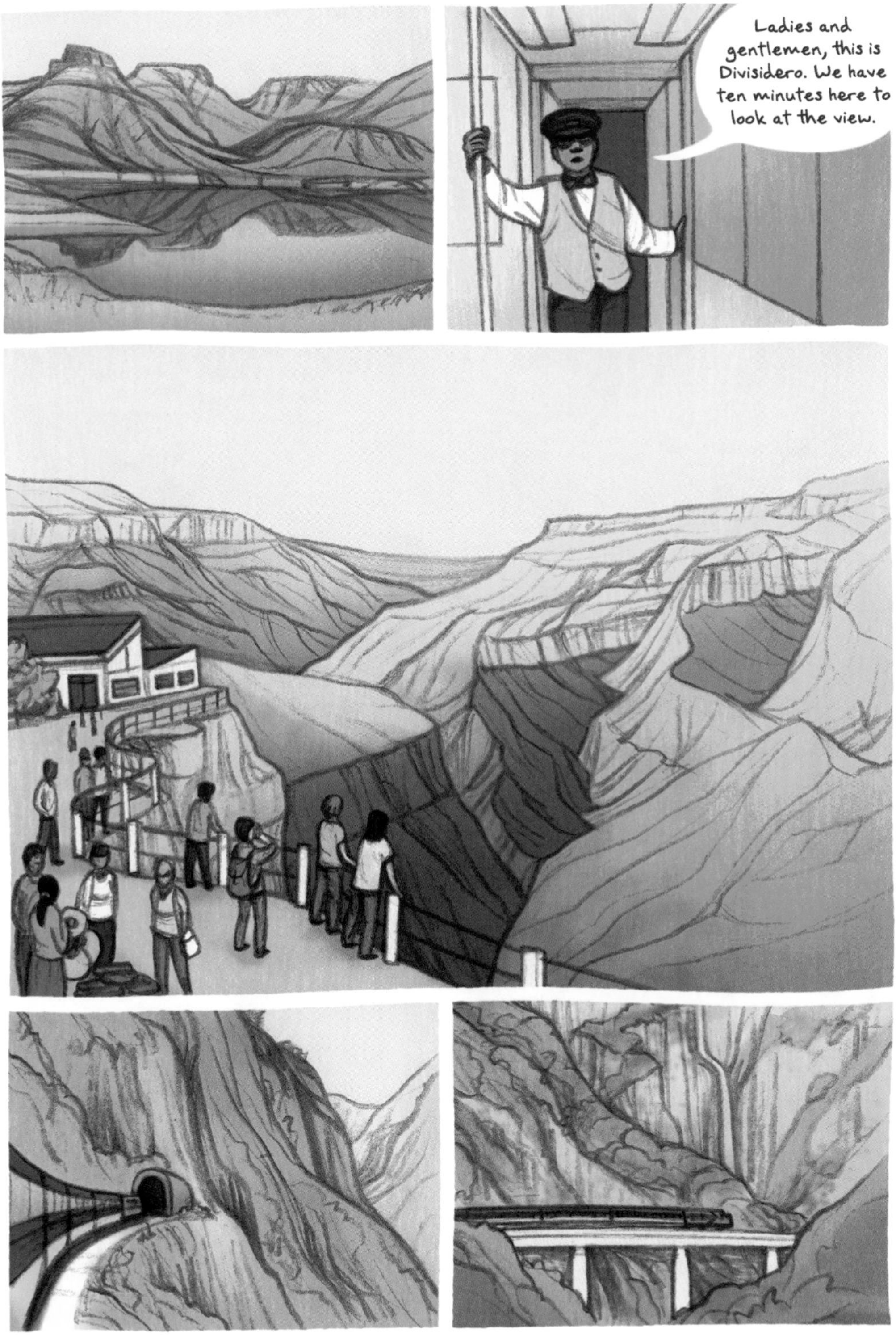
Ladies and gentlemen, this is Divisidero. We have ten minutes here to look at the view.

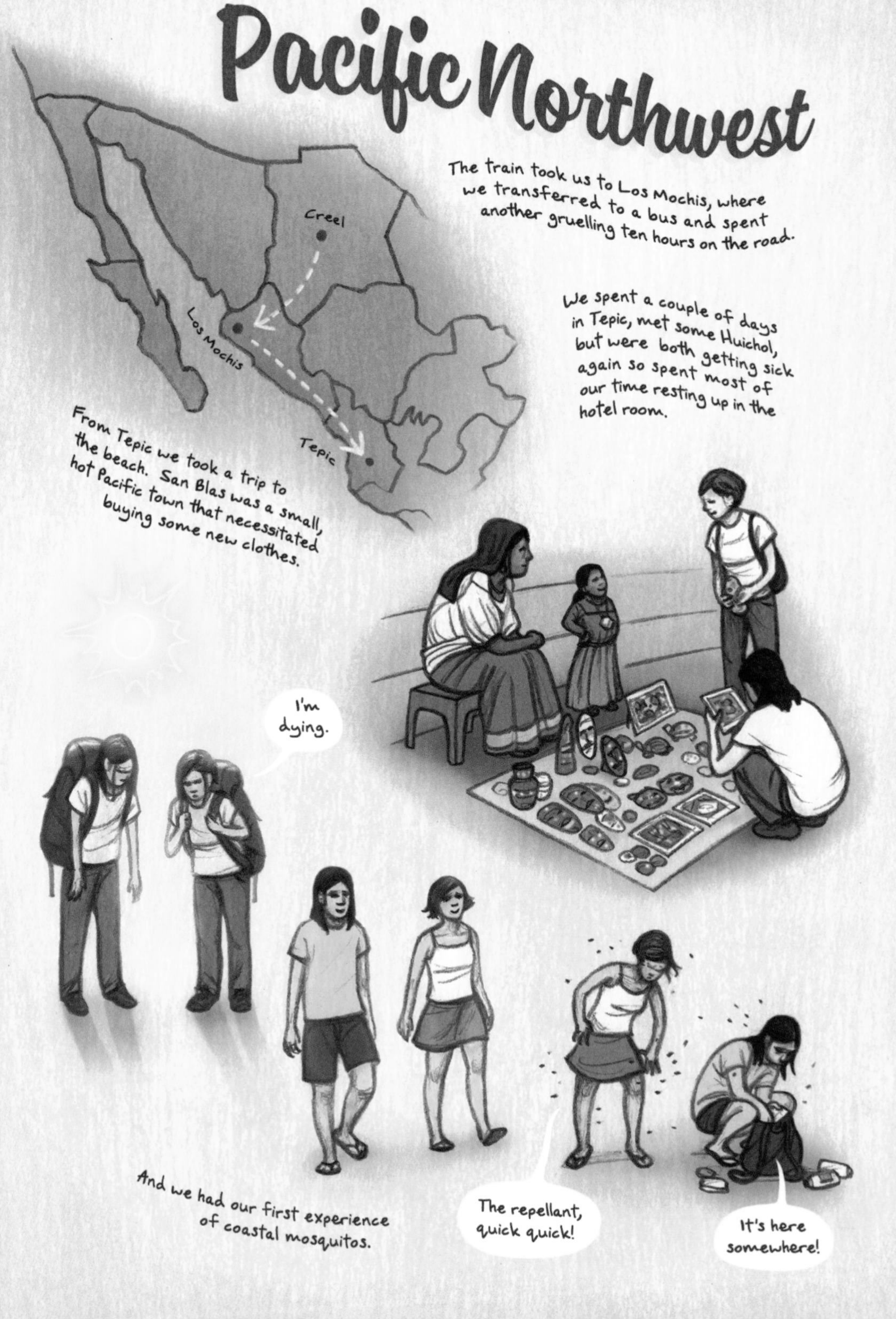
Pacific Northwest
The train took us to Los Mochis, where we transferred to a bus and spent another gruelling ten hours on the road.
Creel
Los Mochis
Tepic
We spent a couple of days in Tepic, met some Huichol, but were both getting sick again so spent most of our time resting up in the hotel room.
From Tepic we took a trip to the beach. San Blas was a small, hot Pacific town that necessitated buying some new clothes.
I'm dying.
And we had our first experience of coastal mosquitos.
The repellant, quick quick!
It's here somewhere!

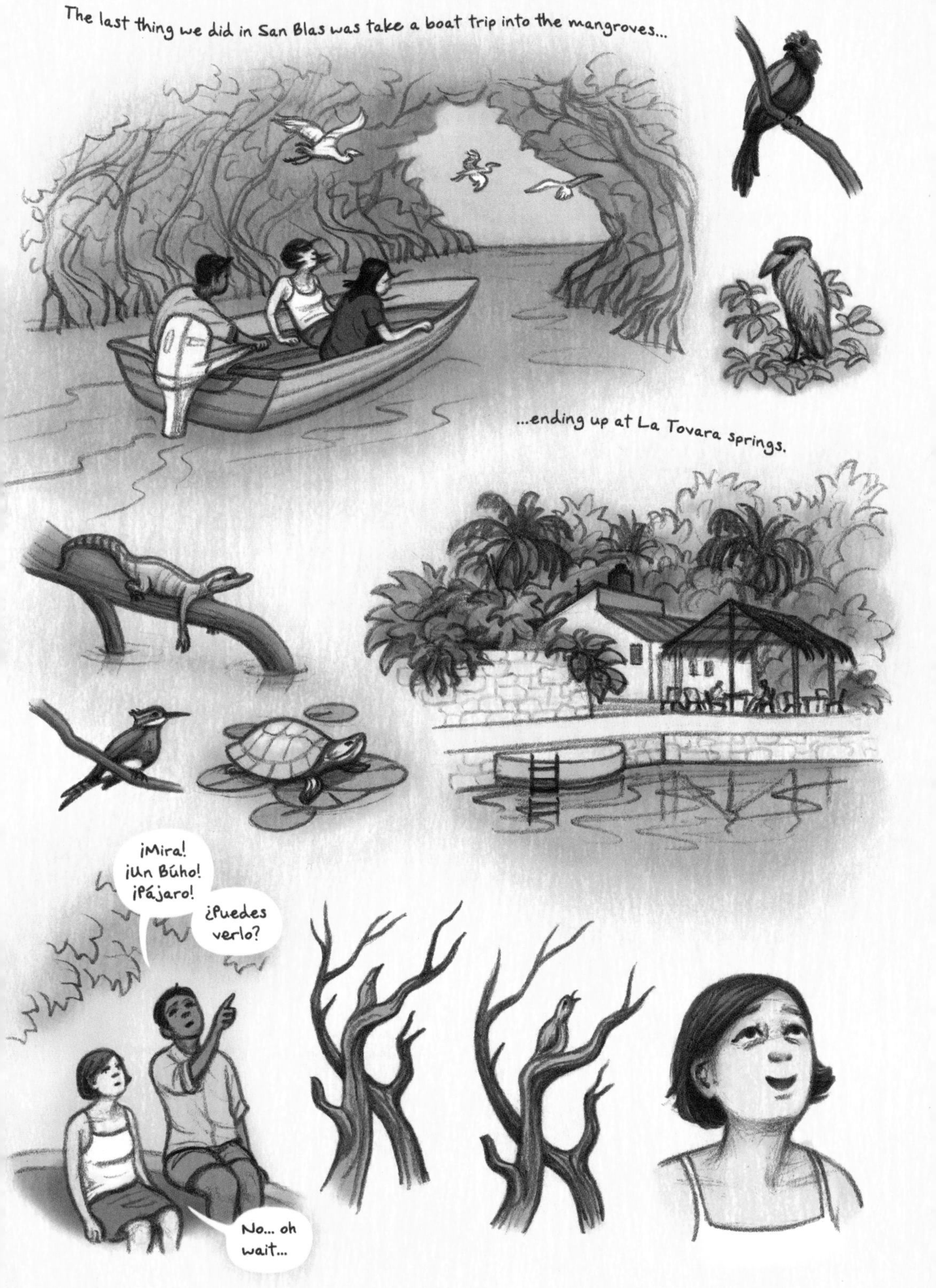
The last thing we did in San Blas was take a boat trip into the mangroves...
...ending up at La Tovara springs.
¡Mira! ¡Un Búho! ¡Pájaro!
¿Puedes verlo?
No... oh wait...

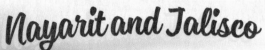

Nayarit and Jalisco

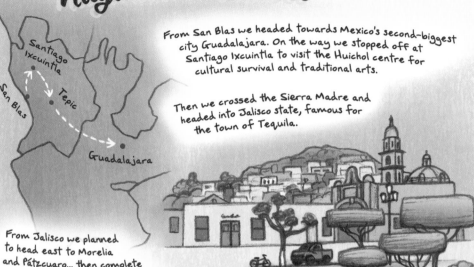

From San Blas we headed towards Mexico's second-biggest city Guadalajara. On the way we stopped off at Santiago Ixcuintla to visit the Huichol centre for cultural survival and traditional arts.

Then we crossed the Sierra Madre and headed into Jalisco state, famous for the town of Tequila.

From Jalisco we planned to head east to Morelia and Pátzcuaro... then complete a huge loop by returning to Mexico City via the small towns of Angangueo and Toluca.

San Blas
Santiago Ixcuintla
Tepic
Guadalajara

Santiago Ixcuintla

What do you think about visiting Tequila while we're here?

Uh

I guess.

TACOS RETO

It'd be a shame not to check it out.

And you've been so good so far – two whole months teetotal.

Cool! We'll go tomorrow.

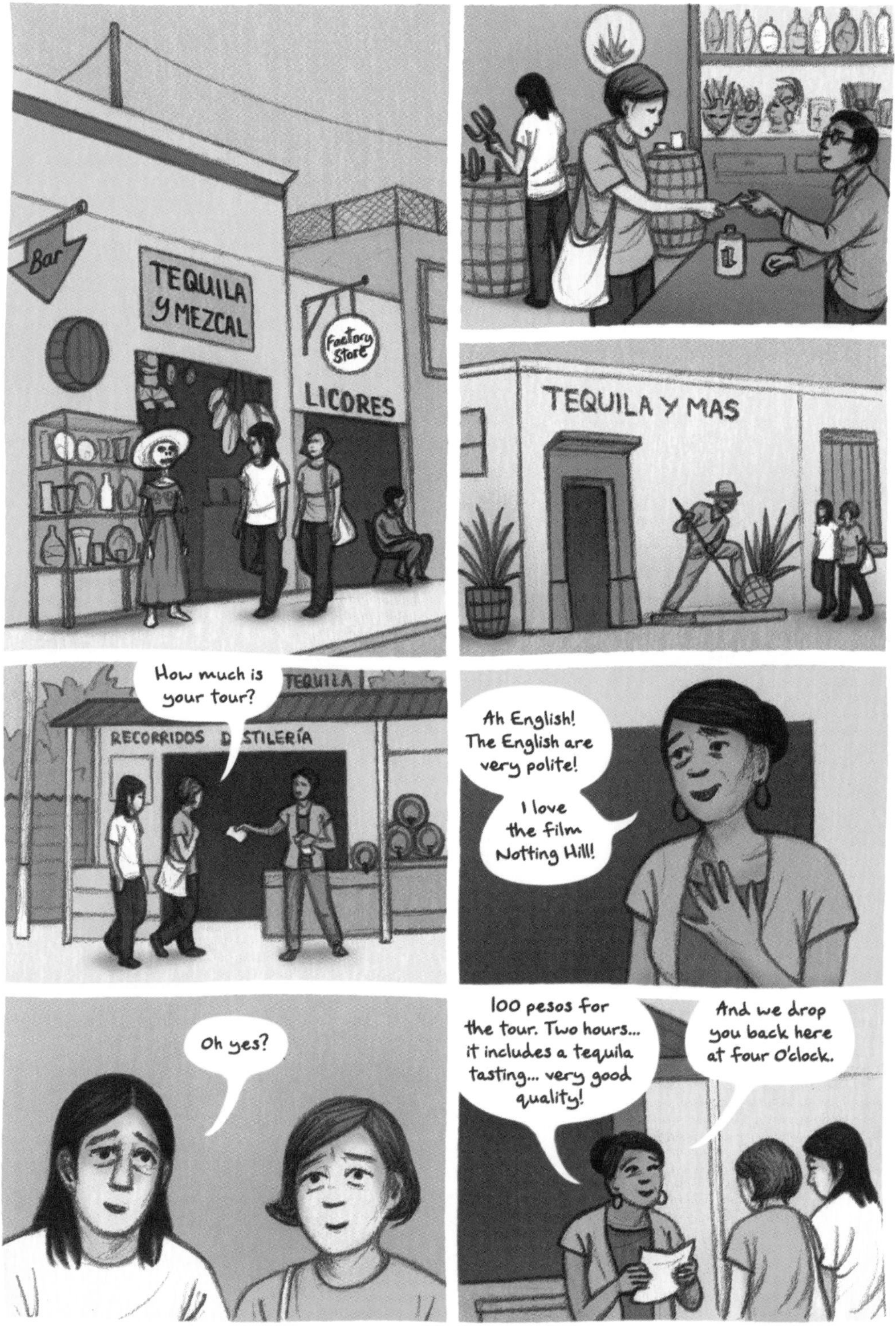

Bar
TEQUILA y MEZCAL
Factory Store
LICORES
TEQUILA Y MAS
TEQUILA
RECORRIDOS DESTILERÍA
How much is your tour?
Ah English! The English are very polite!
I love the film Notting Hill!
Oh yes?
100 pesos for the tour. Two hours... it includes a tequila tasting... very good quality!
And we drop you back here at four O'clock.

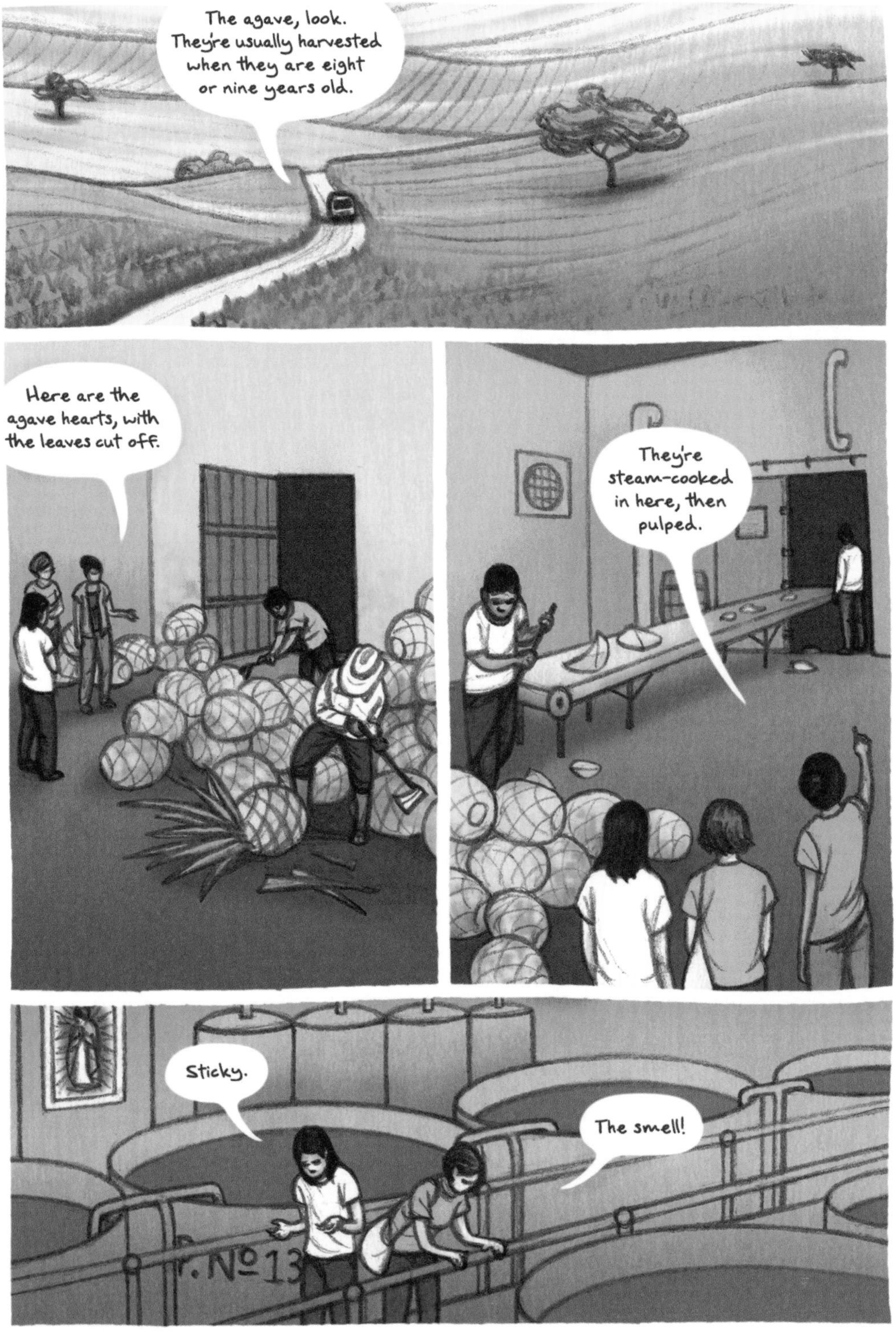
The agave, look. They're usually harvested when they are eight or nine years old.
Here are the agave hearts, with the leaves cut off.
They're steam-cooked in here, then pulped.
Sticky.
The smell!

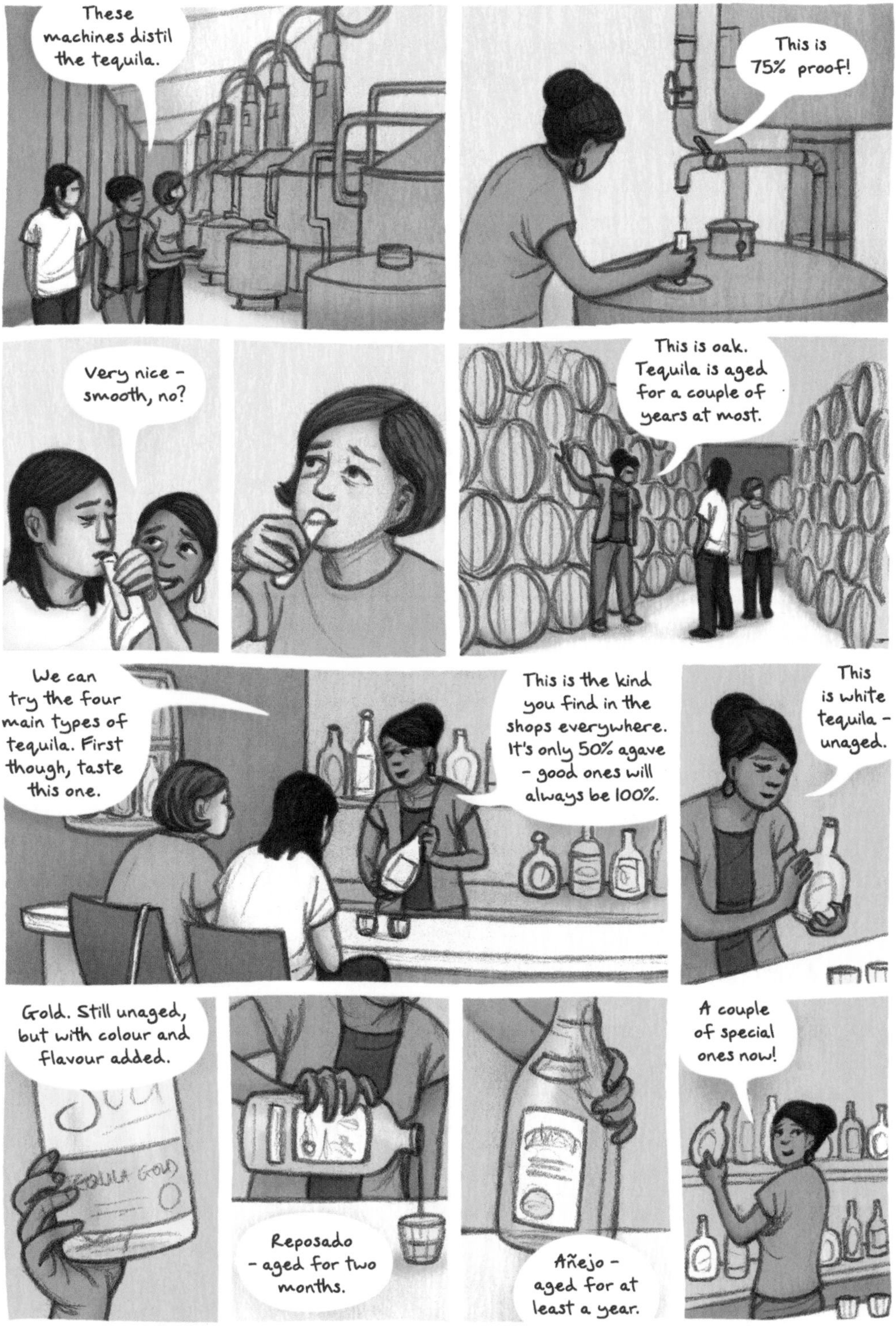
These machines distil the tequila.
This is 75% proof!
Very nice – smooth, no?
This is oak. Tequila is aged for a couple of years at most.
We can try the four main types of tequila. First though, taste this one.
This is the kind you find in the shops everywhere. It's only 50% agave – good ones will always be 100%.
This is white tequila – unaged.
Gold. Still unaged, but with colour and flavour added.
Reposado – aged for two months.
Añejo – aged for at least a year.
A couple of special ones now!

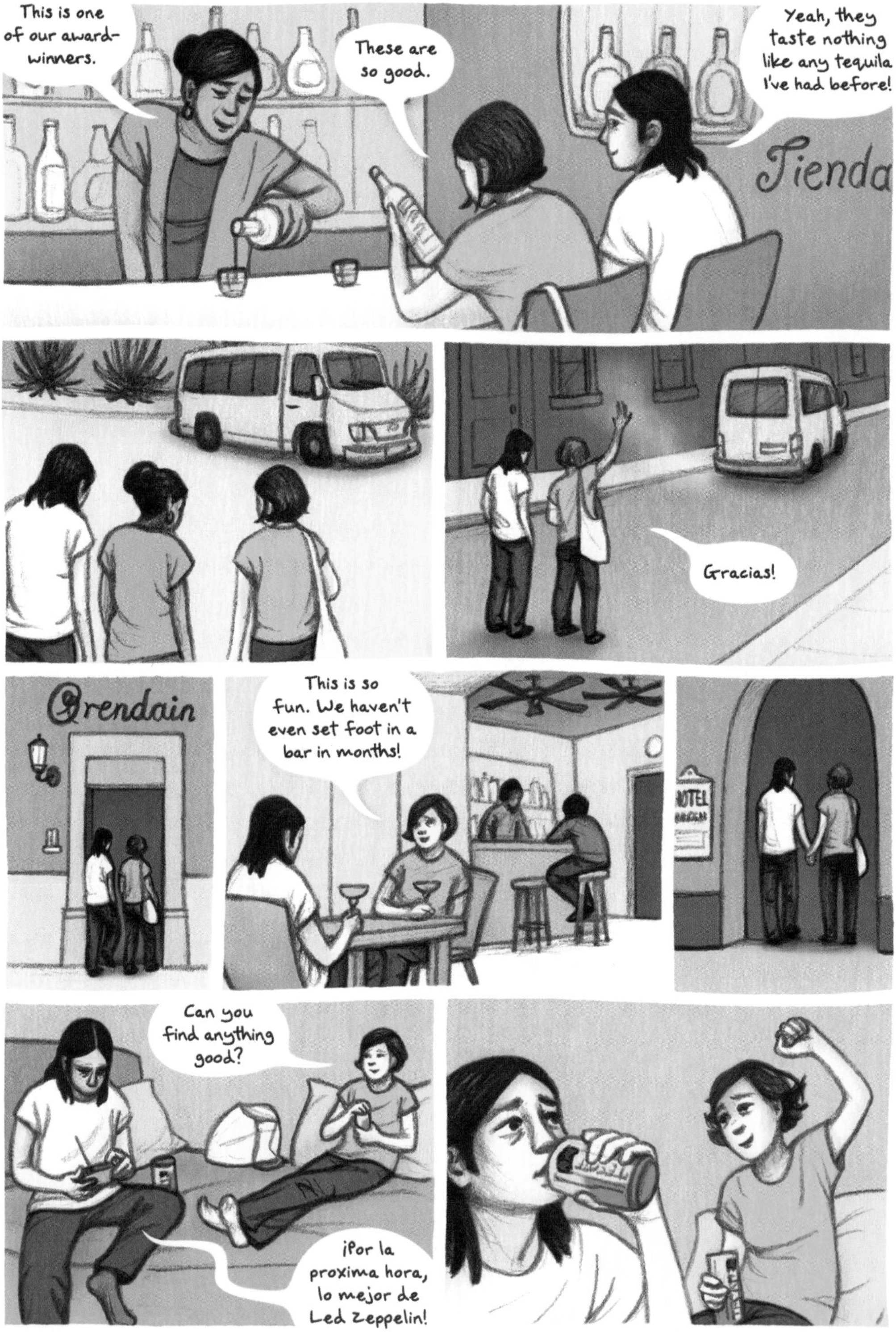
This is one of our award-winners.
These are so good.
Yeah, they taste nothing like any tequila I've had before!
Tienda
Gracias!
Orendain
This is so fun. We haven't even set foot in a bar in months!
HOTEL
Can you find anything good?
¡Por la proxima hora, lo mejor de Led Zeppelin!

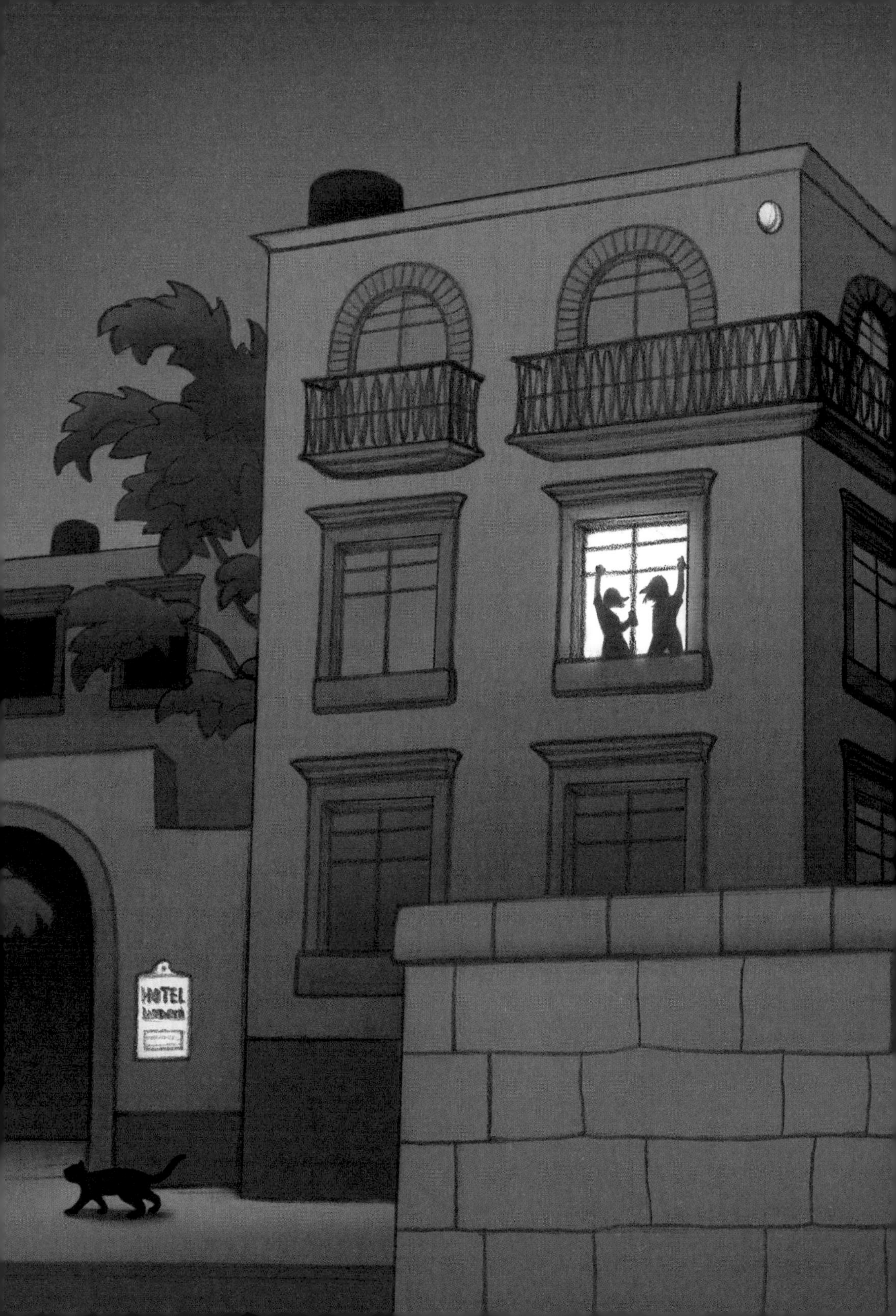
HOTEL

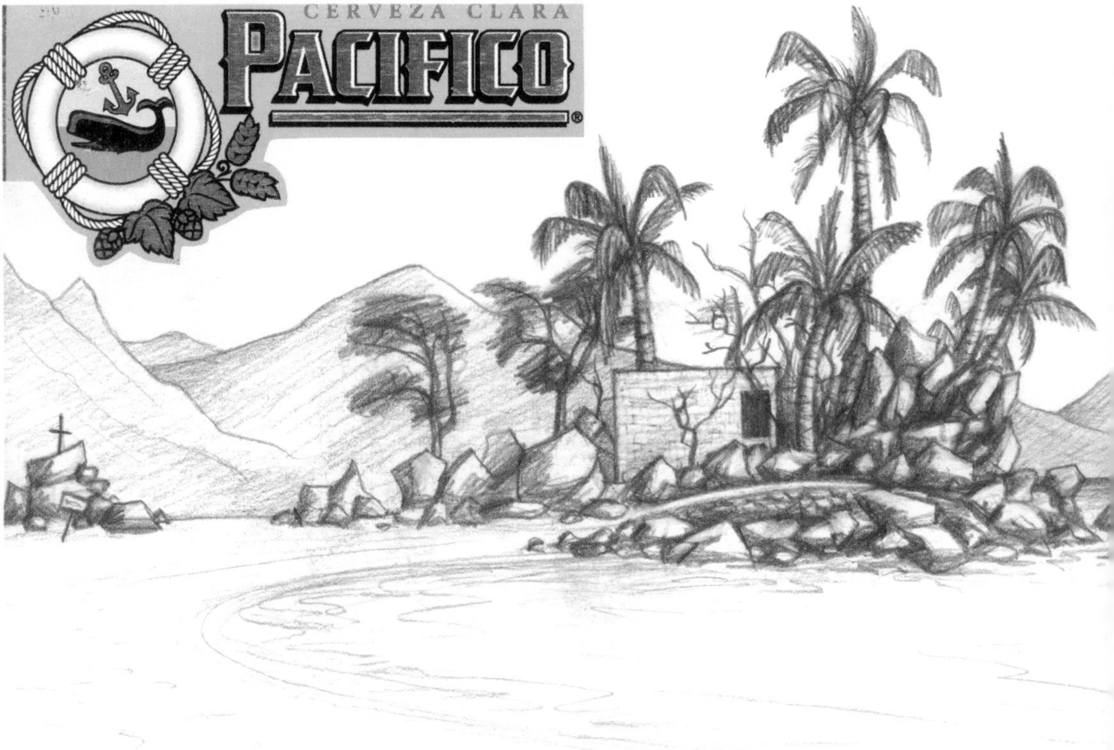
CERVEZA CLARA
PACIFICO

Playa Las Islitas,
near San Blas, 22/10/03

Daily Routine

We settled into a pattern of trying to find a balance between travelling and staying put... between things which cost money and things which didn't.

In money-saving phases, we would look for things to do to pass the time... things to take us out of our often unpleasant budget hotel rooms, but that wouldn't cost much money.

Mexico has wonderful public libraries where we'd draw, read and catch up on our journals.

In particularly hot places, the cinema was an option to kill time and also enjoy some air conditioning. American films were subtitled rather than dubbed, so were easy for us to watch.

The weirdest experience was watching Easy Rider in a free community cinema in Merida, along-side an audience of mostly horrified older ladies.

BEBIDAS   PALOMITAS

DULCE   SALADO

We also spent many long evenings in internet cafes chatting online to friends back home.

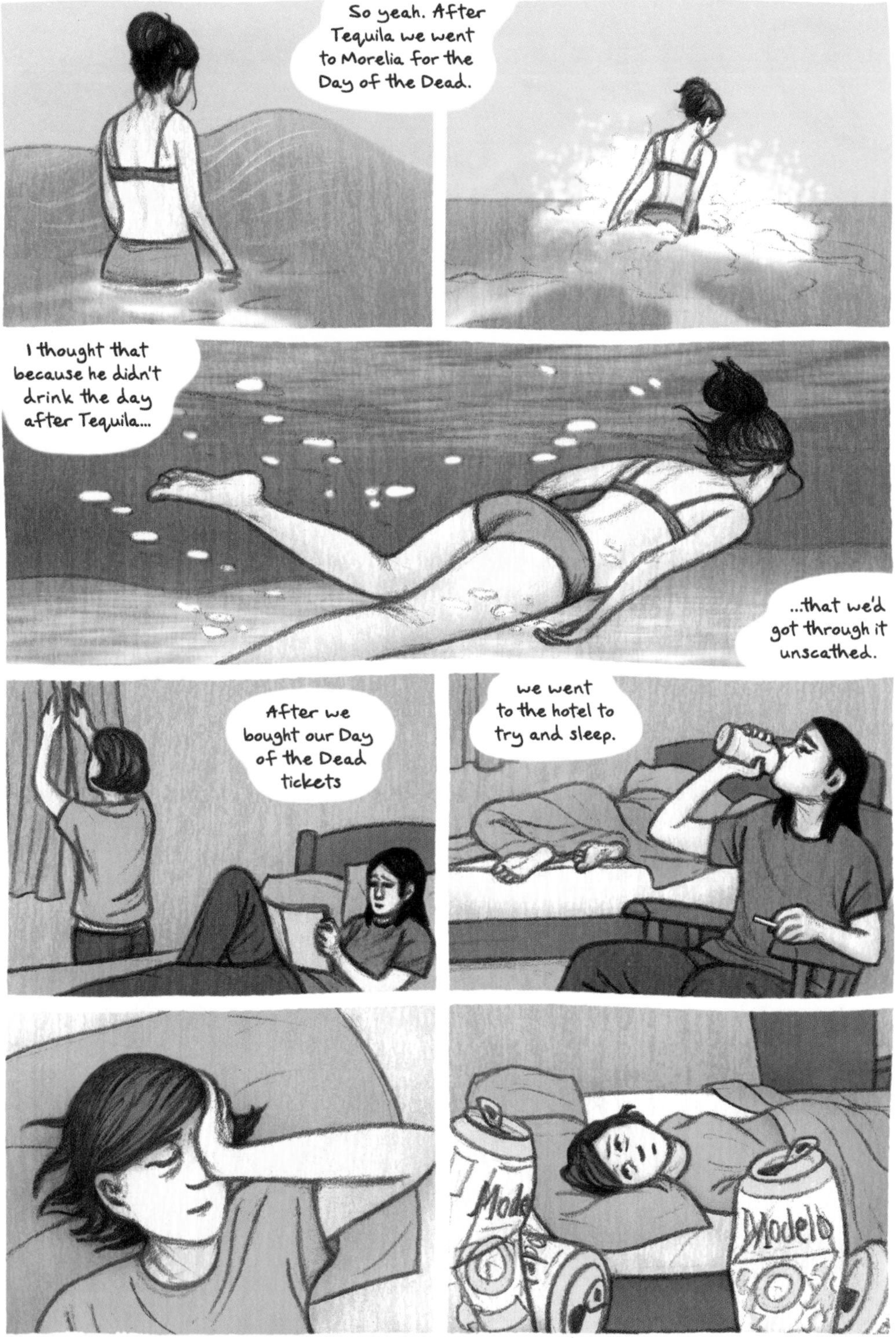
So yeah. After Tequila we went to Morelia for the Day of the Dead.
I thought that because he didn't drink the day after Tequila...
...that we'd got through it unscathed.
After we bought our Day of the Dead tickets
we went to the hotel to try and sleep.
Modelo
Modelo

I think the reason it took me so long to accept that he was an alcoholic

was because of the bingeing.

Because he sometimes went weeks without drinking

I thought he couldn't be one.

Even though he lost jobs to it

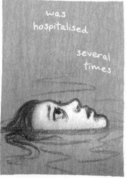

was hospitalised

several times

was prescribed medication

that he didn't take

had his jaw broken in a fight

Even though I woke to the sound of him peeing the bed

even though I was always waiting

for the next disaster.

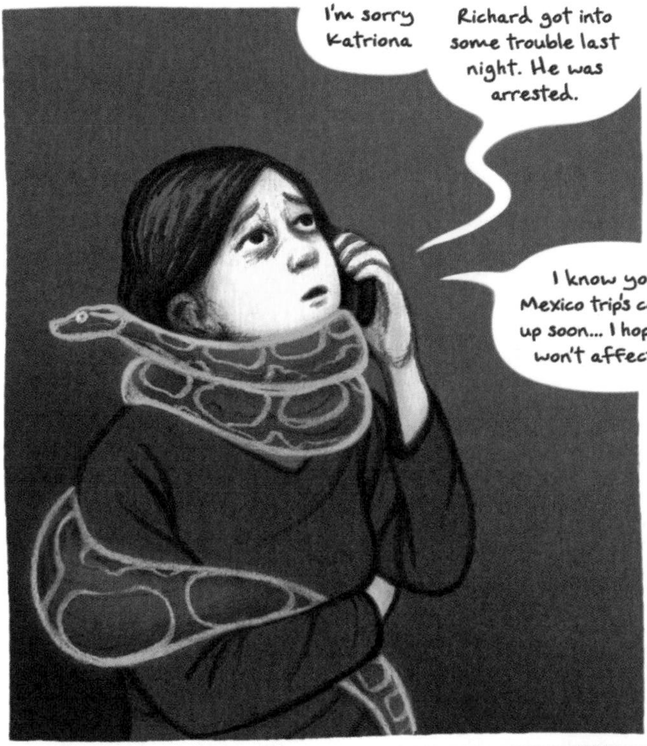
I'm sorry Katriona
Richard got into some trouble last night. He was arrested.
I know your Mexico trip's coming up soon... I hope this won't affect it...

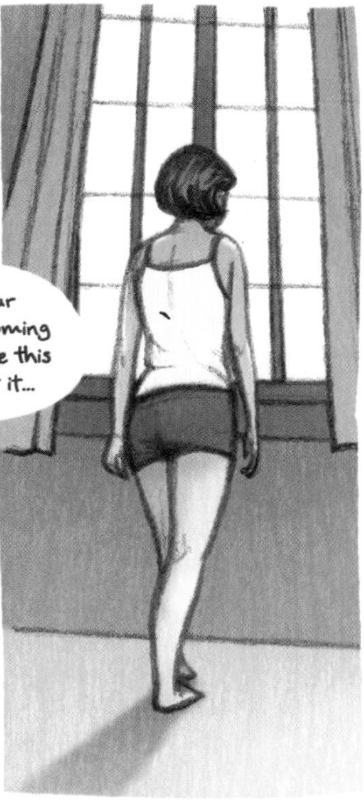

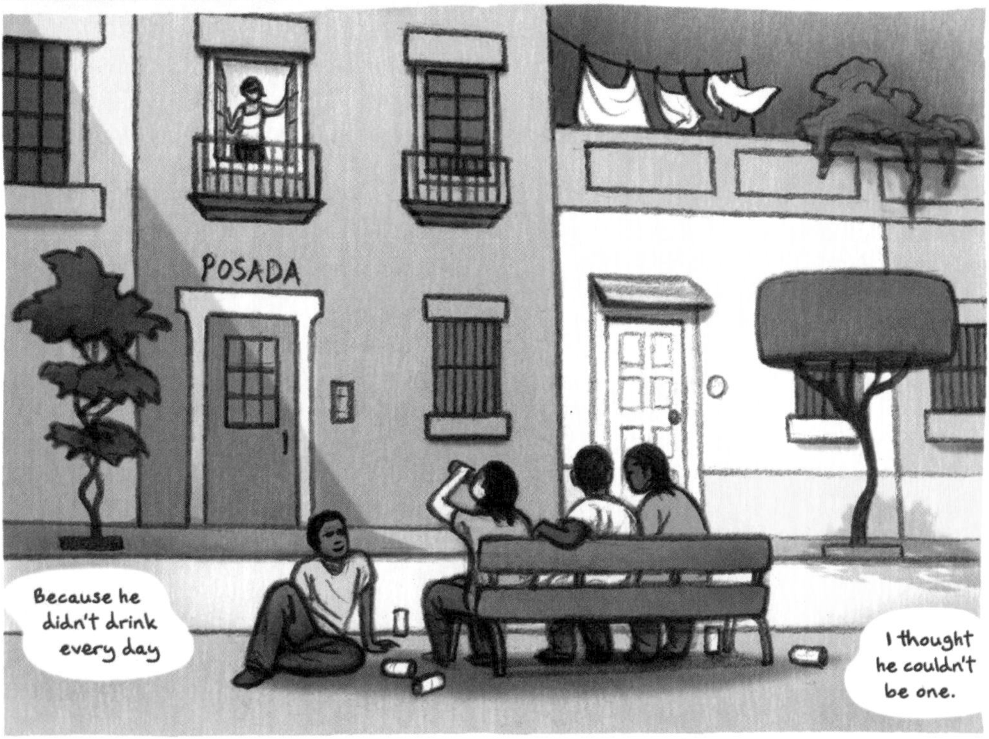
POSADA
Because he didn't drink every day
I thought he couldn't be one.

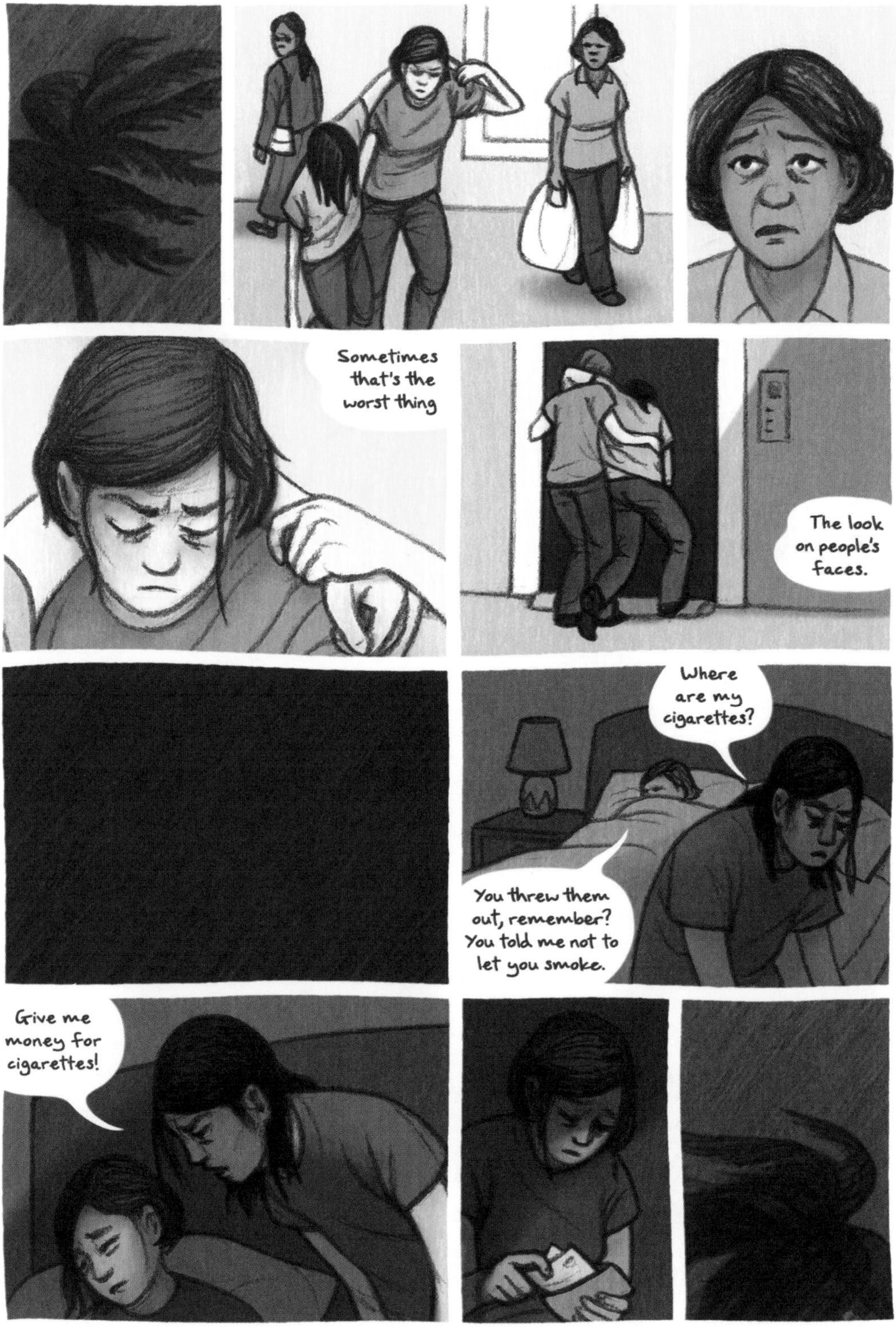
Sometimes that's the worst thing
The look on people's faces.
Where are my cigarettes?
You threw them out, remember? You told me not to let you smoke.
Give me money for cigarettes!

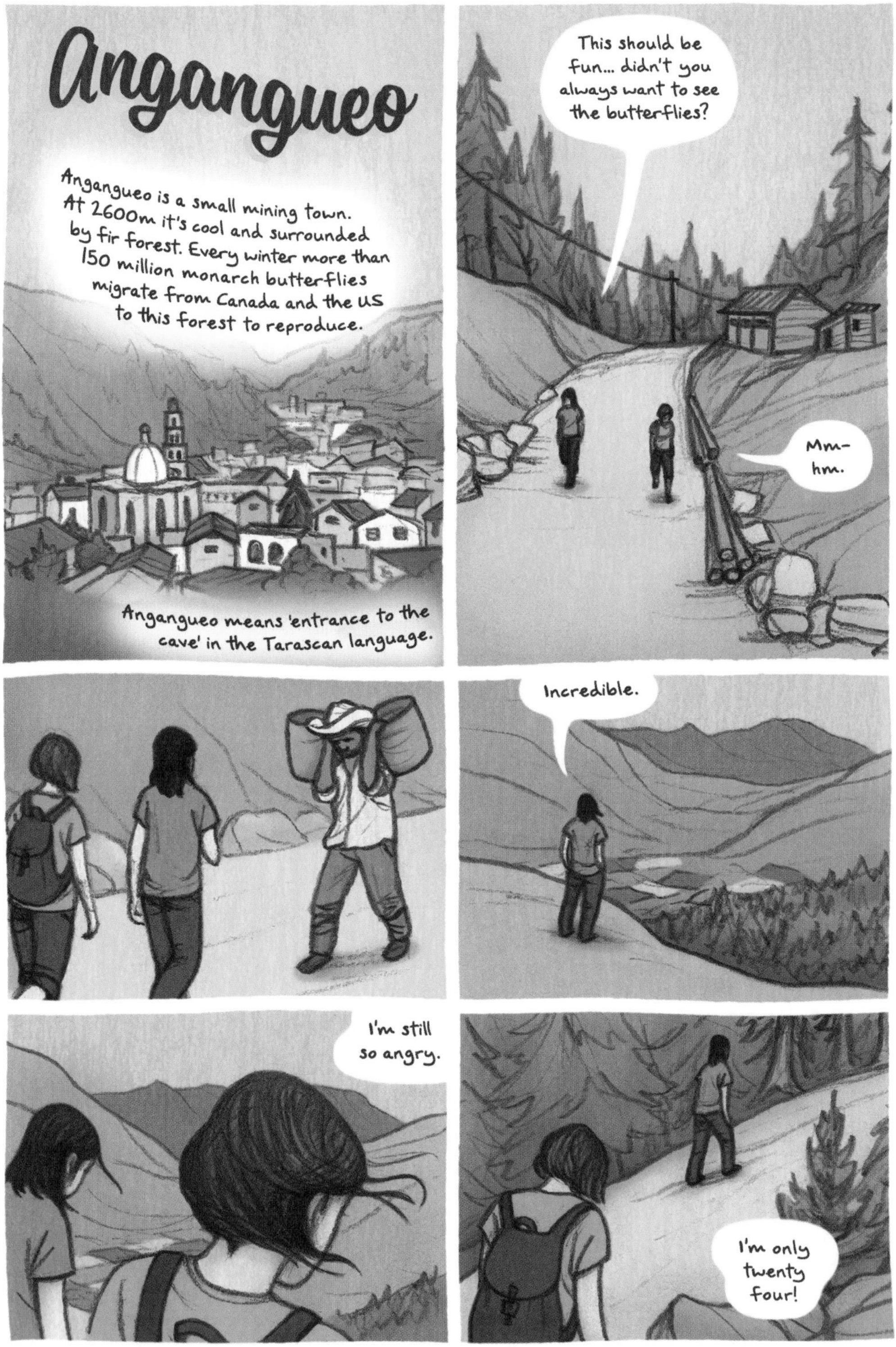

Angangueo
Angangueo is a small mining town. At 2600m it's cool and surrounded by fir forest. Every winter more than 150 million monarch butterflies migrate from Canada and the US to this forest to reproduce.
Angangueo means 'entrance to the cave' in the Tarascan language.
This should be fun... didn't you always want to see the butterflies?
Mm-hm.
Incredible.
I'm still so angry.
I'm only twenty four!

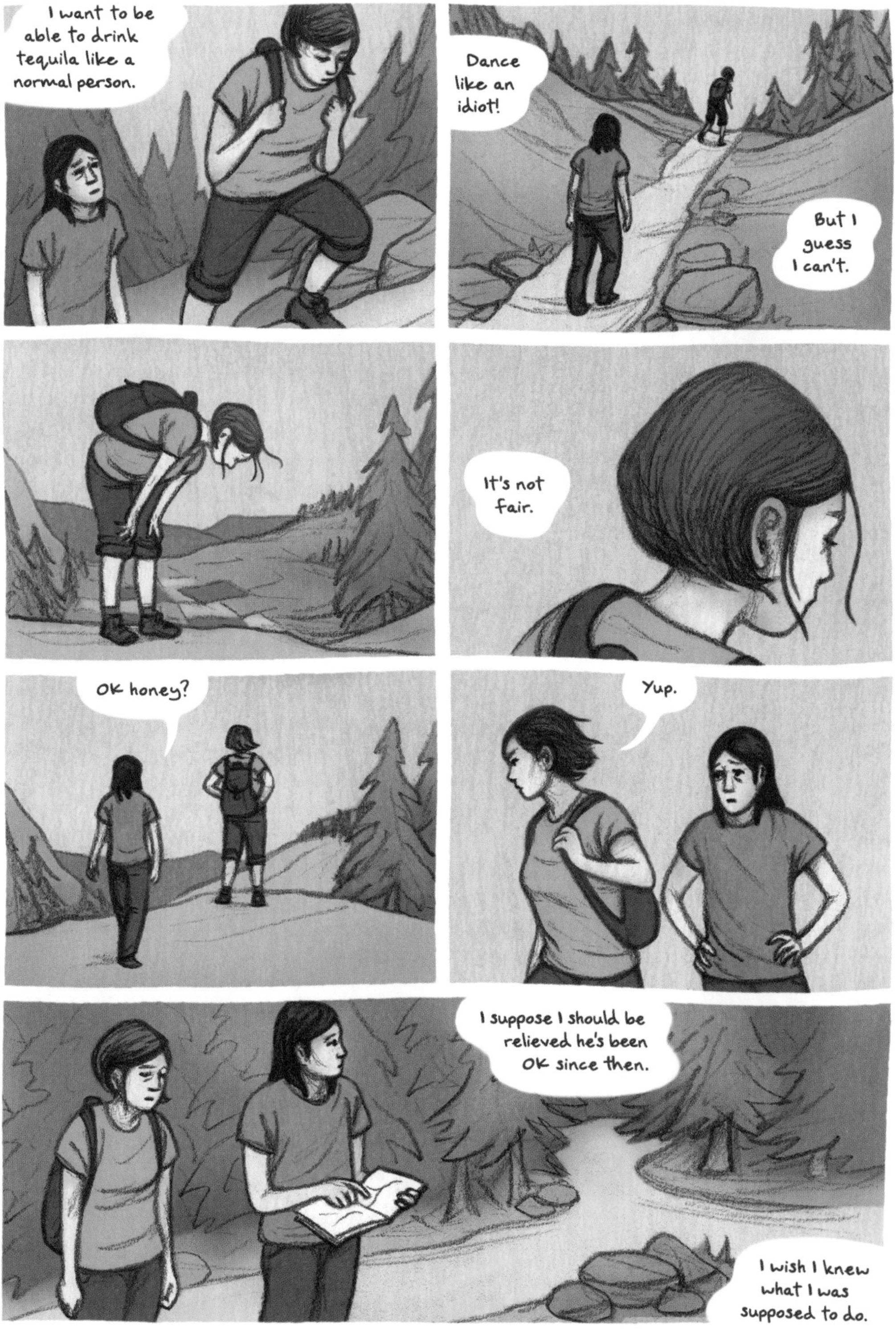
I want to be able to drink tequila like a normal person.
Dance like an idiot!
But I guess I can't.
It's not fair.
OK honey?
Yup.
I suppose I should be relieved he's been OK since then.
I wish I knew what I was supposed to do.

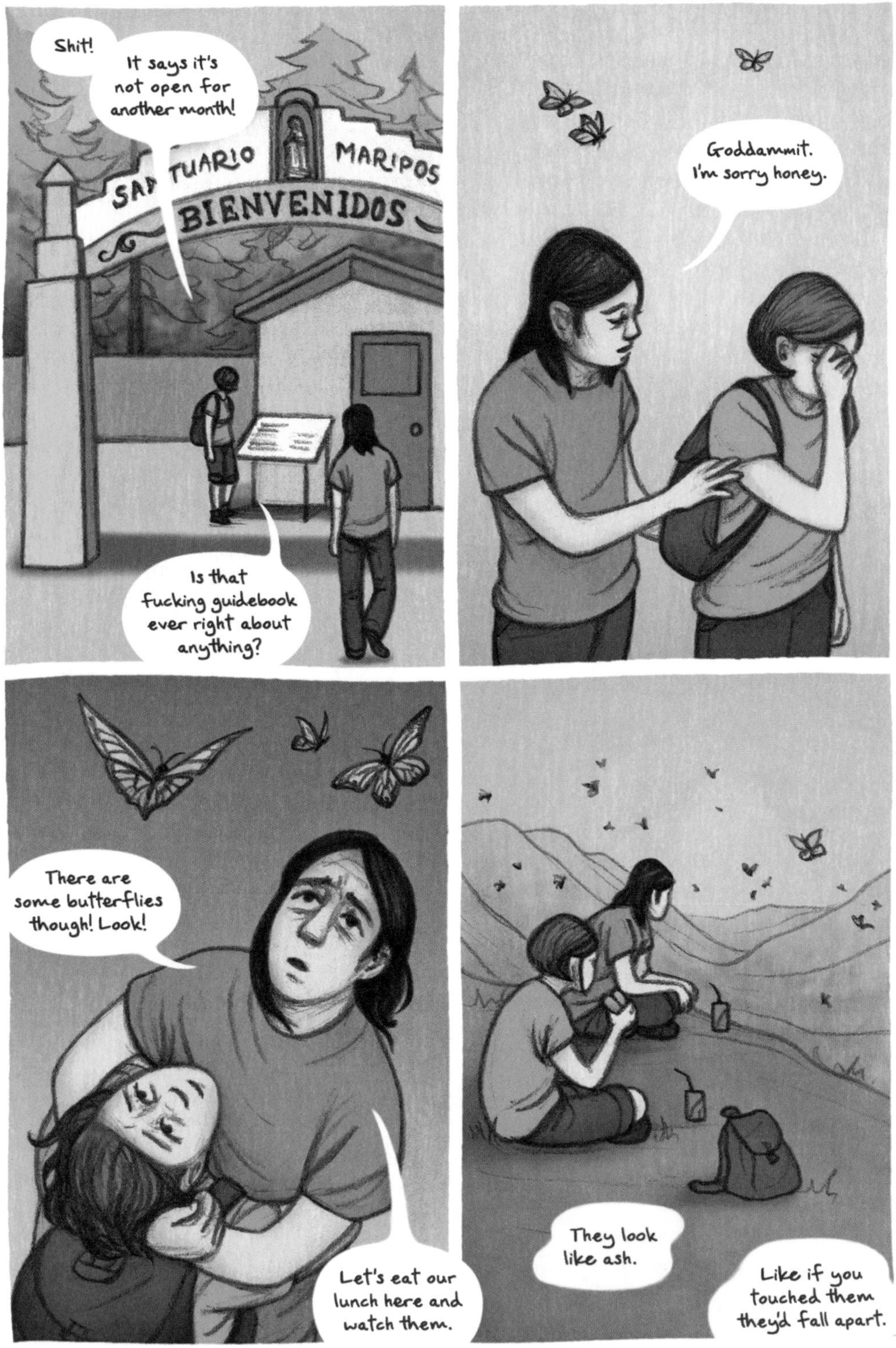
Shit!
It says it's not open for another month!
SANTUARIO MARIPOS
BIENVENIDOS
Is that fucking guidebook ever right about anything?
Goddammit. I'm sorry honey.
There are some butterflies though! Look!
Let's eat our lunch here and watch them.
They look like ash.
Like if you touched them they'd fall apart.

Travel Sketching

Jalisco, Estilo Azteca.
450 BC – 400 BC

Sketchbook rules

- Must draw from life or memory, not from photos
- Exceptions: anything that would be impossible or very difficult to draw from life
- If killing time in a library, I can draw from books but have to credit the source
- It's also OK to copy an artists' work that I like
- Always keep souvenirs to glue in

'Del porfirismo a la Revolución. Don Porfirio y sus cortesanos' Mural by David Alfaro Siqueiros. 17/2/04   1957–1965

Museo de la Medicina Maya
Organización de Médicos Indígenas del Estado de Chiapas, A.C.
Av. Salomon González Blanco Nº 10   Tel. (967) 8-54-38
San Cristóbal de Las Casas, Chiapas; México.

Cooperación $ 40ºº

Nº 000045

Gracias por cooperar al desarrollo de la Medicina Indígena Maya

Favourite media

Detailed drawings:
3B pencil (Faber-Castell)

Coloured pencils (Caran d'Ache)

Charcoal pencil (Conté)
Good for fast blocking-in
of rocks/trees/landscapes

I rarely finish a drawing in one sitting... if I won't have a chance to come back, I put down enough rough information to finish up the drawing later from memory. I might make notes on colour to refer back to.

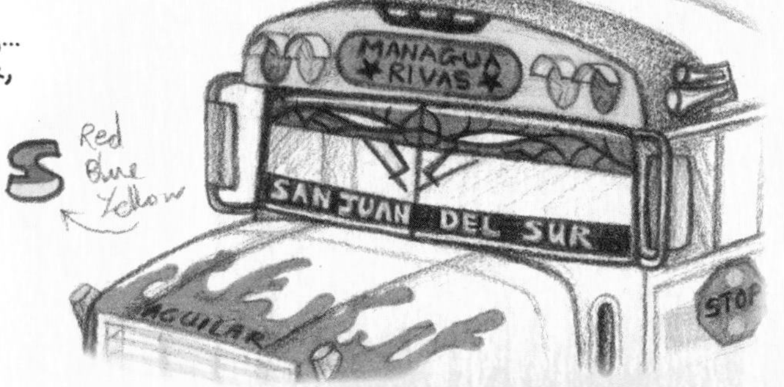
MANAGUA RIVAS
SAN JUAN DEL SUR
AGUILAR
STOP
Red
Blue
Yellow

I don't like being watched while I draw but sometimes it's unavoidable. I was always on the lookout not only for things to draw, but good private spots to draw them from.

The ideal spot is up high, somewhere that people won't notice you... and preferably with something to lean against.

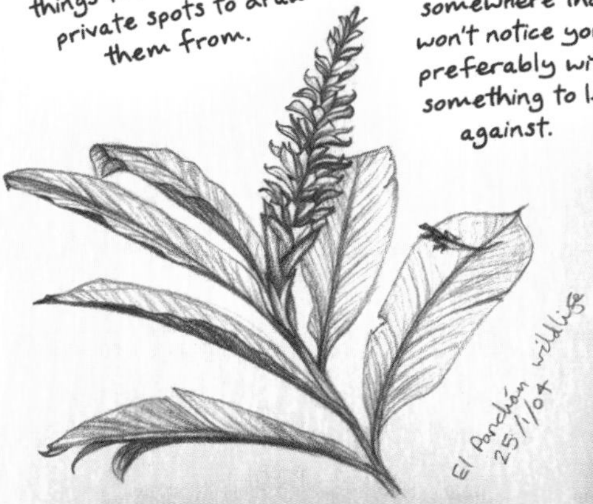
El Panchán wildlife
25/1/04

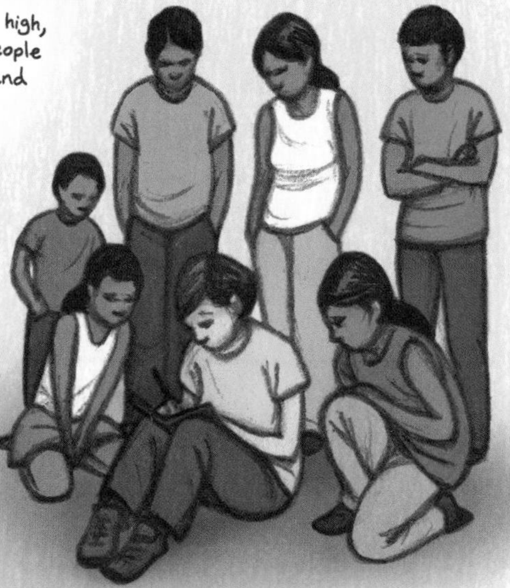

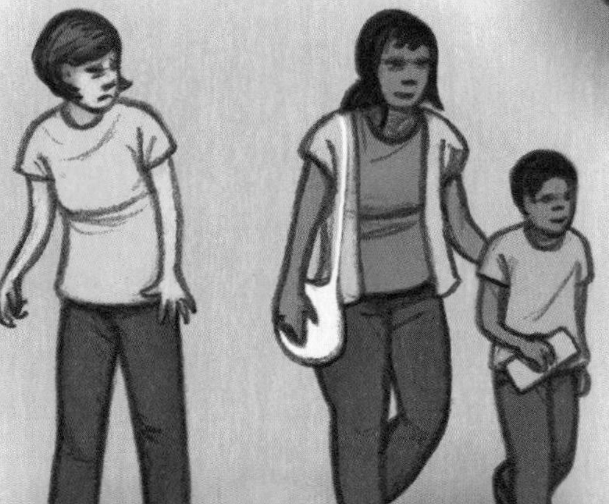

One time in a museum in Puebla I lost my pencil tin. It suddenly dawned on me how hard it would be to replace my favourite materials on the road. Then I saw a young boy about to leave the museum with his mother, carrying my tin. I had to figure out how to tactfully get it back. I told him I was really happy he'd found it for me.

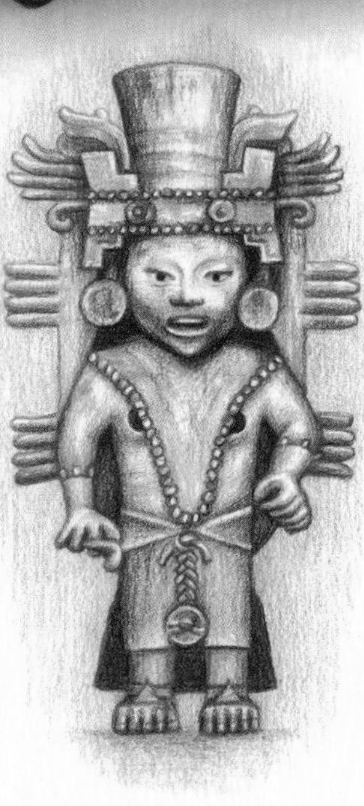

Incense-burner from Mayapan. Post-classic. 20/3/04

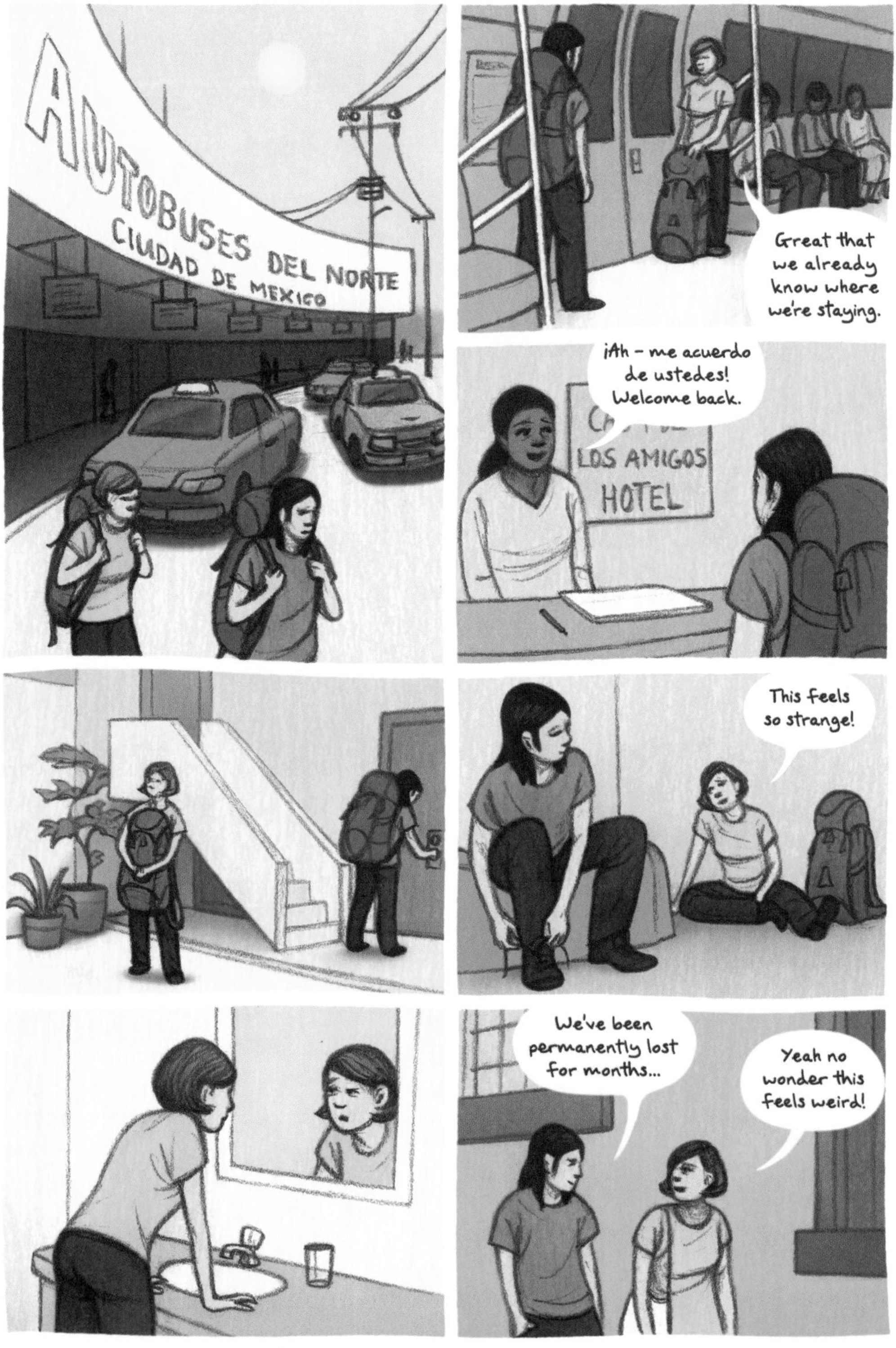
AUTOBUSES DEL NORTE
CIUDAD DE MEXICO
Great that we already know where we're staying.
¡Ah - me acuerdo de ustedes! Welcome back.
LOS AMIGOS
HOTEL
This feels so strange!
We've been permanently lost for months...
Yeah no wonder this feels weird!

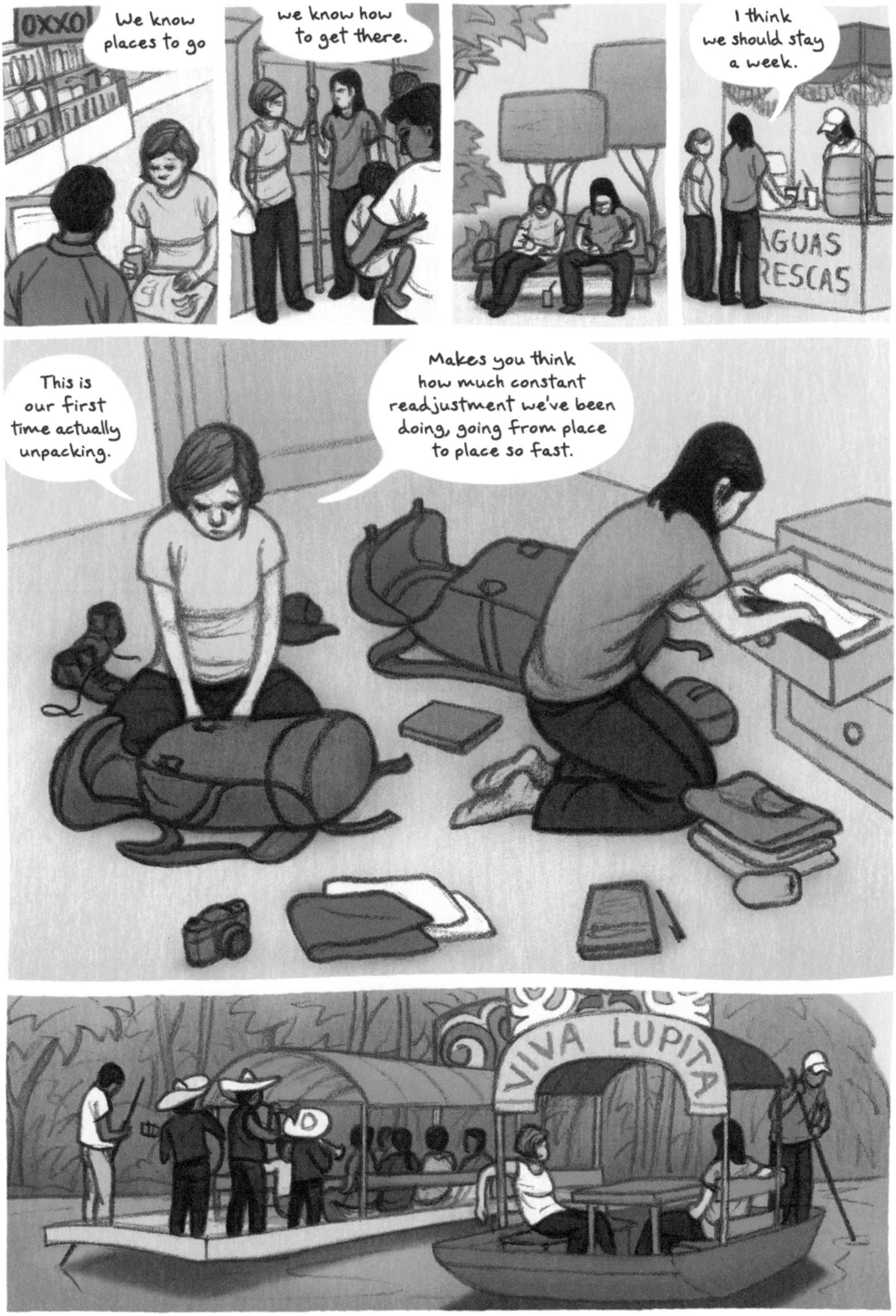
OXXO
We know places to go
we know how to get there.
I think we should stay a week.
AGUAS
RESCAS
This is our first time actually unpacking.
Makes you think how much constant readjustment we've been doing, going from place to place so fast.
VIVA LUPITA

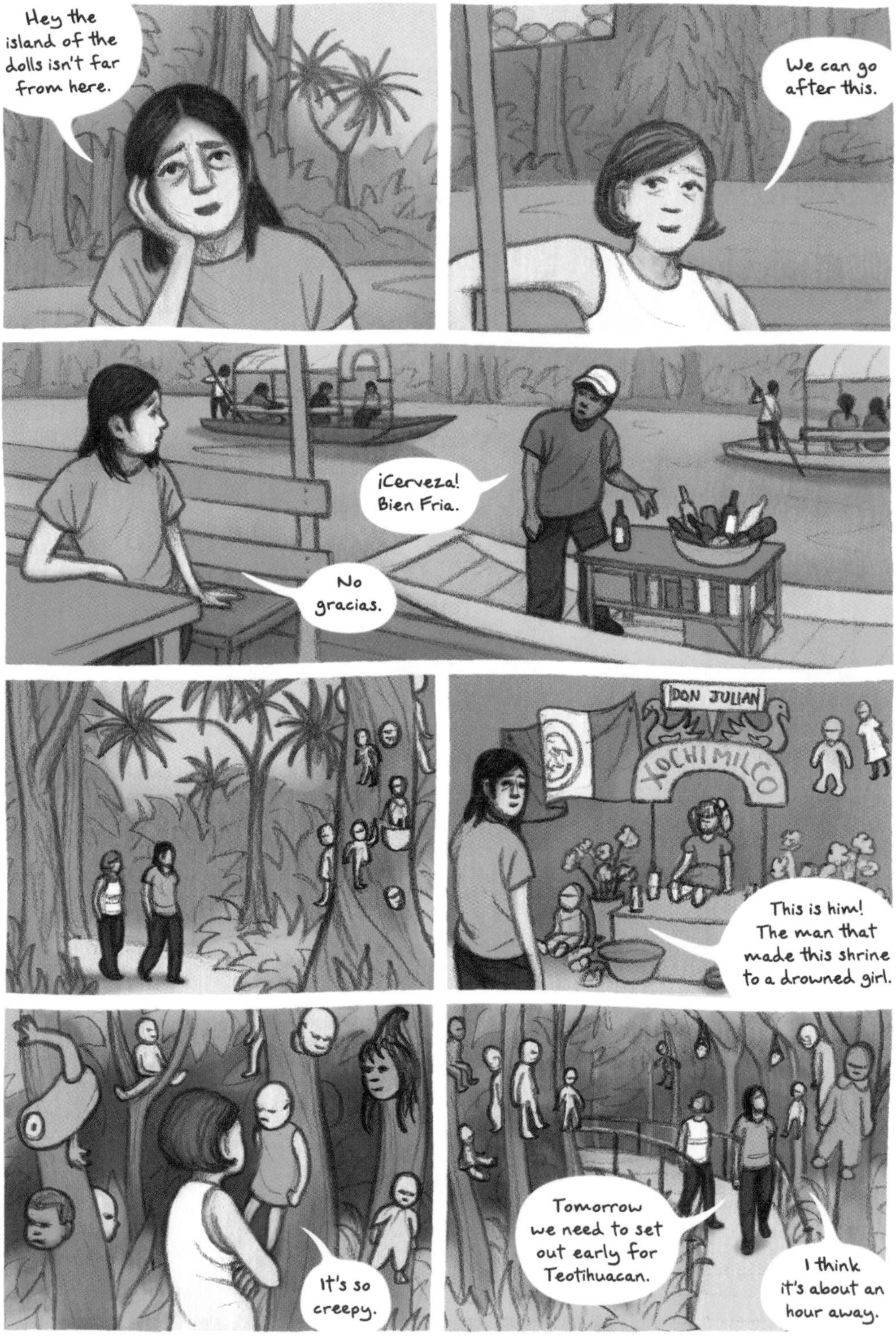
Hey the island of the dolls isn't far from here.
We can go after this.
¡Cerveza! Bien Fria.
No gracias.
DON JULIAN
XOCHIMILCO
This is him! The man that made this shrine to a drowned girl.
It's so creepy.
Tomorrow we need to set out early for Teotihuacan.
I think it's about an hour away.

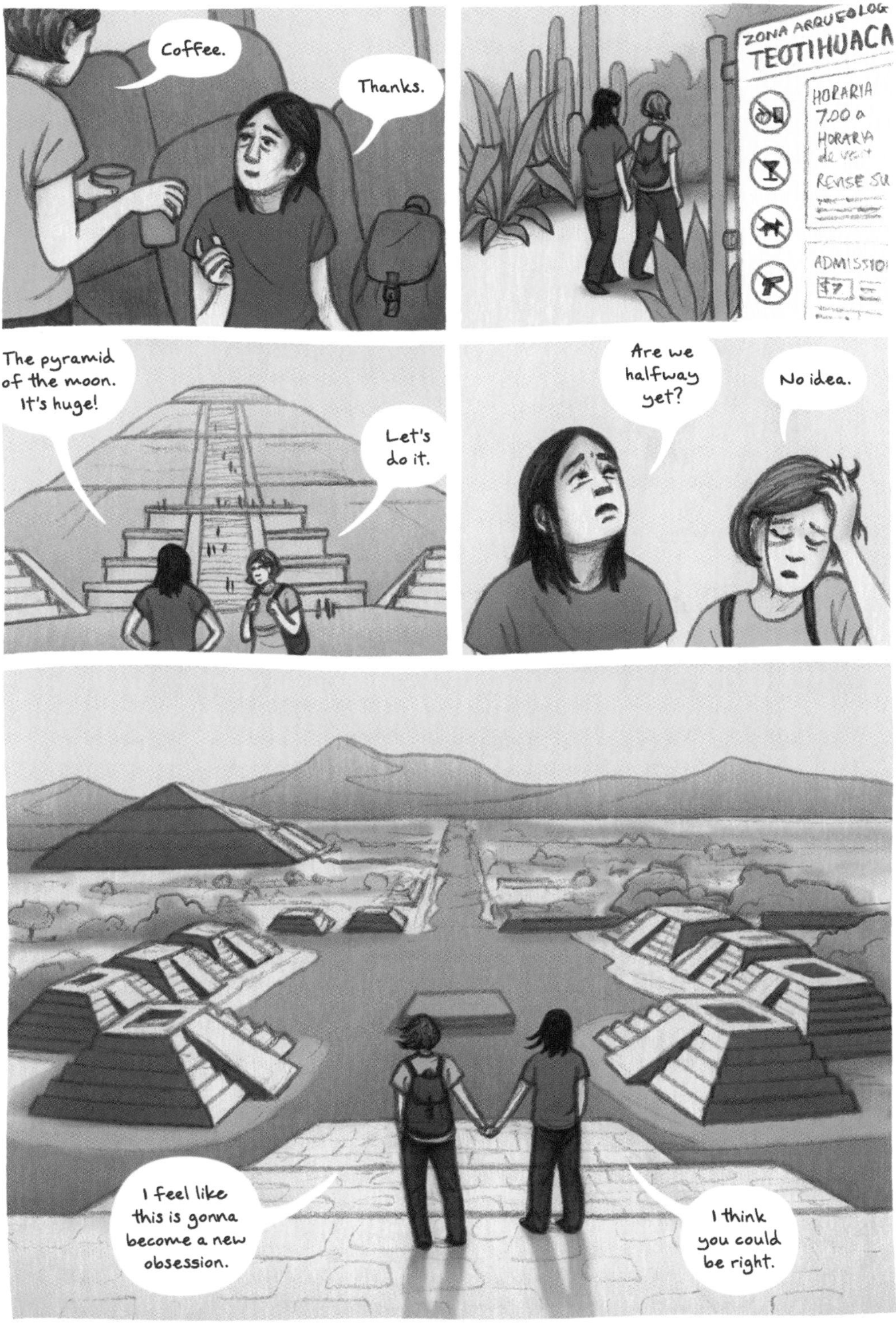

Coffee.
Thanks.
ZONA ARQUEOLOG
TEOTIHUACA
HORARIA
7.00 a
HORARYA
REVISE SU
ADMISSIO
The pyramid of the moon. It's huge!
Let's do it.
Are we halfway yet?
No idea.
I feel like this is gonna become a new obsession.
I think you could be right.

1. La Quemada

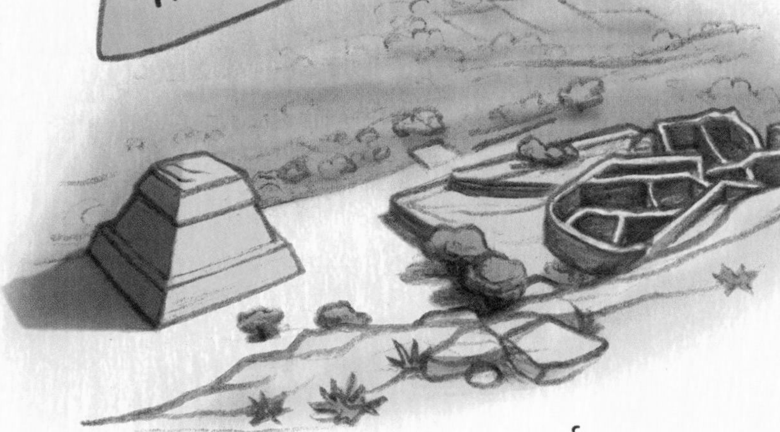

Historians and archeologists struggle to agree on the origins of this site, which is further North than the rest of Mesoamerica (the region where pre-Columbian societies flourished before Spanish colonisation.) In general the further South you travel through Mesoamerica, the more intact and well-preserved the archeological sites are.

We saw four other archeological sites

2. Tula

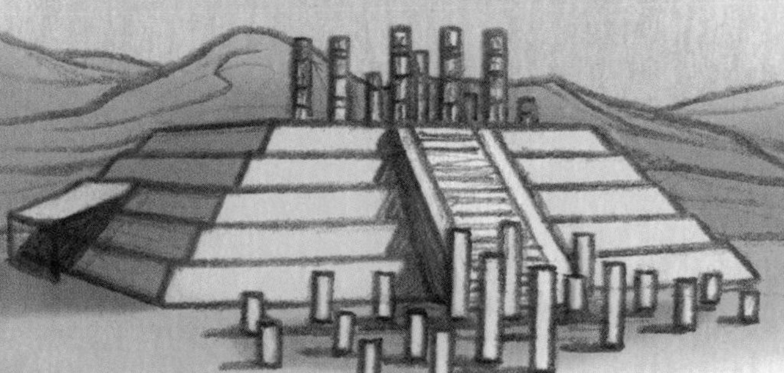

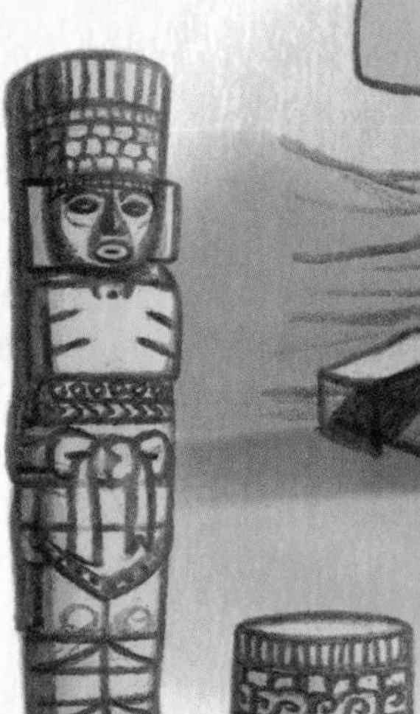

Tula reached its height as the capital of the Toltec Empire between the fall of Teotihuacan and the rise of Tenochtitlan (the capital of the Aztec empire located where downtown Mexico City is today.) Its famous feature is the Pyramid of Quetzalcoatl which is topped by four metre high basalt columns carved in the shape of Toltec warriors.

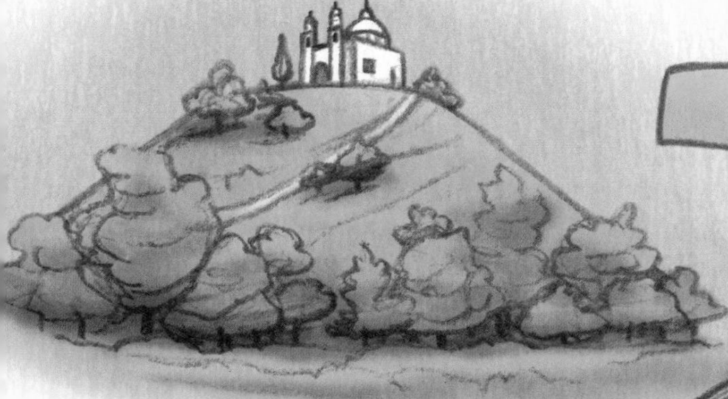

3. Cholula

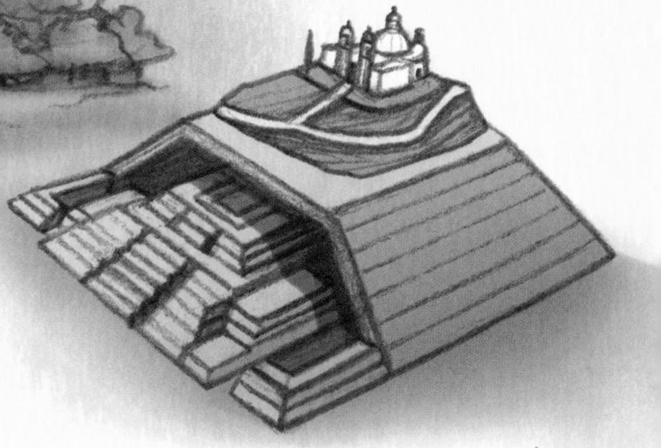

The great pyramid of Cholula is the largest pyramid known to exist in the world today (though not the tallest). It's mostly unrestored, and looks like a hill.

during our time in Central Mexico

Five miles of tunnels have been excavated inside it. In 1594 Spanish colonialists built a church on top of it – The Iglesia de Nuestra Señora de los Remedios. The church is a major Catholic pilgrimage destination, and the site is also used for the celebration of indigenous rites.

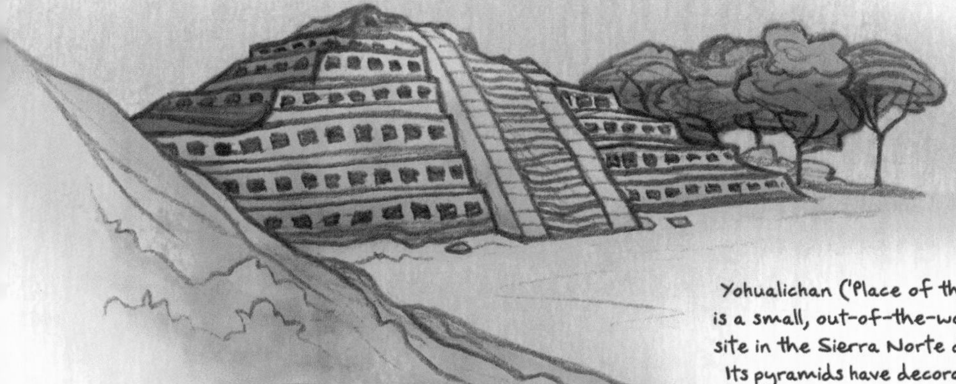

4. Yohualichan

Yohualichan ('Place of the Night') is a small, out-of-the-way Totonac site in the Sierra Norte de Puebla. Its pyramids have decorative niches in the same style as the more famous site El Tajín near Veracruz. We were the only visitors when we went.

Puebla – Central Gulf Coast – Oaxaca

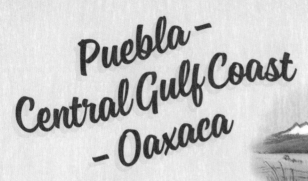

From Mexico City we travelled east past the volcanoes Popocatepetl and Ixtaccihuatl to the city of Puebla.

Mexico City
Jalapa
Veracruz
Puebla
Oaxaca

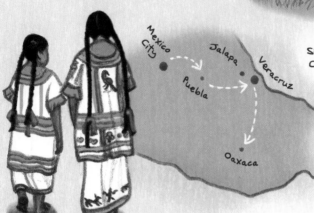

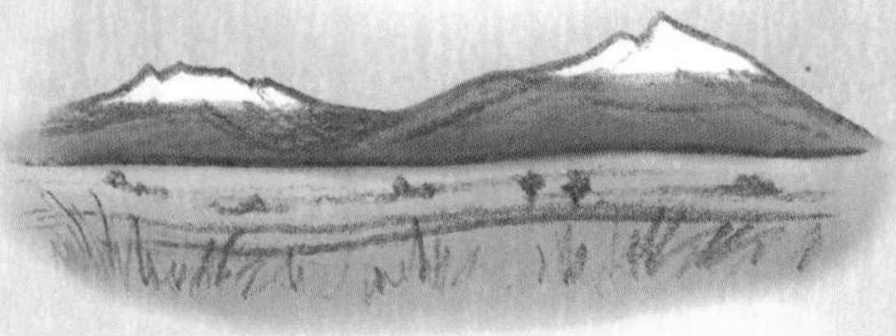

Whilst in Puebla we visited the Sierra Norte and the small town of Cuetzalan where there are Totonac and Nahua populations.

From Puebla we headed East again to the tropical Gulf Coast and the cities of Jalapa and Veracruz... home to the incredible Museo de Antropologia de Xalapa.

After a hot and stormy few days in the port city of Veracruz, we spent eight hours on a bus to Oaxaca.

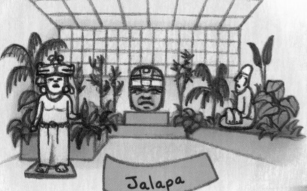

Jalapa

We'll get there two weeks before Christmas. We should look for a cheap apartment for a month! Put down roots.

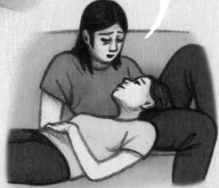

The state of Oaxaca feels like a point of change – the North/Central part of Mexico having a North American feel and the South having more of a Central American feel. We needed a place to have a rest and take a break from travelling... and we settled on Oaxaca.

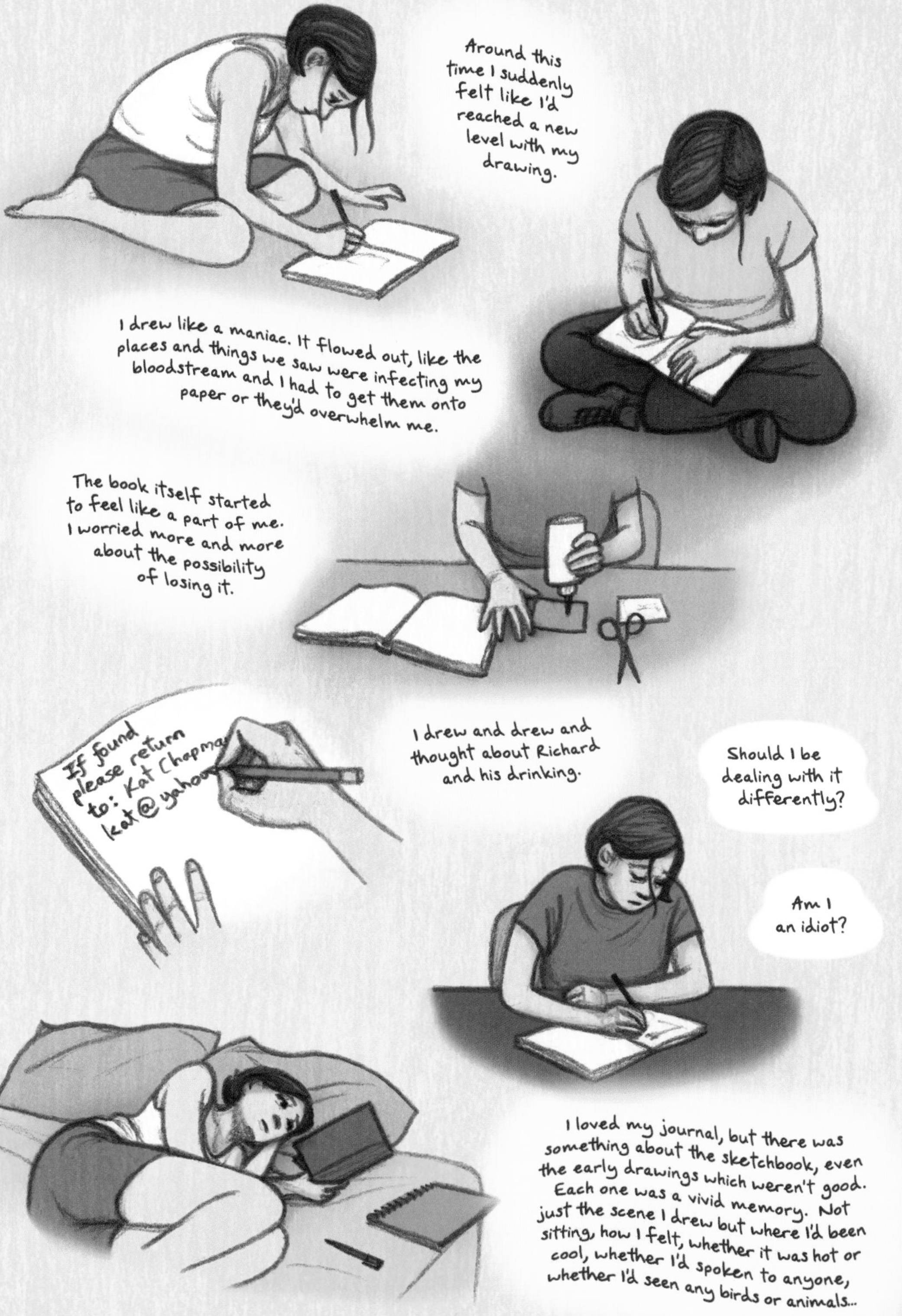

Around this time I suddenly felt like I'd reached a new level with my drawing.
I drew like a maniac. It flowed out, like the
places and things we saw were infecting my
bloodstream and I had to get them onto
paper or they'd overwhelm me.
The book itself started to feel like a part of me. I worried more and more about the possibility of losing it.
If found
please return
to: Kat Chapma
kat@yahoo
I drew and drew and thought about Richard and his drinking.
Should I be dealing with it differently?
Am I an idiot?
I loved my journal, but there was
something about the sketchbook, even
the early drawings which weren't good.
Each one was a vivid memory. Not
just the scene I drew but where I'd been
sitting, how I felt, whether it was hot or
cool, whether I'd spoken to anyone,
whether I'd seen any birds or animals...

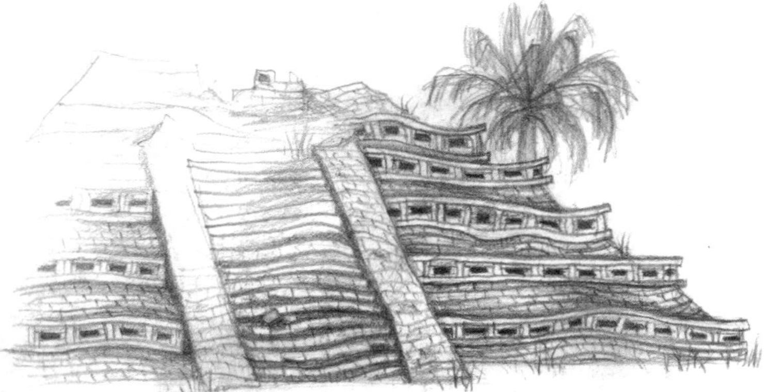

Niche pyramid at Yohualichán.
19/11/03

Implements for use in the ball-game. Museo de Antropología, Xalapa.

23/11/03

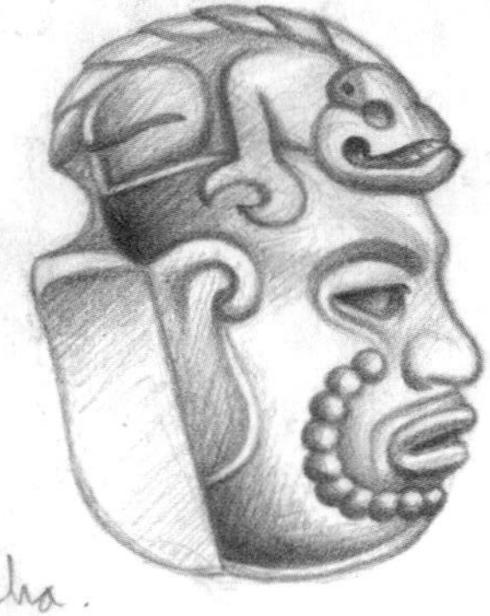

Hacha.
600 - 900 d.c,
Veracruz.

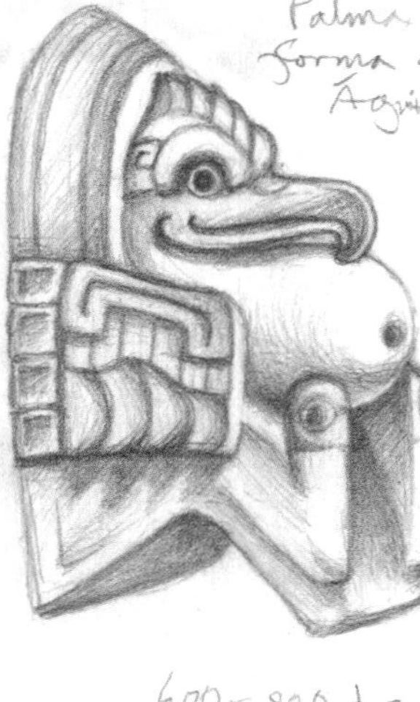

Palma con forma de Águila.

600 - 900 d.c
Gutiérrez Zamora, Veracruz

18/11/03

Zócalo, from Posada Jaqueline.

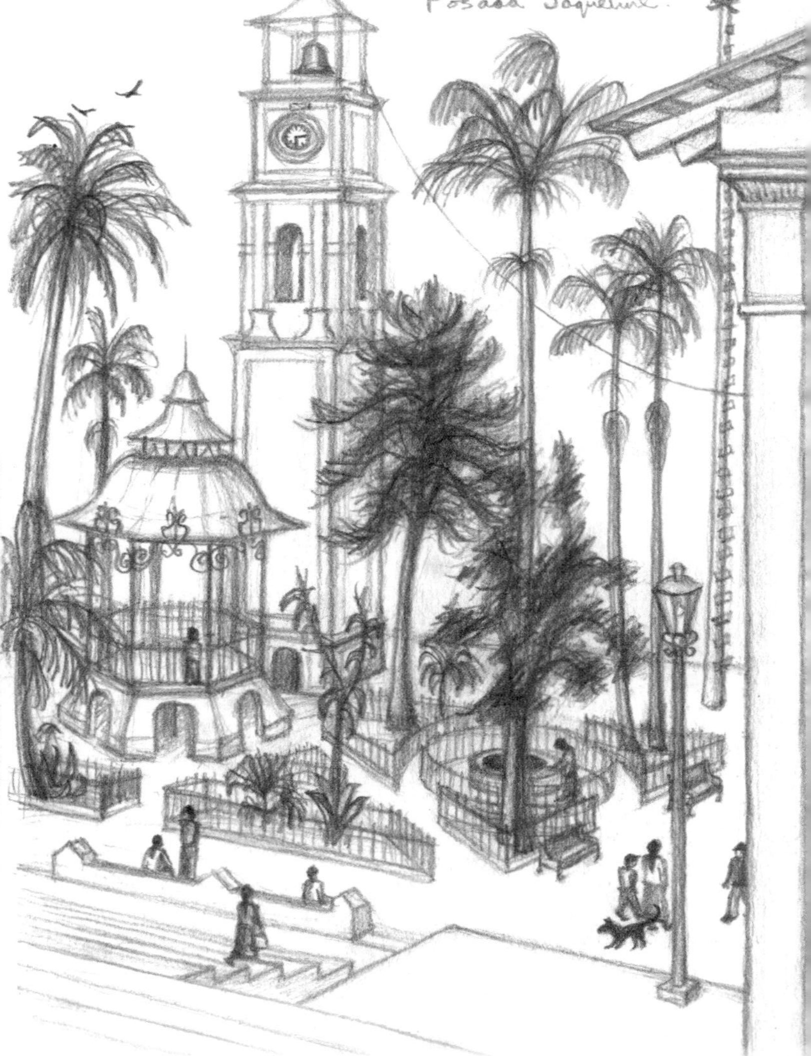

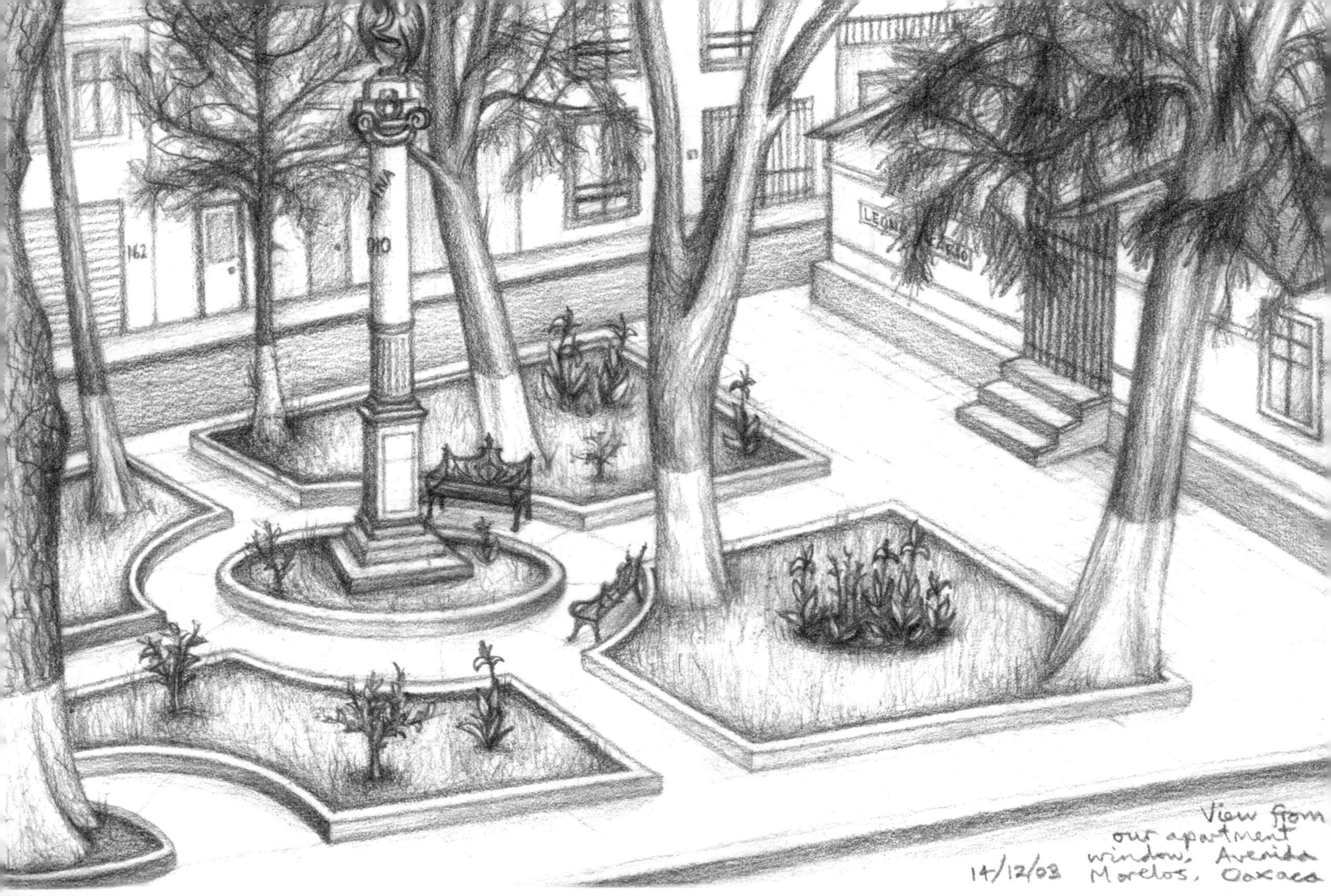
162
View from
our apartment
window, Avenida
Morelos, Oaxaca
14/12/03

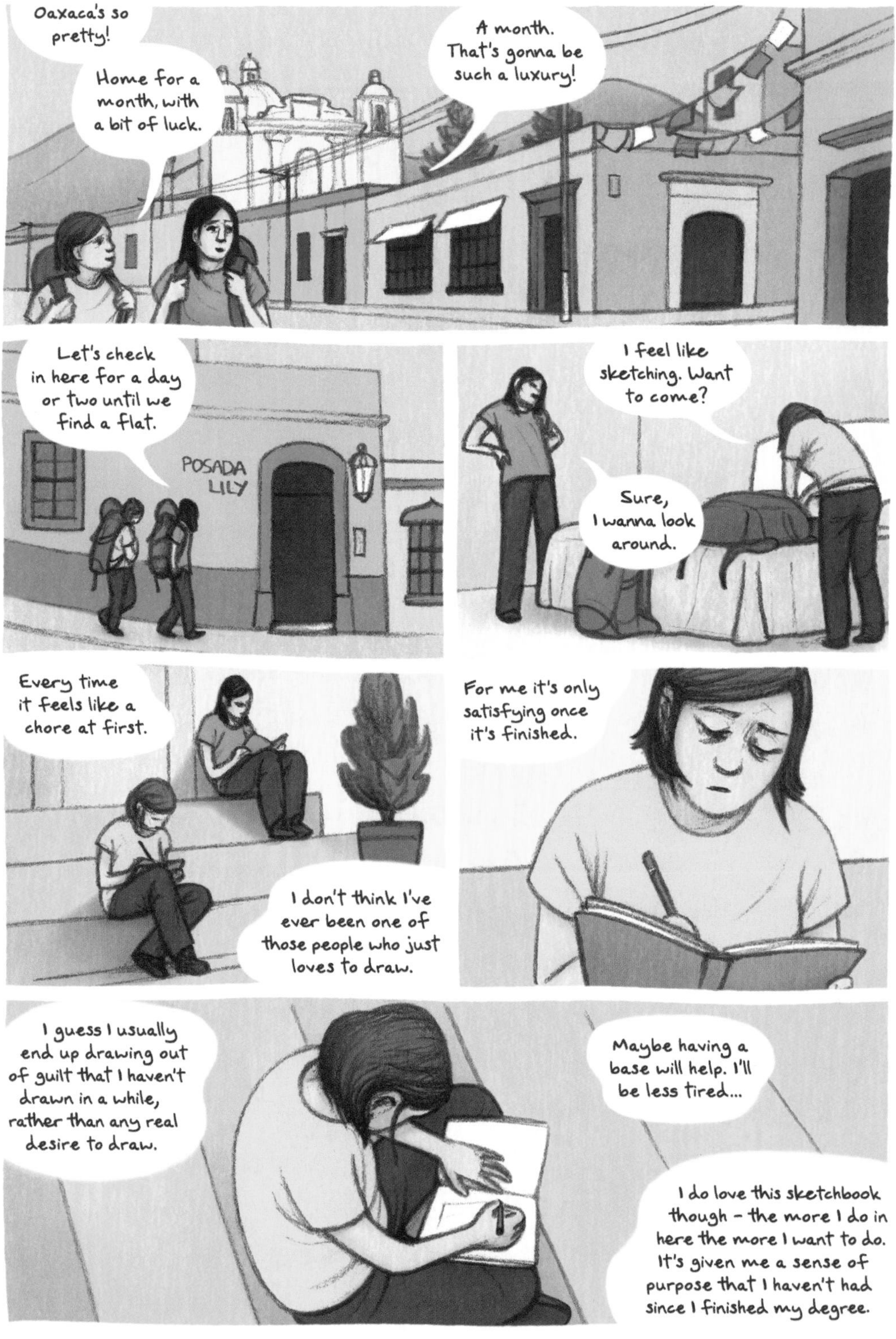
Oaxaca's so pretty!
Home for a month, with a bit of luck.
A month. That's gonna be such a luxury!
Let's check in here for a day or two until we find a flat.
POSADA LILY
I feel like sketching. Want to come?
Sure, I wanna look around.
Every time it feels like a chore at first.
I don't think I've ever been one of those people who just loves to draw.
For me it's only satisfying once it's finished.
I guess I usually end up drawing out of guilt that I haven't drawn in a while, rather than any real desire to draw.
Maybe having a base will help. I'll be less tired...
I do love this sketchbook though - the more I do in here the more I want to do. It's given me a sense of purpose that I haven't had since I finished my degree.

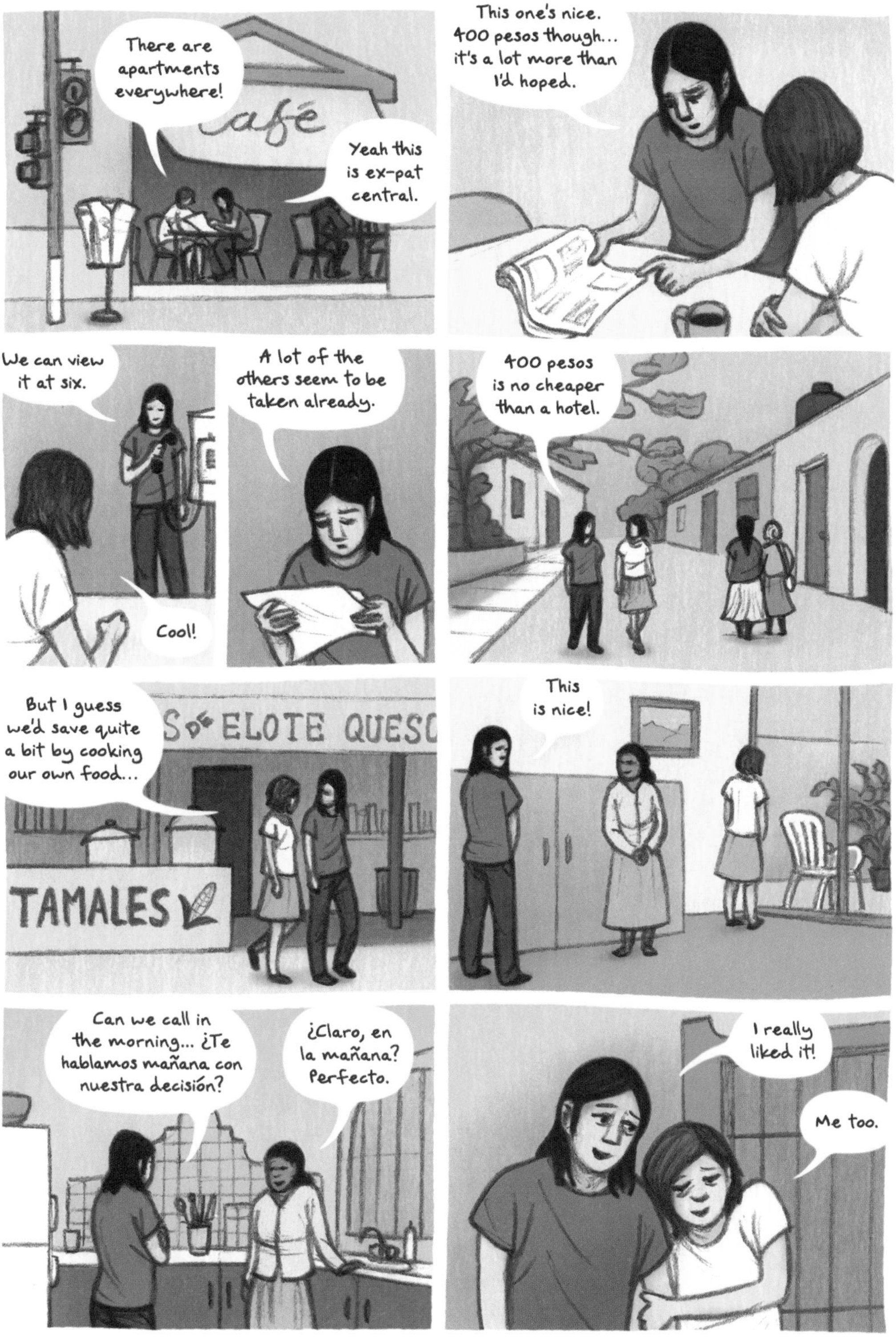
There are apartments everywhere!
Café
Yeah this is ex-pat central.
This one's nice. 400 pesos though... it's a lot more than I'd hoped.
We can view it at six.
Cool!
A lot of the others seem to be taken already.
400 pesos is no cheaper than a hotel.
But I guess we'd save quite a bit by cooking our own food...
S DE ELOTE QUESO
TAMALES
This is nice!
Can we call in the morning... ¿Te hablamos mañana con nuestra decisión?
¿Claro, en la mañana? Perfecto.
I really liked it!
Me too.

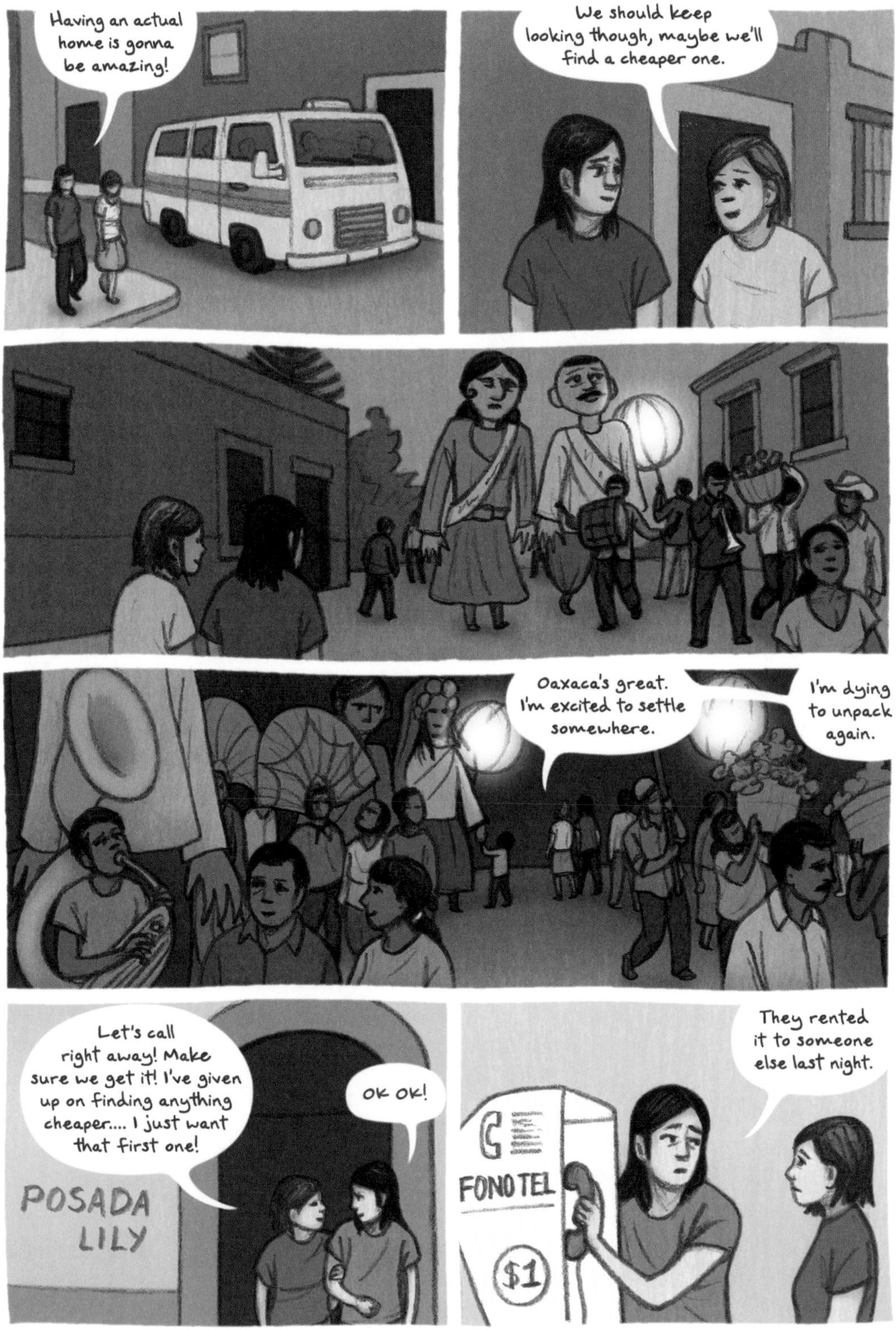
Having an actual home is gonna be amazing!
We should keep looking though, maybe we'll find a cheaper one.
Oaxaca's great. I'm excited to settle somewhere.
I'm dying to unpack again.
Let's call right away! Make sure we get it! I've given up on finding anything cheaper.... I just want that first one!
OK OK!
POSADA LILY
They rented it to someone else last night.
FONOTEL
$1

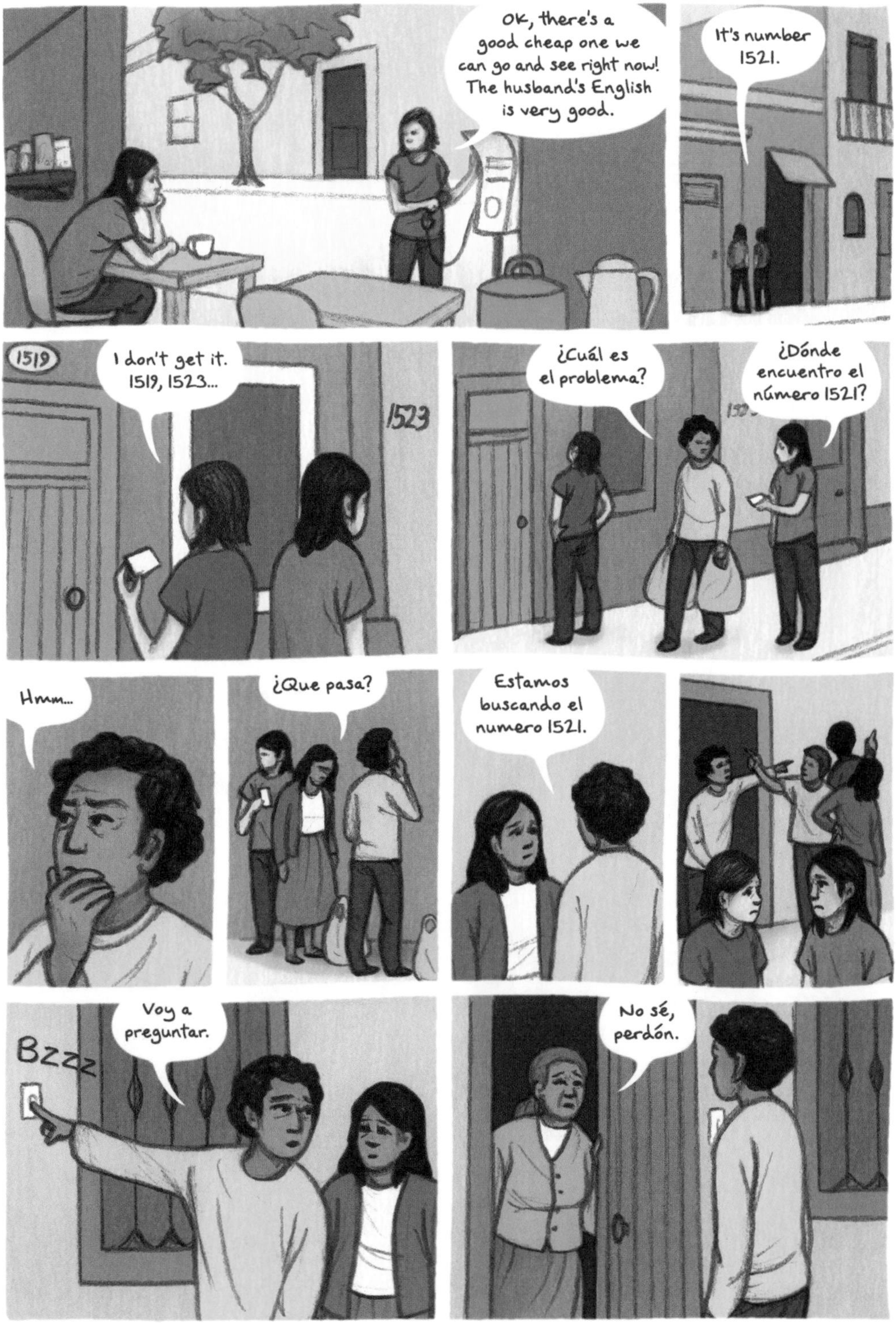
OK, there's a good cheap one we can go and see right now! The husband's English is very good.
It's number 1521.
1519
I don't get it. 1519, 1523...
1523
¿Cuál es el problema?
¿Dónde encuentro el número 1521?
Hmm...
¿Que pasa?
Estamos buscando el numero 1521.
Voy a preguntar.
Bzzz
No sé, perdón.

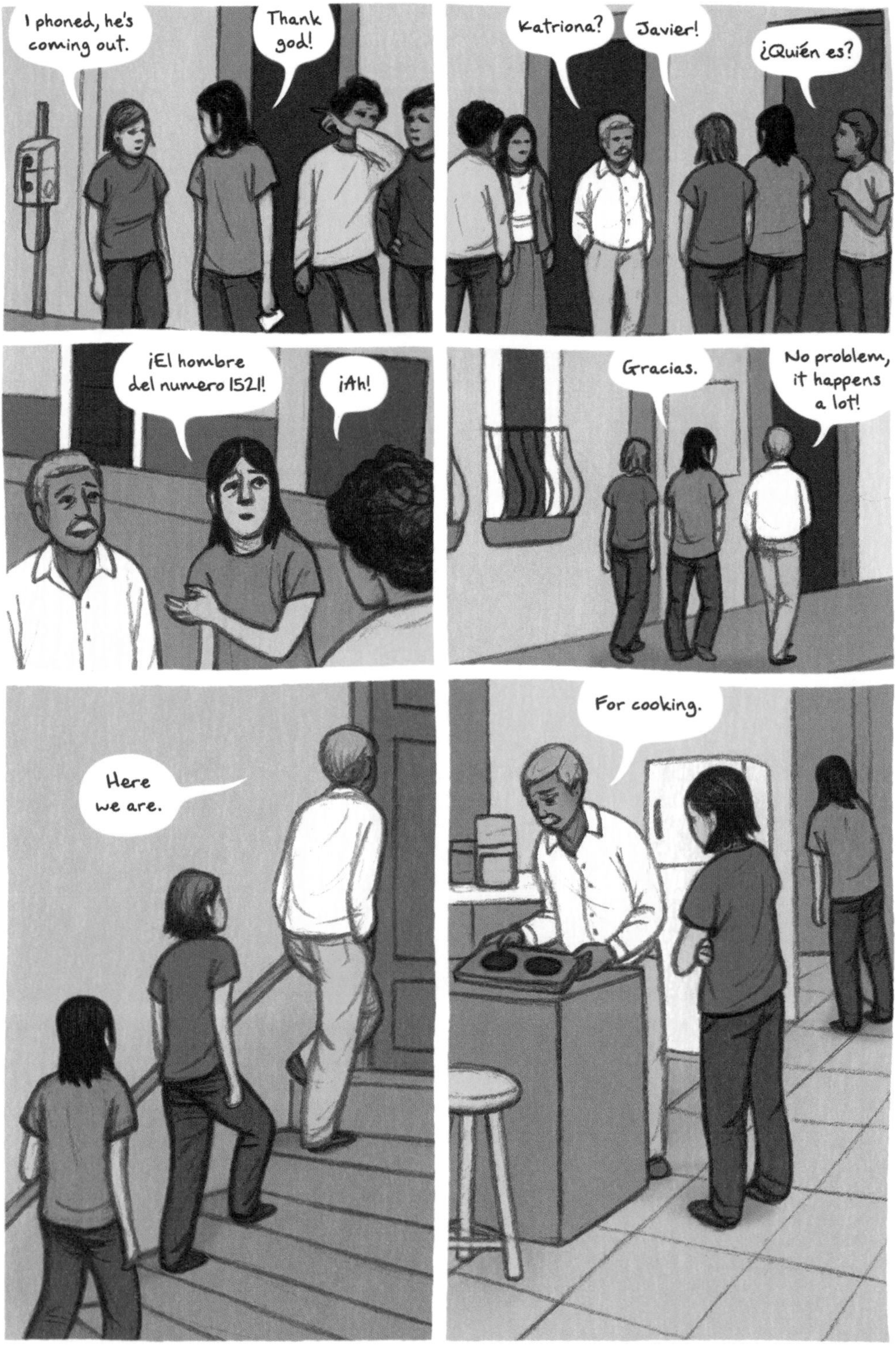
I phoned, he's coming out.
Thank god!
Katriona?
Javier!
¿Quién es?
¡El hombre del numero 1521!
¡Ah!
Gracias.
No problem, it happens a lot!
Here we are.
For cooking.

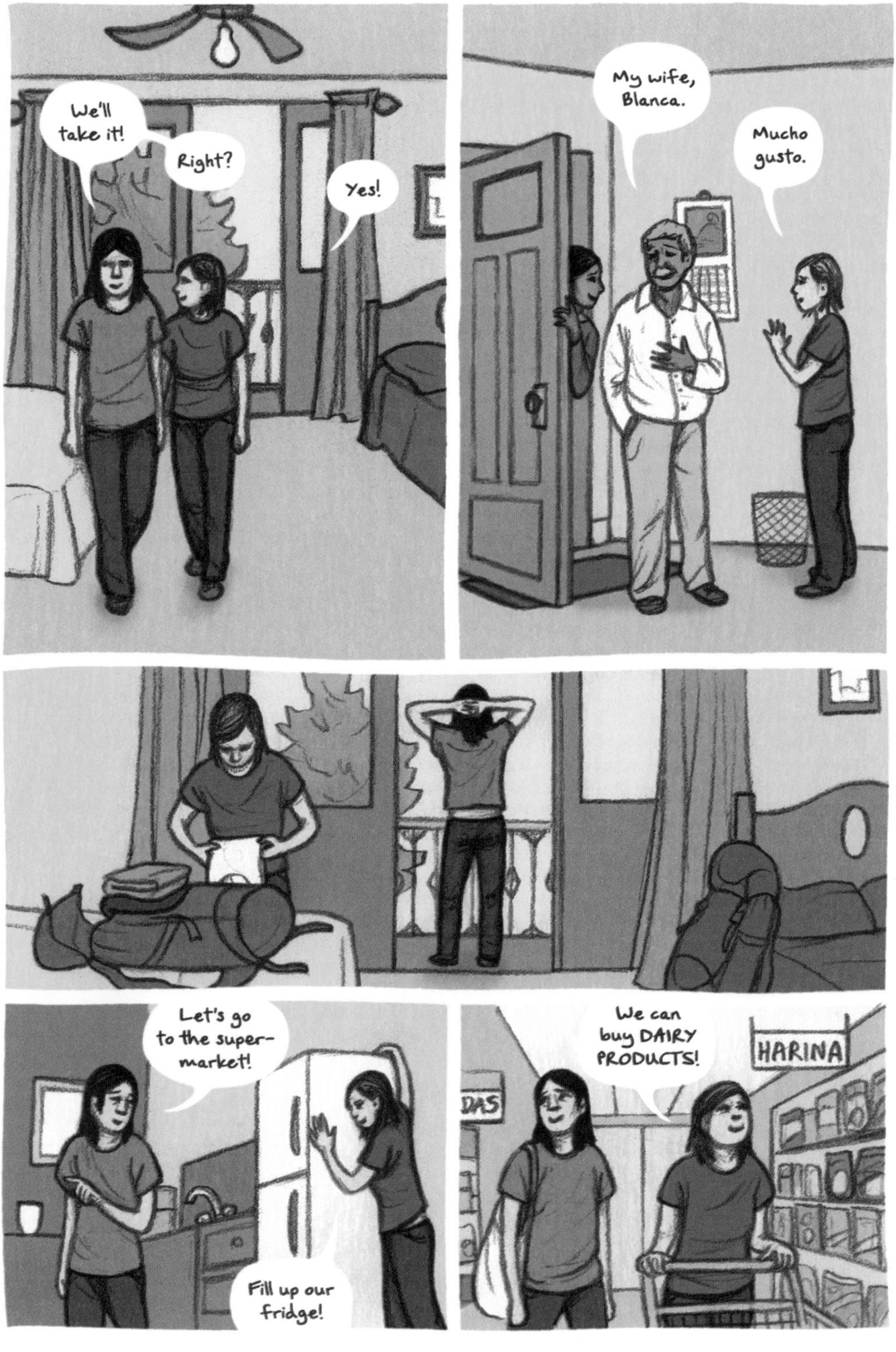
We'll take it!
Right?
Yes!
My wife, Blanca.
Mucho gusto.
Let's go to the super-market!
Fill up our fridge!
We can buy DAIRY PRODUCTS!
DAS
HARINA

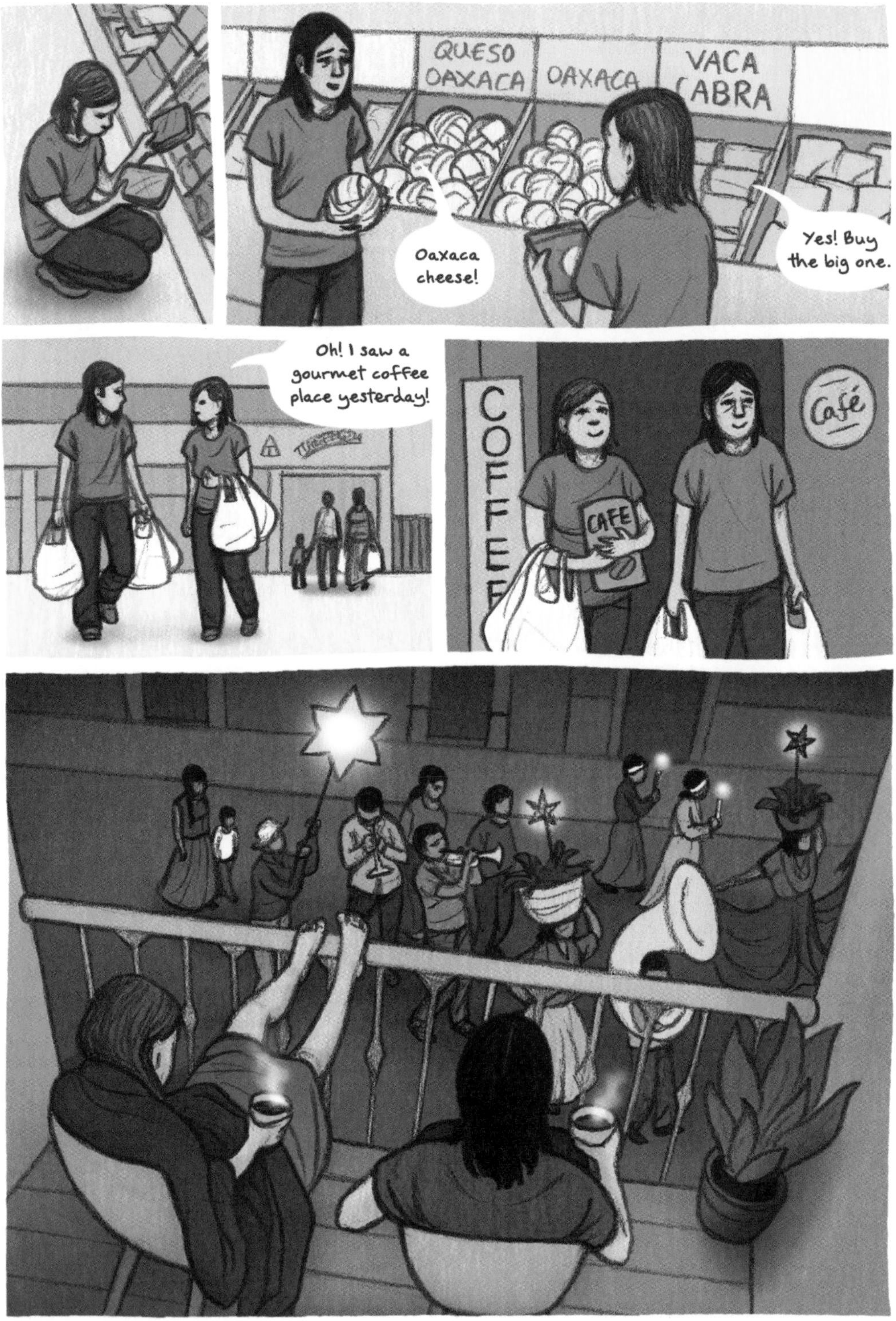
QUESO OAXACA
OAXACA
VACA CABRA
Oaxaca cheese!
Yes! Buy the big one.
Oh! I saw a gourmet coffee place yesterday!
COFFEE
CAFE
Café

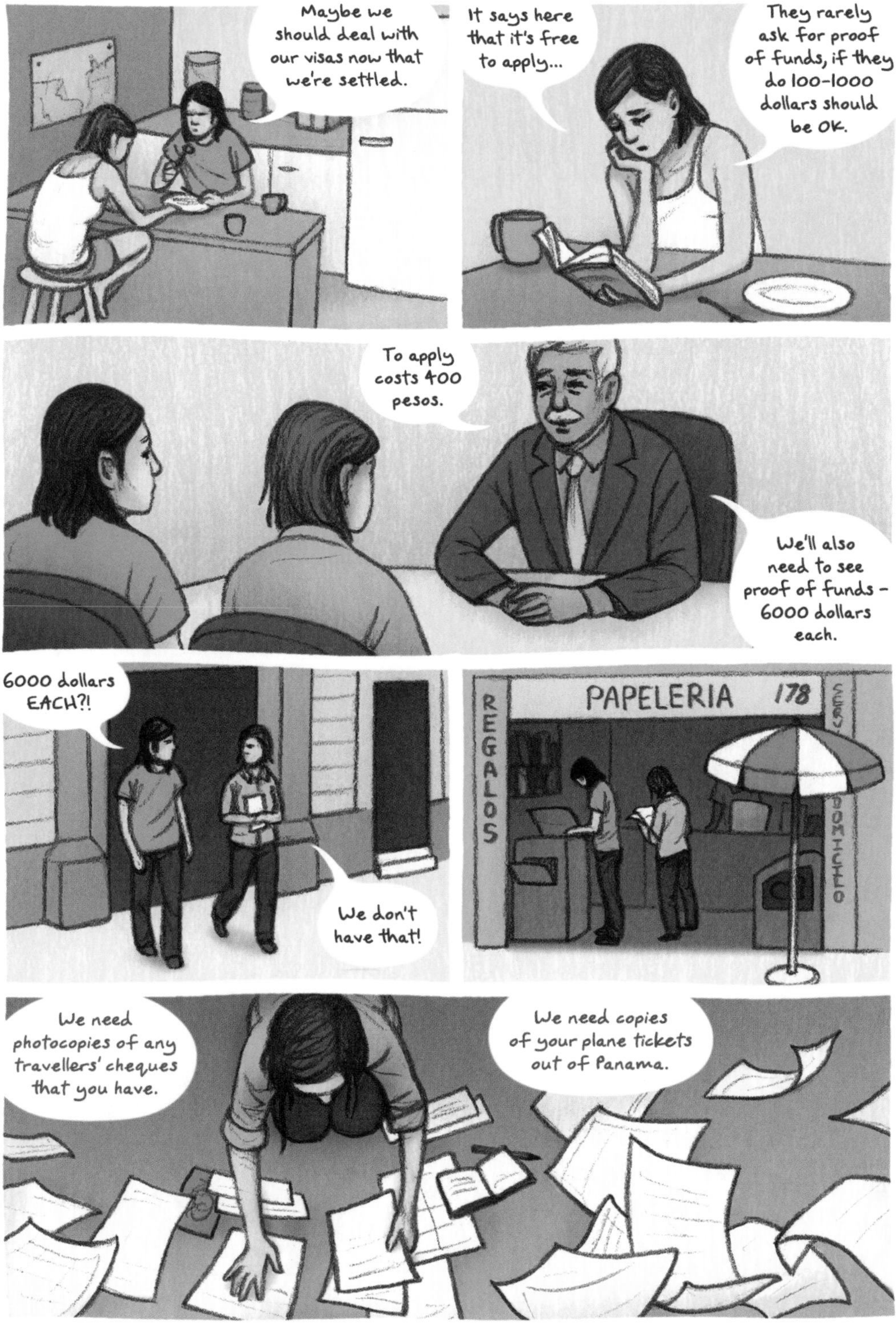
Maybe we should deal with our visas now that we're settled.
It says here that it's free to apply...
They rarely ask for proof of funds, if they do 100-1000 dollars should be OK.
To apply costs 400 pesos.
We'll also need to see proof of funds - 6000 dollars each.
6000 dollars EACH?!
We don't have that!
PAPELERIA 178
REGALOS
DOMICILIO
We need photocopies of any travellers' cheques that you have.
We need copies of your plane tickets out of Panama.

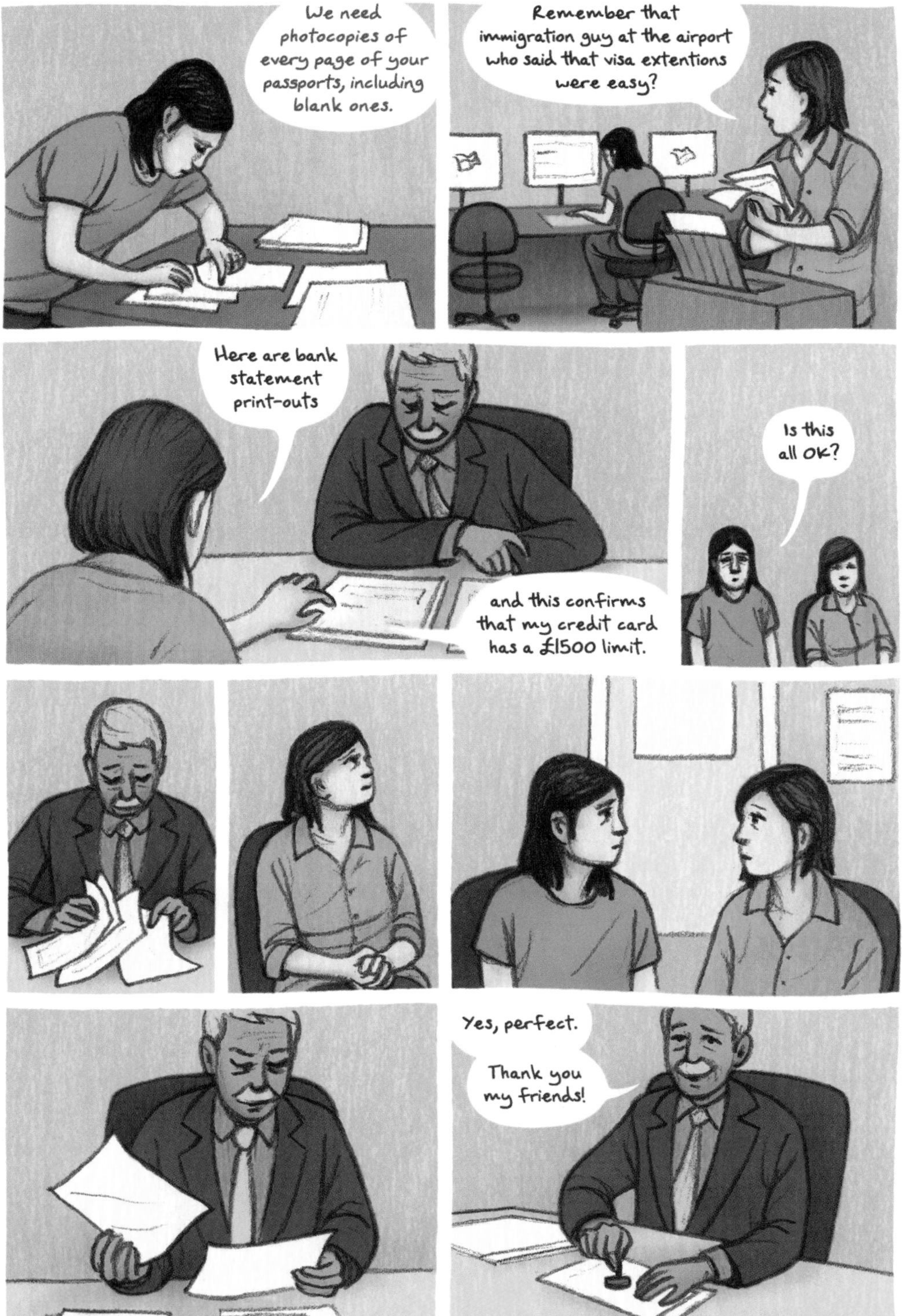
We need photocopies of every page of your passports, including blank ones.
Remember that immigration guy at the airport who said that visa extentions were easy?
Here are bank statement print-outs
and this confirms that my credit card has a £1500 limit.
Is this all OK?
Yes, perfect.
Thank you my friends!

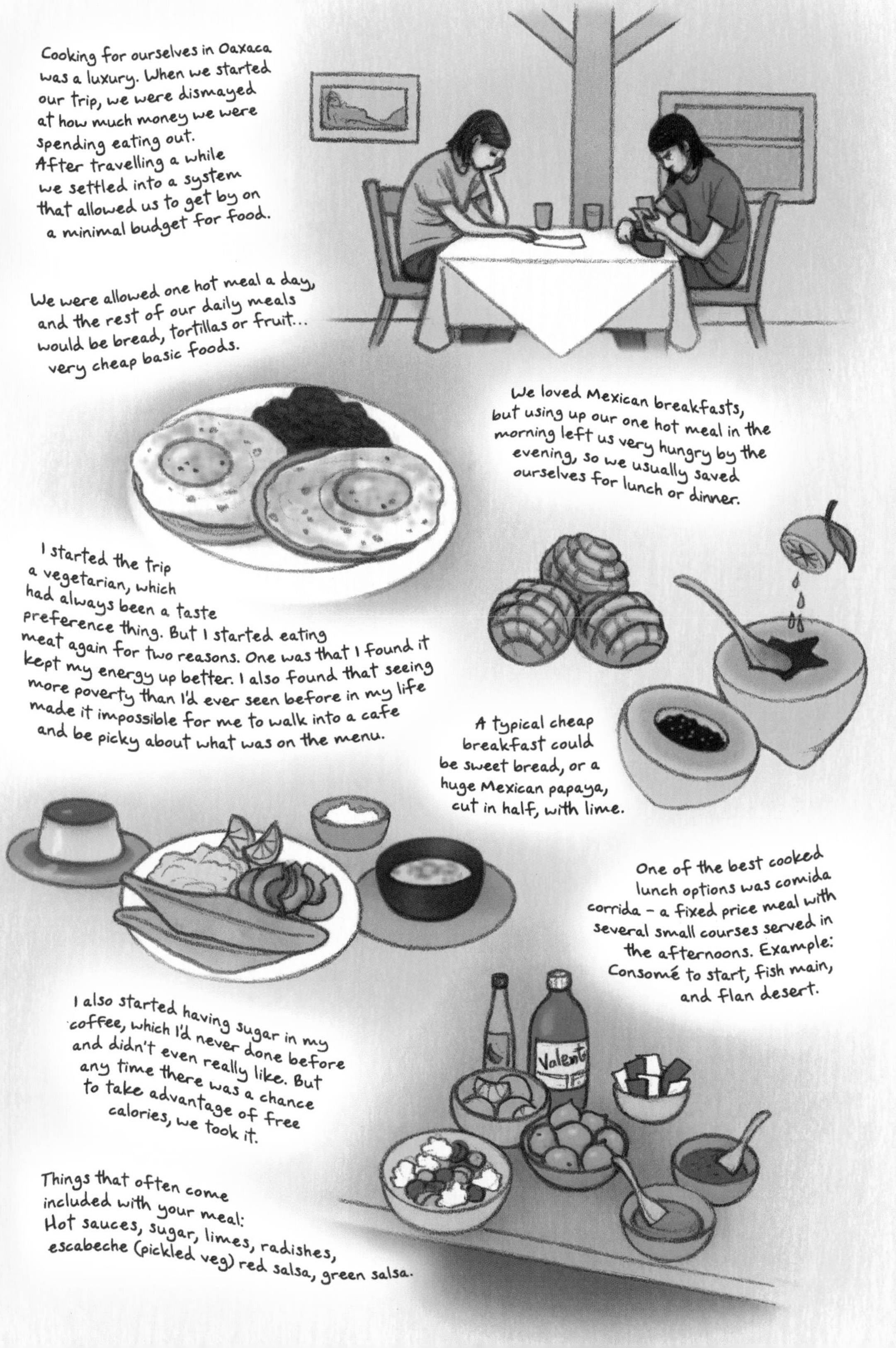
Cooking for ourselves in Oaxaca was a luxury. When we started our trip, we were dismayed at how much money we were spending eating out.
After travelling a while we settled into a system that allowed us to get by on a minimal budget for food.
We were allowed one hot meal a day, and the rest of our daily meals would be bread, tortillas or fruit... very cheap basic foods.
We loved Mexican breakfasts, but using up our one hot meal in the morning left us very hungry by the evening, so we usually saved ourselves for lunch or dinner.
I started the trip a vegetarian, which had always been a taste preference thing. But I started eating meat again for two reasons. One was that I found it kept my energy up better. I also found that seeing more poverty than I'd ever seen before in my life made it impossible for me to walk into a cafe and be picky about what was on the menu.
A typical cheap breakfast could be sweet bread, or a huge Mexican papaya, cut in half, with lime.
One of the best cooked lunch options was comida corrida – a fixed price meal with several small courses served in the afternoons. Example: Consomé to start, fish main, and flan desert.
I also started having sugar in my coffee, which I'd never done before and didn't even really like. But any time there was a chance to take advantage of free calories, we took it.
Valenti
Things that often come included with your meal: Hot sauces, sugar, limes, radishes, escabeche (pickled veg) red salsa, green salsa.

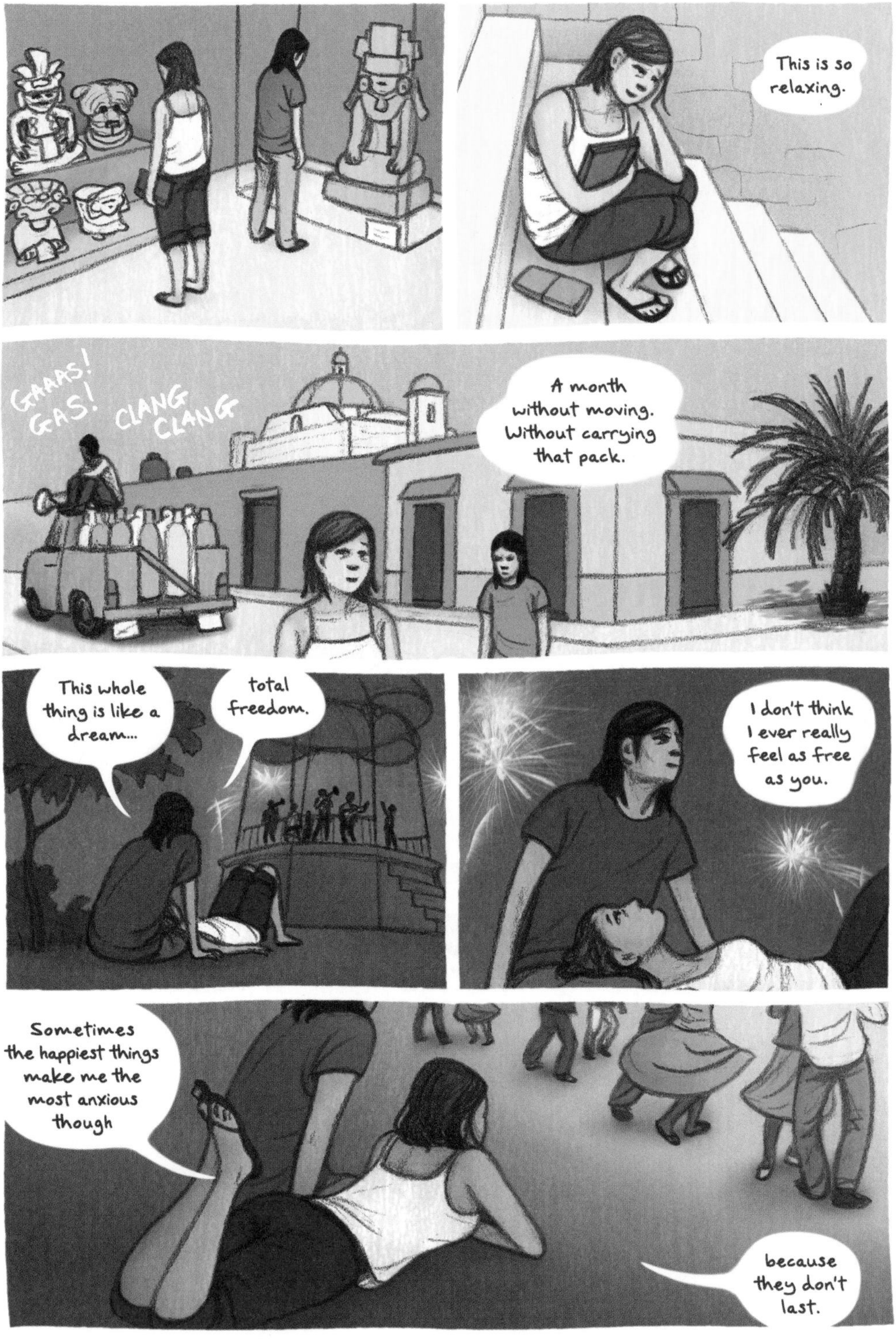
This is so relaxing.
GAAAS! GAS!
CLANG CLANG
A month without moving. Without carrying that pack.
This whole thing is like a dream...
total freedom.
I don't think I ever really feel as free as you.
Sometimes the happiest things make me the most anxious though
because they don't last.

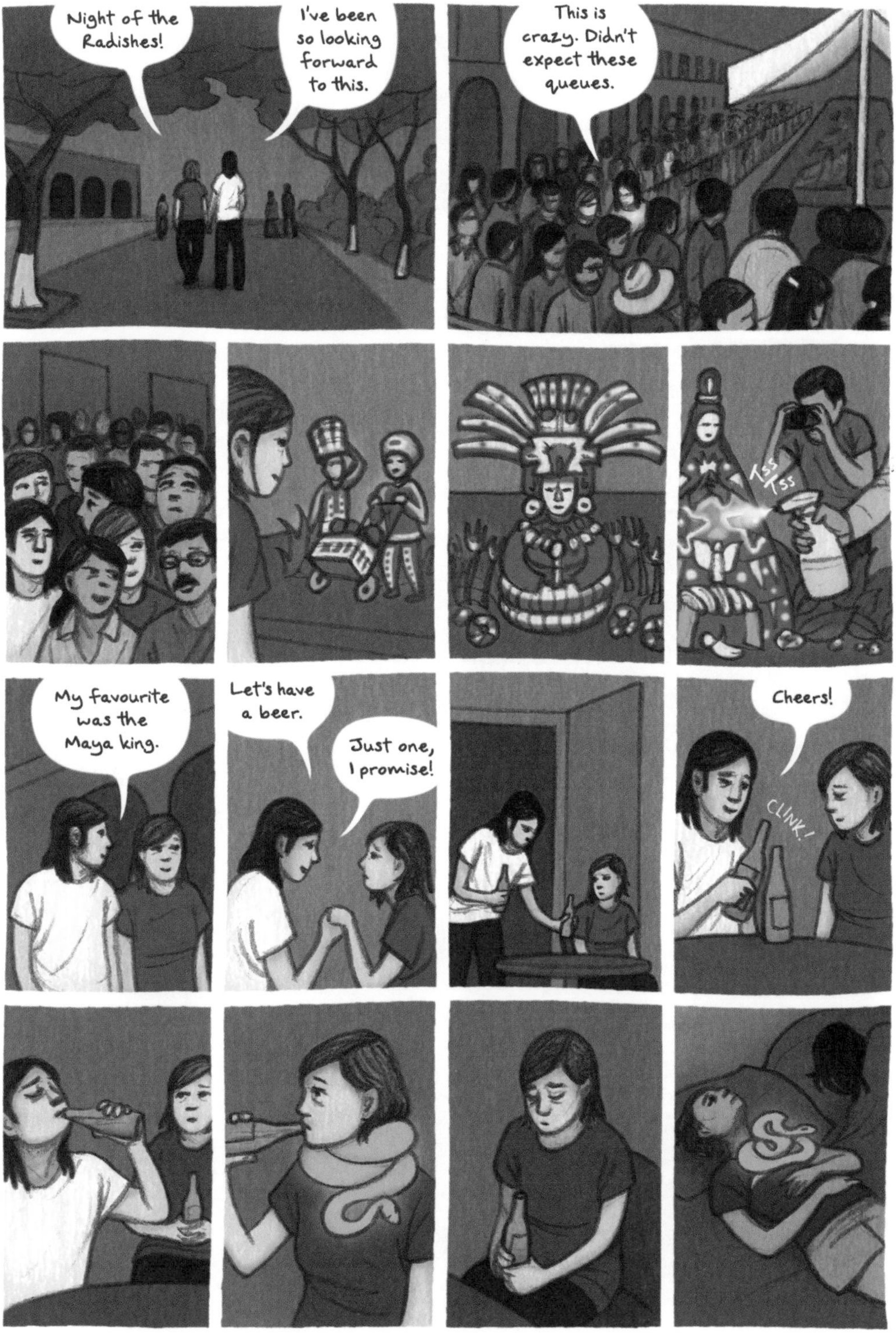

Night of the Radishes!
I've been so looking forward to this.
This is crazy. Didn't expect these queues.
TSS TSS
My favourite was the Maya king.
Let's have a beer.
Just one, I promise!
Cheers!
CLINK!

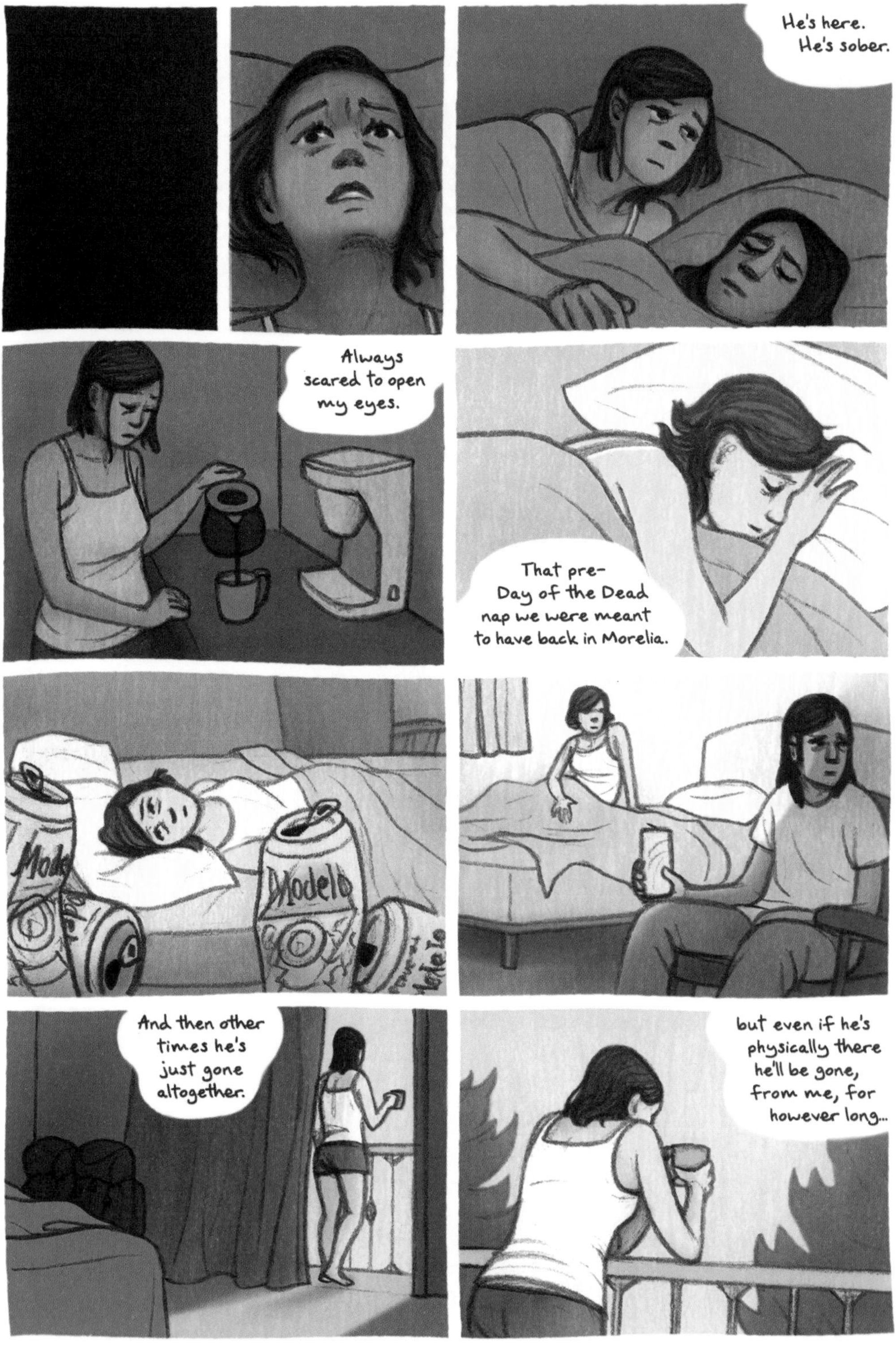
He's here.
He's sober.
Always scared to open my eyes.
That pre-Day of the Dead nap we were meant to have back in Morelia.
Modelo
Modelo
And then other times he's just gone altogether.
but even if he's physically there he'll be gone, from me, for however long...

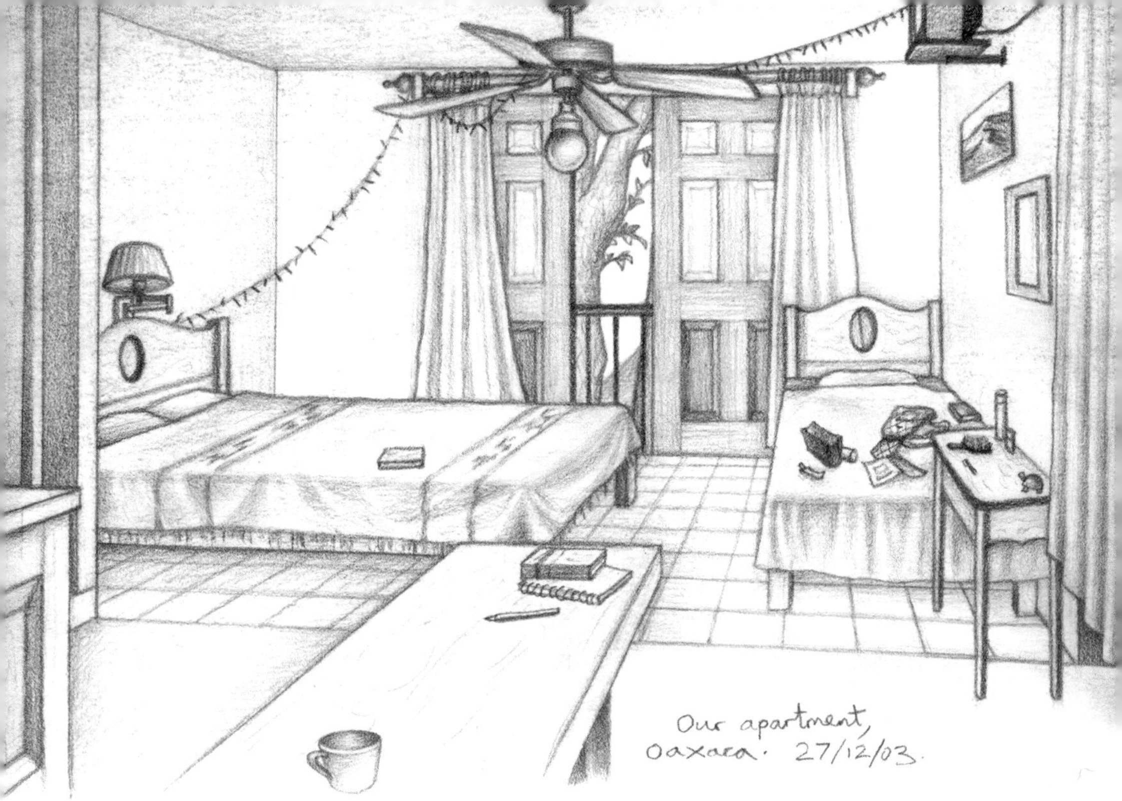

Our apartment, Oaxaca. 27/12/03.

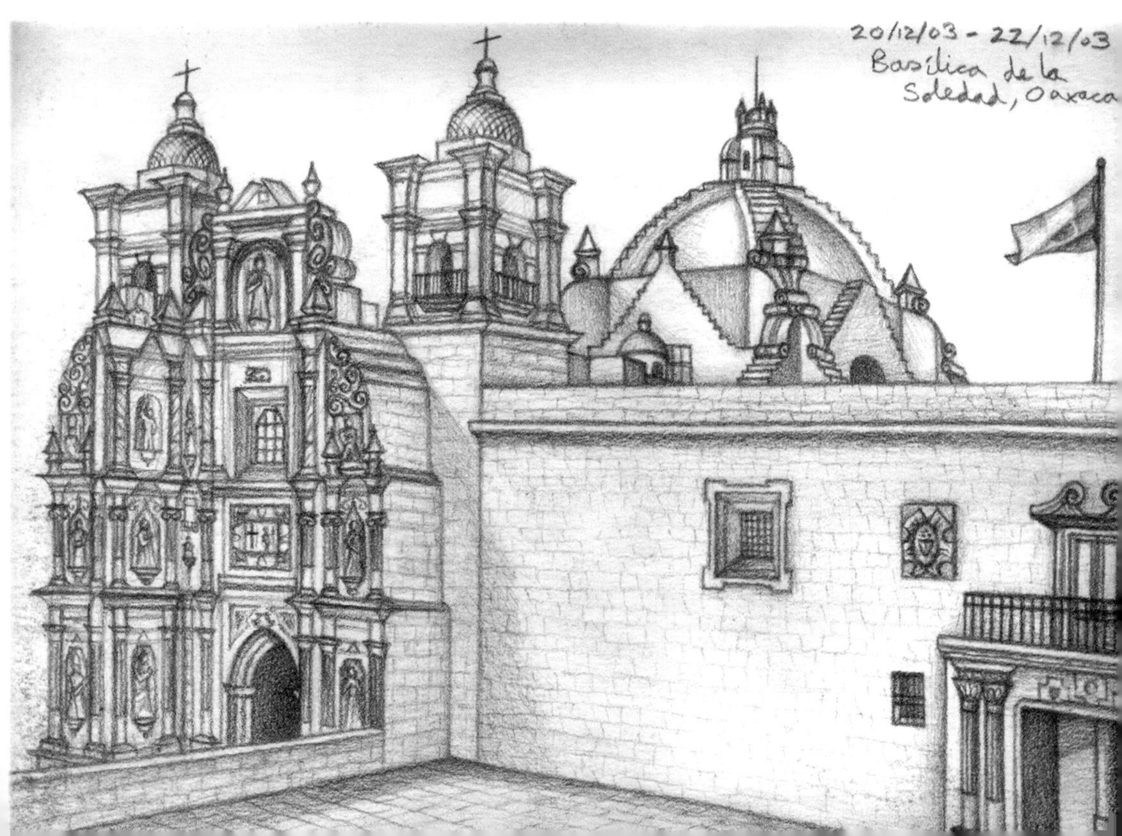

20/12/03 – 22/12/03 Basílica de la Soledad, Oaxaca

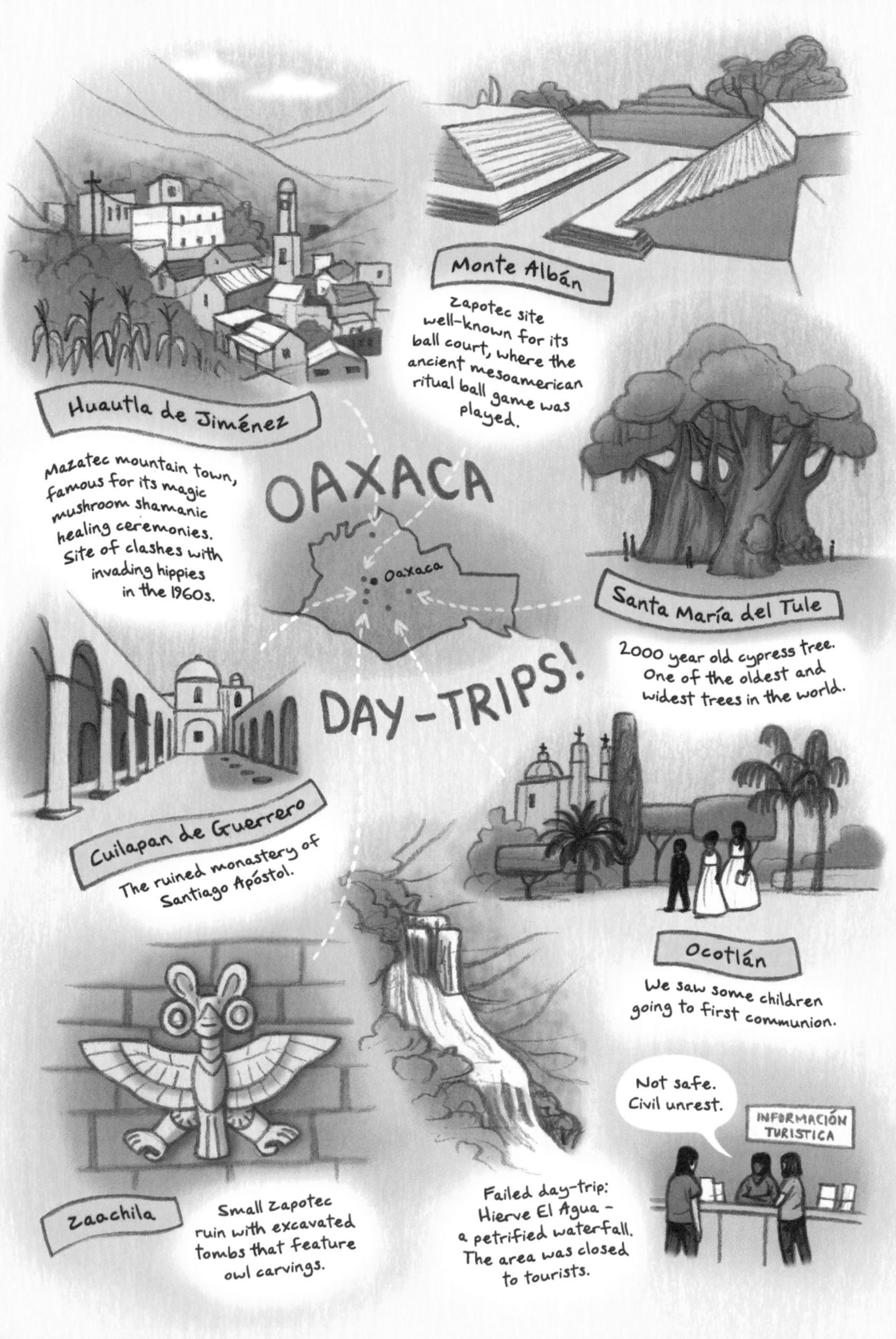

OAXACA
DAY-TRIPS!
Oaxaca
Huautla de Jiménez
Mazatec mountain town, famous for its magic mushroom shamanic healing ceremonies. Site of clashes with invading hippies in the 1960s.
Monte Albán
Zapotec site well-known for its ball court, where the ancient mesoamerican ritual ball game was played.
Santa María del Tule
2000 year old cypress tree. One of the oldest and widest trees in the world.
Cuilapan de Guerrero
The ruined monastery of Santiago Apóstol.
Ocotlán
We saw some children going to first communion.
Zaachila
Small Zapotec ruin with excavated tombs that feature owl carvings.
Failed day-trip: Hierve El Agua – a petrified waterfall. The area was closed to tourists.
Not safe. Civil unrest.
INFORMACIÓN TURISTICA

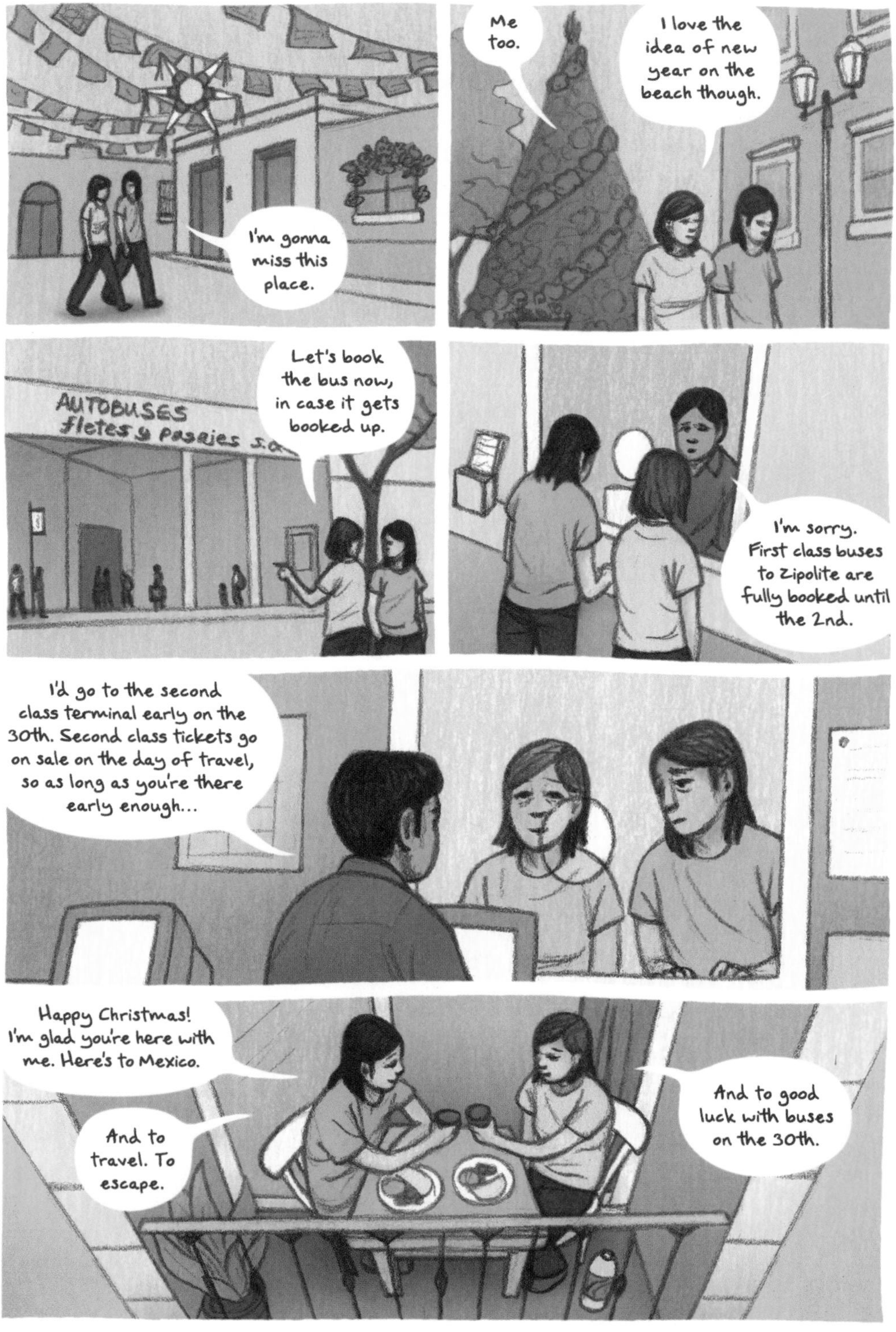
I'm gonna miss this place.
Me too.
I love the idea of new year on the beach though.
AUTOBUSES
fletes y pasajes S.A.
Let's book the bus now, in case it gets booked up.
I'm sorry. First class buses to Zipolite are fully booked until the 2nd.
I'd go to the second class terminal early on the 30th. Second class tickets go on sale on the day of travel, so as long as you're there early enough...
Happy Christmas! I'm glad you're here with me. Here's to Mexico.
And to good luck with buses on the 30th.
And to travel. To escape.

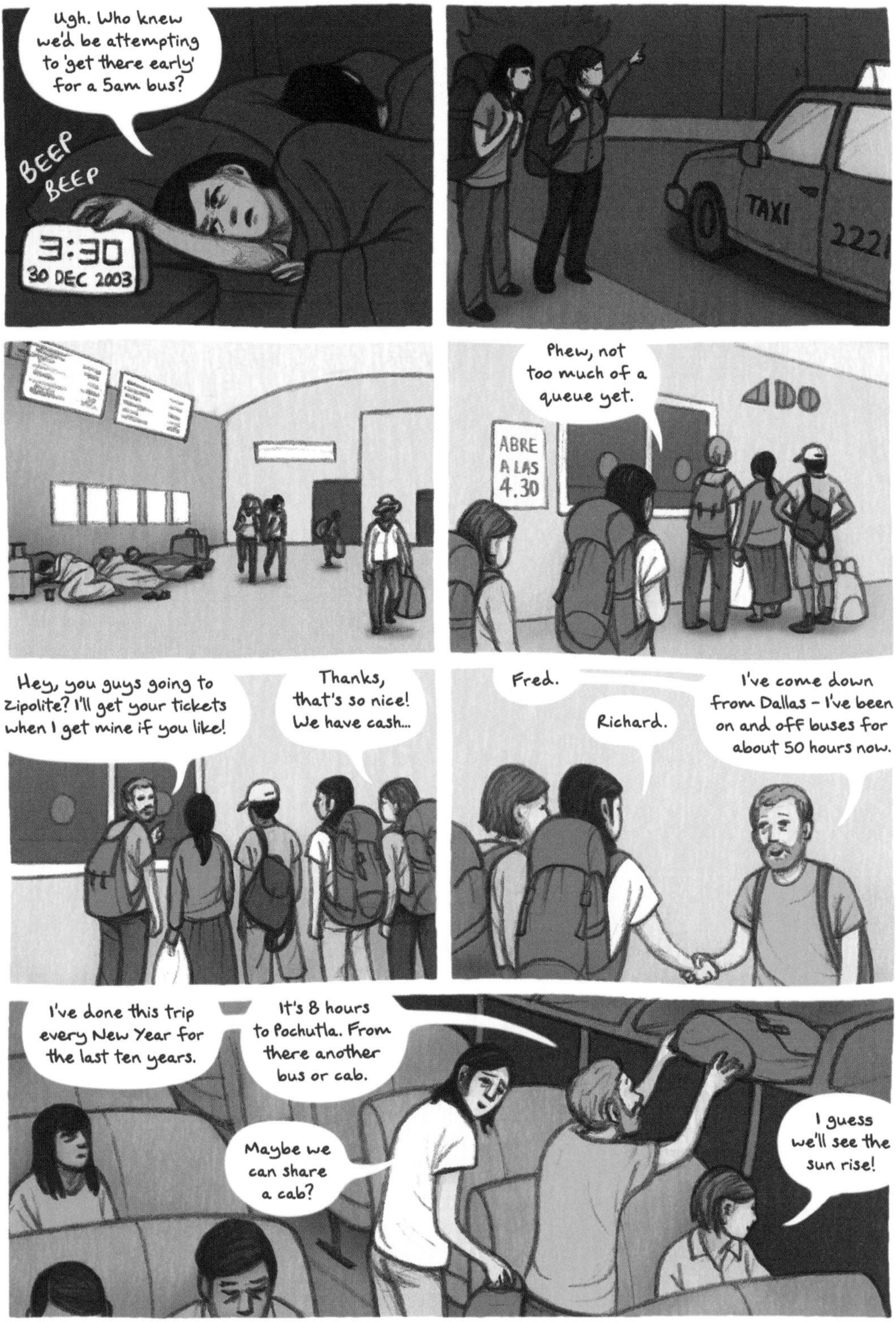
Ugh. Who knew we'd be attempting to 'get there early' for a 5am bus?
BEEP BEEP
3:30
30 DEC 2003
TAXI
Phew, not too much of a queue yet.
ADO
ABRE A LAS 4.30
Hey, you guys going to Zipolite? I'll get your tickets when I get mine if you like!
Thanks, that's so nice! We have cash...
Fred.
Richard.
I've come down from Dallas - I've been on and off buses for about 50 hours now.
I've done this trip every New Year for the last ten years.
It's 8 hours to Pochutla. From there another bus or cab.
Maybe we can share a cab?
I guess we'll see the sun rise!

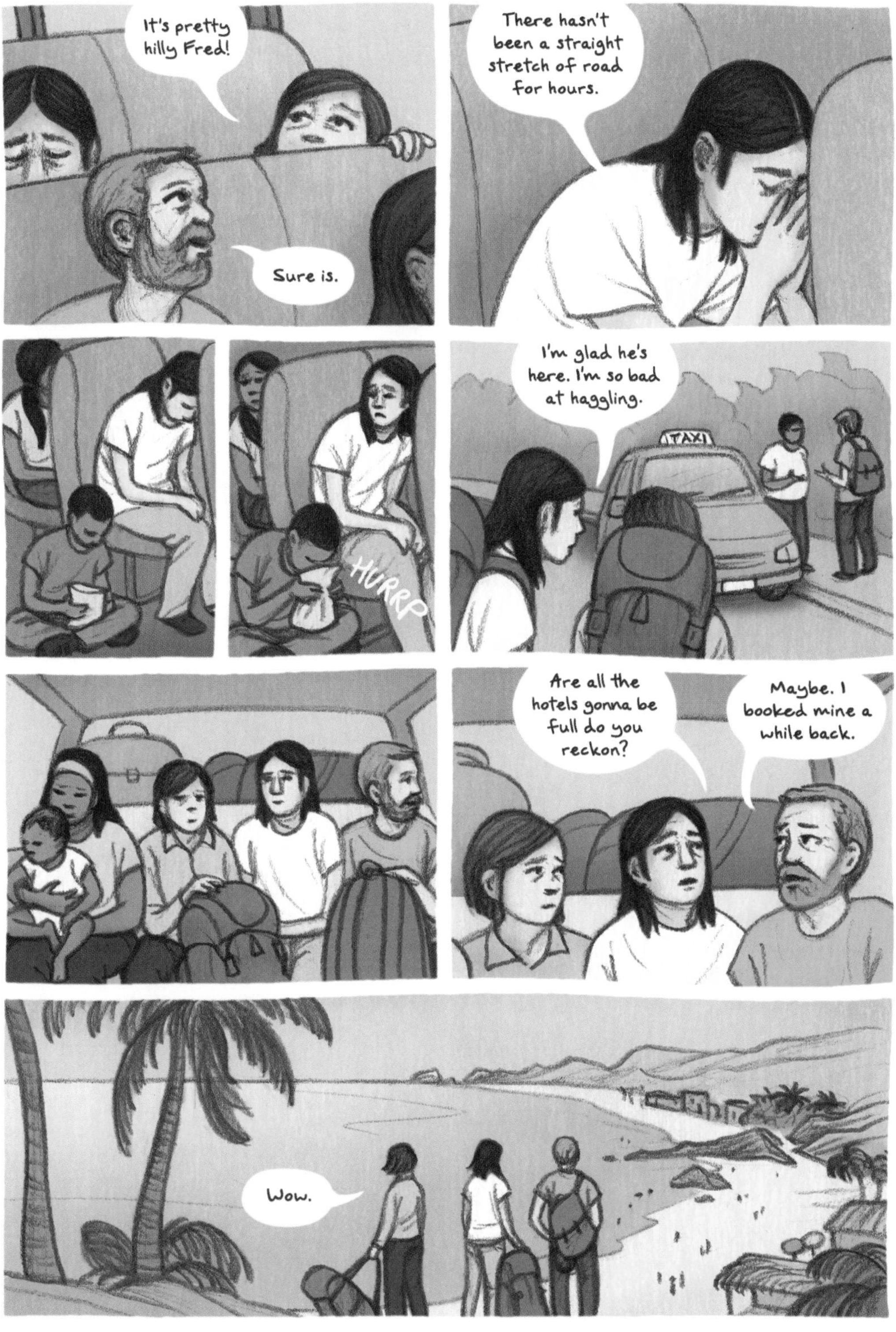
It's pretty hilly Fred!
Sure is.
There hasn't been a straight stretch of road for hours.
HURRP
I'm glad he's here. I'm so bad at haggling.
TAXI
Are all the hotels gonna be full do you reckon?
Maybe. I booked mine a while back.
Wow.

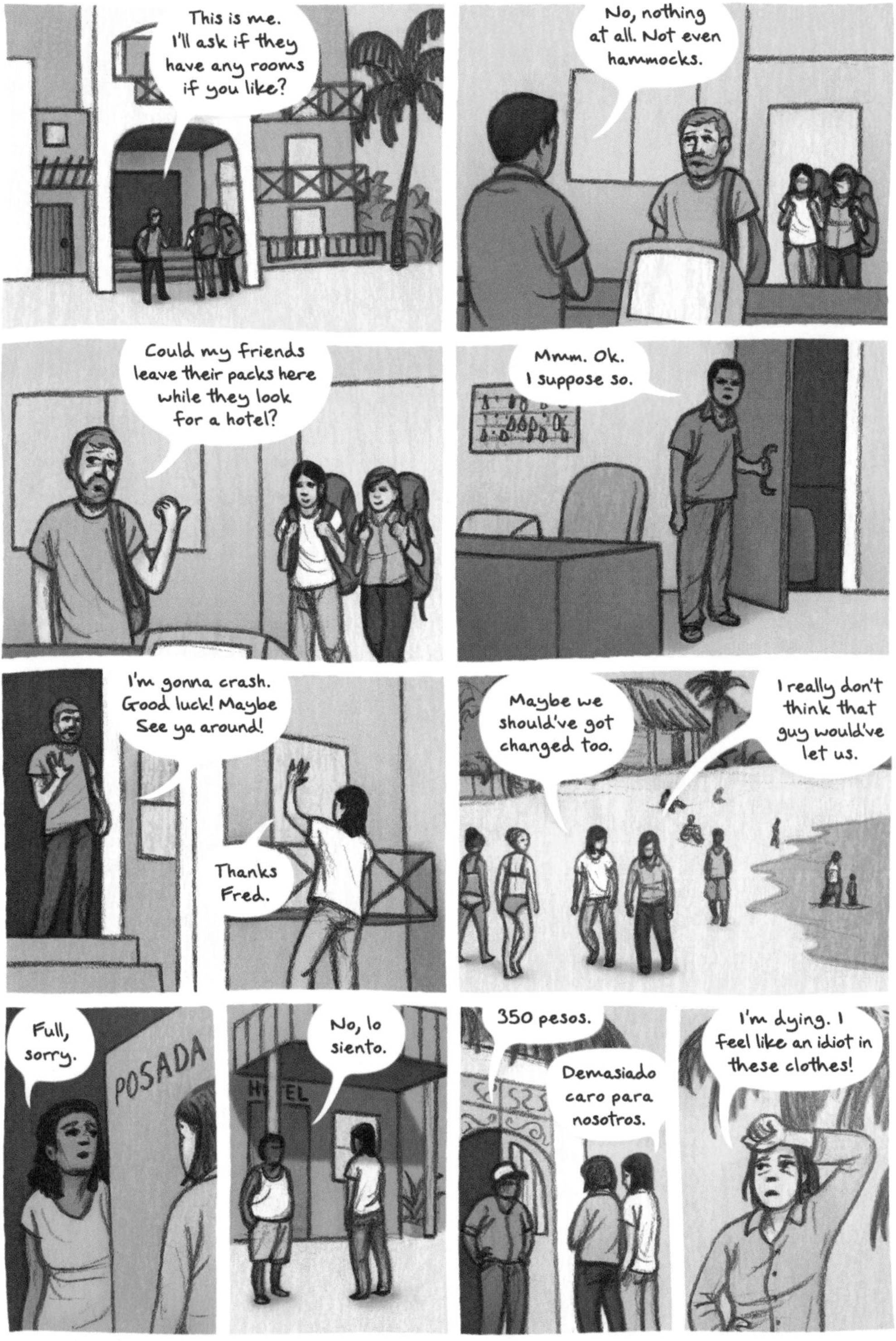
This is me. I'll ask if they have any rooms if you like?
No, nothing at all. Not even hammocks.
Could my friends leave their packs here while they look for a hotel?
Mmm. Ok. I suppose so.
I'm gonna crash. Good luck! Maybe See ya around!
Thanks Fred.
Maybe we should've got changed too.
I really don't think that guy would've let us.
Full, sorry.
POSADA
No, lo siento.
HOTEL
350 pesos.
Demasiado caro para nosotros.
I'm dying. I feel like an idiot in these clothes!

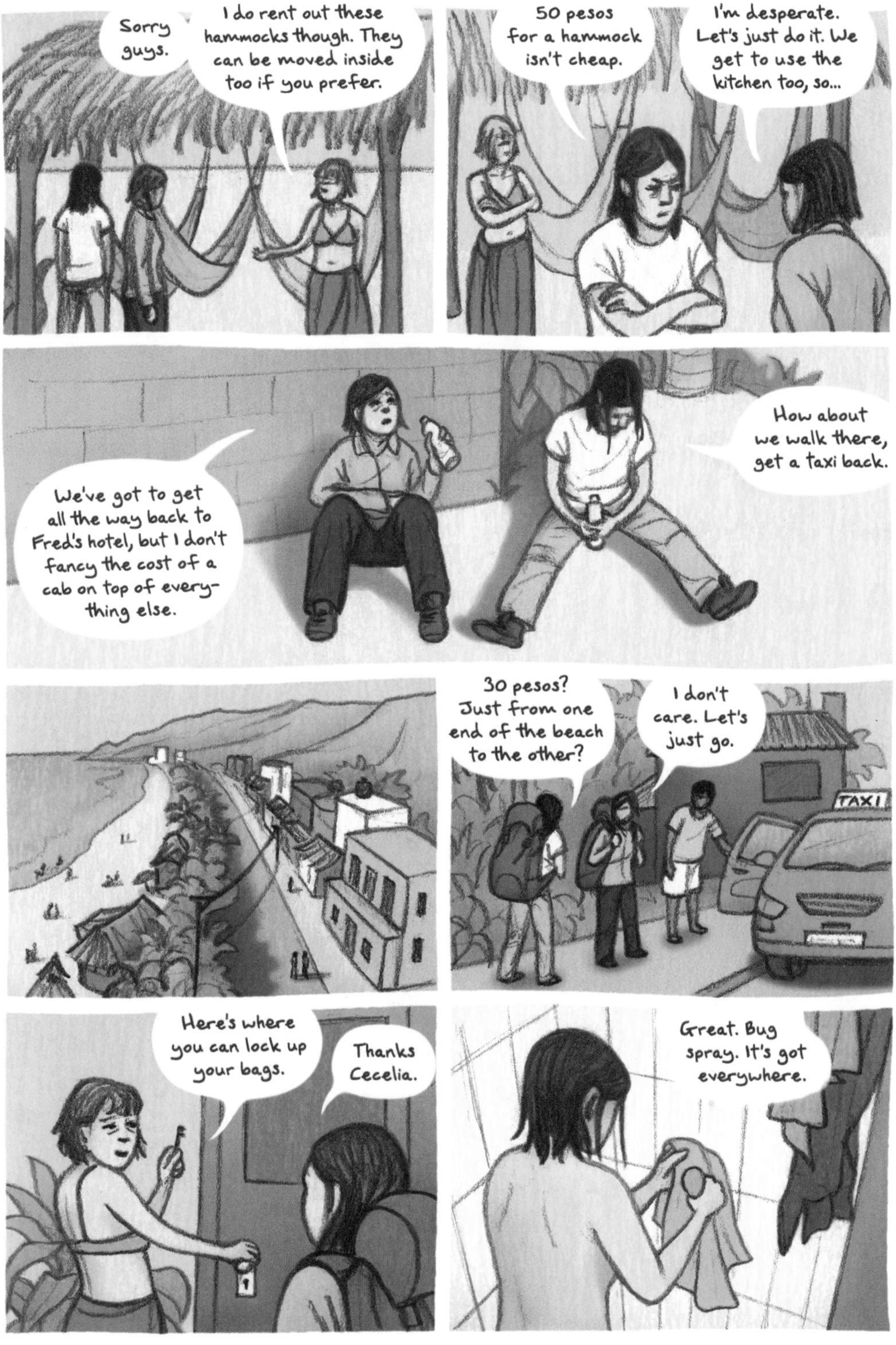
Sorry guys.
I do rent out these hammocks though. They can be moved inside too if you prefer.
50 pesos for a hammock isn't cheap.
I'm desperate. Let's just do it. We get to use the kitchen too, so...
We've got to get all the way back to Fred's hotel, but I don't fancy the cost of a cab on top of every-thing else.
How about we walk there, get a taxi back.
30 pesos? Just from one end of the beach to the other?
I don't care. Let's just go.
TAXI
Here's where you can lock up your bags.
Thanks Cecelia.
Great. Bug spray. It's got everywhere.

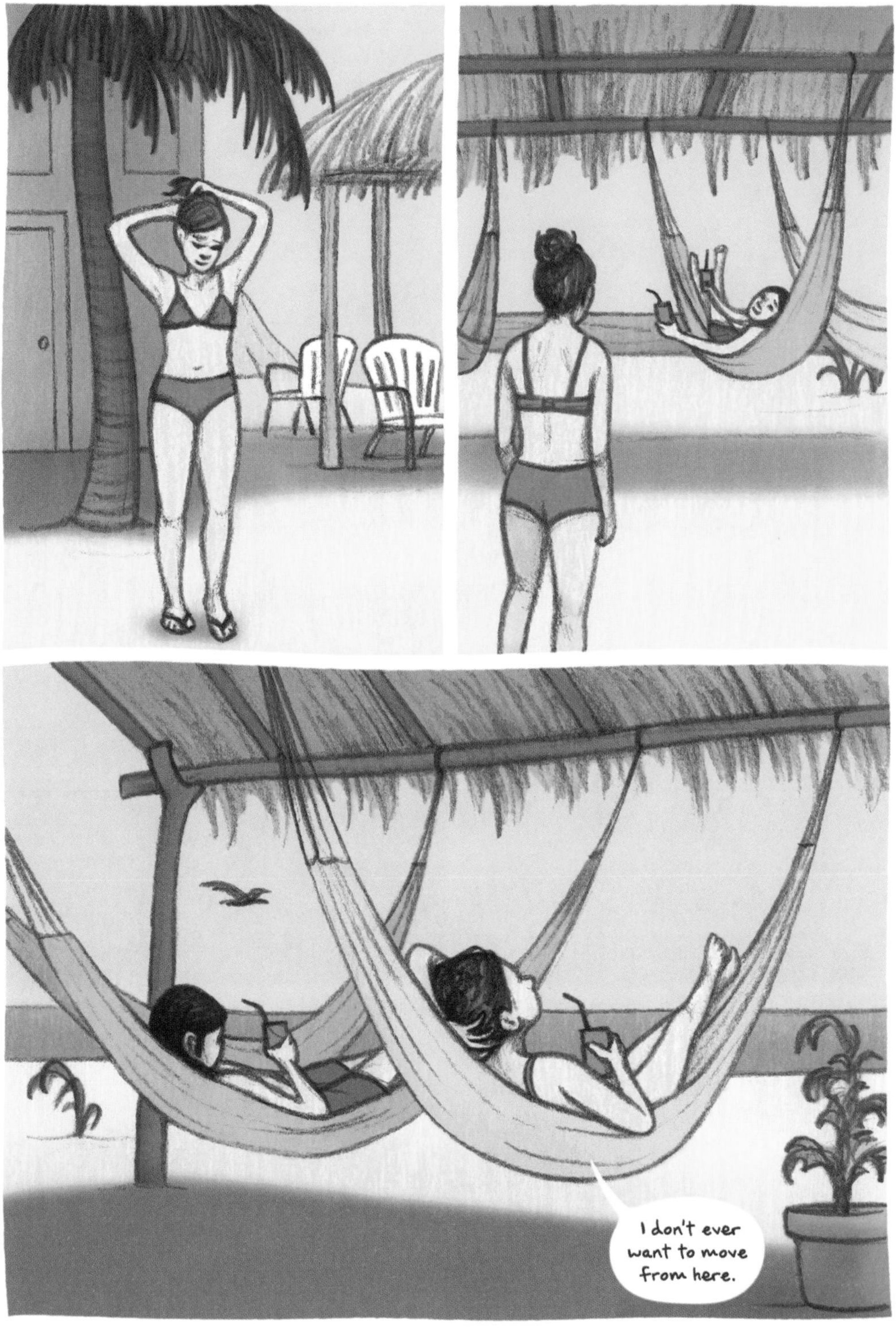
I don't ever want to move from here.

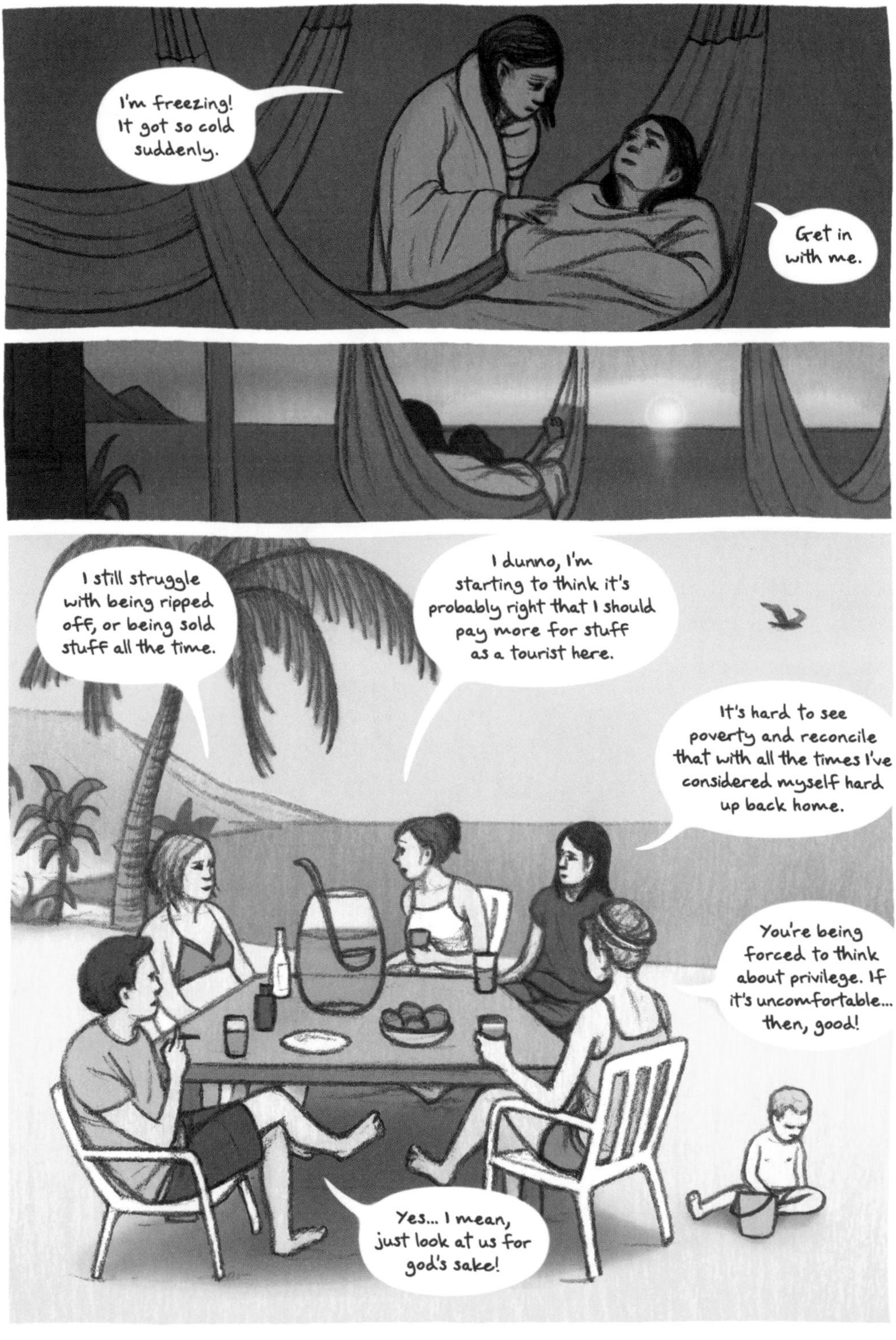
I'm freezing! It got so cold suddenly.
Get in with me.
I still struggle with being ripped off, or being sold stuff all the time.
I dunno, I'm starting to think it's probably right that I should pay more for stuff as a tourist here.
It's hard to see poverty and reconcile that with all the times I've considered myself hard up back home.
You're being forced to think about privilege. If it's uncomfortable... then, good!
Yes... I mean, just look at us for god's sake!

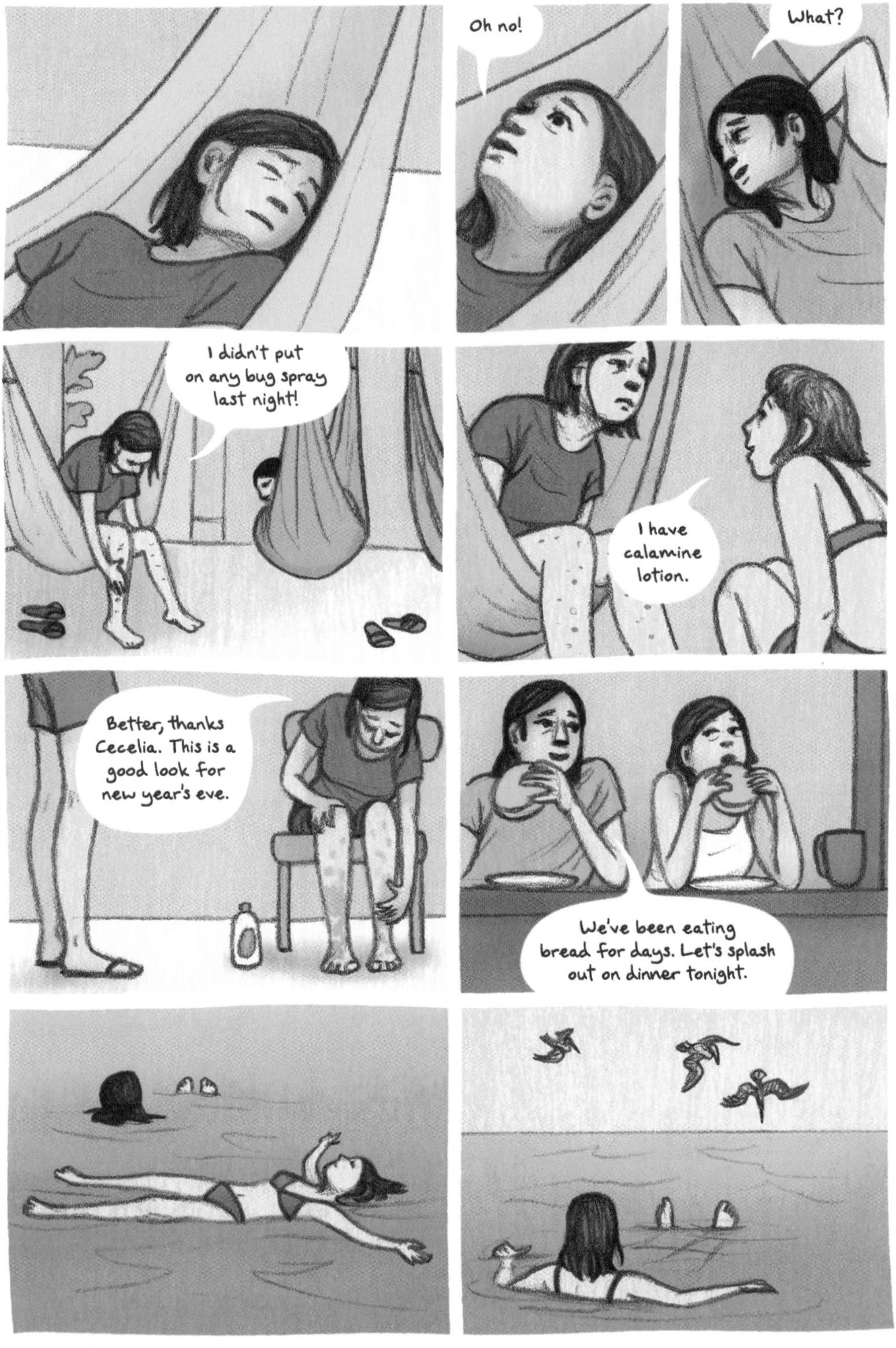
Oh no!
What?
I didn't put on any bug spray last night!
I have calamine lotion.
Better, thanks Cecelia. This is a good look for new year's eve.
We've been eating bread for days. Let's splash out on dinner tonight.

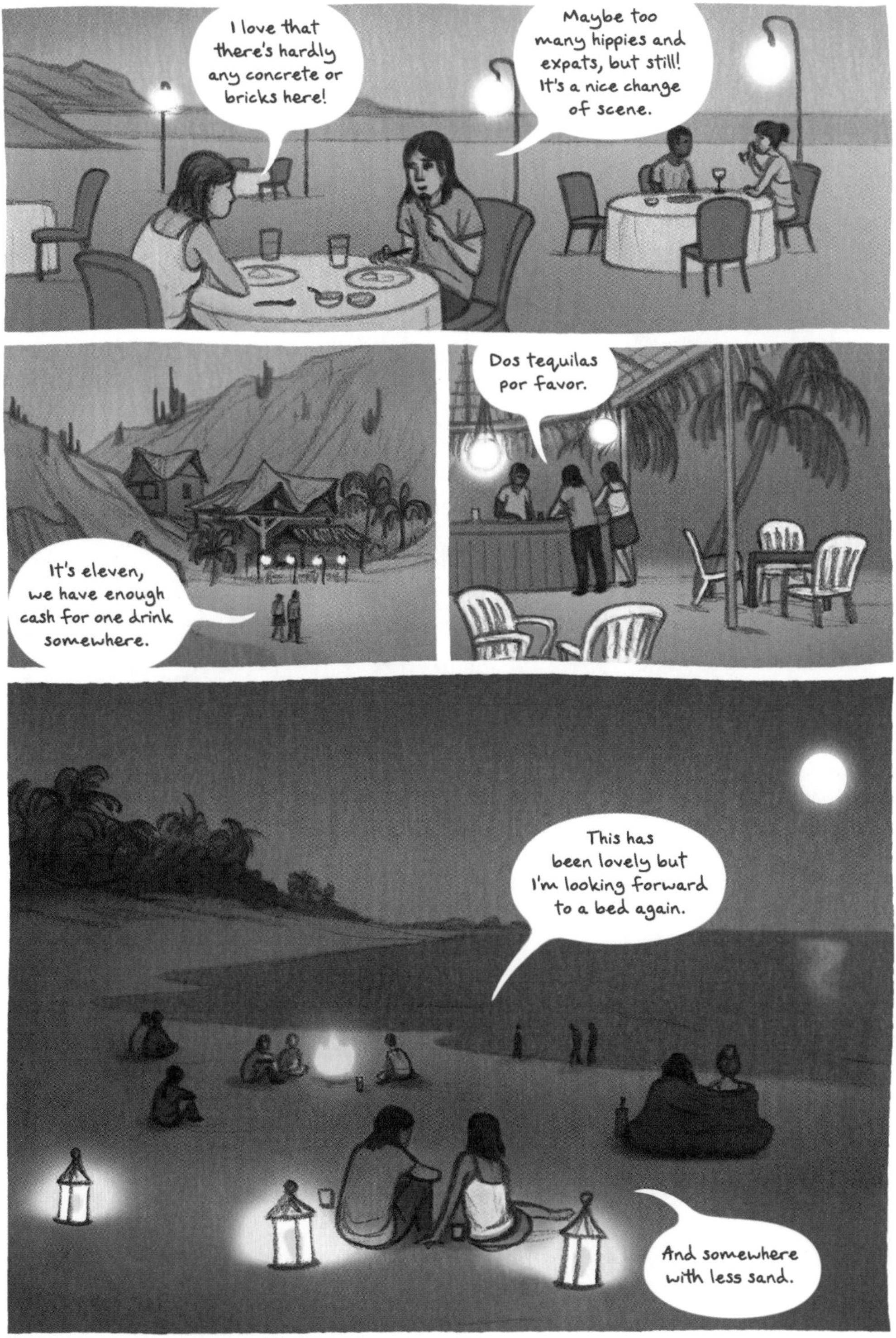

I love that there's hardly any concrete or bricks here!
Maybe too many hippies and expats, but still! It's a nice change of scene.
It's eleven, we have enough cash for one drink somewhere.
Dos tequilas por favor.
This has been lovely but I'm looking forward to a bed again.
And somewhere with less sand.

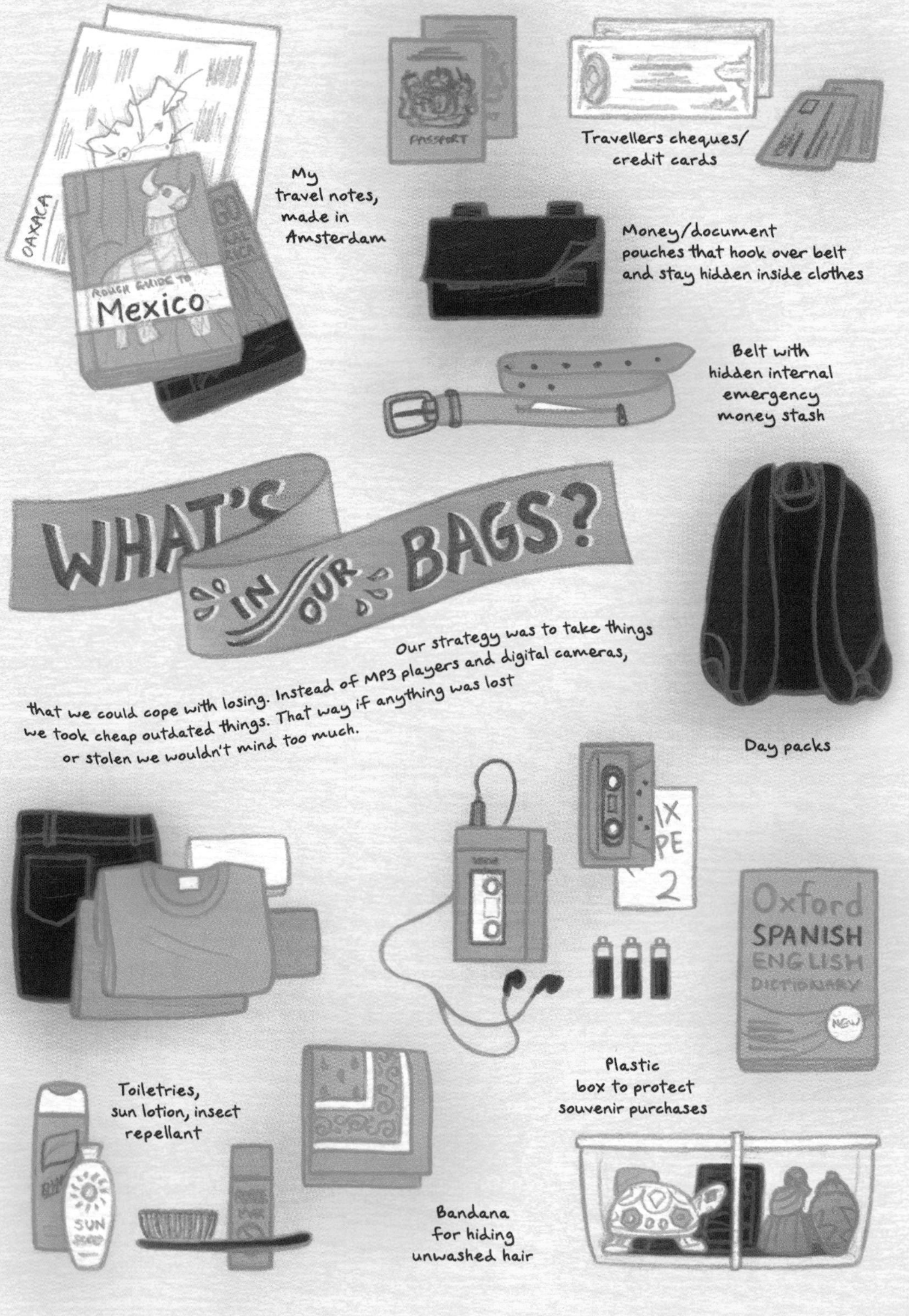
OAXACA
ROUGH GUIDE TO
Mexico
My travel notes, made in Amsterdam
PASSPORT
Travellers cheques/ credit cards
Money/document pouches that hook over belt and stay hidden inside clothes
Belt with hidden internal emergency money stash
WHAT'S IN OUR BAGS?
Our strategy was to take things that we could cope with losing. Instead of MP3 players and digital cameras, we took cheap outdated things. That way if anything was lost or stolen we wouldn't mind too much.
Day packs
Oxford SPANISH ENGLISH DICTIONARY
NEW
Plastic box to protect souvenir purchases
Toiletries, sun lotion, insect repellant
SUN
Bandana for hiding unwashed hair

'Incidents of Travel in Central America, Chiapas, and Yucatán'. by John L. Stephens (1841.) An account of early exploration of Mesoamerican archeological sites, by one of the first Americans to see and document them.

Incidents of Travel in Central America, Chiapas & Yucatan

John L. Stephens

with illustrations

Volume 1

MEXICO
GUIDE
DEVICES
HISTORY

AMONG THE MAYA
RONALD WRIGHT

'A Hiker's Guide to Mexico's Natural History' by Jim Conrad. Bought before I discovered that I loved hiking.

'Time Among the Maya: Travels in Belize, Guatemala, and Mexico' by Ronald Wright. About pre-Hispanic traditions in modern Maya culture.

Pencil case: scissors, glue, hairspray for fixing charcoal and pencil drawings

putty

PVA

AE1 CANON

Mosquito net

Plastic bag to protect rolls of film

Cheap point n' shoot for use on beach/boats

San Cristóbal de las Casas

Another all-night coach journey took us east from the coast into the jungles of Chiapas and then the chilly highland town of San Cristóbal de las Casas.

Puebla

Veracruz

Campeche

Oaxaca

Tabasco

Guatemala

Guerrero

San Cristóbal
de las Casas

Santa Maria
Huatulco

Chiapas

Zipolite   (Overnight
stay)

Chiapas is known for its Maya ruins and for its high concentration of indigenous groups – twelve federally recognised ethnicities. It has also historically been a hotbed of anti-government activity and uprisings.

Chiapas is also home to stunning pockets of cloud forest, where persistent low-level cloud keeps the air wet, and mosses and bromeliads thrive.

BIENVENIDOS

ESTA USTED EN TERRITORIO
ZAPATISTA
EN REBELDIA AQUI MANDA EL
ELG... ...RDECE

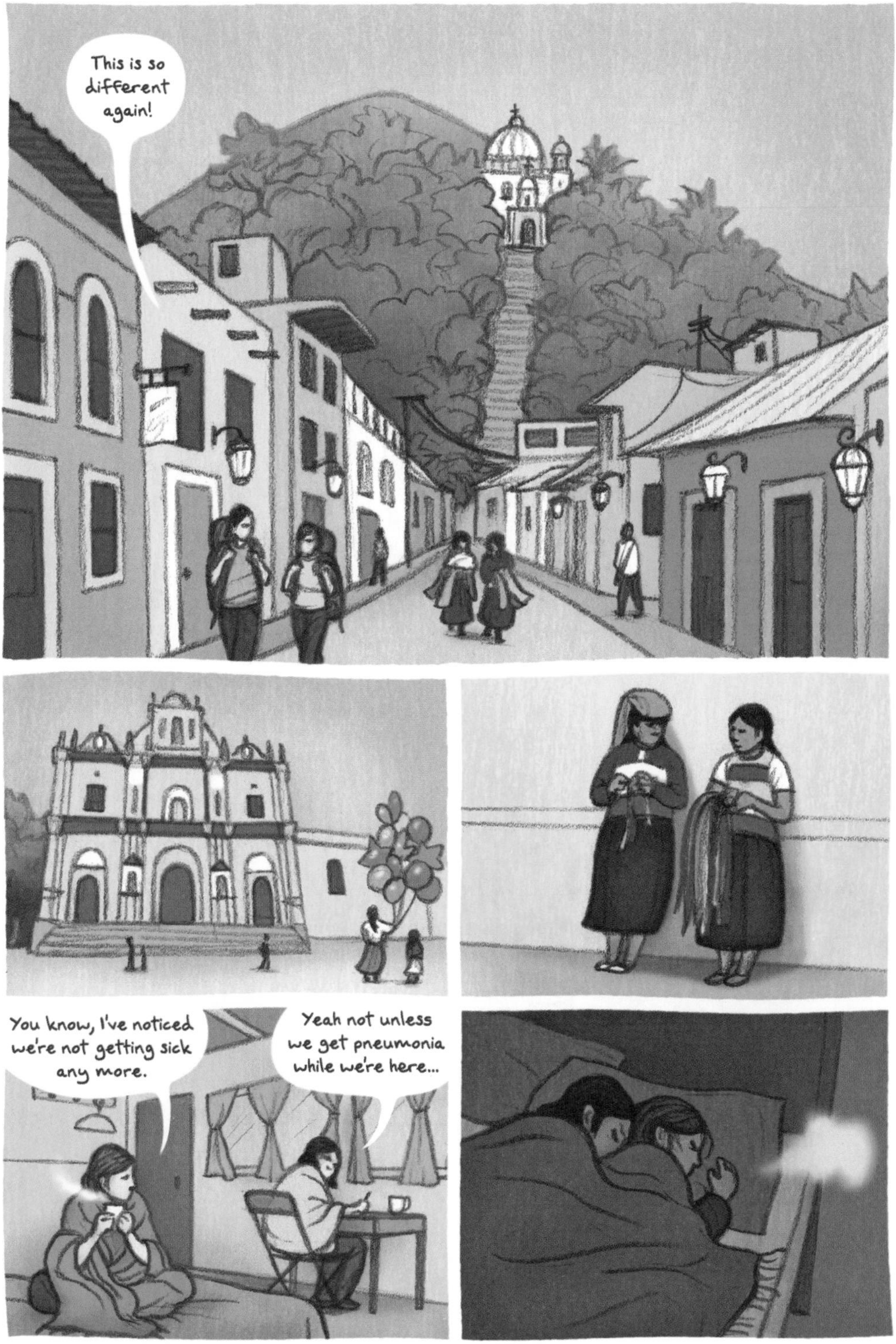
This is so different again!
You know, I've noticed we're not getting sick any more.
Yeah not unless we get pneumonia while we're here...

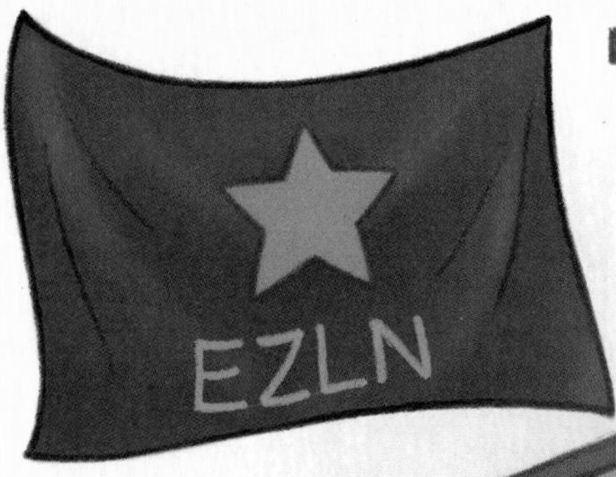
EZLN

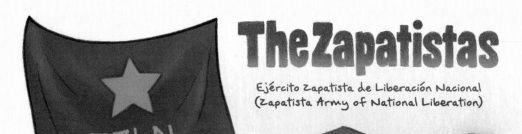

The Zapatistas

Ejército Zapatista de Liberación Nacional
(Zapatista Army of National Liberation)

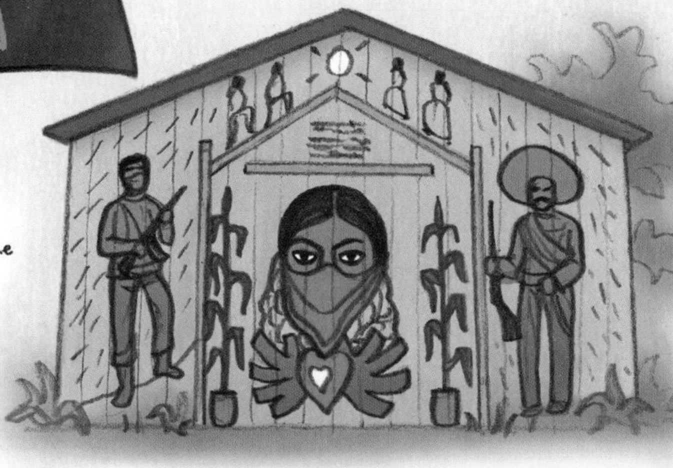

Roughly a third of the population of Chiapas is made up of indigenous groups.

The Zapatistas are a mostly indigenous revolutionary leftist political and militant group based in Chiapas. Since 1994 they've been in a declared war against the Mexican state. In recent years they've focused on a strategy of civil resistance.

Their name comes from Emiliano Zapata, the agrarian reformer and commander of the Liberation Army of the South during the Mexican Revolution. Their principles reflect libertarian socialism, though they reject political classification due to distinctions arising from their unique Maya heritage. Their main concerns are issues of land reform, indigenous autonomy, women's rights and the rights of indigenous groups to control their local resources.

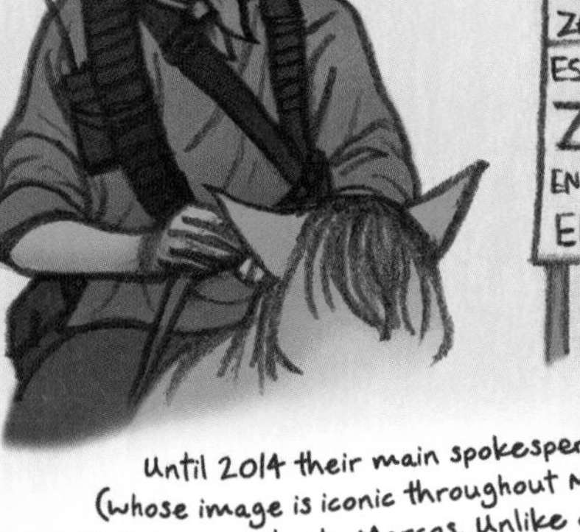

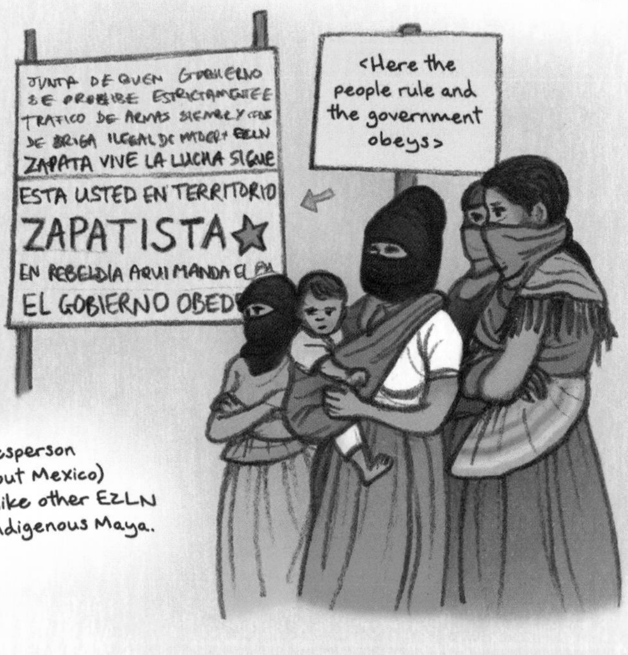
ZAPATA VIVE LA LUCHA SIGUE
ESTA USTED EN TERRITORIO
ZAPATISTA
EN REBELDIA AQUI MANDA EL
EL GOBIERNO OBED
<Here the people rule and the government obeys>

Until 2014 their main spokesperson (whose image is iconic throughout Mexico) was Subcomandante Marcos. Unlike other EZLN spokespeople, Marcos was not indigenous Maya.

The Chiapas Conflict

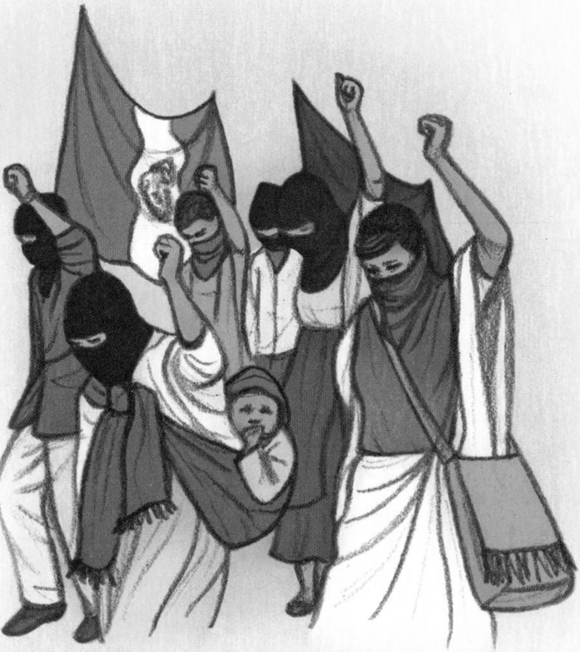

The EZLN gained global attention on January 1st 1994 – the day the North American Free Trade Agreement came into effect. They issued a declaration against corruption in the Mexican government and began an uprising.

300 armed insurgents seized towns and cities in Chiapas. Armed clashes ended on January 12th, with a ceasefire brokered by the Catholic diocese in San Cristóbal de las Casas. Since then the EZLN has ceased military offensives and adopted a strategy of generating local and international support for their cause through the media and internet campaigns.

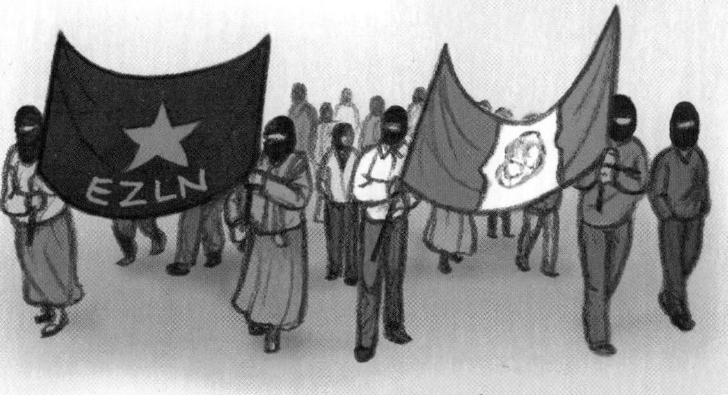
EZLN

They've created thirty two autonomous municipalities in Chiapas, partially implementing their demands without government support but with some funding from international organisations.

The Zapatista rebellion not only raised questions about globalisation and free trade, it also challenged long-standing ideas created by the Spanish colonial system.

"We didn't go to war to kill or be killed. We went to war in order to be heard."
—Subcomandante Marcos

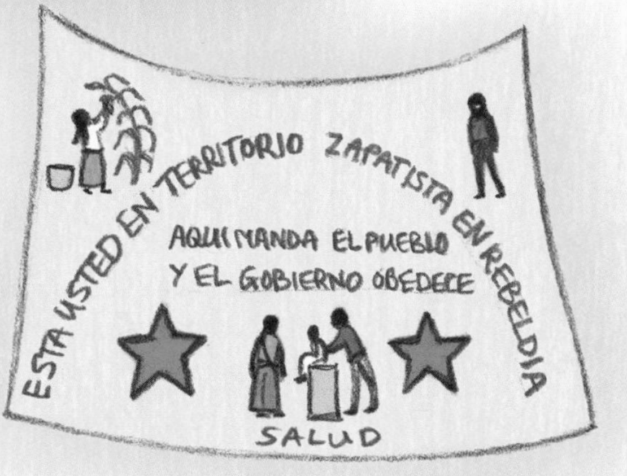
ESTA USTED EN TERRITORIO ZAPATISTA EN REBELDIA
AQUI MANDA EL PUEBLO
Y EL GOBIERNO OBEDECE
SALUD

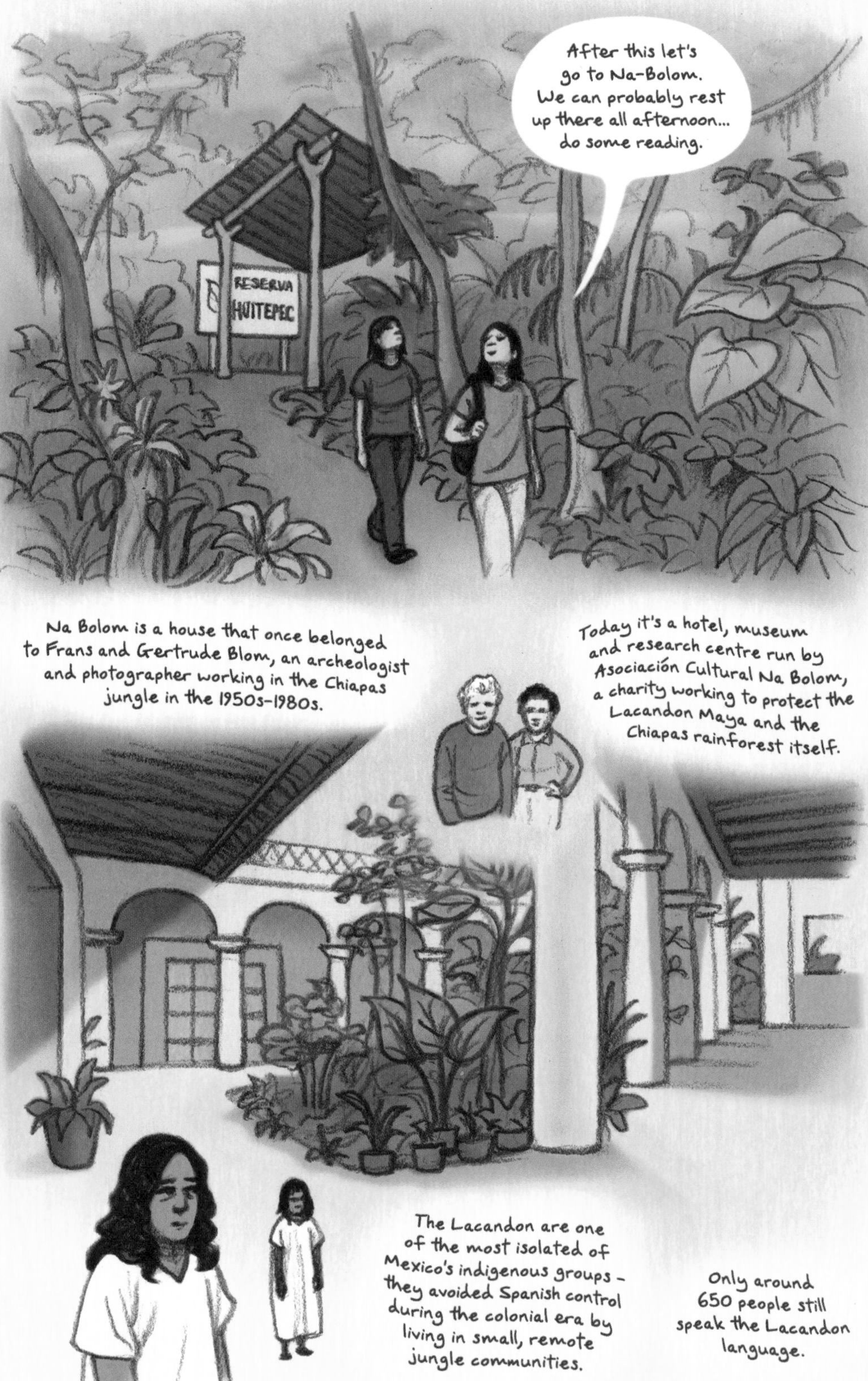
After this let's go to Na-Bolom. We can probably rest up there all afternoon... do some reading.
RESERVA HUITEPEC
Na Bolom is a house that once belonged to Frans and Gertrude Blom, an archeologist and photographer working in the Chiapas jungle in the 1950s-1980s.
Today it's a hotel, museum and research centre run by Asociación Cultural Na Bolom, a charity working to protect the Lacandon Maya and the Chiapas rainforest itself.
The Lacandon are one of the most isolated of Mexico's indigenous groups - they avoided Spanish control during the colonial era by living in small, remote jungle communities.
Only around 650 people still speak the Lacandon language.

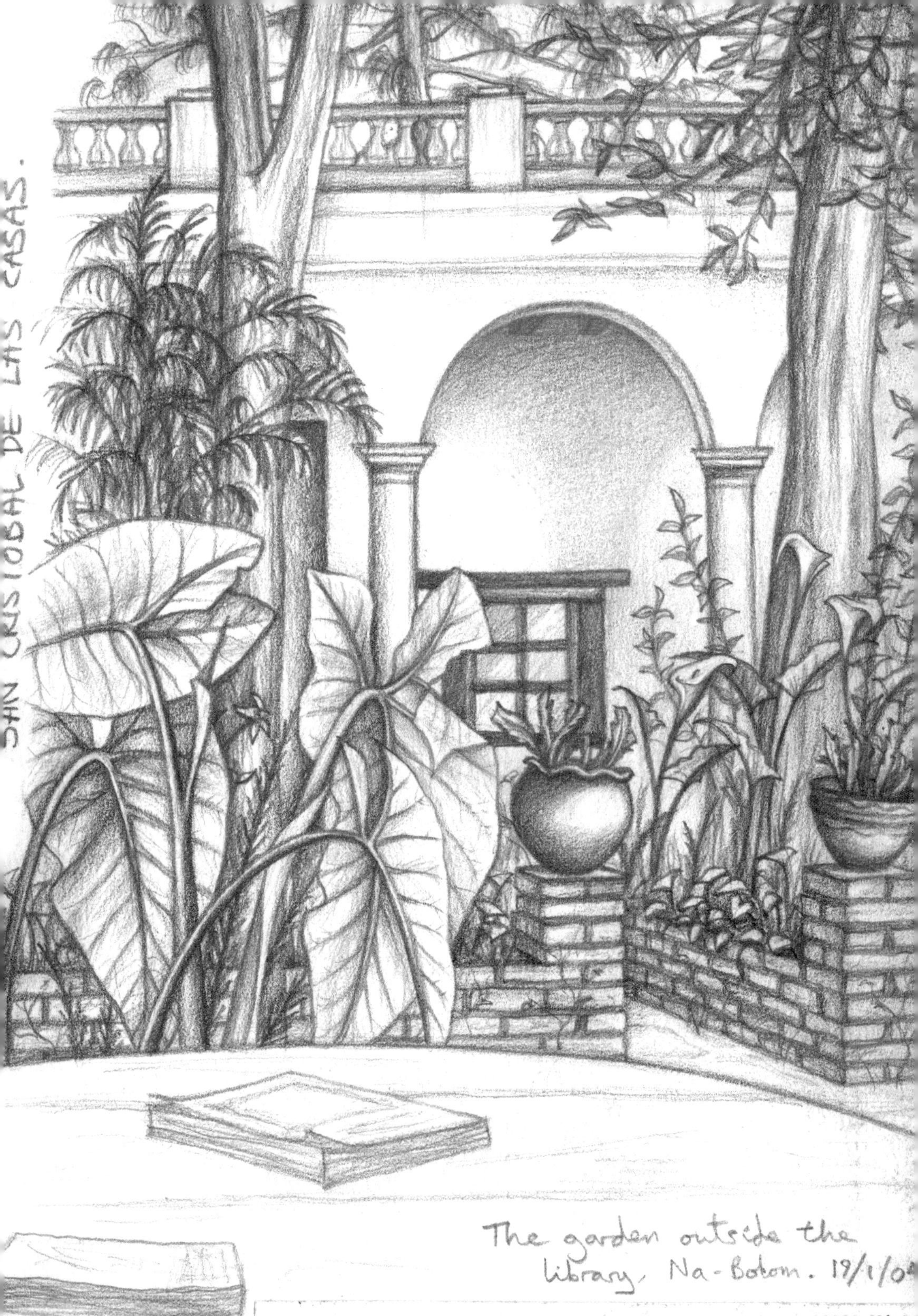
SAN CRISTOBAL DE LAS CASAS.

The garden outside the library, Na-Bolom. 19/1/04

Av. Vicente Guerrero No. 33, San Cristobal de Las Casas, Chiapas. 29220, Méxic
Tel. (967) 8 14 18 Fax (967) 8 55 86 E-mail nabolom@sclc.ecosur.mx

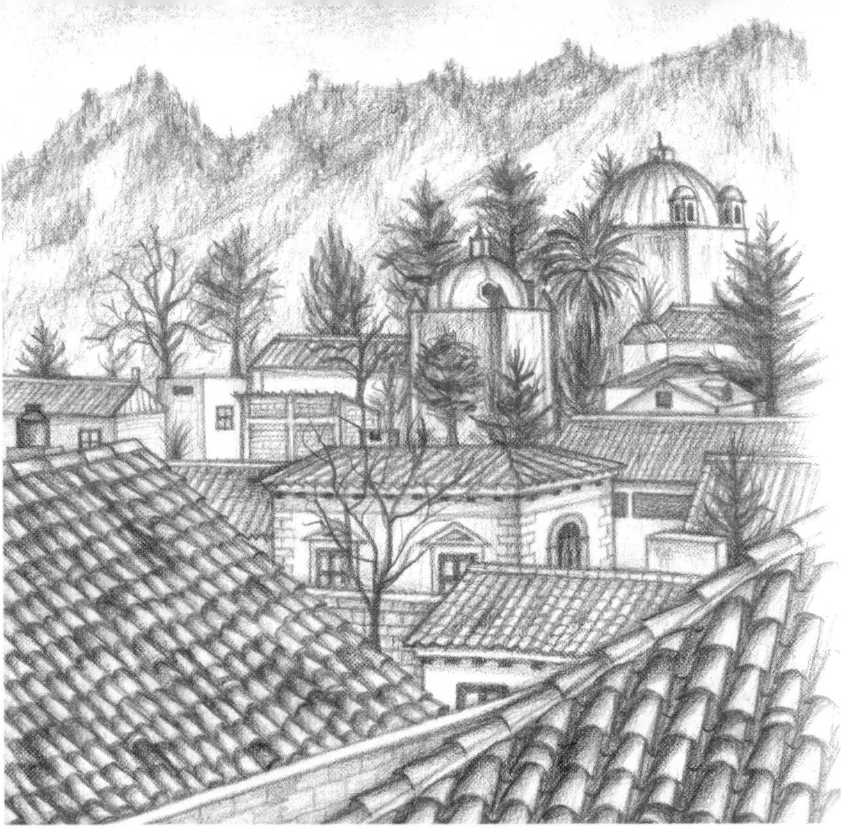

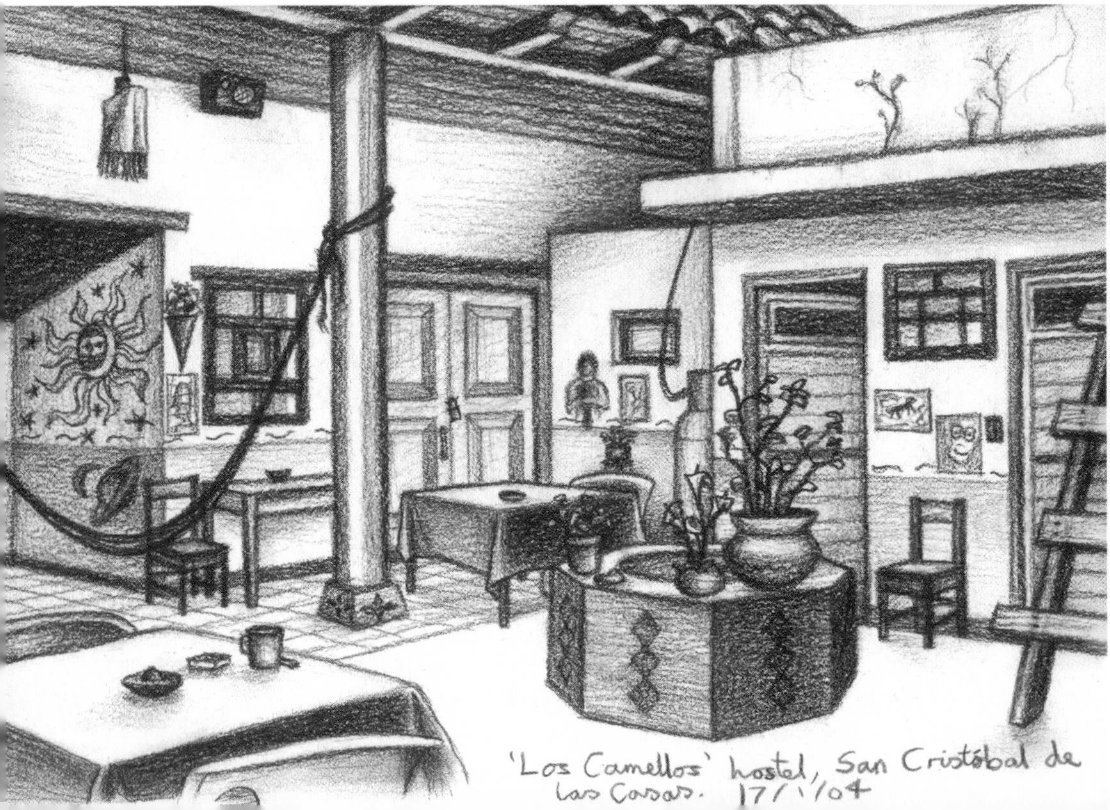
'Los Camellos' hostel, San Cristóbal de las Casas. 17/1/04

San Juan Chamula y San Lorenzo Zinacantán

With a guide, César, we visited these two nearby Tzotzil Maya towns. The people are very private and photography isn't tolerated.

Chamula is autonomous within Mexico – no outside military or police are allowed in and the town has its own justice system (part of which César told us involves wrongdoers doing compulsory duty in the role of law enforcement.)

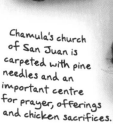

Chamula's church of San Juan is carpeted with pine needles and an important centre for prayer, offerings and chicken sacrifices.

We went on a fiesta day and there were parades, music, games and homemade fireworks. People in Tzotzil society earn status and serve the community by participating in a system of rotating administrative/religious offices ('cargo-holding.') We saw inside the house of a man who was serving a religious cargo by maintaining an altar which had to have three daily offerings made throughout the year.

Zinacantán means 'land of bats.' The church there was also fascinating... they were in the process of hanging incredible fruit and foliage arrangements from the ceiling.

They gave us fermented sugarcane moonshine, and we saw a demonstration of back-strap weaving there. We felt like we'd spent the day in an entirely different country.

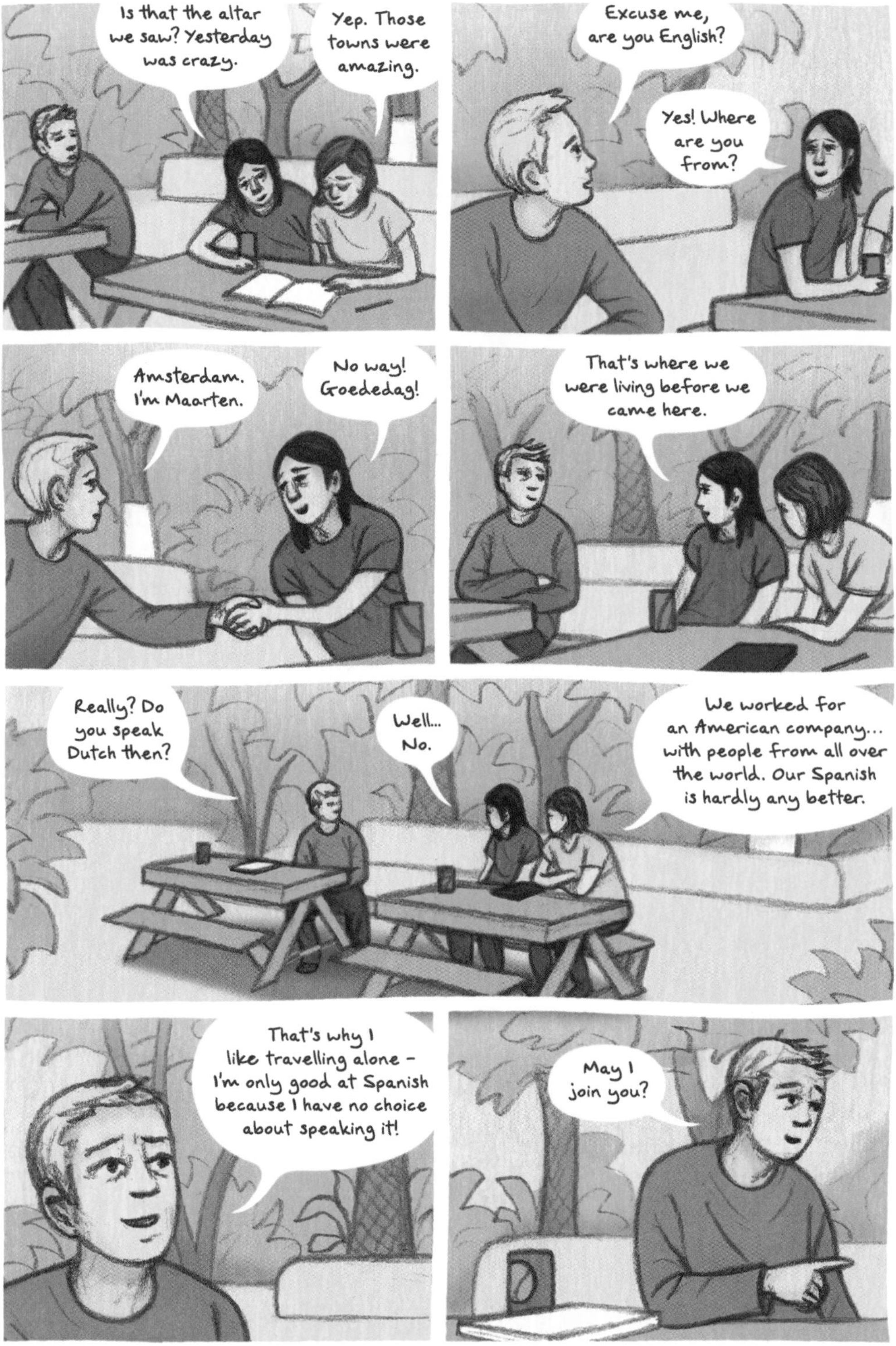
Is that the altar we saw? Yesterday was crazy.
Yep. Those towns were amazing.
Excuse me, are you English?
Yes! Where are you from?
Amsterdam. I'm Maarten.
No way! Goededag!
That's where we were living before we came here.
Really? Do you speak Dutch then?
Well... No.
We worked for an American company... with people from all over the world. Our Spanish is hardly any better.
That's why I like travelling alone – I'm only good at Spanish because I have no choice about speaking it!
May I join you?

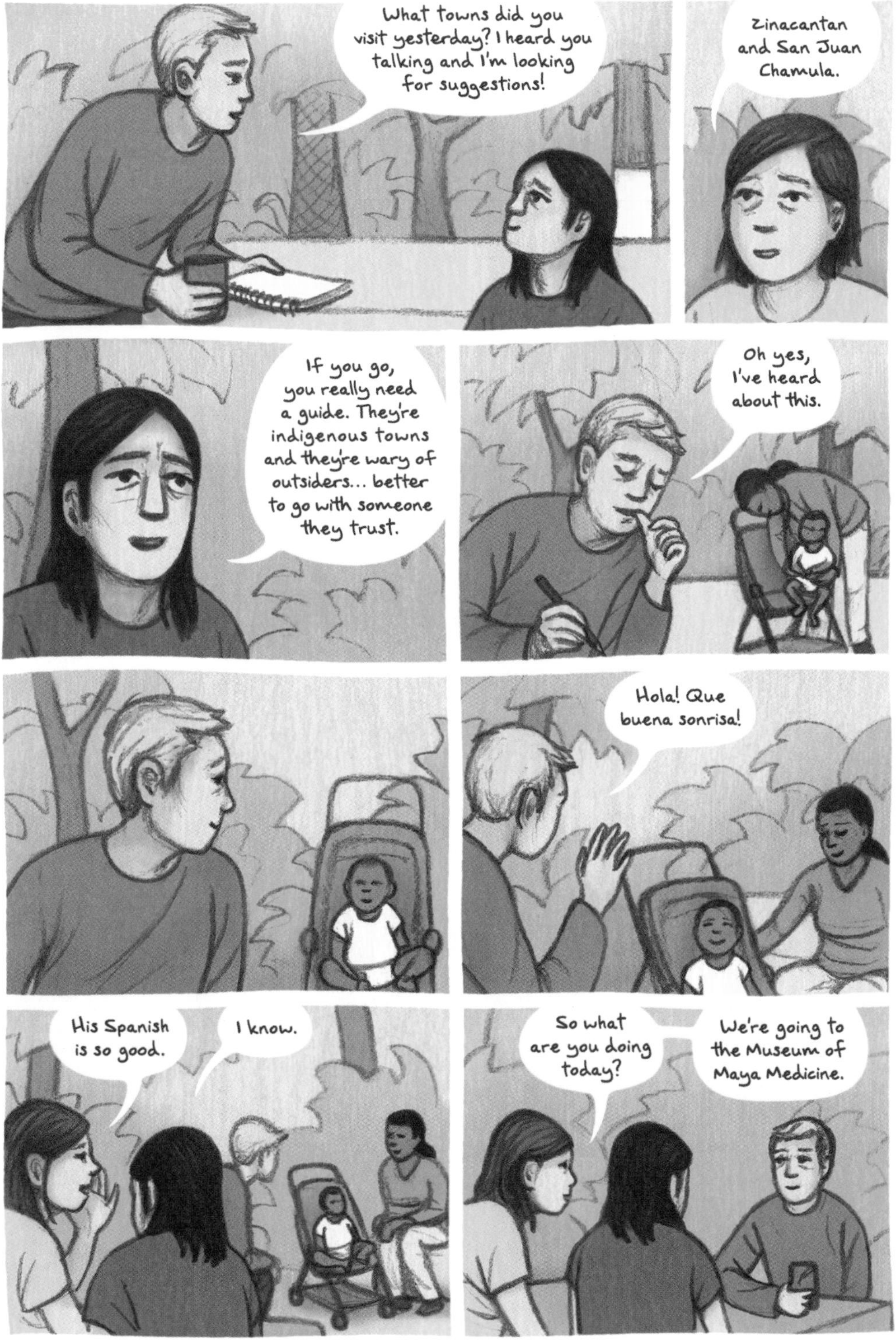
What towns did you visit yesterday? I heard you talking and I'm looking for suggestions!
Zinacantan and San Juan Chamula.
If you go, you really need a guide. They're indigenous towns and they're wary of outsiders… better to go with someone they trust.
Oh yes, I've heard about this.
Hola! Que buena sonrisa!
His Spanish is so good.
I know.
So what are you doing today?
We're going to the Museum of Maya Medicine.

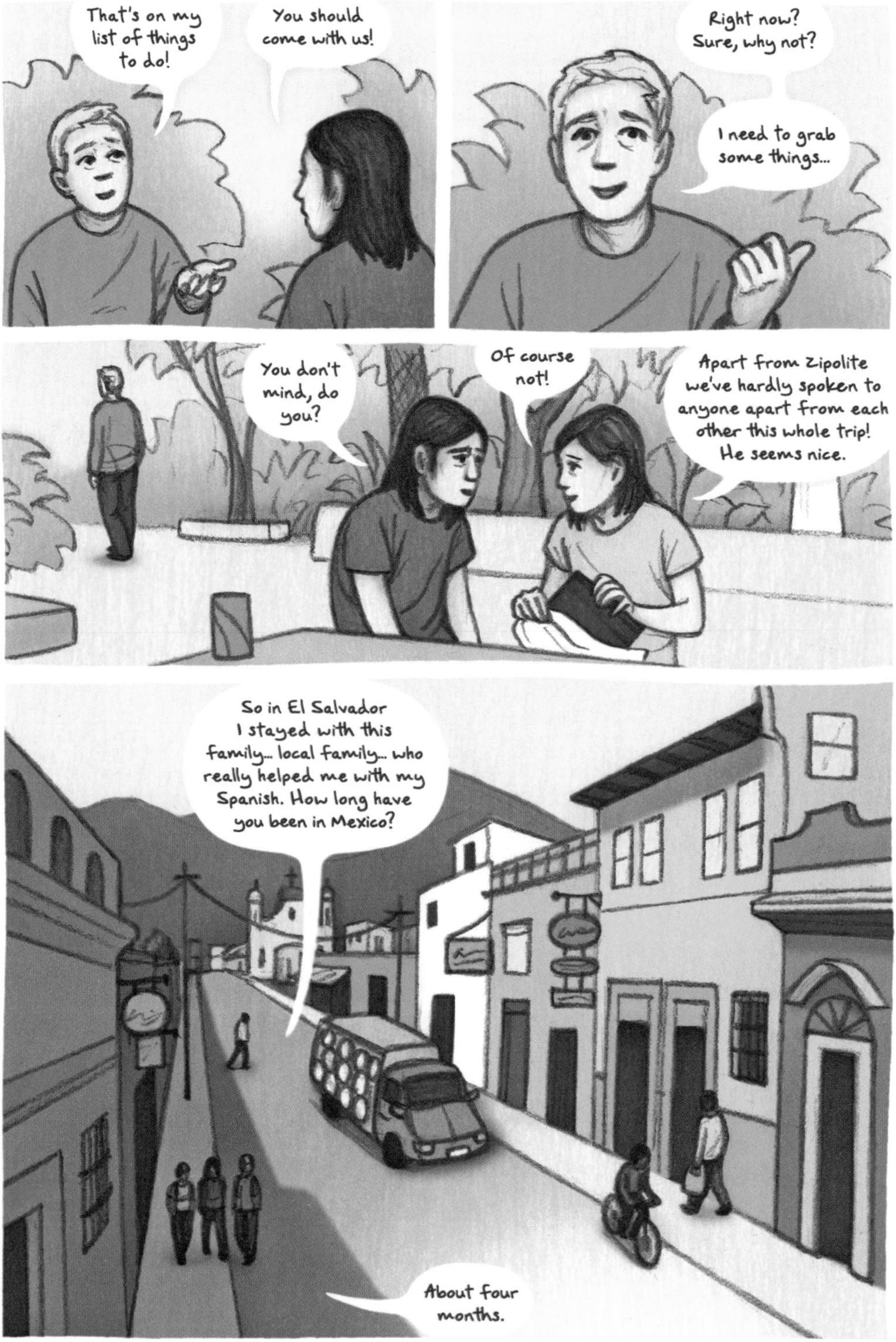
That's on my list of things to do!
You should come with us!
Right now? Sure, why not?
I need to grab some things...
You don't mind, do you?
Of course not!
Apart from Zipolite we've hardly spoken to anyone apart from each other this whole trip! He seems nice.
So in El Salvador I stayed with this family... local family... who really helped me with my Spanish. How long have you been in Mexico?
About four months.

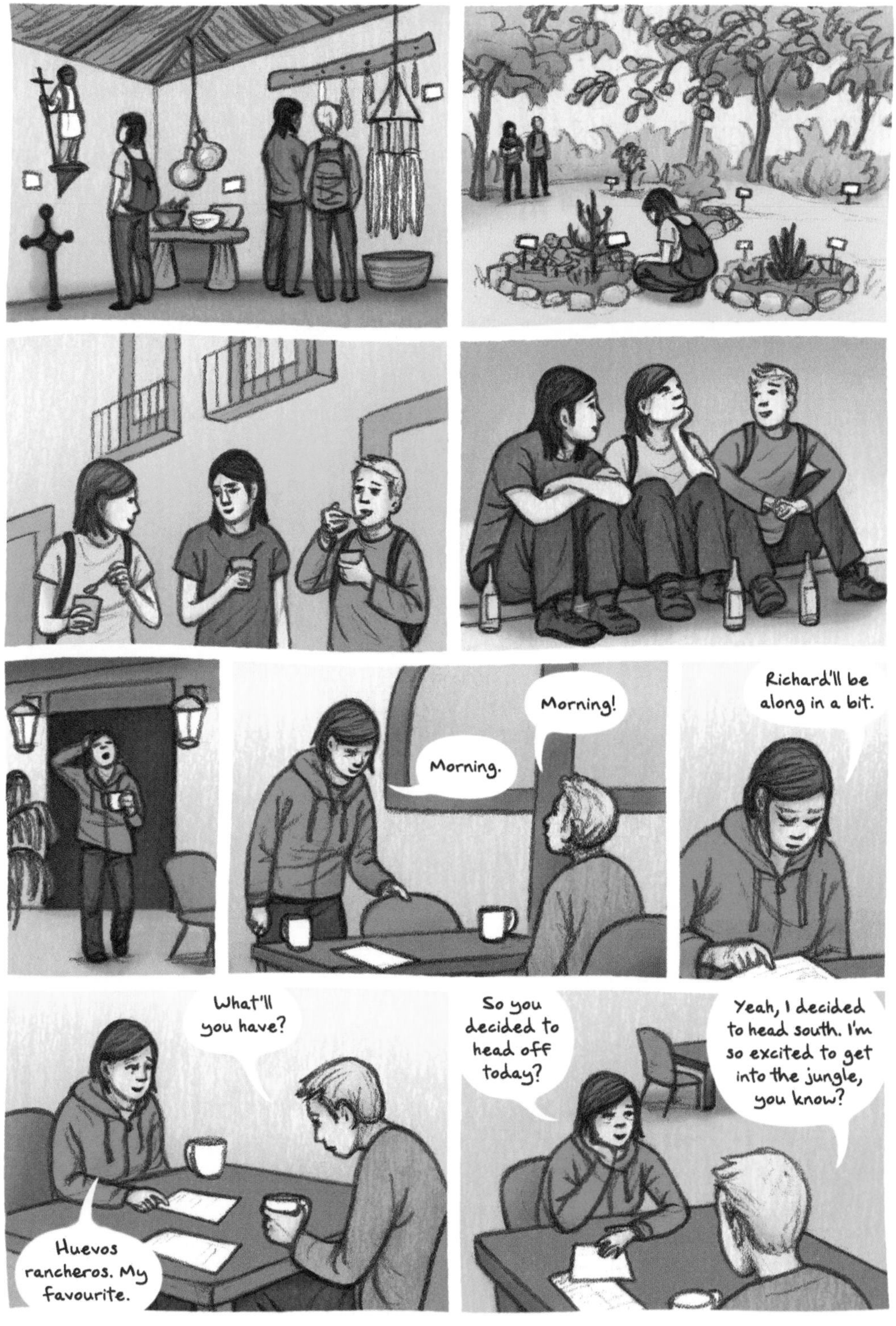
Morning.
Morning!
Richard'll be along in a bit.
What'll you have?
Huevos rancheros. My favourite.
So you decided to head off today?
Yeah, I decided to head south. I'm so excited to get into the jungle, you know?

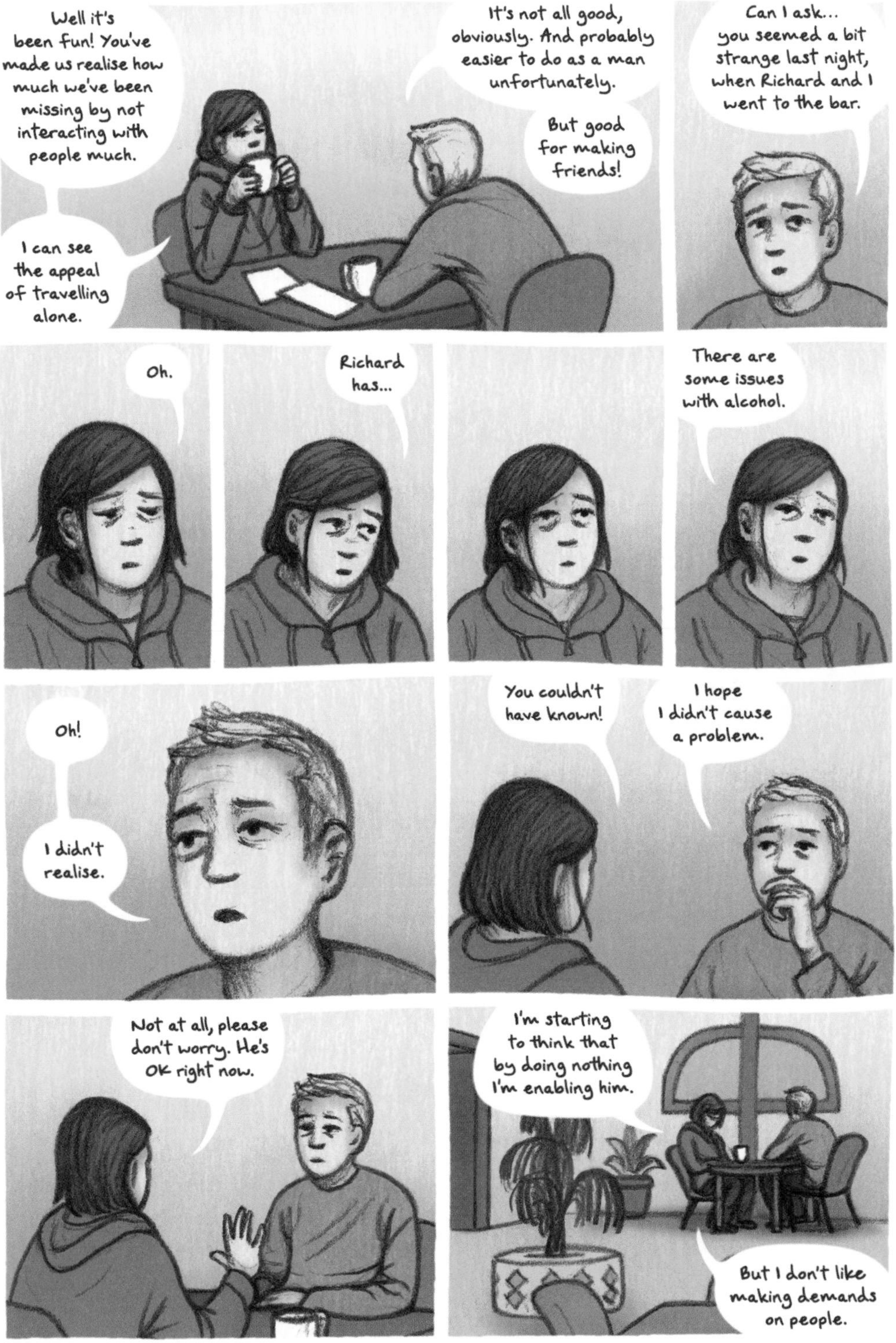
Well it's been fun! You've made us realise how much we've been missing by not interacting with people much.
I can see the appeal of travelling alone.
It's not all good, obviously. And probably easier to do as a man unfortunately.
But good for making friends!
Can I ask... you seemed a bit strange last night, when Richard and I went to the bar.
Oh.
Richard has...
There are some issues with alcohol.
Oh!
I didn't realise.
You couldn't have known!
I hope I didn't cause a problem.
Not at all, please don't worry. He's OK right now.
I'm starting to think that by doing nothing I'm enabling him.
But I don't like making demands on people.

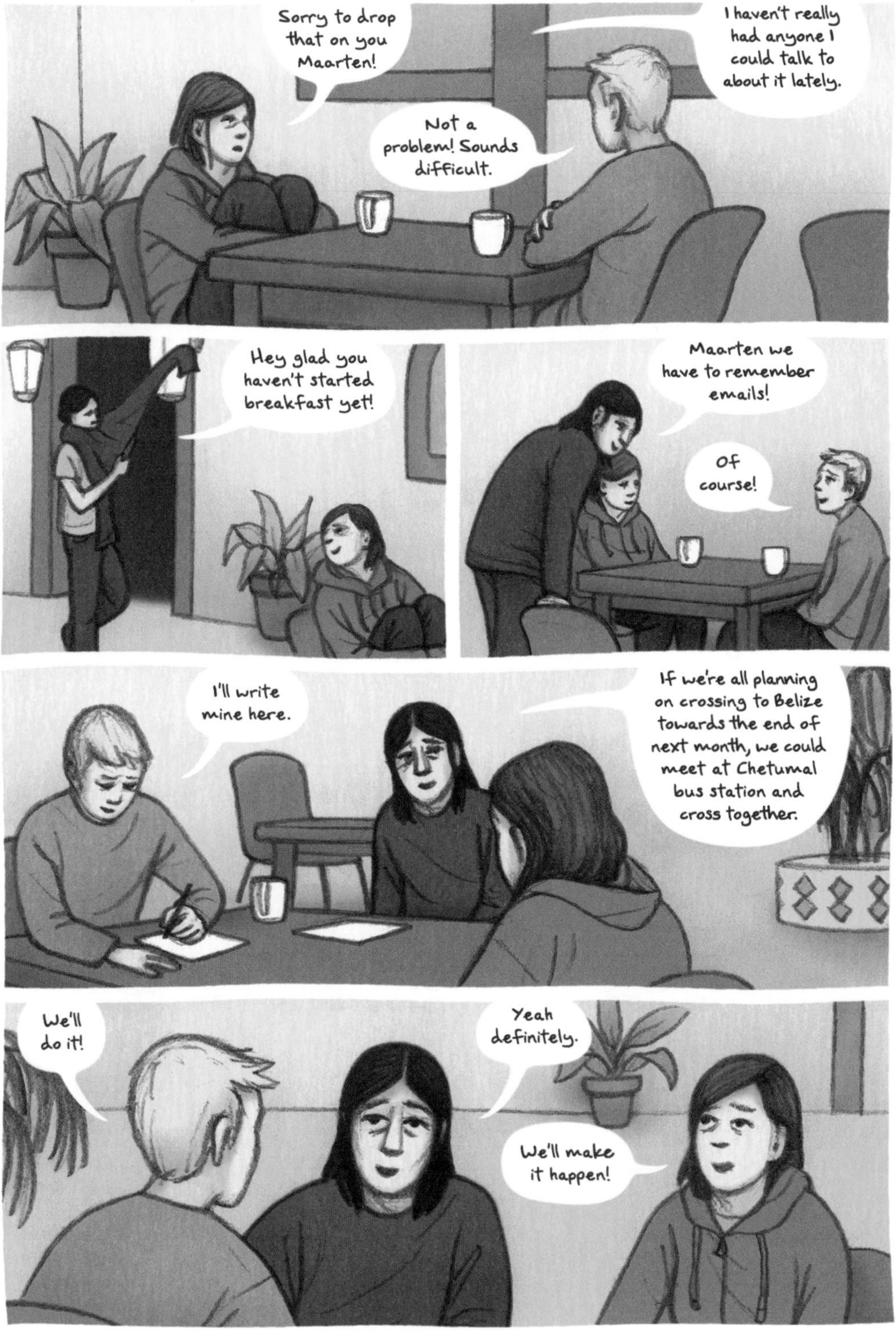
Sorry to drop that on you Maarten!
I haven't really had anyone I could talk to about it lately.
Not a problem! Sounds difficult.
Hey glad you haven't started breakfast yet!
Maarten we have to remember emails!
Of course!
I'll write mine here.
If we're all planning on crossing to Belize towards the end of next month, we could meet at Chetumal bus station and cross together.
We'll do it!
Yeah definitely.
We'll make it happen!

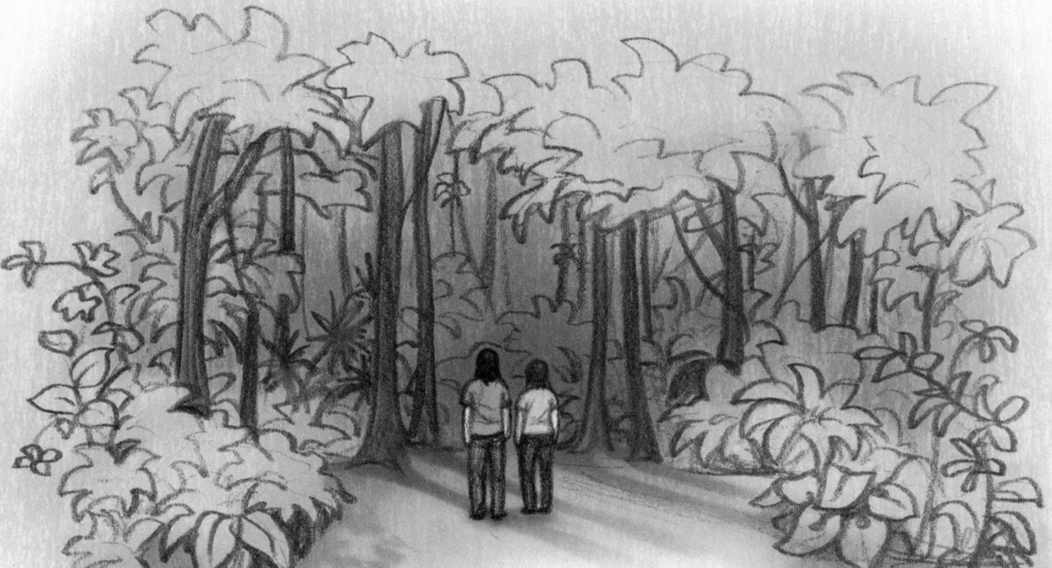

We were bewitched by this part of Mexico.

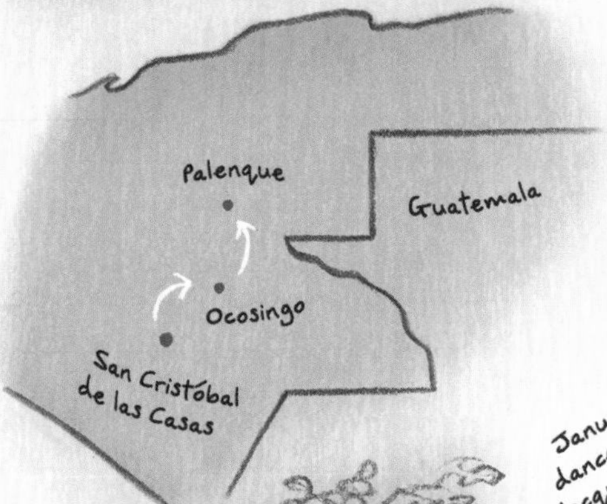
Palenque
Guatemala
Ocosingo
San Cristóbal de las Casas

From our San Cristóbal base we visited Chiapas's urban hub Tuxtla Guttierez. We also took a boat through the Sumidero Canyon and went to the Fiesta de Enero in Chiapa de Corzo.

January Feast Parachicos dancers – they wear lacquered masks and wigs that mimic Caucasian looks.

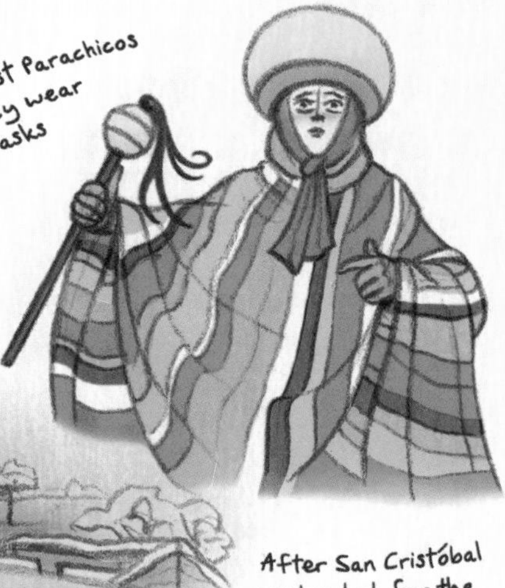

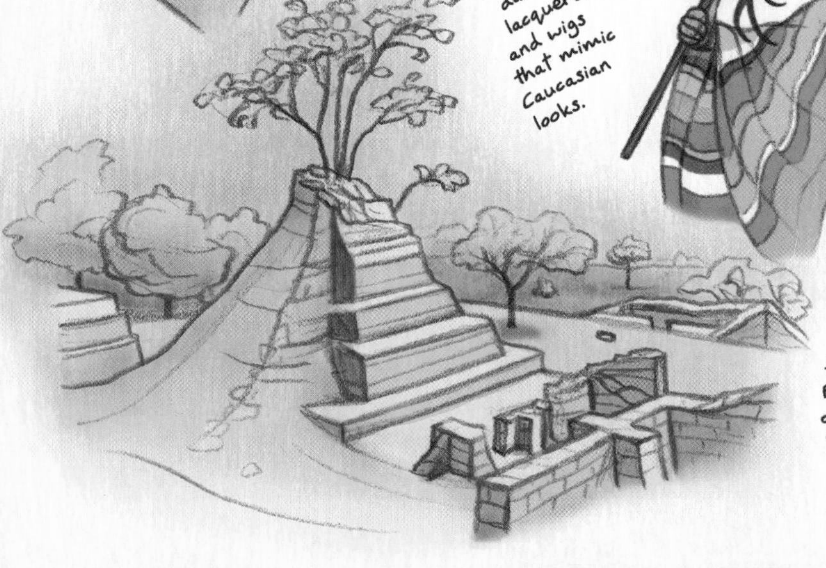

After San Cristóbal we headed for the famous ruins of Palenque. We stopped on the way in Ocosingo to see the smaller ruins of Toniná.

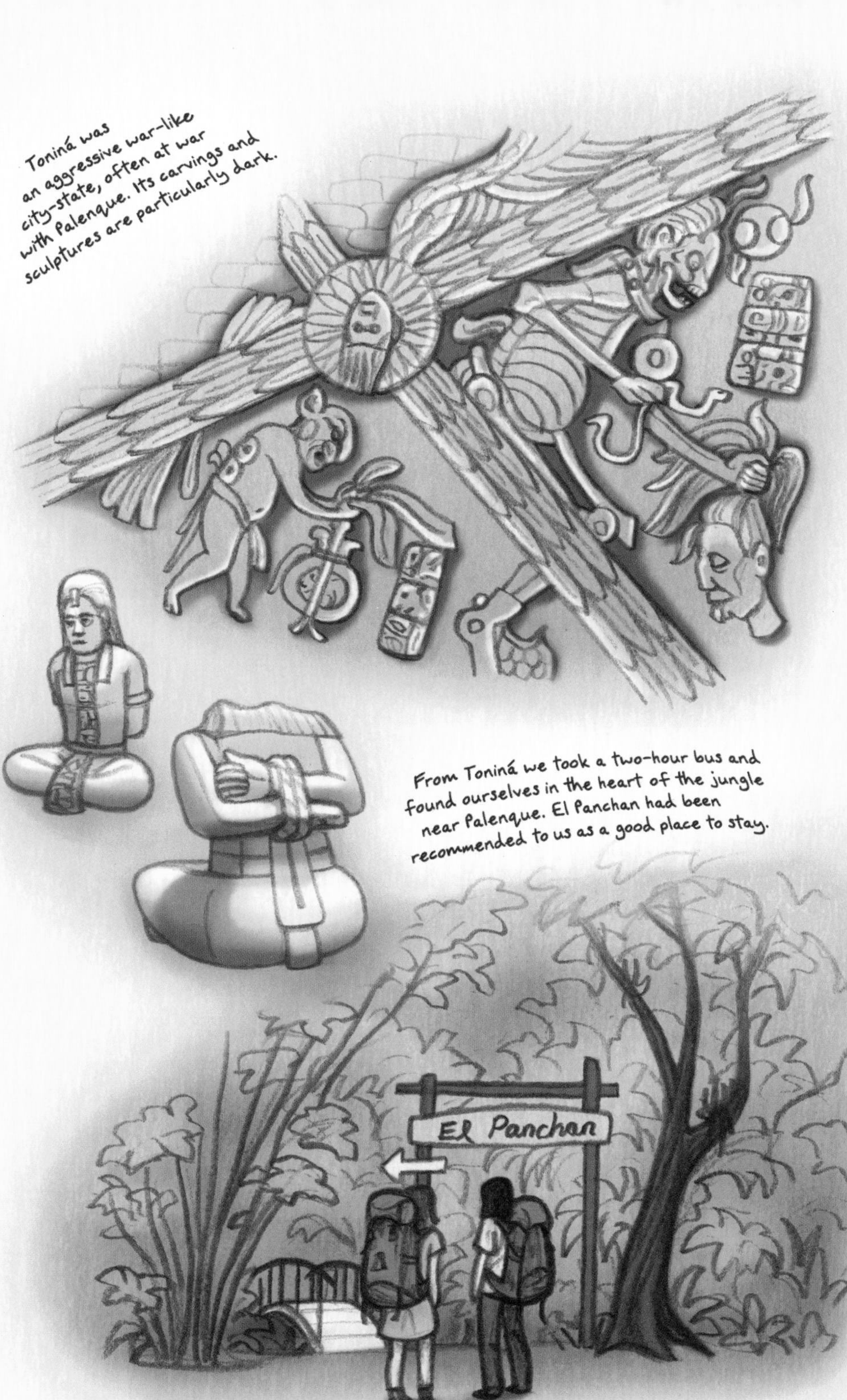
Toniná was an aggressive war-like city-state, often at war with Palenque. Its carvings and sculptures are particularly dark.
From Toniná we took a two-hour bus and found ourselves in the heart of the jungle near Palenque. El Panchan had been recommended to us as a good place to stay.
El Panchan

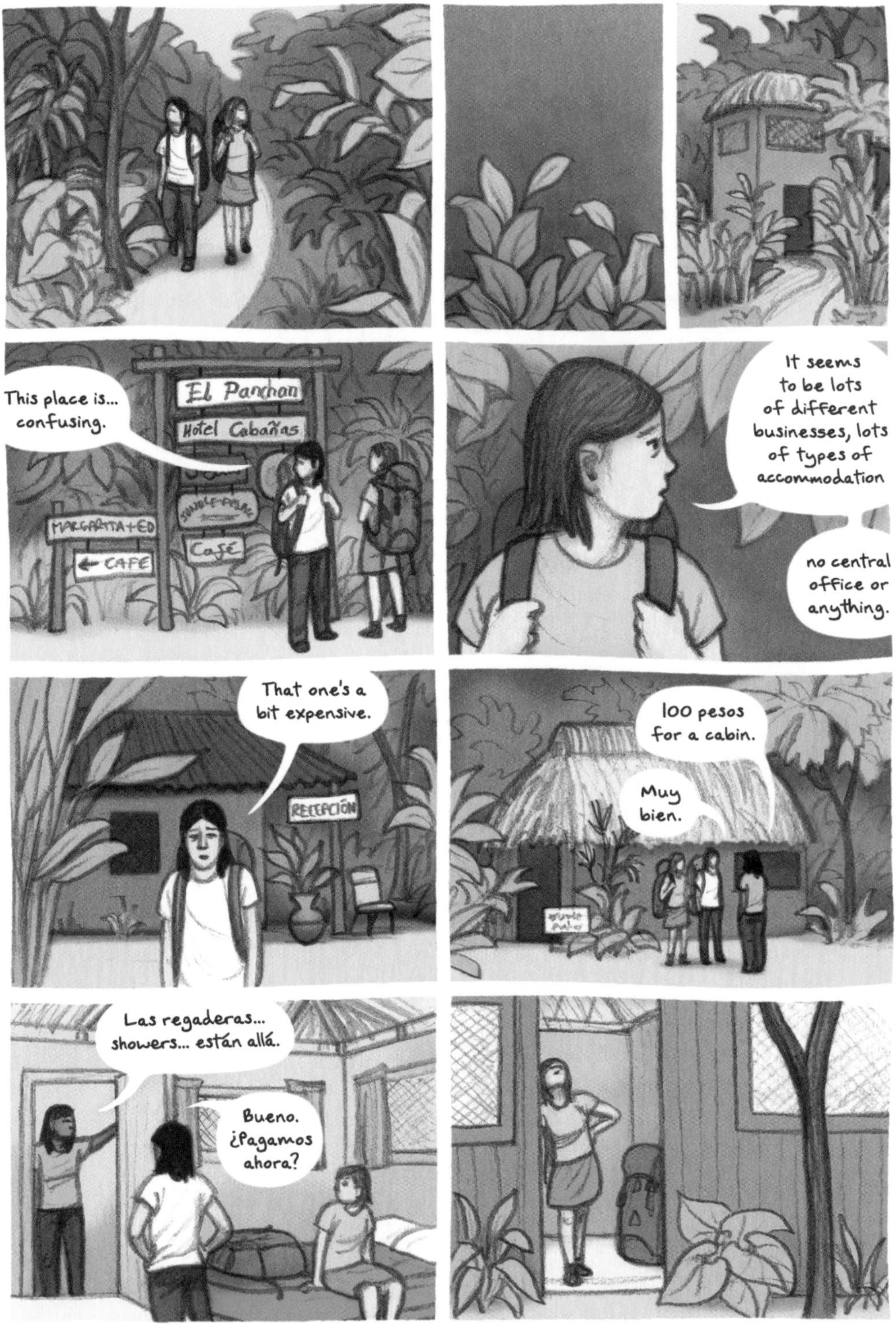
El Panchan
Hotel Cabañas
MARGARITA+ED
CAFE
Café
This place is... confusing.
It seems to be lots of different businesses, lots of types of accommodation
no central office or anything.
That one's a bit expensive.
RECEPCIÓN
100 pesos for a cabin.
Muy bien.
Las regaderas... showers... están allá.
Bueno. ¿Pagamos ahora?

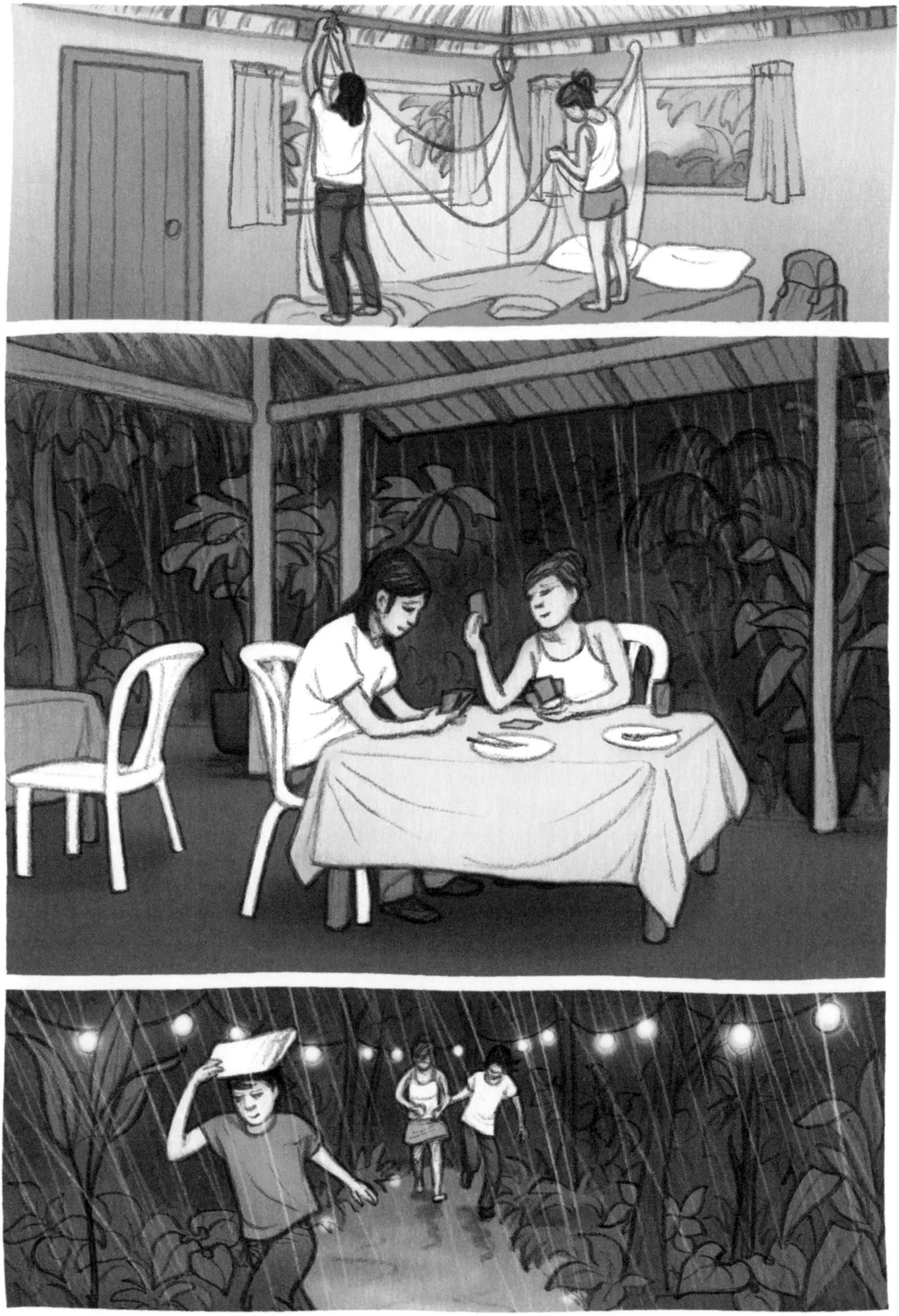

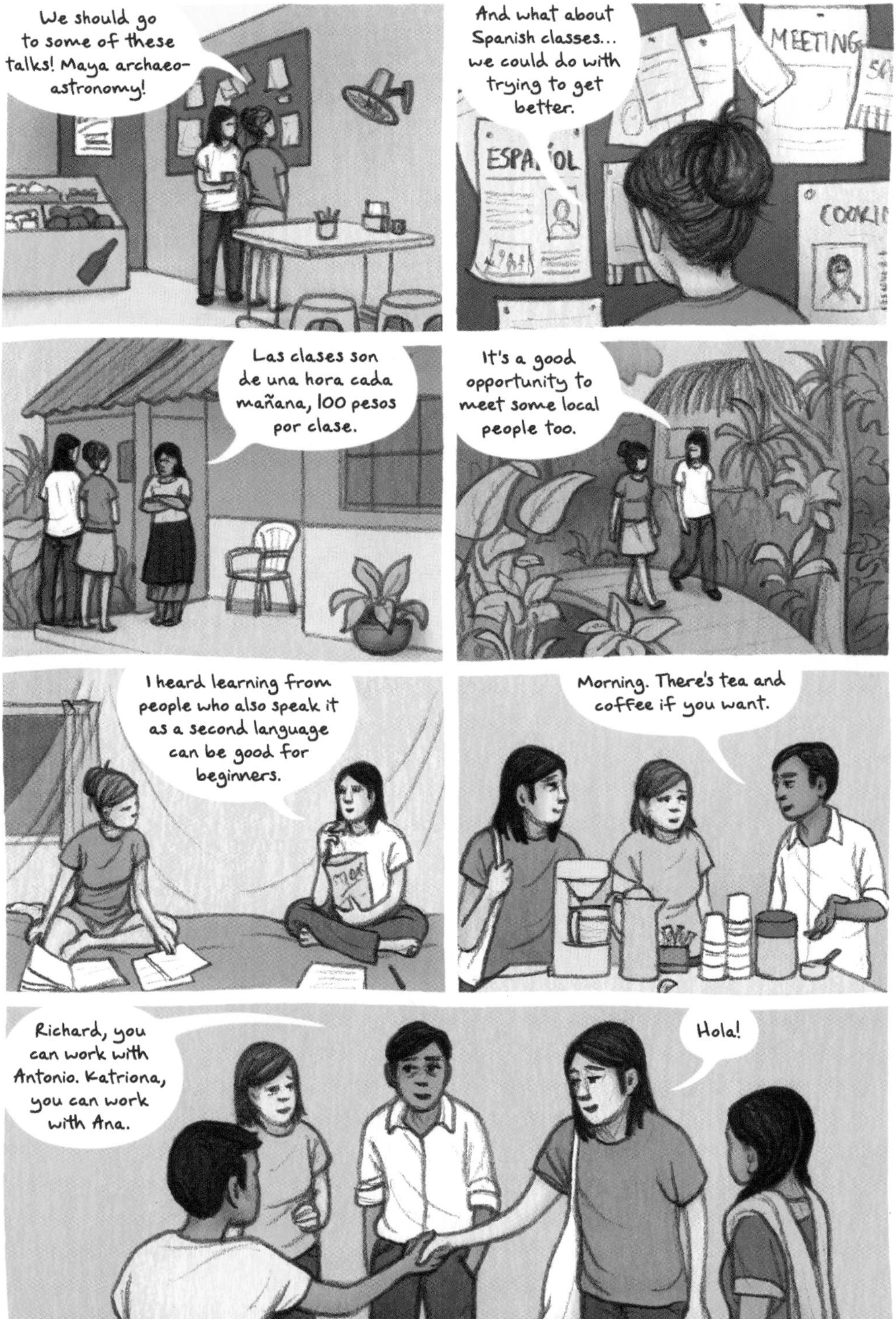
We should go to some of these talks! Maya archaeo-astronomy!
And what about Spanish classes... we could do with trying to get better.
MEETING
ESPAÑOL
COOKI
Las clases son de una hora cada mañana, 100 pesos por clase.
It's a good opportunity to meet some local people too.
I heard learning from people who also speak it as a second language can be good for beginners.
Morning. There's tea and coffee if you want.
Richard, you can work with Antonio. Katriona, you can work with Ana.
Hola!

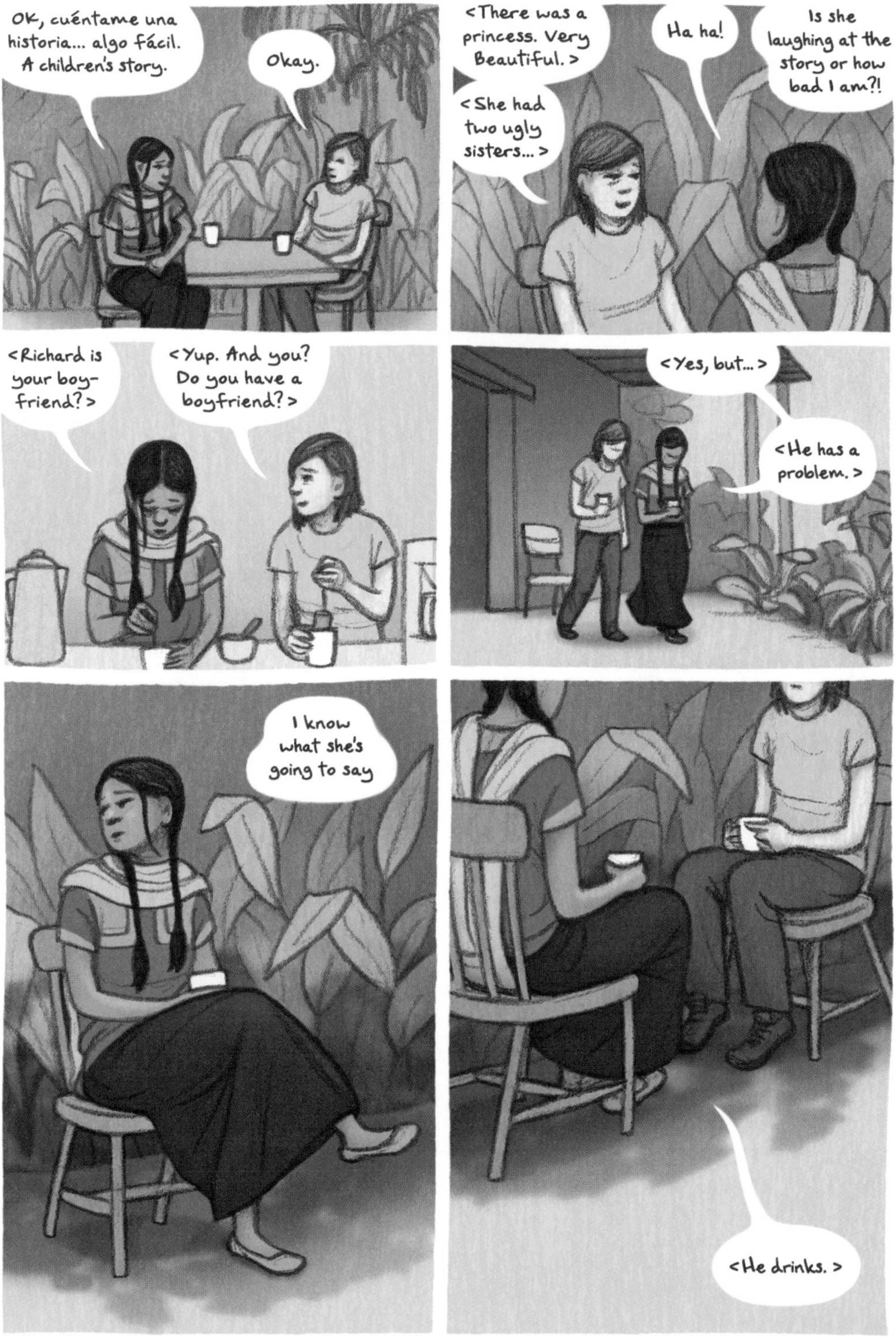
OK, cuéntame una historia... algo fácil. A children's story.
Okay.
<There was a princess. Very Beautiful.>
<She had two ugly sisters...>
Ha ha!
Is she laughing at the story or how bad I am?!
<Richard is your boy-friend?>
<Yup. And you? Do you have a boyfriend?>
<Yes, but...>
<He has a problem.>
I know what she's going to say
<He drinks.>

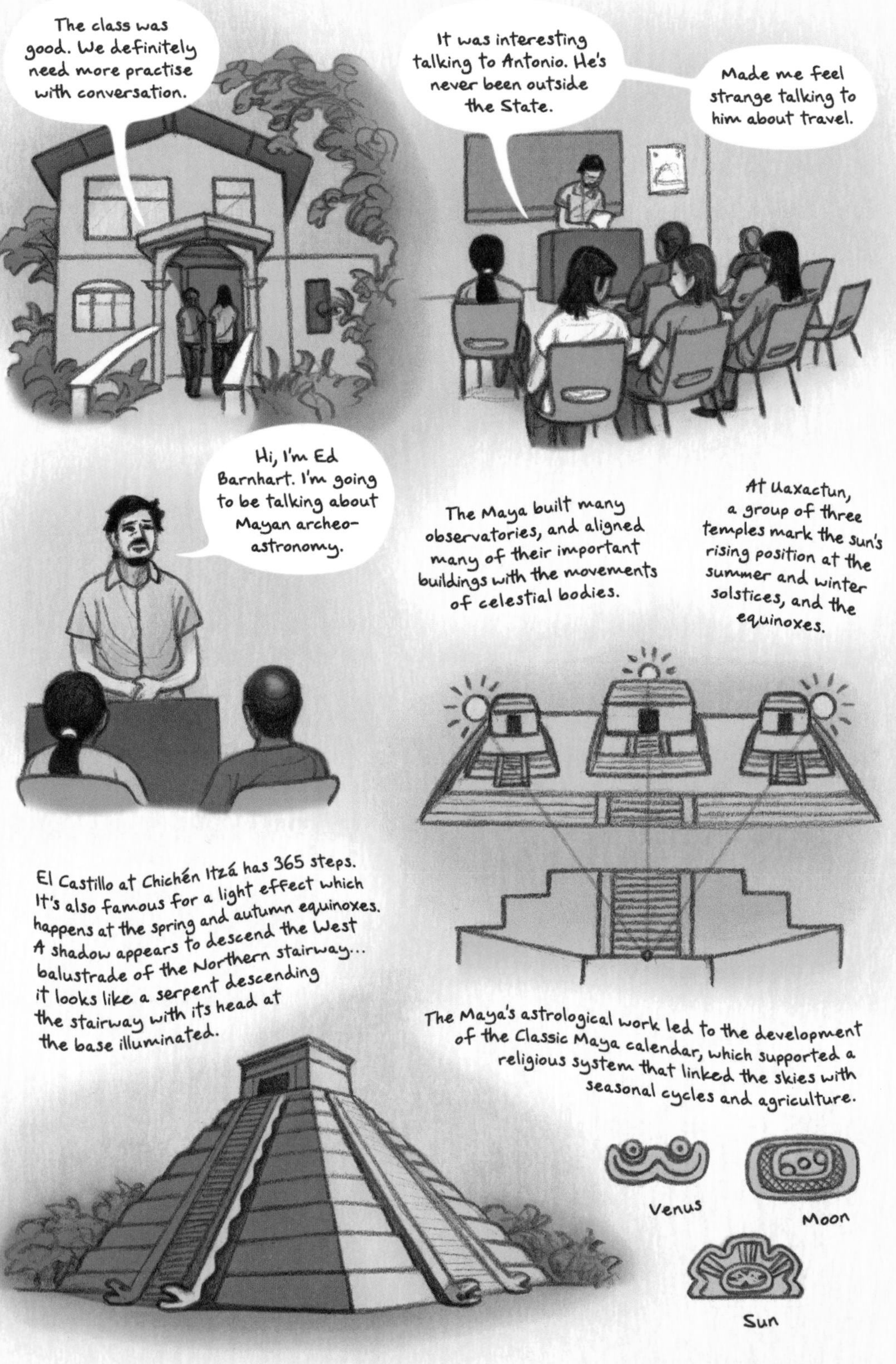

The class was good. We definitely need more practise with conversation.
It was interesting talking to Antonio. He's never been outside the State.
Made me feel strange talking to him about travel.
Hi, I'm Ed Barnhart. I'm going to be talking about Mayan archeo-astronomy.
The Maya built many observatories, and aligned many of their important buildings with the movements of celestial bodies.
At Uaxactun, a group of three temples mark the sun's rising position at the summer and winter solstices, and the equinoxes.
El Castillo at Chichén Itzá has 365 steps. It's also famous for a light effect which happens at the spring and autumn equinoxes. A shadow appears to descend the West balustrade of the Northern stairway... it looks like a serpent descending the stairway with its head at the base illuminated.
The Maya's astrological work led to the development of the Classic Maya calendar, which supported a religious system that linked the skies with seasonal cycles and agriculture.
Venus
Moon
Sun

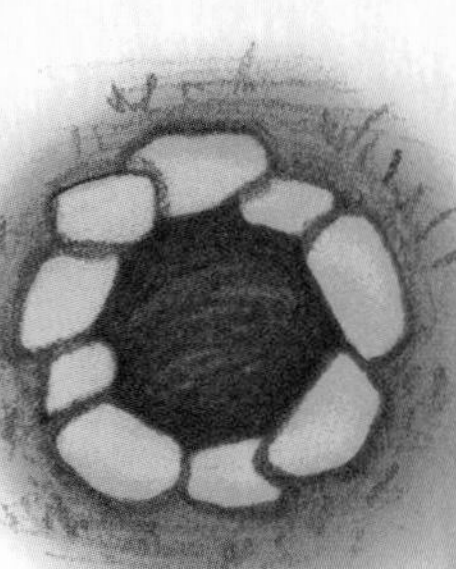

There are vertical 'zenith sighting tubes' at sites like Monte Alban and Xochicalco, which allow a shaft of light to illuminate underground rooms when the sun passes directly overhead. Zenith days were believed to herald rainfall and so were important for agriculture.

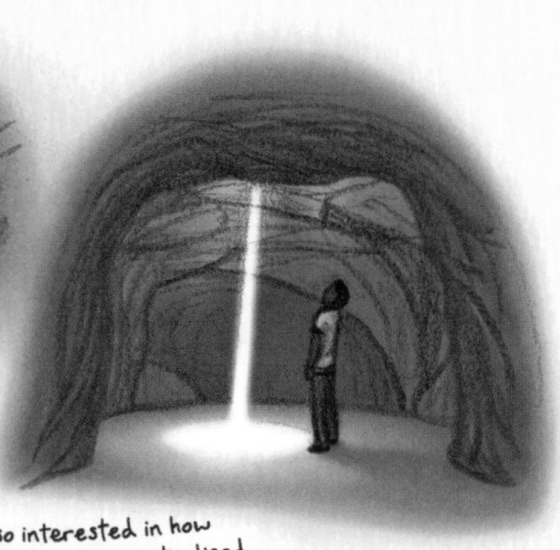

We're also interested in how Maya royalty may have ritualised celestial events to help cement their status as divine rulers. Transfers of power often seem to have been timed to coincide with solstices.

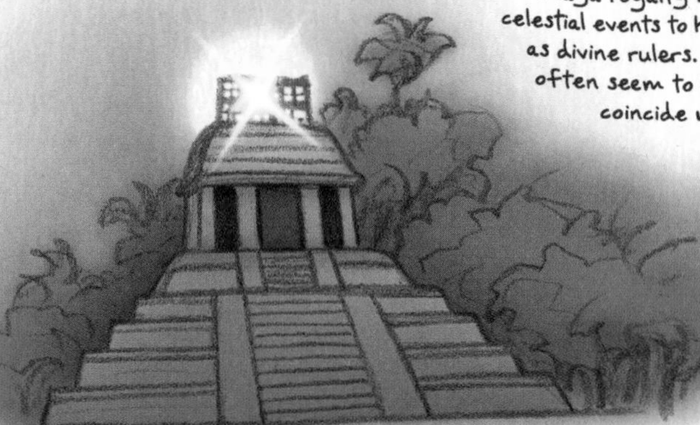

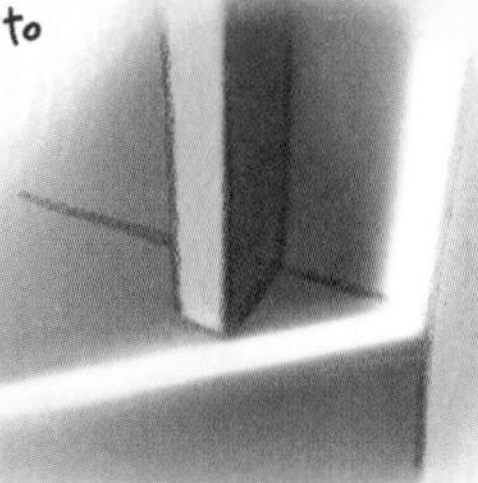

At Palenque, during the winter solstice the sun setting behind the Temple of the Inscriptions sends a shaft of light that mounts the terraces of the Temple of the Cross, enters the temple and illuminates a carving of God L. The transfer of royal power from Janahb Pakal to his son Kan B'ahlam II occurred under the aegis of God L.

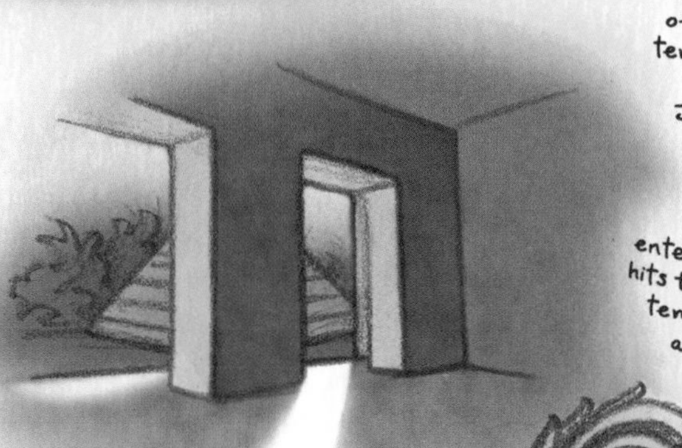

At sunset on the winter solstice, the Sun enters a doorway in the temple of Inscriptions, hits the back wall and, appears to descend the temple stairway into Pakal's tomb. His death and entry into the Underworld are thus equated with The Sun's 'death.'

We believe that these displays must have been incorporated into public ceremonies, designed to invoke awe in the people and confirm the power of the rulers.

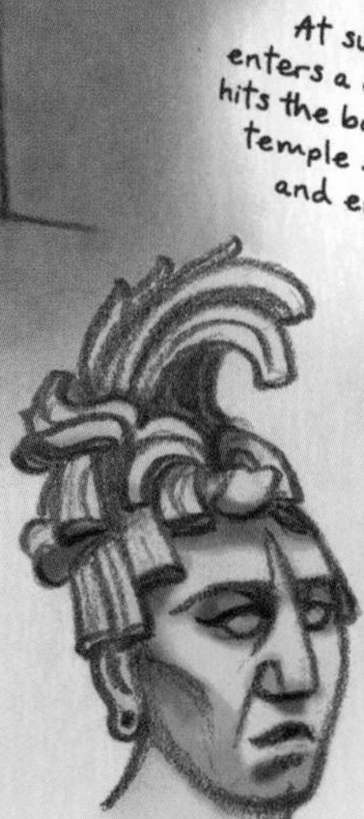

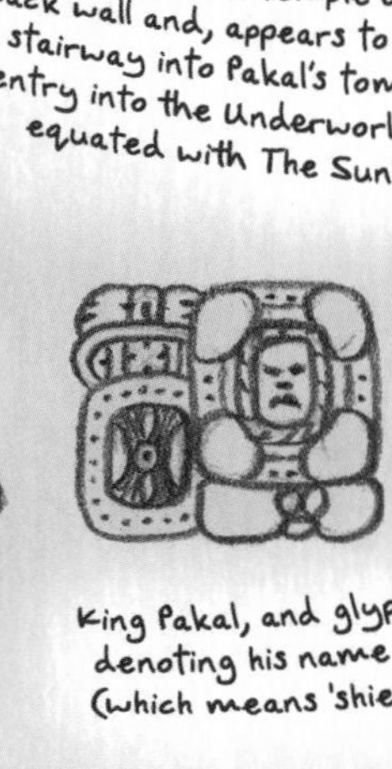

King Pakal, and glyphs denoting his name (which means 'shield')

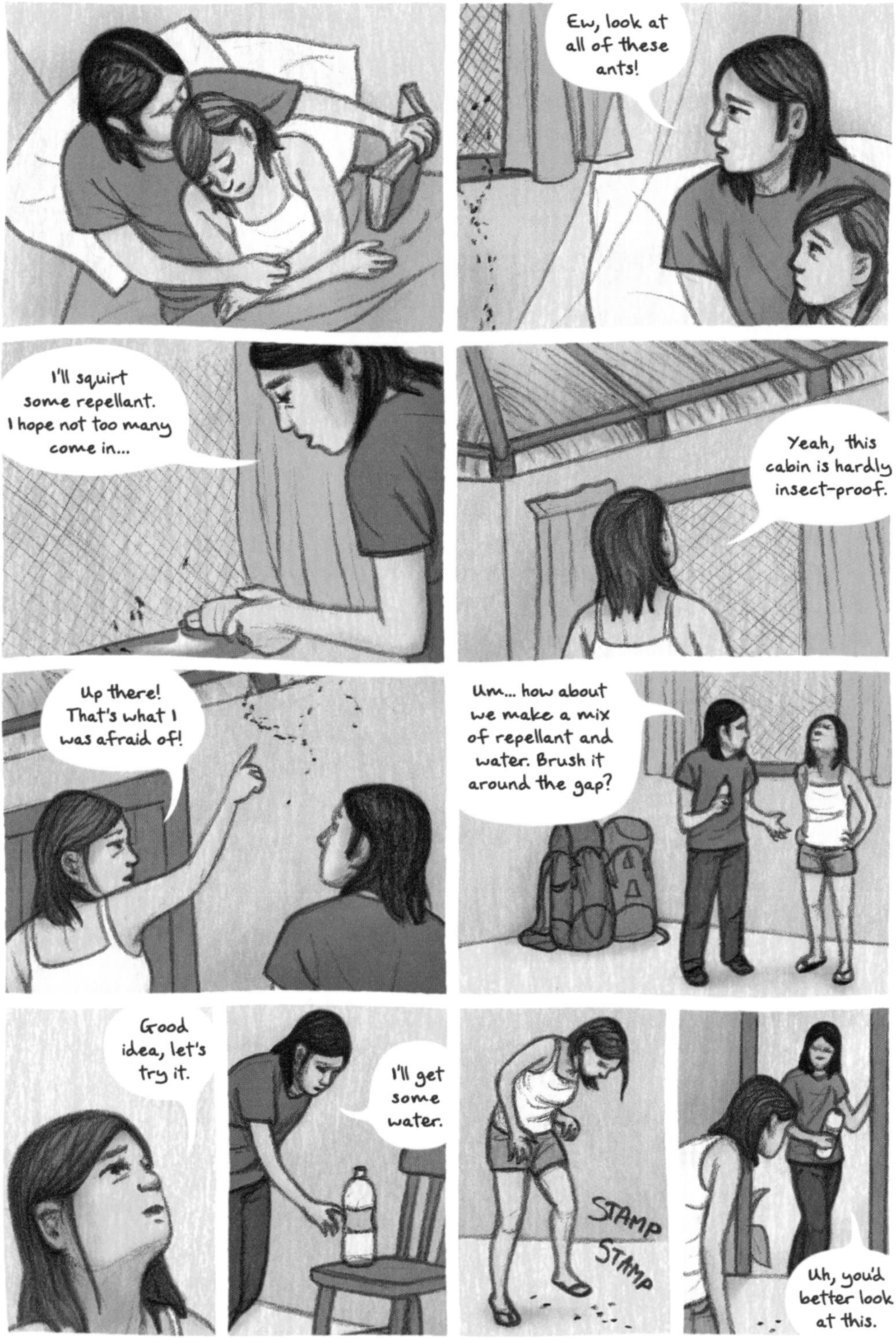
Ew, look at all of these ants!
I'll squirt some repellant. I hope not too many come in...
Yeah, this cabin is hardly insect-proof.
Up there! That's what I was afraid of!
Um... how about we make a mix of repellant and water. Brush it around the gap?
Good idea, let's try it.
I'll get some water.
STAMP
STAMP
Uh, you'd better look at this.

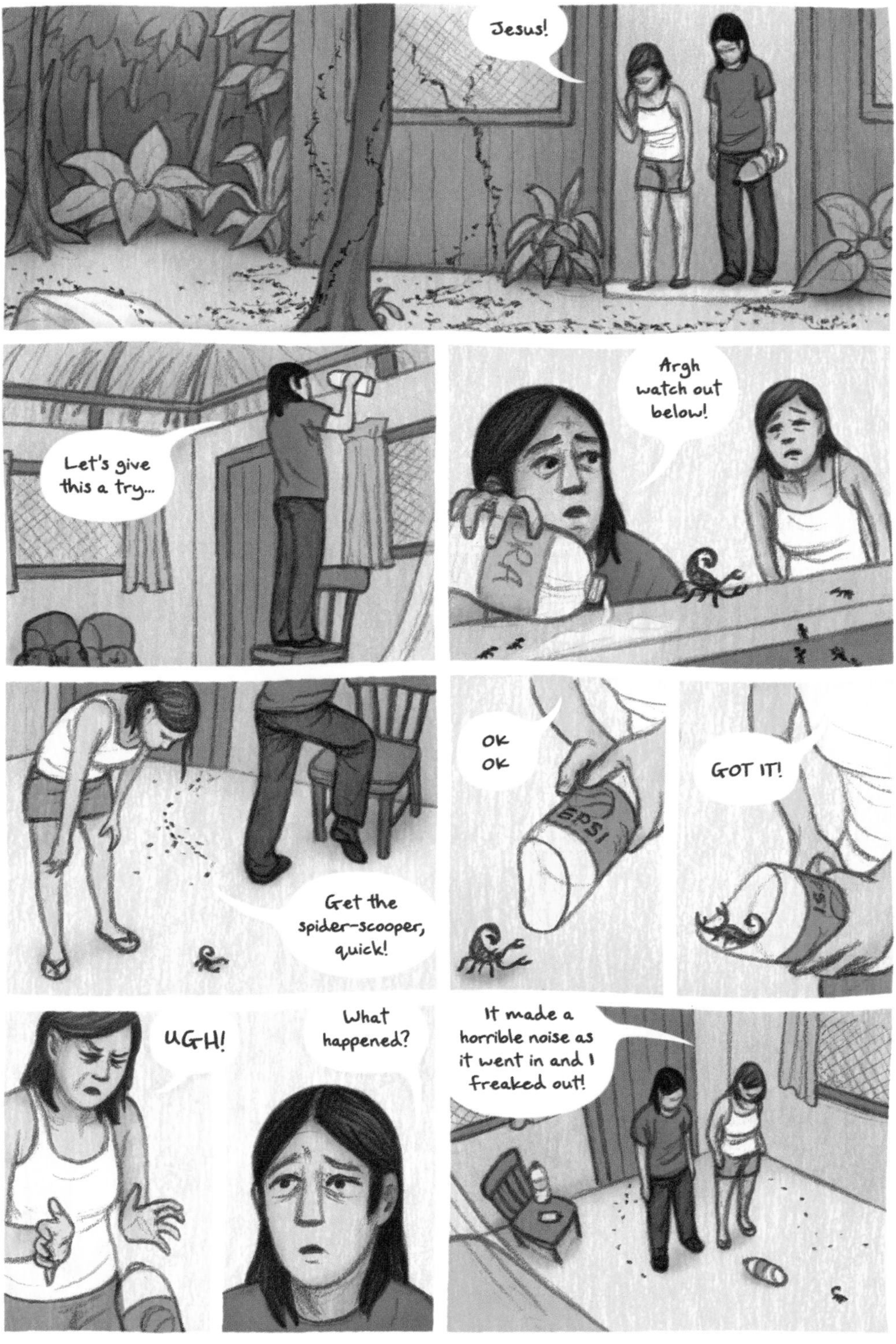
Jesus!
Let's give this a try...
Argh watch out below!
Get the spider-scooper, quick!
OK OK
GOT IT!
UGH!
What happened?
It made a horrible noise as it went in and I freaked out!

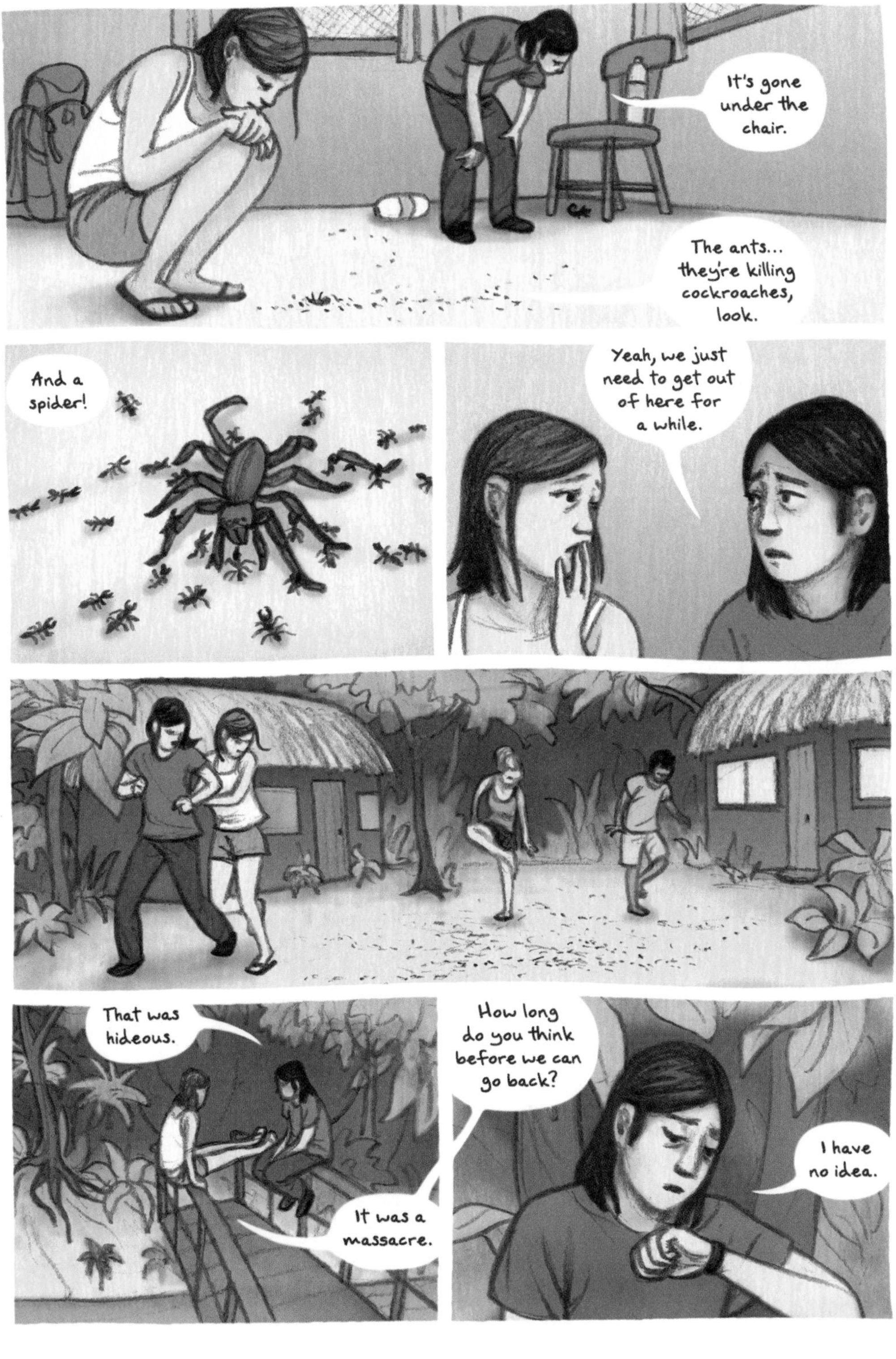
It's gone under the chair.
The ants... they're killing cockroaches, look.
And a spider!
Yeah, we just need to get out of here for a while.
That was hideous.
It was a massacre.
How long do you think before we can go back?
I have no idea.

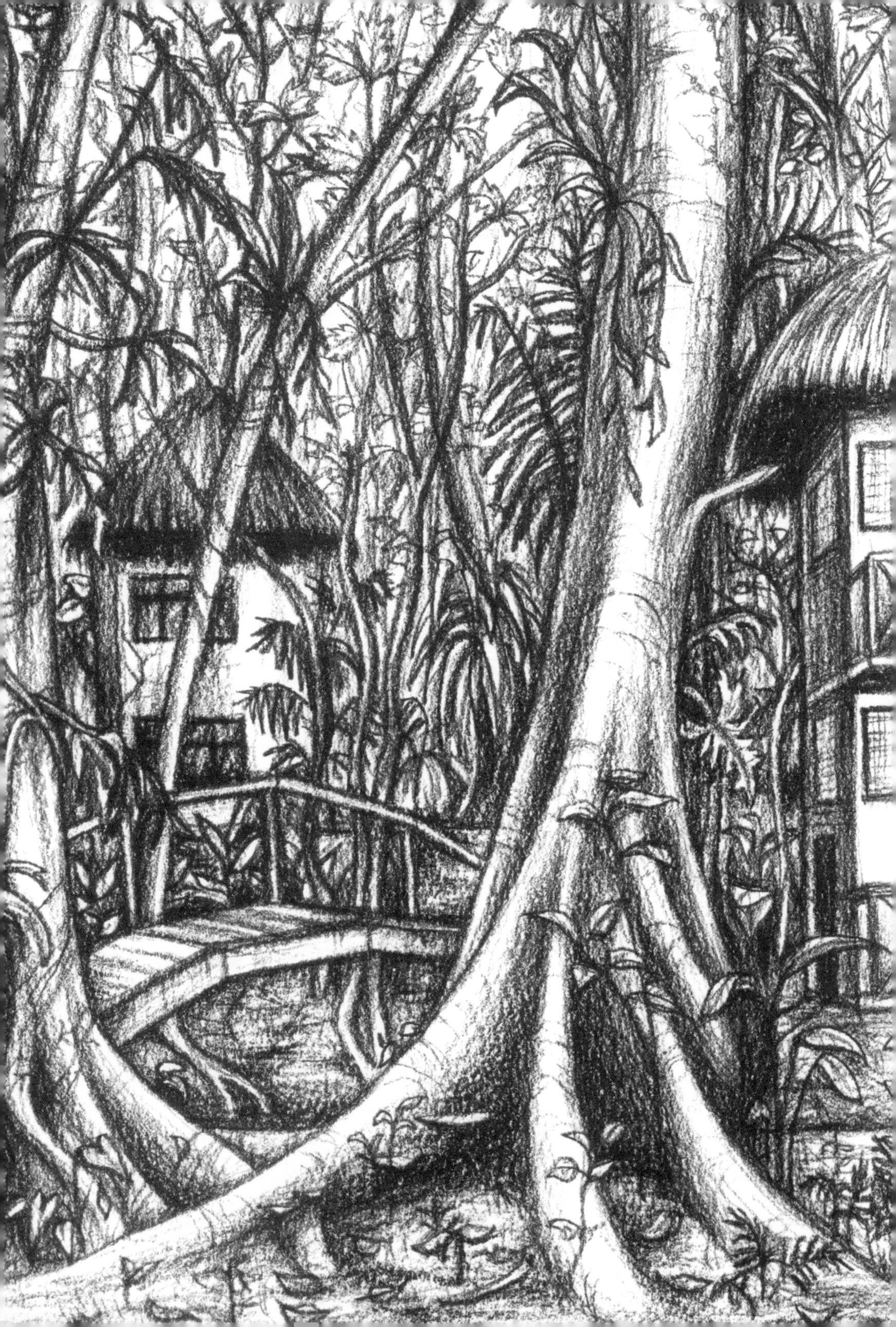

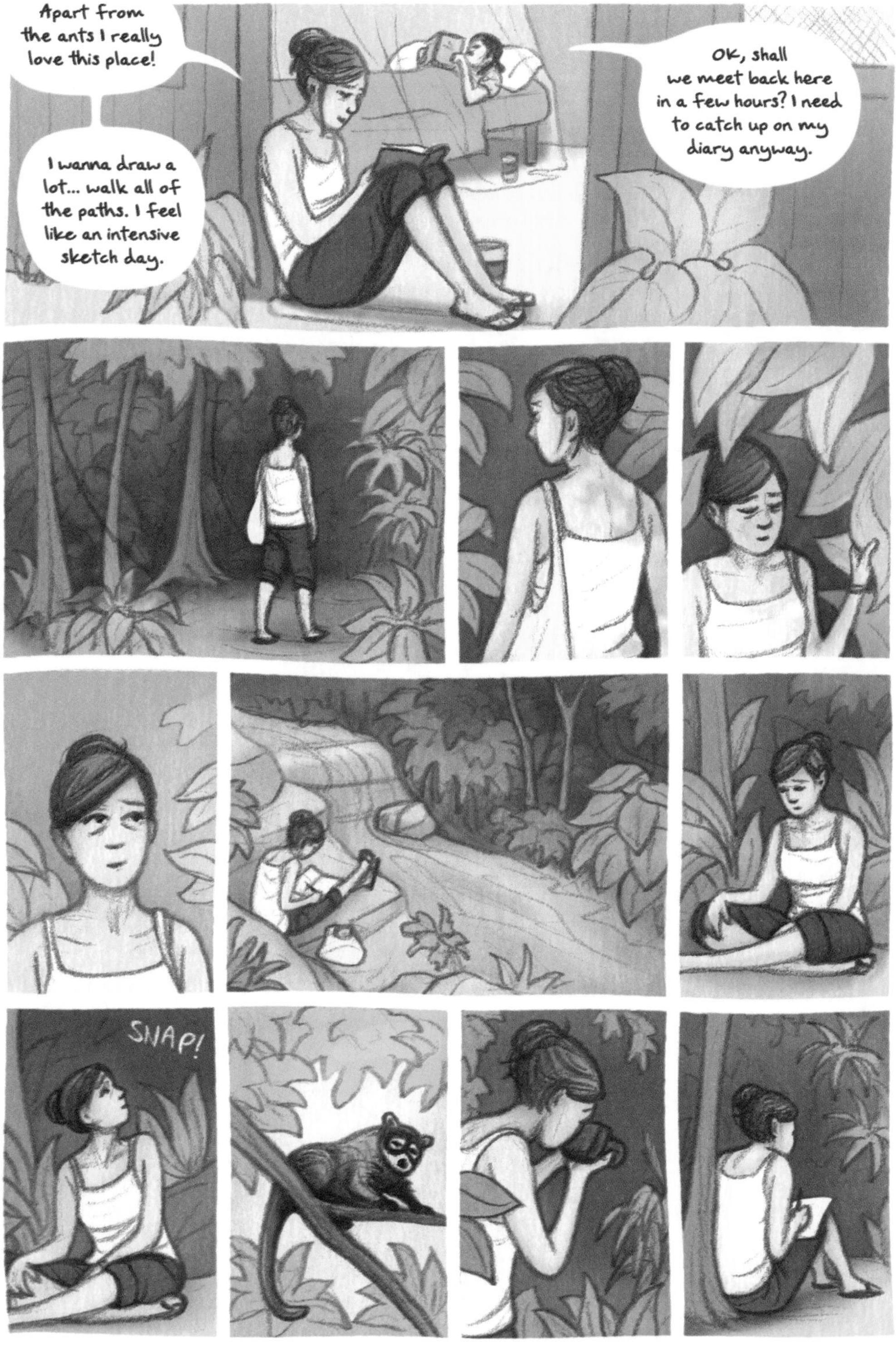
Apart from the ants I really love this place!
I wanna draw a lot... walk all of the paths. I feel like an intensive sketch day.
OK, shall we meet back here in a few hours? I need to catch up on my diary anyway.
SNAP!

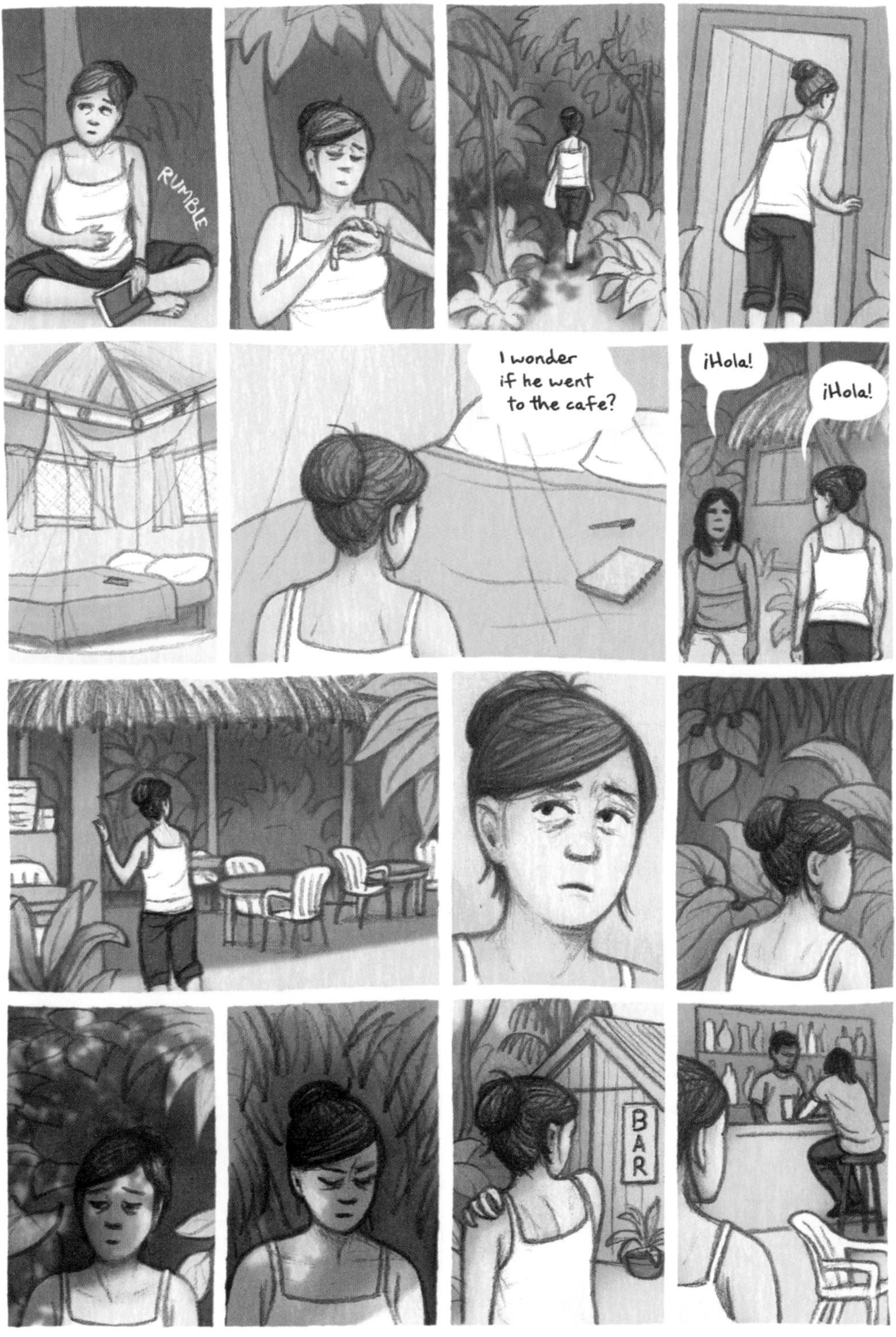
RUMBLE
I wonder if he went to the cafe?
¡Hola!
¡Hola!
BAR

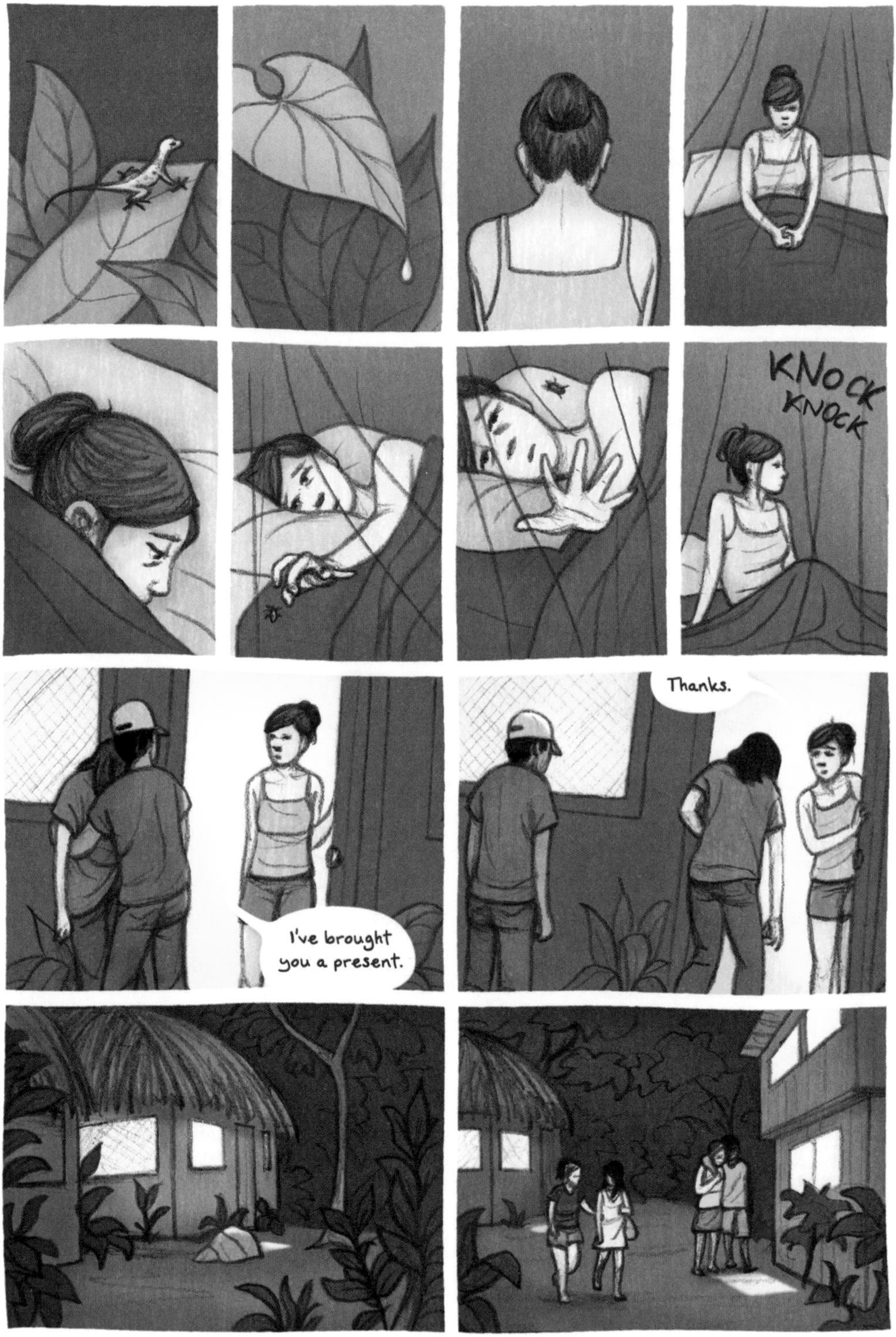
KNOCK
KNOCK
I've brought you a present.
Thanks.

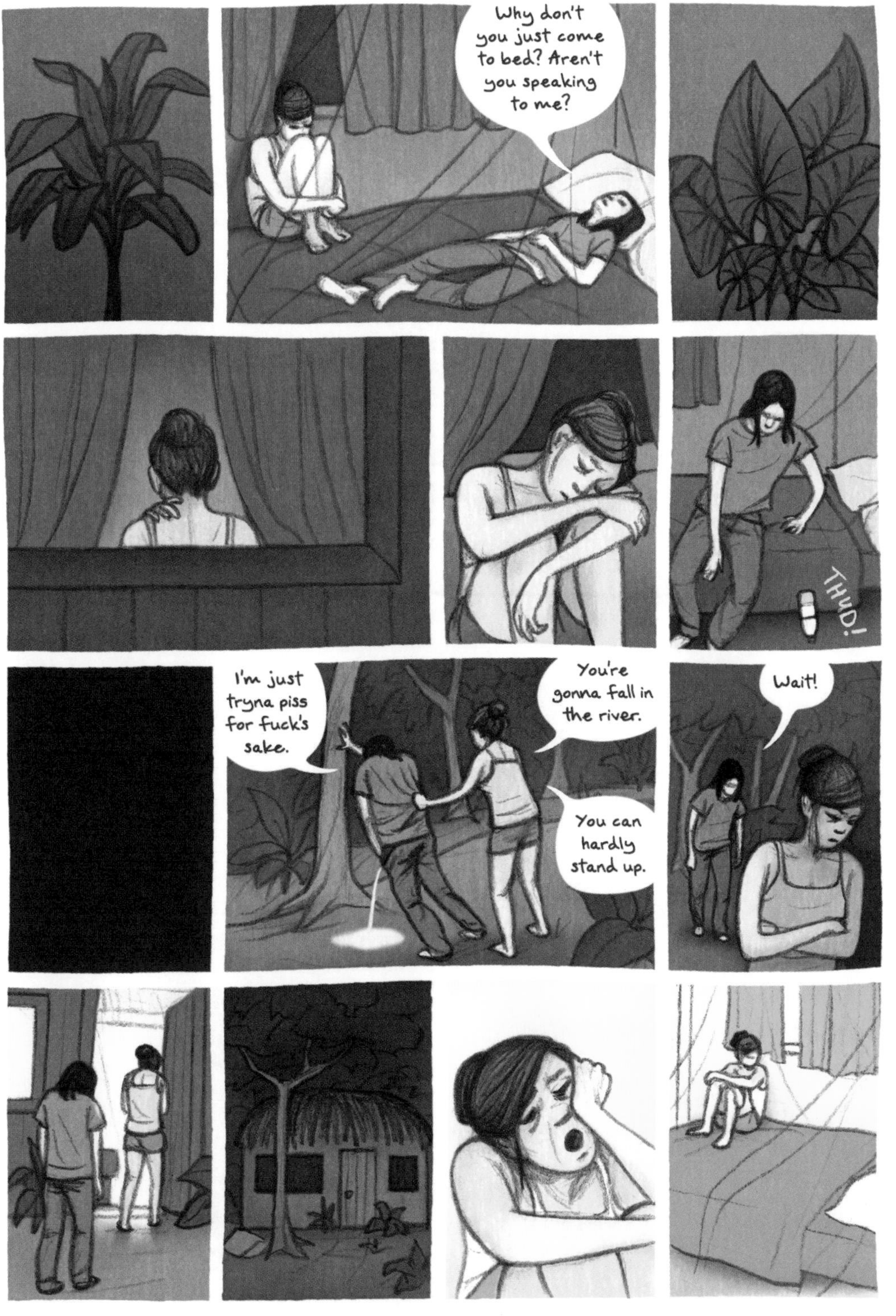
Why don't you just come to bed? Aren't you speaking to me?
THUD!
I'm just tryna piss for fuck's sake.
You're gonna fall in the river.
You can hardly stand up.
Wait!

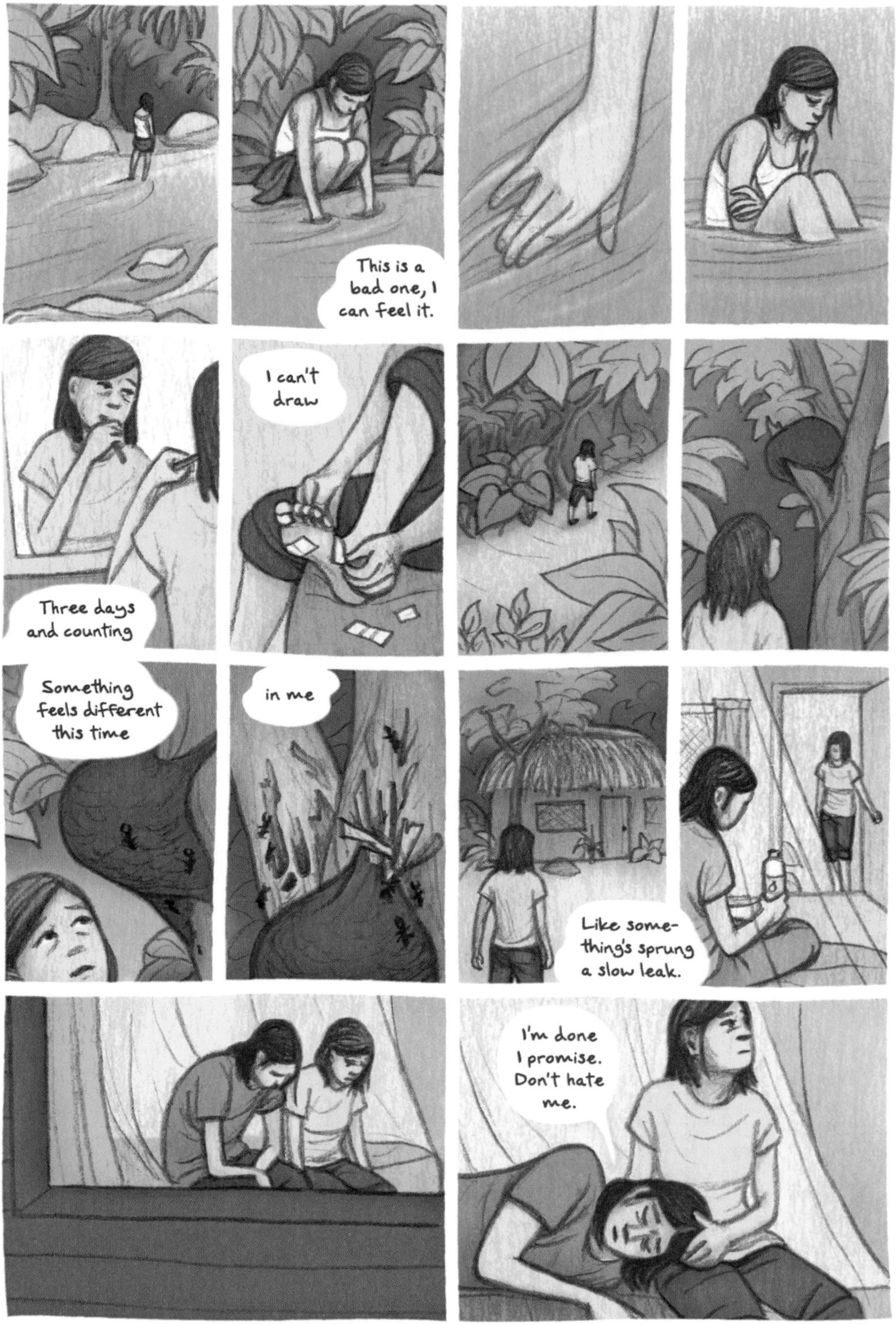
This is a bad one, I can feel it.
Three days and counting
I can't draw
Something feels different this time
in me
Like something's sprung a slow leak.
I'm done I promise. Don't hate me.

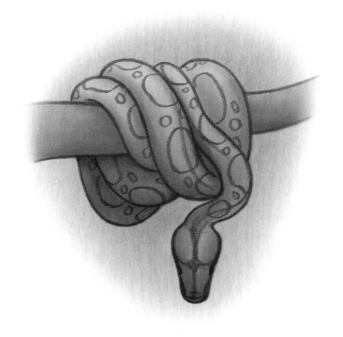

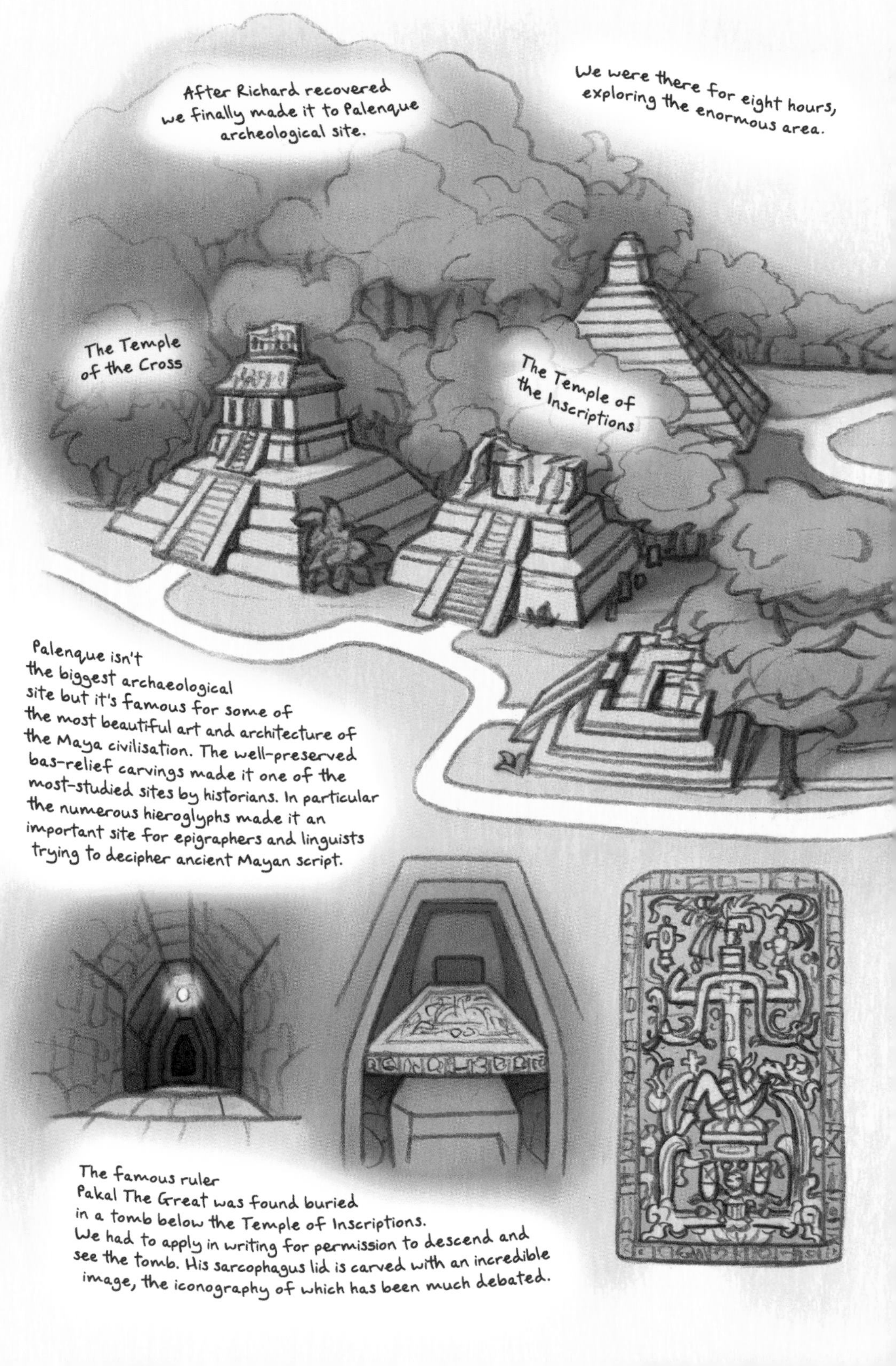
After Richard recovered we finally made it to Palenque archeological site.
We were there for eight hours, exploring the enormous area.
The Temple of the Cross
The Temple of the Inscriptions
Palenque isn't the biggest archaeological site but it's famous for some of the most beautiful art and architecture of the Maya civilisation. The well-preserved bas-relief carvings made it one of the most-studied sites by historians. In particular the numerous hieroglyphs made it an important site for epigraphers and linguists trying to decipher ancient Mayan script.
The famous ruler Pakal The Great was found buried in a tomb below the Temple of Inscriptions. We had to apply in writing for permission to descend and see the tomb. His sarcophagus lid is carved with an incredible image, the iconography of which has been much debated.

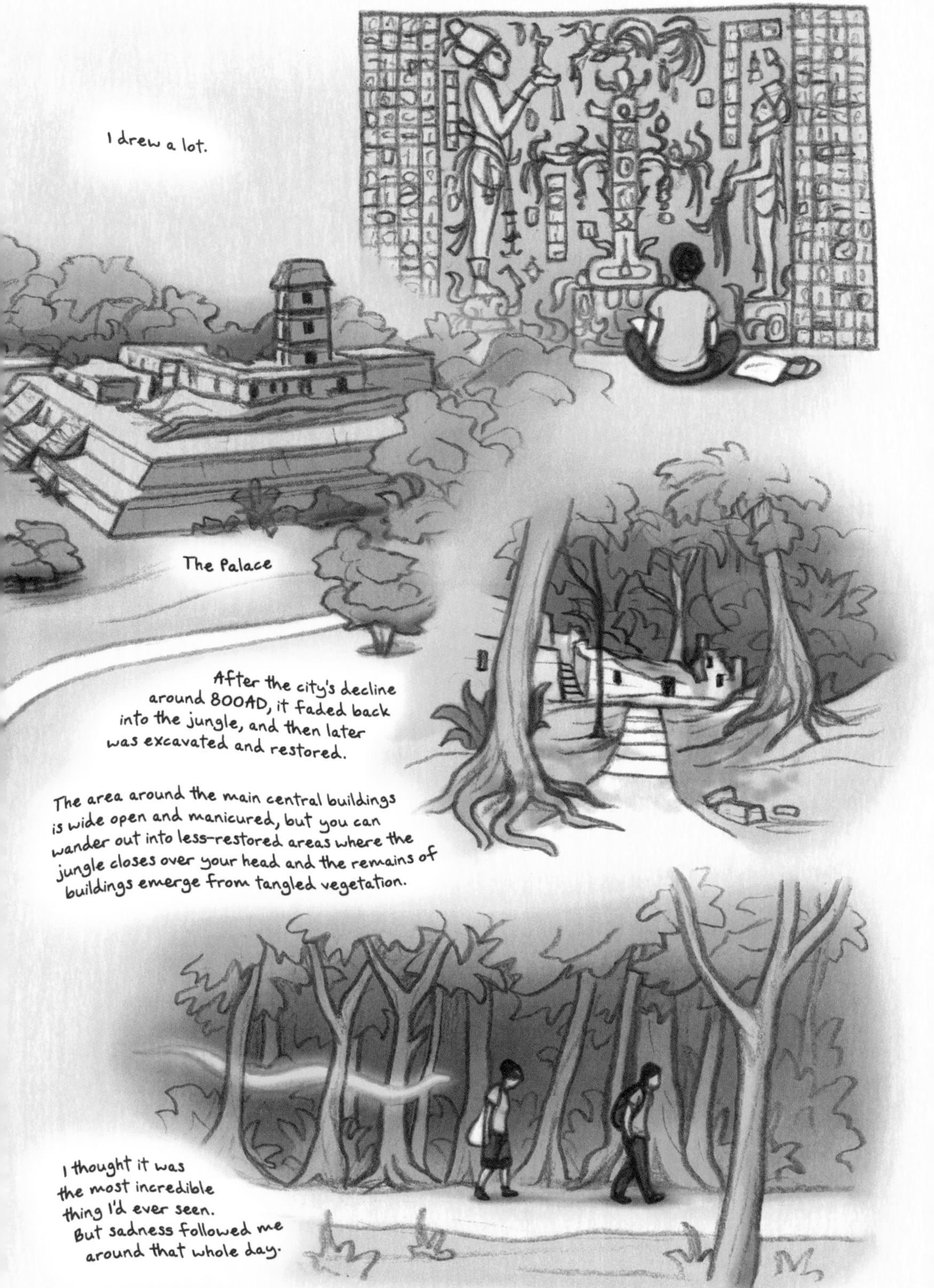

I drew a lot.
The Palace
After the city's decline around 800AD, it faded back into the jungle, and then later was excavated and restored.
The area around the main central buildings is wide open and manicured, but you can wander out into less-restored areas where the jungle closes over your head and the remains of buildings emerge from tangled vegetation.
I thought it was the most incredible thing I'd ever seen. But sadness followed me around that whole day.

Maya art and script

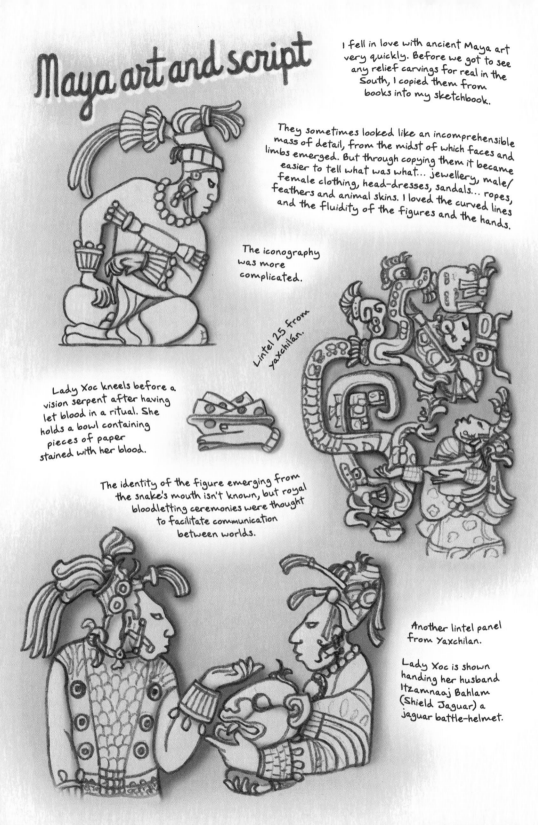

I fell in love with ancient Maya art very quickly. Before we got to see any relief carvings for real in the South, I copied them from books into my sketchbook.

They sometimes looked like an incomprehensible mass of detail, from the midst of which faces and limbs emerged. But through copying them it became easier to tell what was what... jewellery, male/female clothing, head-dresses, sandals... ropes, feathers and animal skins. I loved the curved lines and the fluidity of the figures and the hands.

The iconography was more complicated.

Lintel 25 from Yaxchilán.

Lady Xoc kneels before a vision serpent after having let blood in a ritual. She holds a bowl containing pieces of paper stained with her blood.

The identity of the figure emerging from the snake's mouth isn't known, but royal bloodletting ceremonies were thought to facilitate communication between worlds.

Another lintel panel from Yaxchilan.

Lady Xoc is shown handing her husband Itzamnaaj Bahlam (Shield Jaguar) a jaguar battle-helmet.

Maya script dates from the 3rd century BC and was used right up until the Spanish conquest. It used logograms (characters like Egyptian hieroglyphs/Japanese Kanji,) and syllabic glyphs. About 90% of it can now be translated, with varying degrees of certainty.

Two different ways of writing the word 'jaguar.' First as a logogram representing the entire word with the single glyph B'ALAM. Then phonetically using the three syllable signs b'a, la, and ma.

As well as stone carvings and painted ceramics, Maya scribes wrote in folded books made of bark paper (codices.) Spanish bishop Diego de Landa Calderón collected and destroyed a massive number of the codices in his campaign to eradicate pagan material. Only four survived, the most famous being the Dresden Codex – a book from the Yucatán which related local history and astronomical tables.

"Now it still ripples, now it still murmurs, ripples, it still sighs, still hums, and it is empty under the sky."

Few texts documenting early mesoamerican mythology/religion survived the conquest, but the Popul Vuh (a mytho-historical narrative of the K'iche' Maya) was preserved by Francisco Ximénez, a Dominican priest who transcribed and translated it while living in Guatemala.

Another famous text that survived is The Books of Chilam Balam, from the Yucatán (author/s unknown.) They include literal content like medical texts and records of daily life, mixed with esoteric riddles and metaphor, making them hard to interpret.

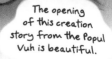

The opening of this creation story from the Popul Vuh is beautiful.

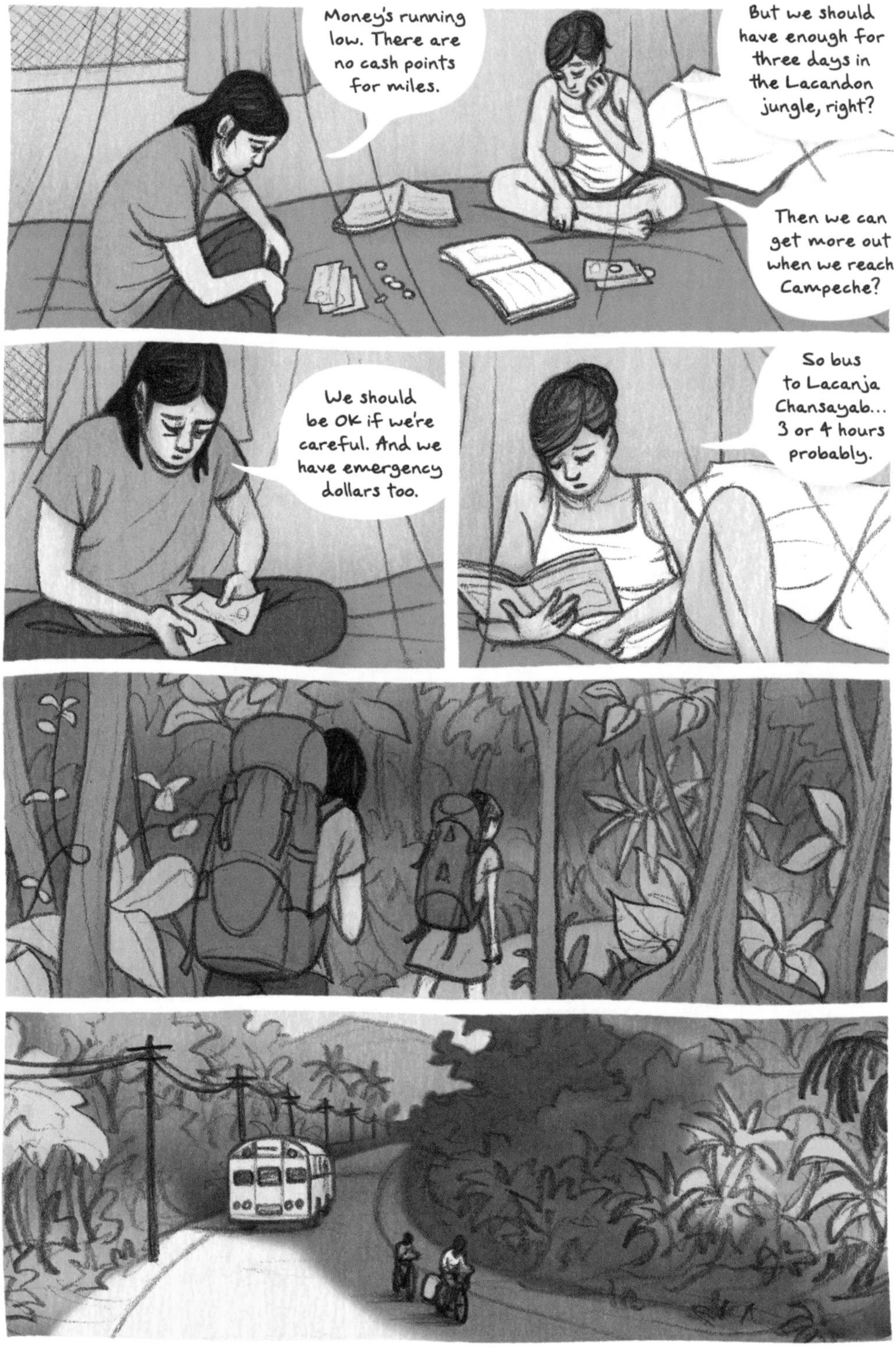
Money's running low. There are no cash points for miles.
But we should have enough for three days in the Lacandon jungle, right?
Then we can get more out when we reach Campeche?
We should be OK if we're careful. And we have emergency dollars too.
So bus to Lacanja Chansayab... 3 or 4 hours probably.

The Usamacinta Valley and the Selva Lacandona

Continuing through verdant rural Chiapas, we headed towards the Lacandón jungle on the border with Guatemala. We planned to stay in the Lacandón village of Lacanja Chansayab and see the ruins of Bonampak and Yaxchilán.

The area's known for its biodiversity, containing 1500 species of trees, 33% of Mexico's bird species and 25% of Mexico's animal species. It's one of the last Mexican forest areas large enough to support jaguars.

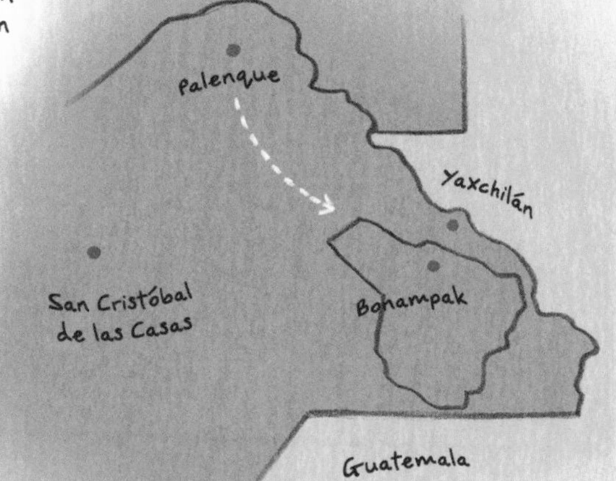

Palenque
Yaxchilán
San Cristóbal de las Casas
Bonampak
Guatemala

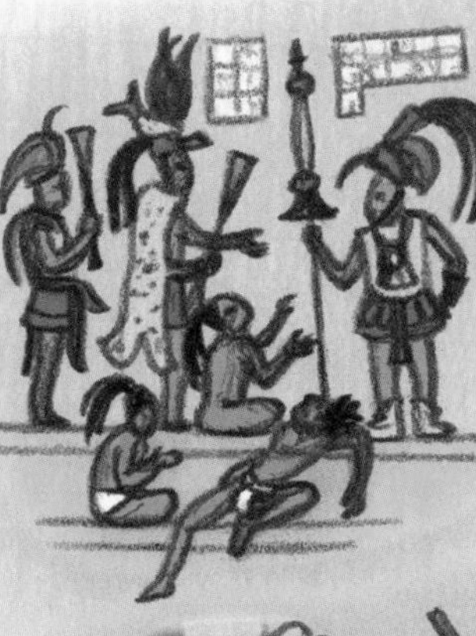

The archeological site of Bonampak is a relatively small one, that became a satellite city of the much larger Yaxchilán (one of the most powerful Maya city-states, and a rival of Palenque.) In spite of its small size it's significant for its famous murals, painted at the end of the 8th Century AD.

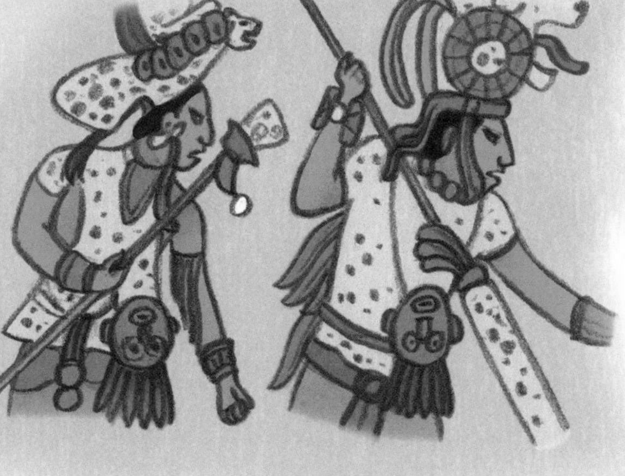

Now very degraded and hard to make out, the murals depict scenes of tribute, dressing, war, music, dancing and ritual bloodletting across the walls of three rooms.

The ruins were first seen by outsiders from the US in 1946. Lacandón people were still worshipping in the ruined city. Similarly at other archeological sites across Mexico and Central America, Maya communities claim the ruins as part of their heritage and use them in their religious practise.

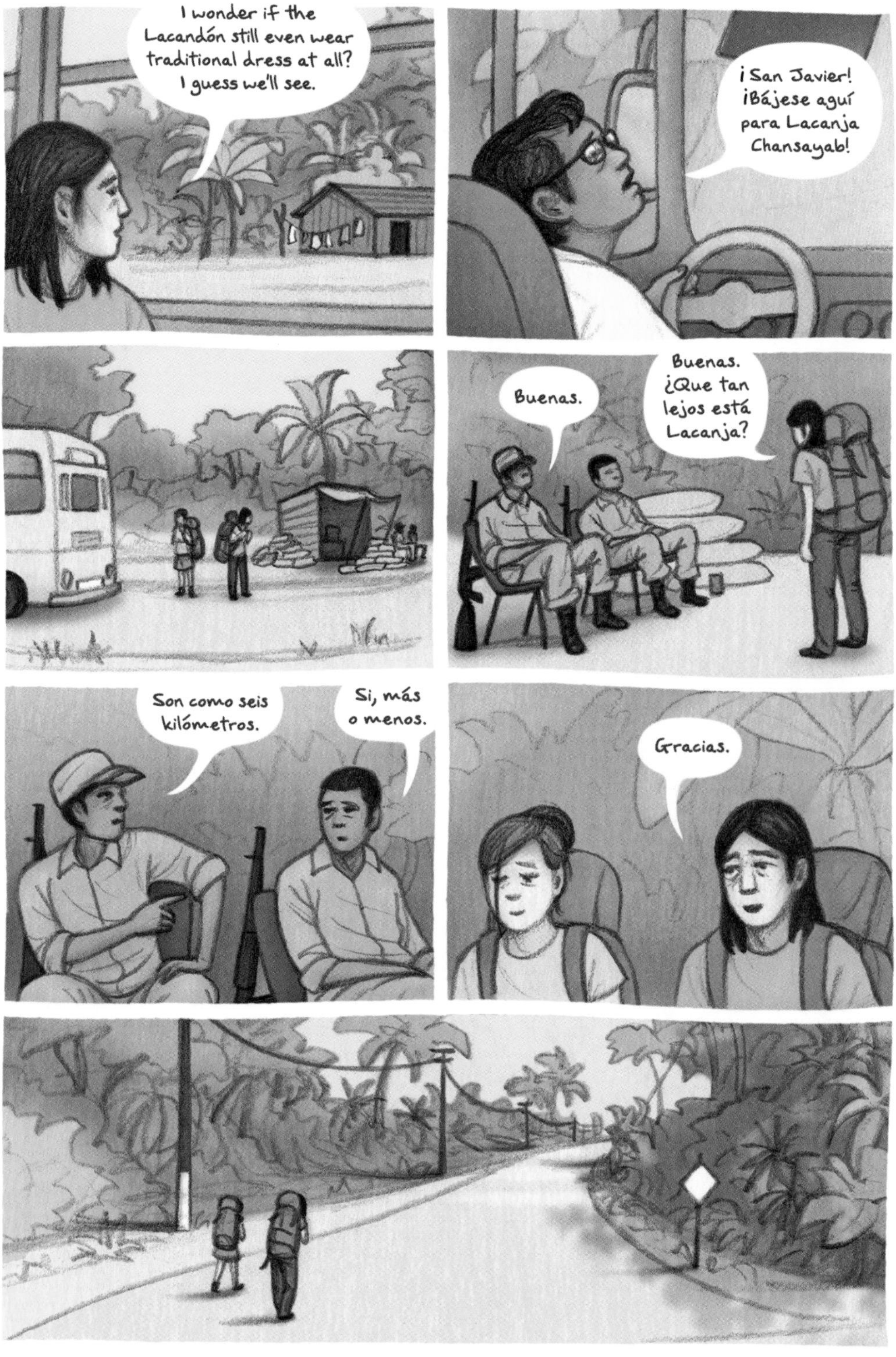
I wonder if the Lacandón still even wear traditional dress at all? I guess we'll see.
¡San Javier! ¡Bájese aguí para Lacanja Chansayab!
Buenas.
Buenas. ¿Que tan lejos está Lacanja?
Son como seis kilómetros.
Si, más o menos.
Gracias.

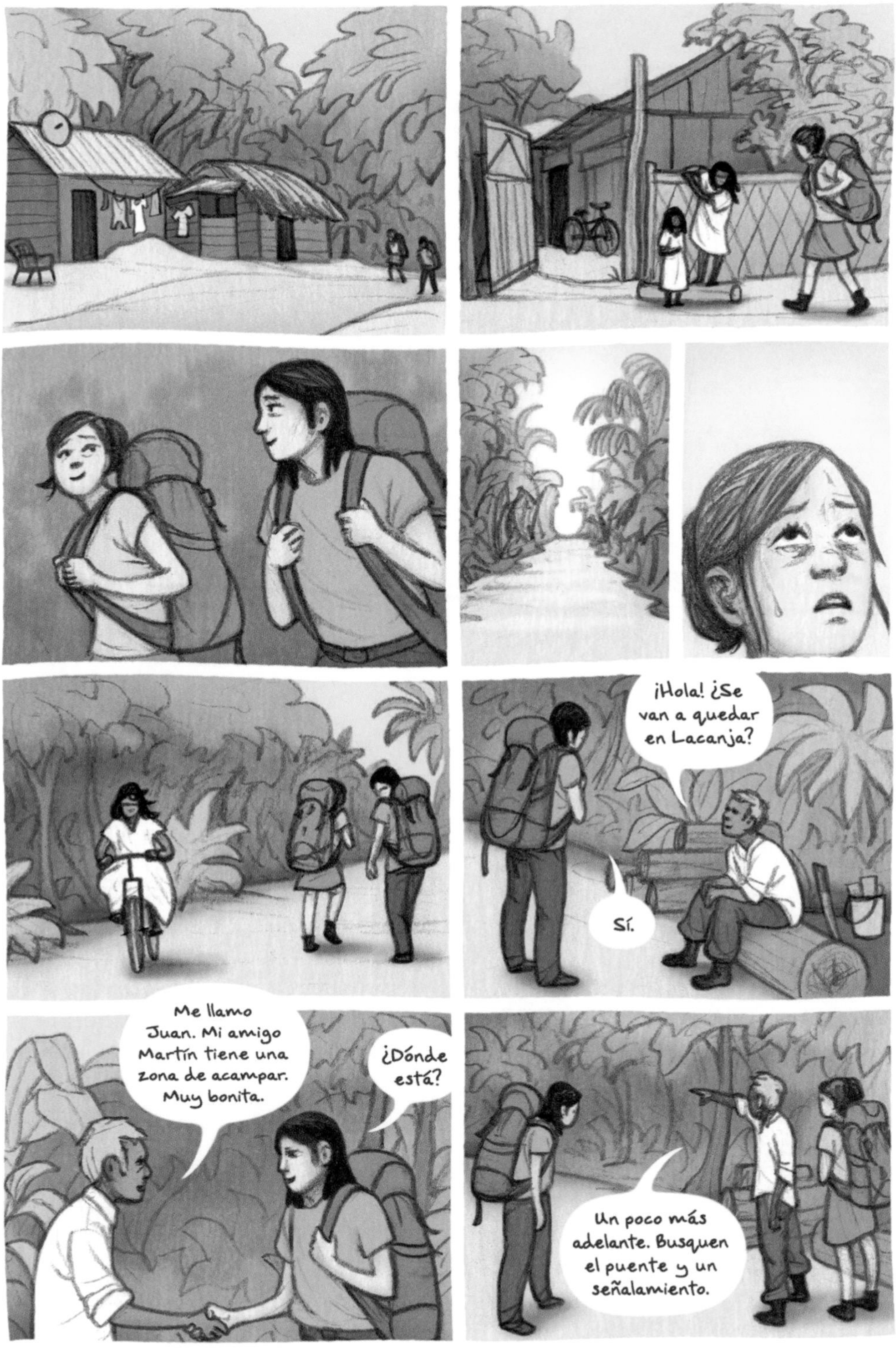
¡Hola! ¿Se van a quedar en Lacanja?
Sí.
Me llamo Juan. Mi amigo Martín tiene una zona de acampar. Muy bonita.
¿Dónde está?
Un poco más adelante. Busquen el puente y un señalamiento.

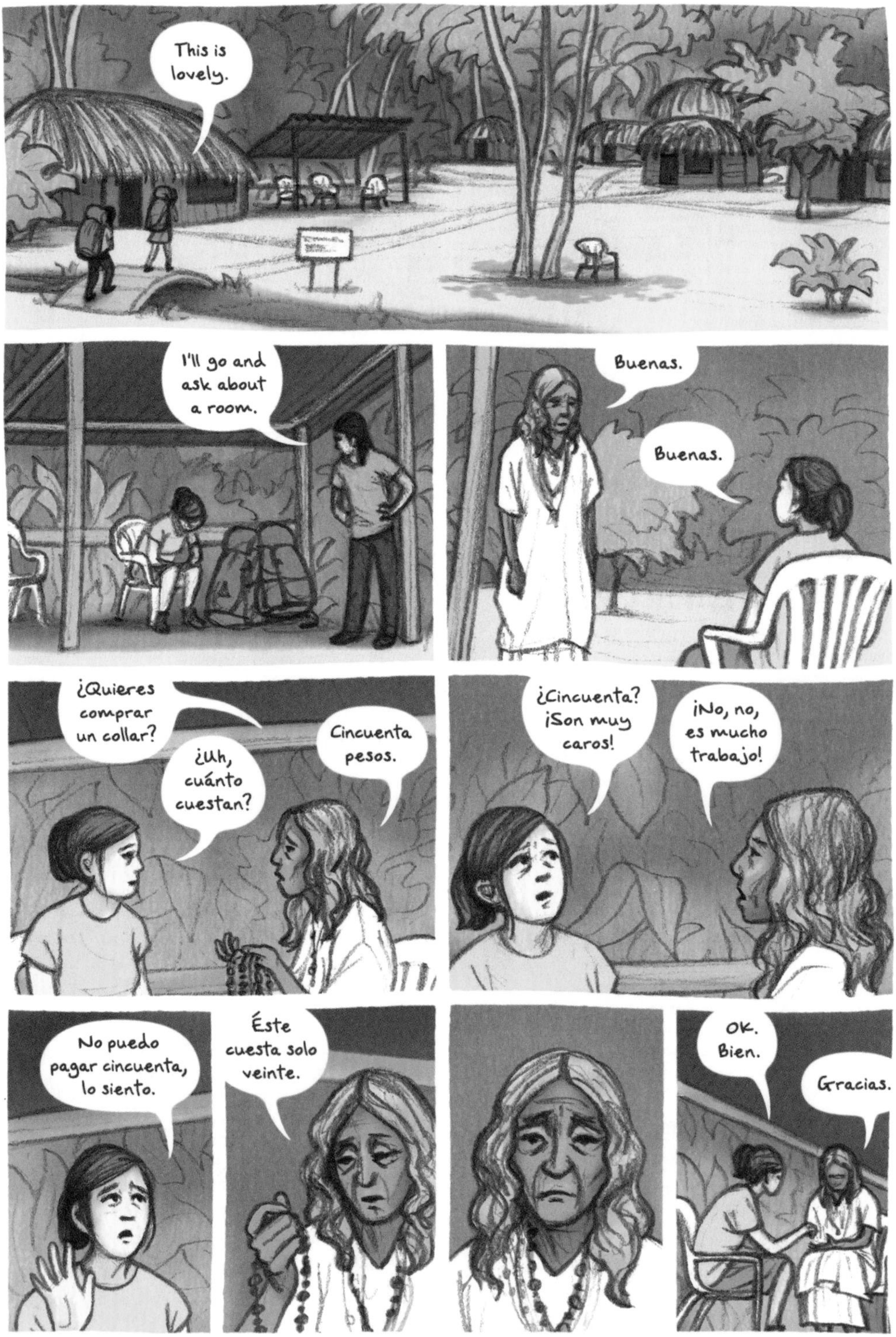
This is lovely.
I'll go and ask about a room.
Buenas.
Buenas.
¿Quieres comprar un collar?
¿Uh, cuánto cuestan?
Cincuenta pesos.
¿Cincuenta? ¡Son muy caros!
¡No, no, es mucho trabajo!
No puedo pagar cincuenta, lo siento.
Éste cuesta solo veinte.
OK. Bien.
Gracias.

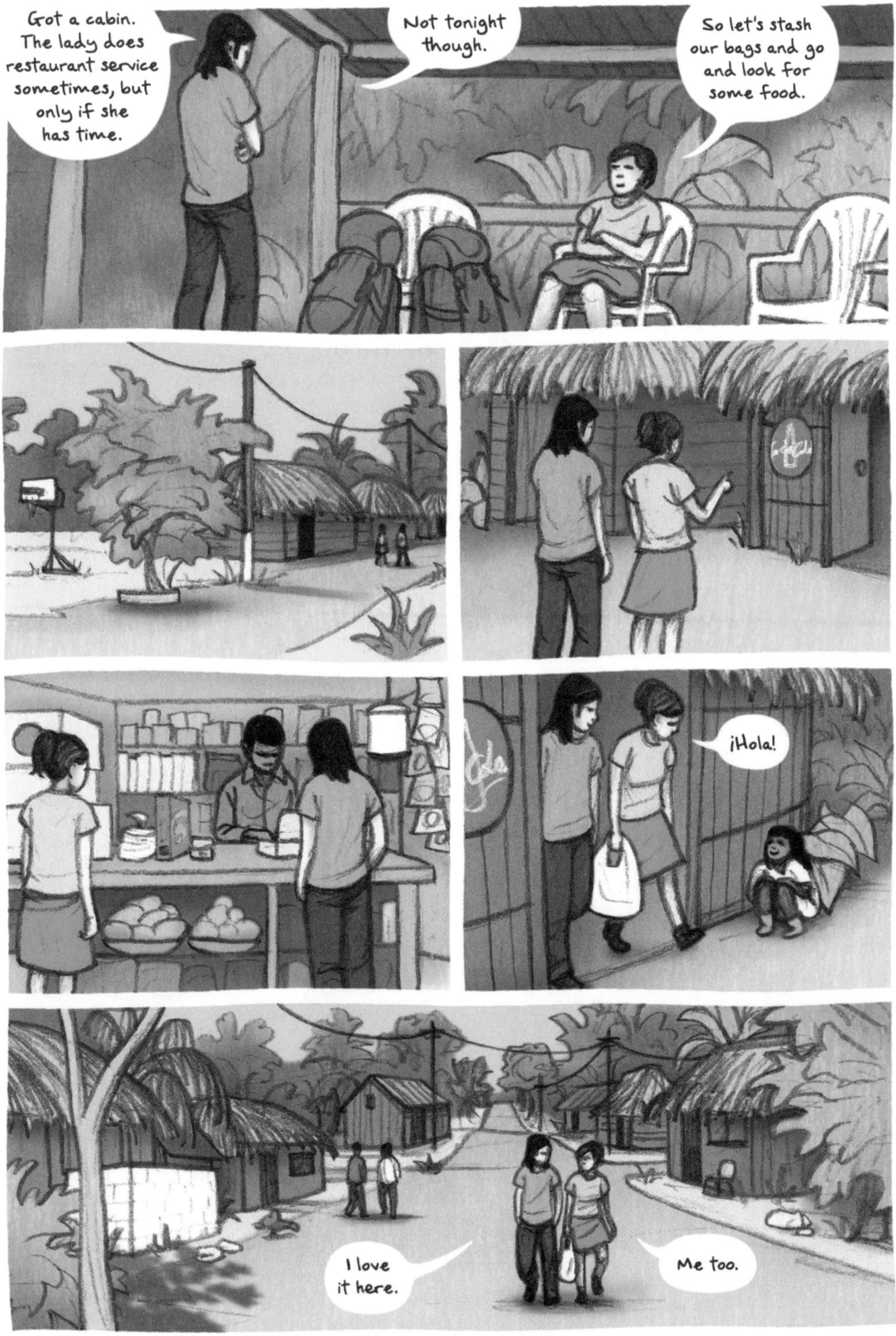

Got a cabin. The lady does restaurant service sometimes, but only if she has time.
Not tonight though.
So let's stash our bags and go and look for some food.
¡Hola!
I love it here.
Me too.

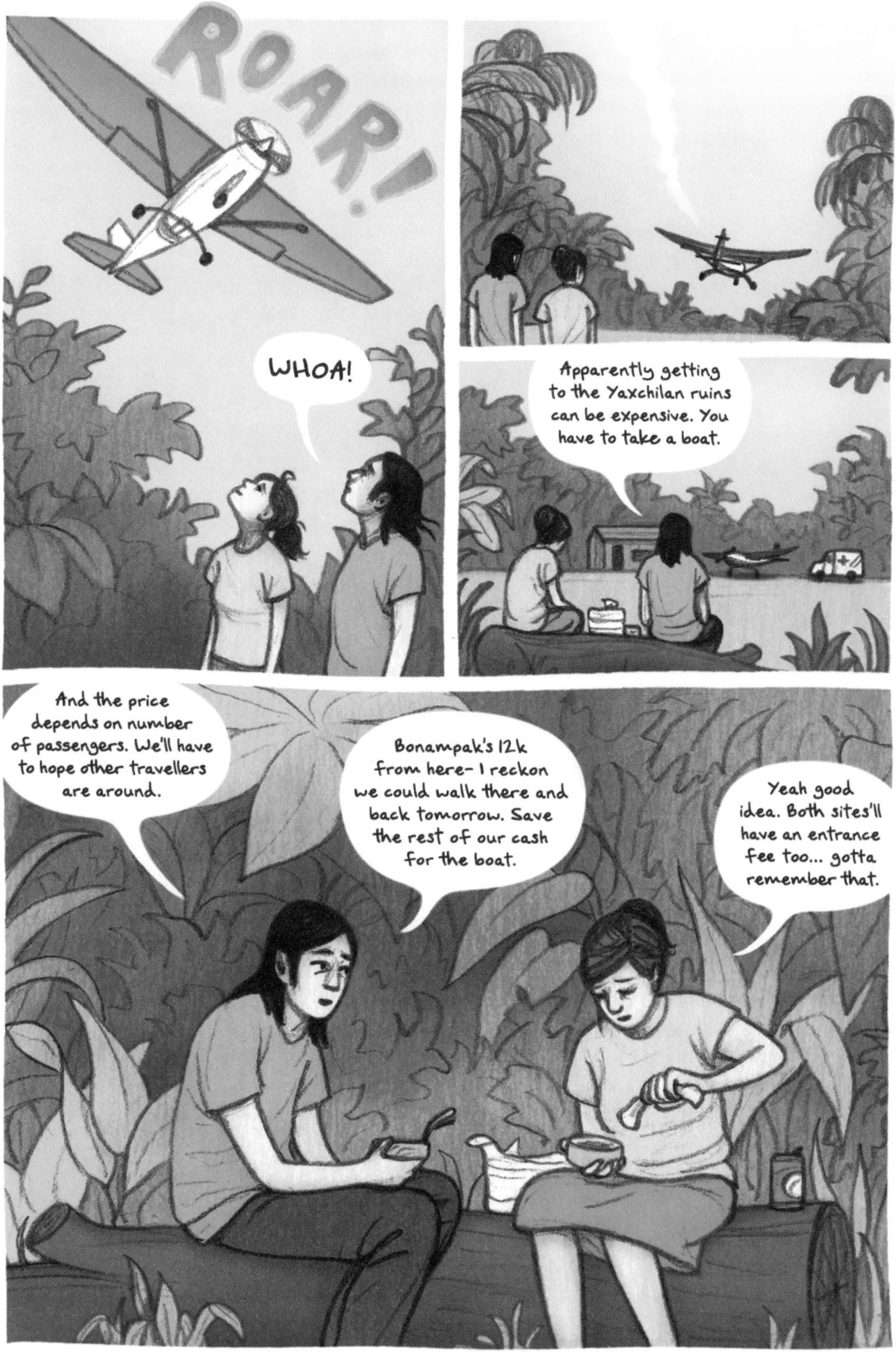
ROAR!
WHOA!
Apparently getting to the Yaxchilan ruins can be expensive. You have to take a boat.
And the price depends on number of passengers. We'll have to hope other travellers are around.
Bonampak's 12k from here- I reckon we could walk there and back tomorrow. Save the rest of our cash for the boat.
Yeah good idea. Both sites'll have an entrance fee too... gotta remember that.

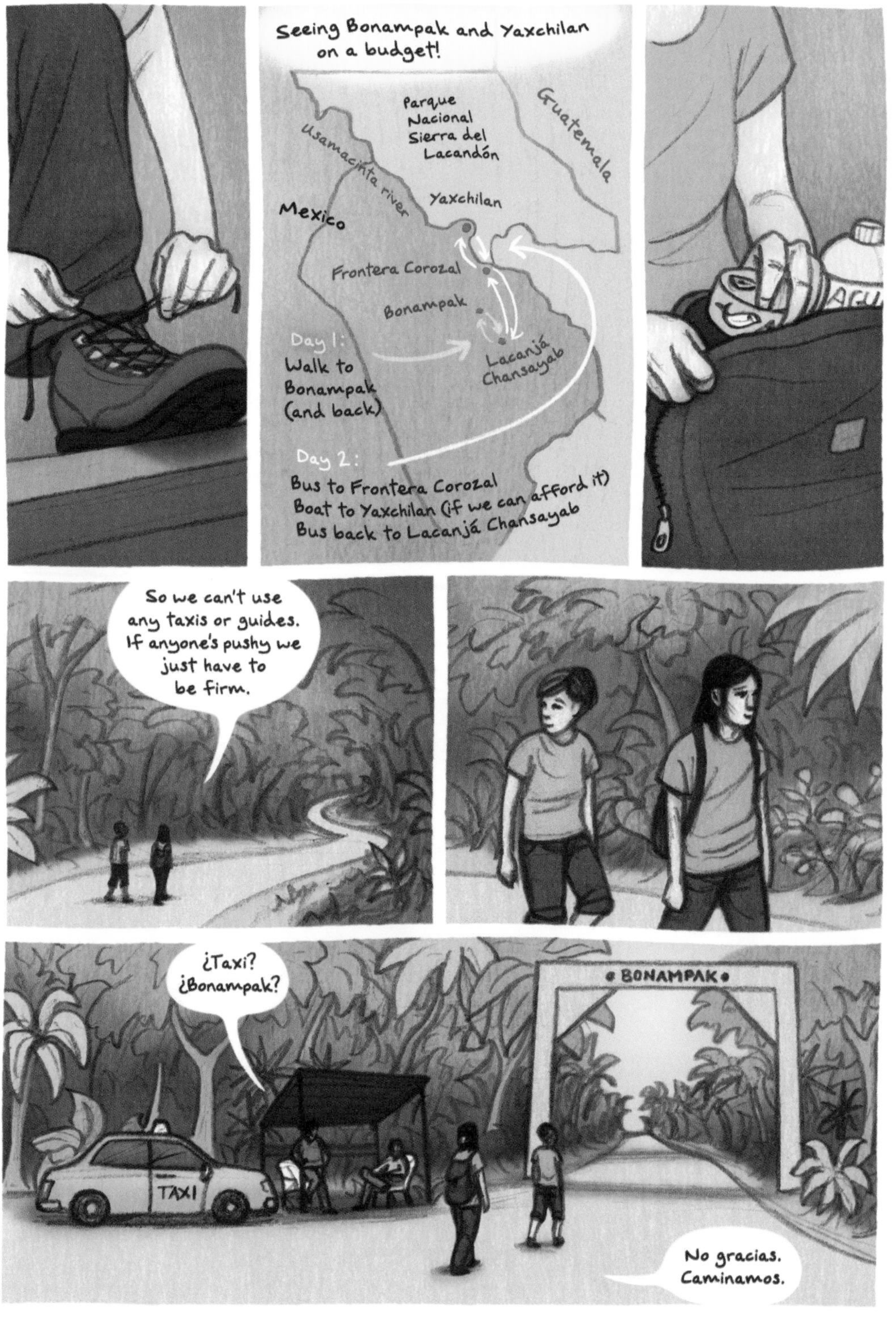
Seeing Bonampak and Yaxchilan on a budget!
Parque Nacional Sierra del Lacandón
Guatemala
Usamacinta river
Mexico
Yaxchilan
Frontera Corozal
Bonampak
Lacanjá Chansayab
Day 1:
Walk to Bonampak (and back)
Day 2:
Bus to Frontera Corozal
Boat to Yaxchilan (if we can afford it)
Bus back to Lacanjá Chansayab
So we can't use any taxis or guides. If anyone's pushy we just have to be firm.
¿Taxi? ¿Bonampak?
BONAMPAK
TAXI
No gracias. Caminamos.

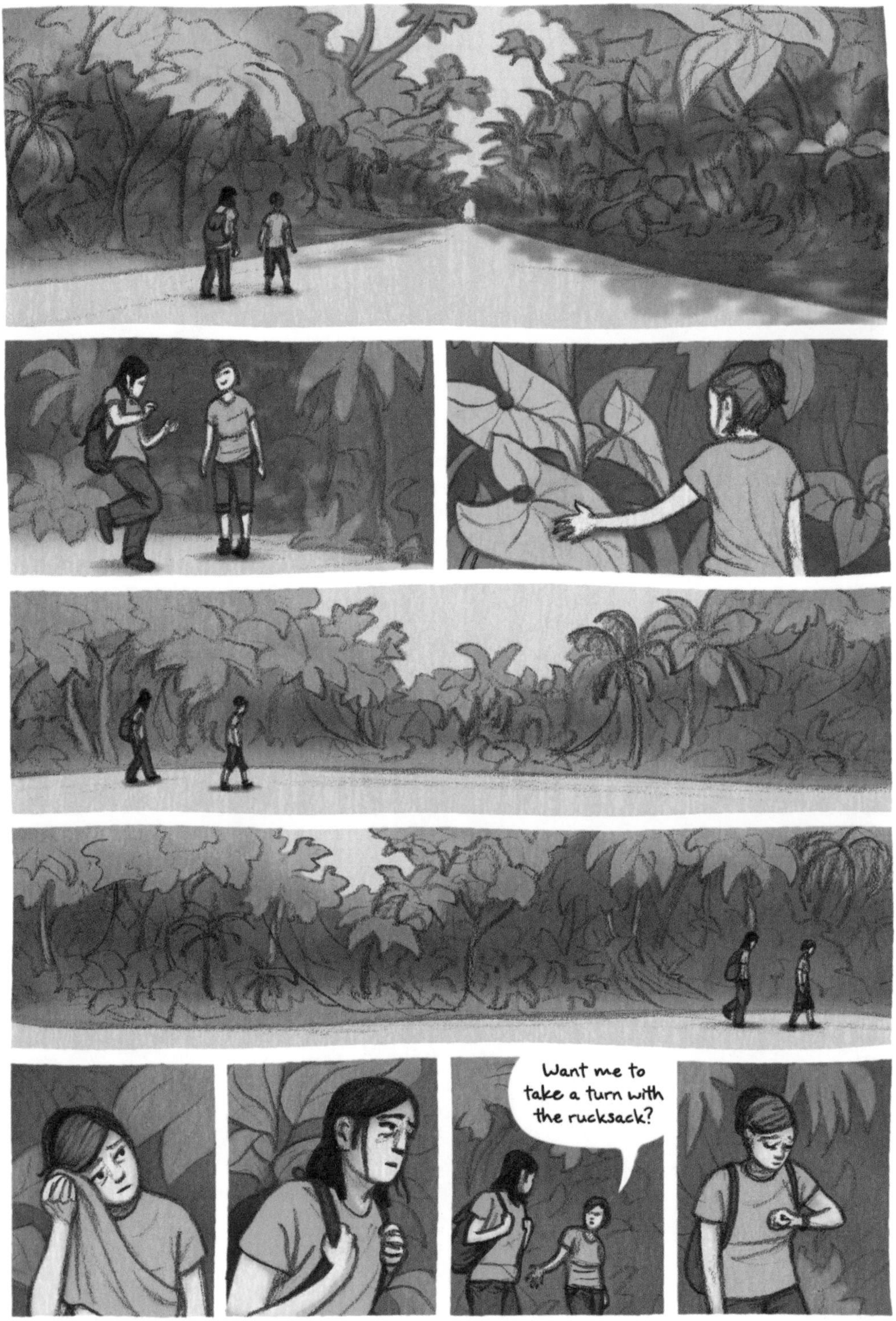
Want me to take a turn with the rucksack?

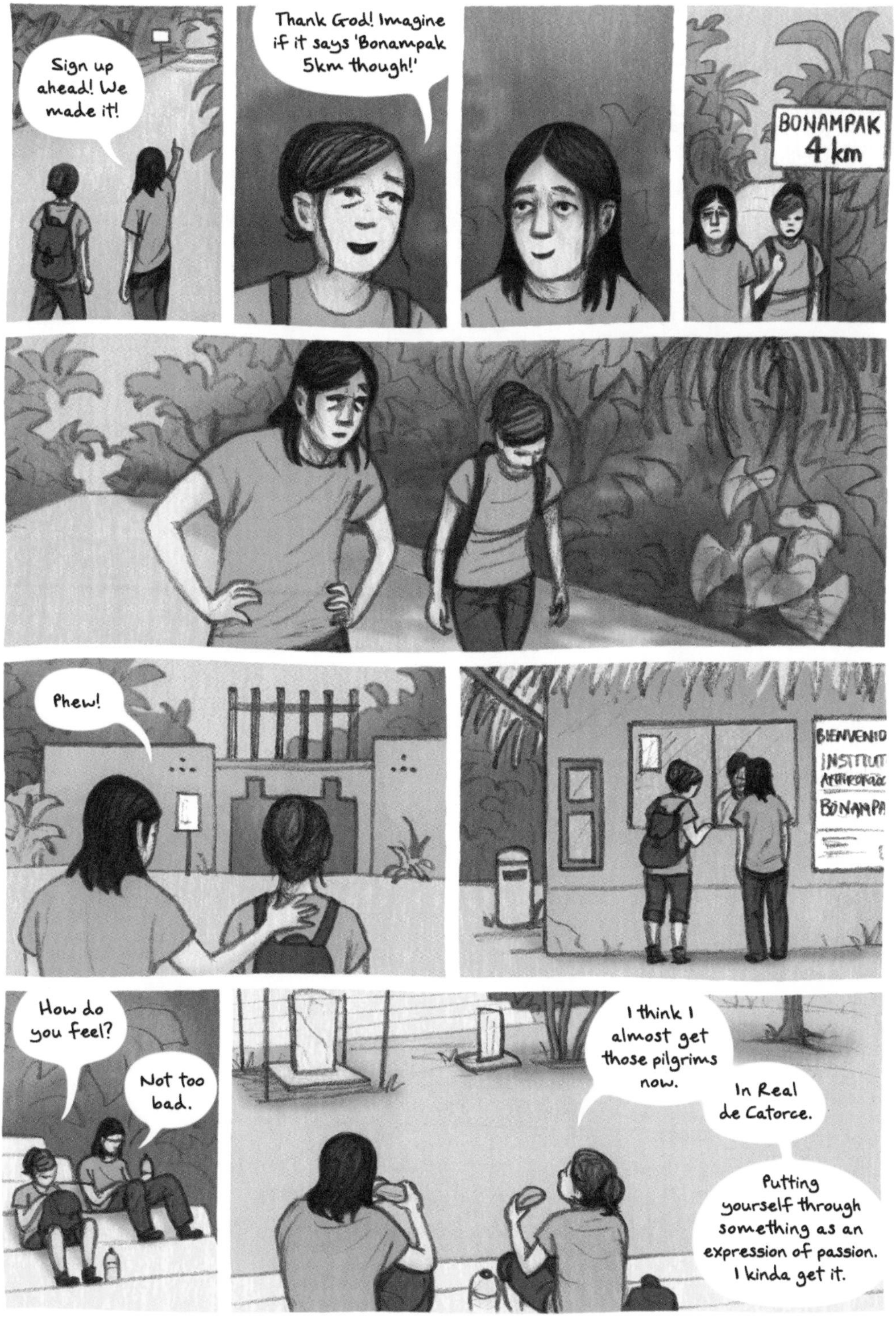
Sign up ahead! We made it!
Thank God! Imagine if it says 'Bonampak 5km though!'
BONAMPAK 4 km
Phew!
BIENVENID
INSTITUT
BONAMPA
How do you feel?
Not too bad.
I think I almost get those pilgrims now.
In Real de Catorce.
Putting yourself through something as an expression of passion. I kinda get it.

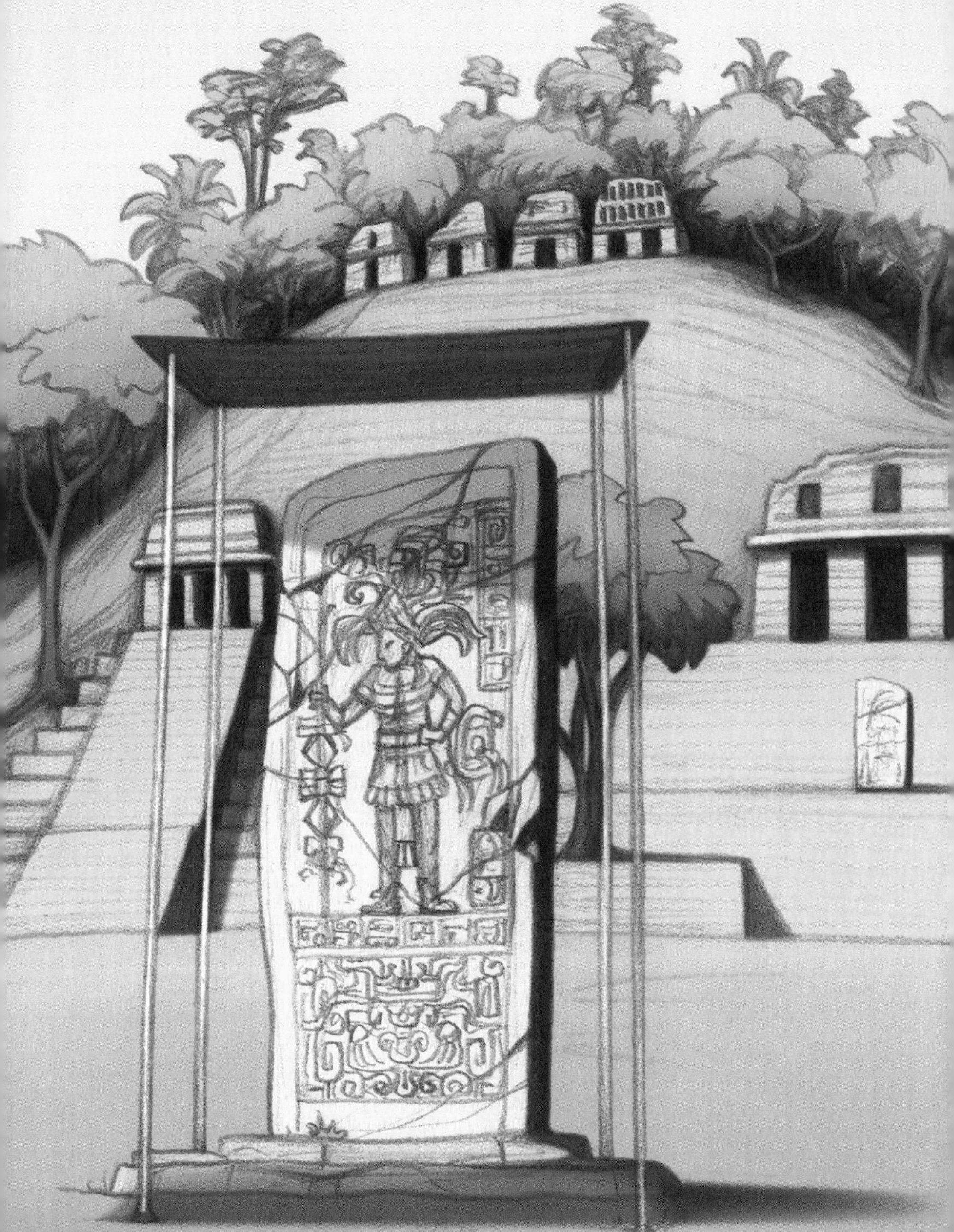

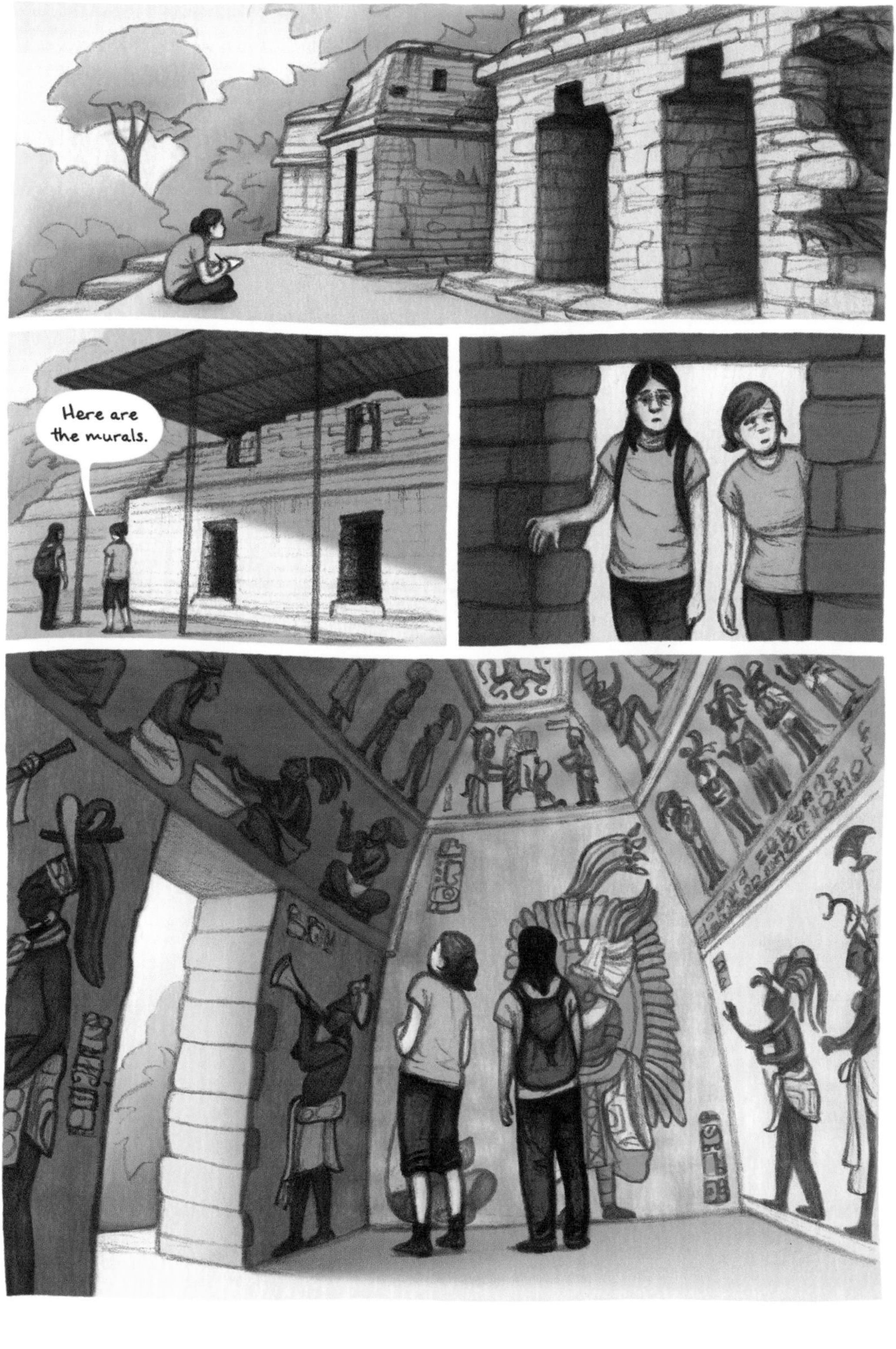
Here are the murals.

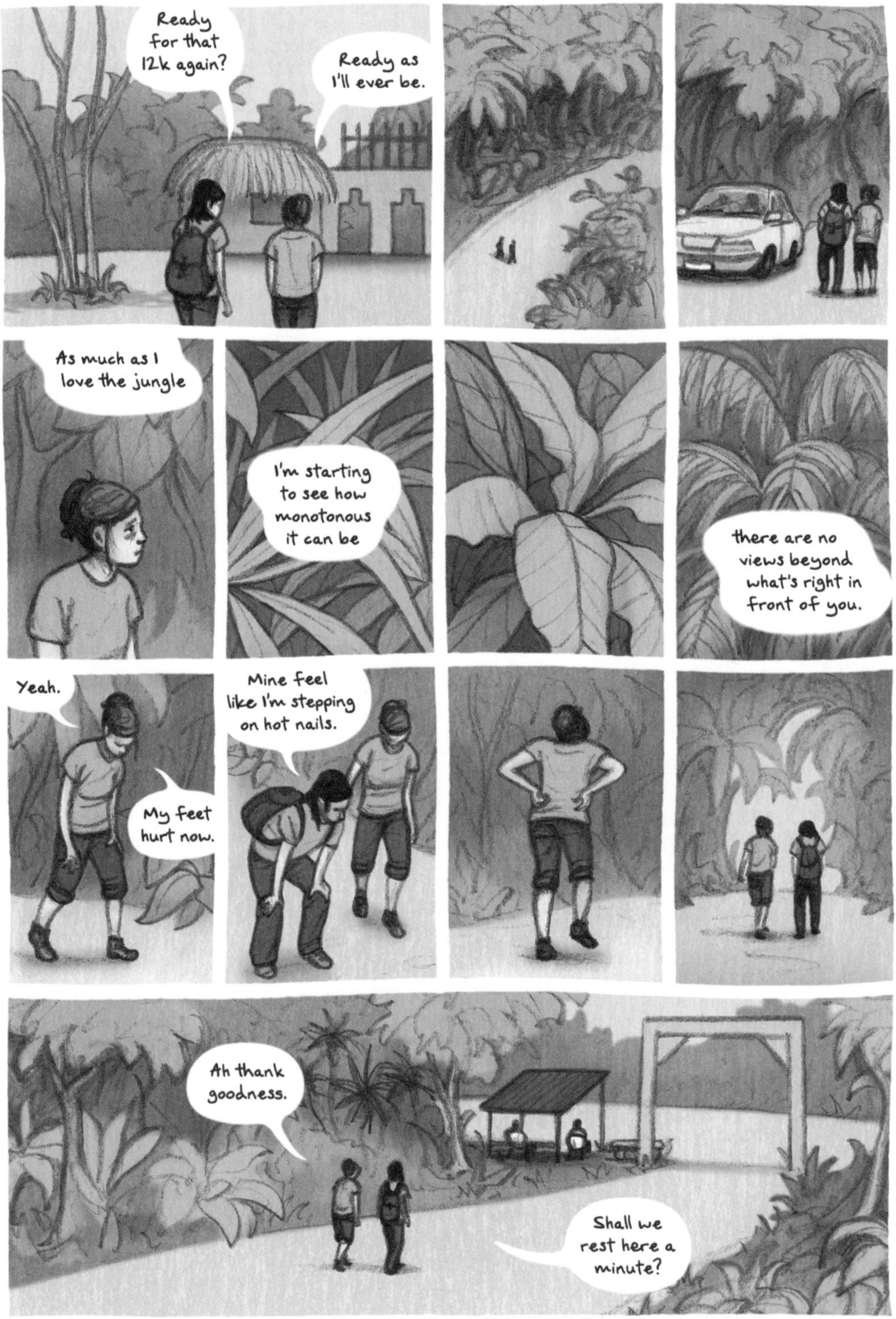
Ready for that 12k again?
Ready as I'll ever be.
As much as I love the jungle
I'm starting to see how monotonous it can be
there are no views beyond what's right in front of you.
Yeah.
My feet hurt now.
Mine feel like I'm stepping on hot nails.
Ah thank goodness.
Shall we rest here a minute?

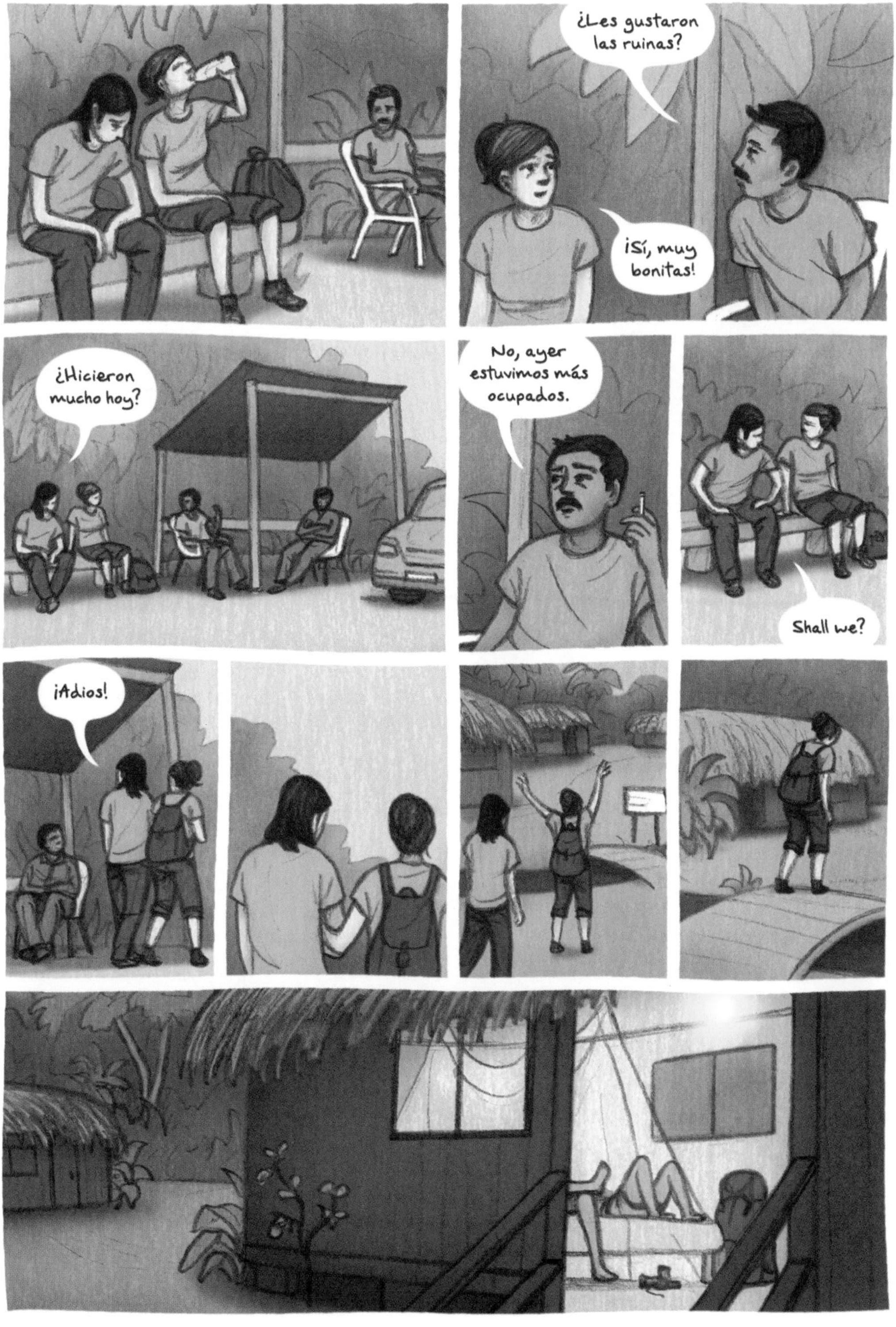
¿Les gustaron las ruinas?
¡Sí, muy bonitas!
¿Hicieron mucho hoy?
No, ayer estuvimos más ocupados.
Shall we?
¡Adios!

THE CONQUESTS

Following the explorations of Columbus, Europeans began permanently settling in the Caribbean around the turn of the 16th Century. Spain stepped up their drive for the conquest of new territory, and in 1519 Hernán Cortés led the expedition which ended with the 1521 overthrow of the Aztec Empire.

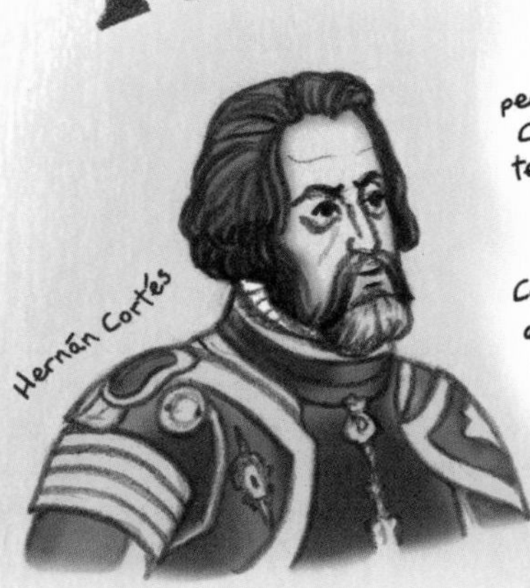
Hernán Cortés

Cortés' expedition was recalled at the last moment, after he clashed with the Governor of Cuba, Diego Velázquez de Cuéllar, but Cortés ignored the order from Spain.

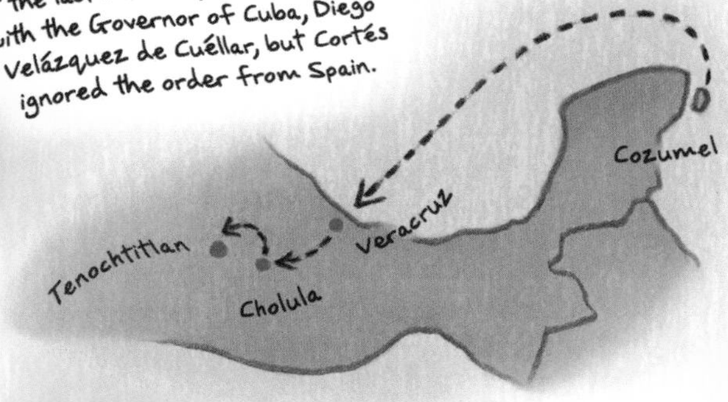
Cozumel
Veracruz
Tenochtitlan
Cholula

He landed on the Yucatán coast via the island of Cozumel, where he enlisted a valuable translator – a Nahua woman who became his mistress and is known as La Malinche (the traitor.)

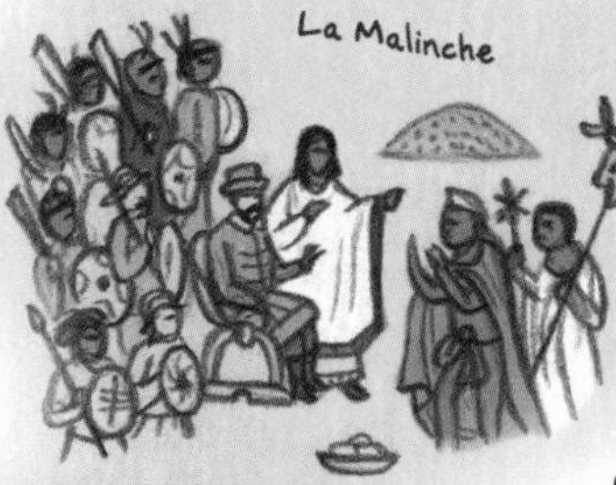
La Malinche

He travelled to the location of the modern-day state of Veracruz, and established the Spanish settlement Veracruz.

He then began his strategy of allying with certain indigenous groups against others, persuading the Totonac chiefs to rebel against the Aztecs and also allying with the Tlaxcalan enemies of the Aztec empire.

On reaching Cholula, he suspected the Aztec leader Moctezuma of ordering an ambush. He launched a pre-emptive attack, massacring the Cholula leaders and burning the city. The show of force convinced other local city-states affiliated with the Aztec empire to switch allegiances and join him.

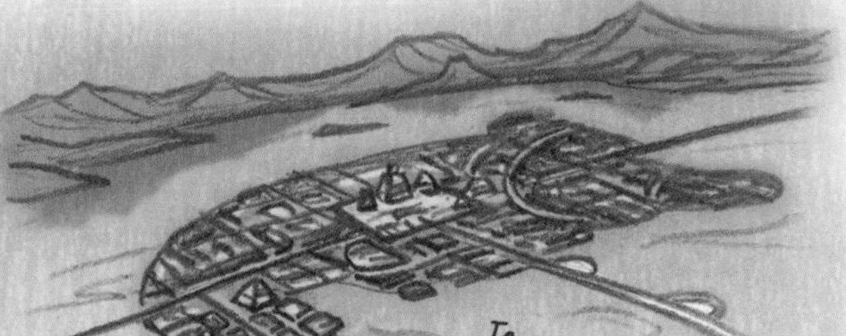
Tenochtitlan

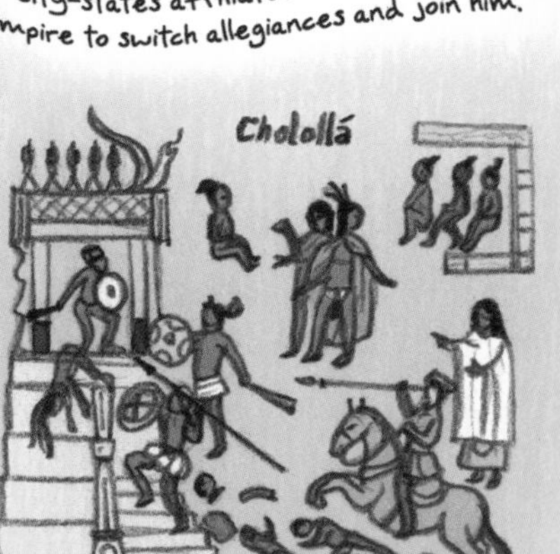
Chololla

When he reached Tenochtitlan, the capital of the Aztec Empire, Moctezuma was uncertain what strategy to take. Initially he welcomed Cortés, but was quickly imprisoned, continuing to act as Emperor subject to Cortés' control.

In April 1520 Cortés learned that Spain had sent troops to arrest him, and left to fight them off, leaving some of his soldiers in charge. In his absence the soldiers massacred many of the city's nobility during a religious festival. Fighting ensued, Moctezuma was killed and the Spanish were forced to flee, suffering heavy casualties. They were welcomed in Tlaxcala, where they regrouped. Cortés sent representatives back to Spain to plead his case.

Moctezuma

In September 1520 the Aztecs were struck by a smallpox epidemic, losing their new emperor. Cortés and his Tlaxcalan allies defeated city after city, until only Tenochtitlan and one other remained. Cortés mounted an eight-month siege of the city, at the end of which the new Emperor Cuauhtémoc was captured trying to escape in a canoe. Both cities fell, Tenochtitlan almost totally destroyed by fire. The Spanish ordered the population out and founded modern-day Mexico City.

Cuauhtémoc

The integration of Mexico into the Spanish empire began. Representatives of the Catholic church started to convert the indigenous population. The people of Central Mexico were already used to rendering labour and tribute to the Aztec overlords, and the Spanish conquerors exploited this to generate wealth for Spain.

There was also terrible cruelty at the hands of the clergy. Bishop Diego de Landa became notorious for his extreme mistreatment of the indigenous people in the name of religious conversion.

In the 16th century about 240,000 Spanish settlers entered American ports, followed by 450,000 in the next century.

Unlike the English-speaking colonists of North America, the majority of the Spanish colonists were single men who were encouraged to marry or make concubines of the indigenous women. As a result, the vast majority of the current population of Mexico are mixed race (mestizo.)

It took almost 60 years of war to suppress the resistance of the indigenous population across the whole of Mesoamerica.

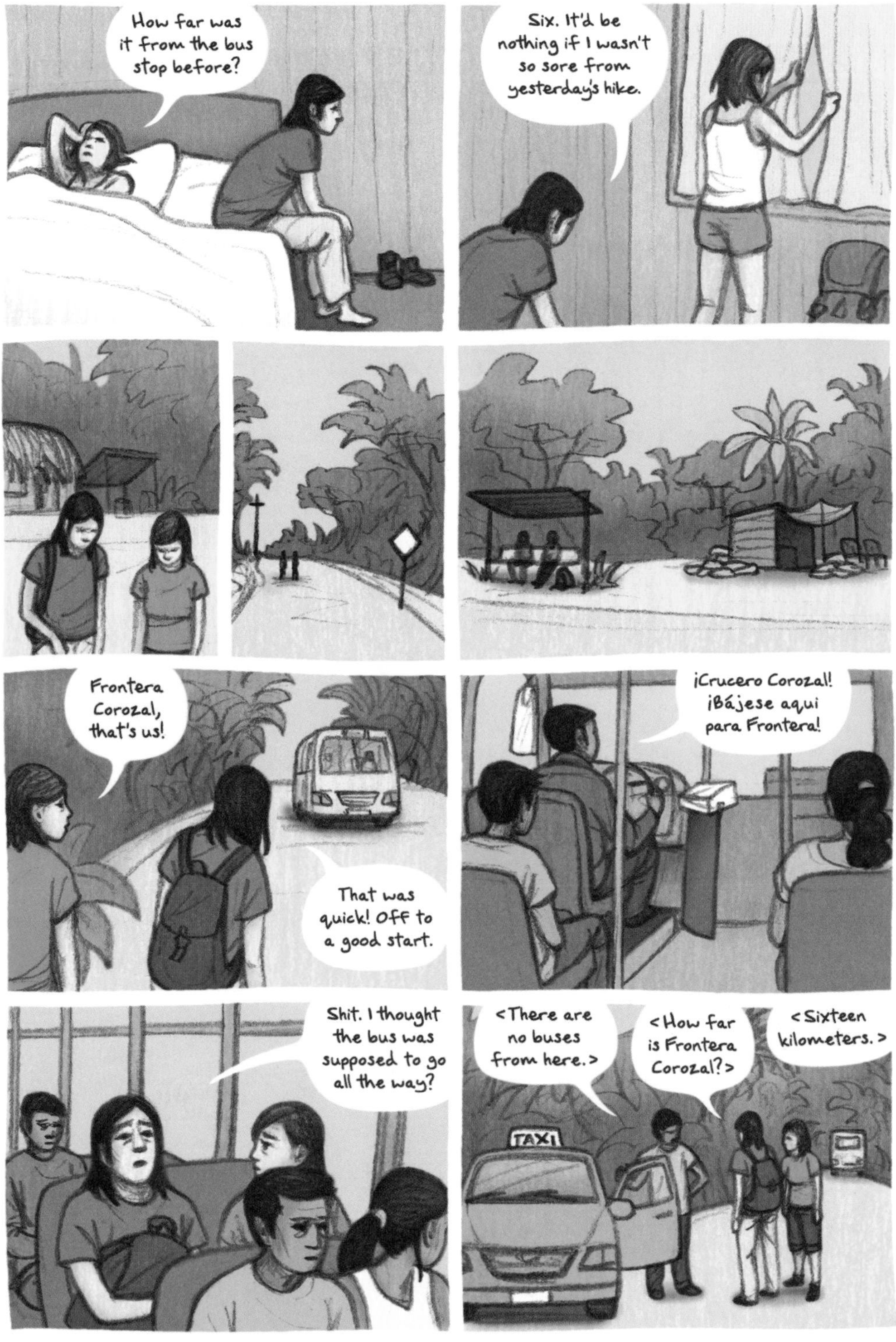
How far was it from the bus stop before?
Six. It'd be nothing if I wasn't so sore from yesterday's hike.
Frontera Corozal, that's us!
That was quick! Off to a good start.
¡Crucero Corozal! ¡Bájese aqui para Frontera!
Shit. I thought the bus was supposed to go all the way?
<There are no buses from here.>
<How far is Frontera Corozal?>
<Sixteen kilometers.>
TAXI

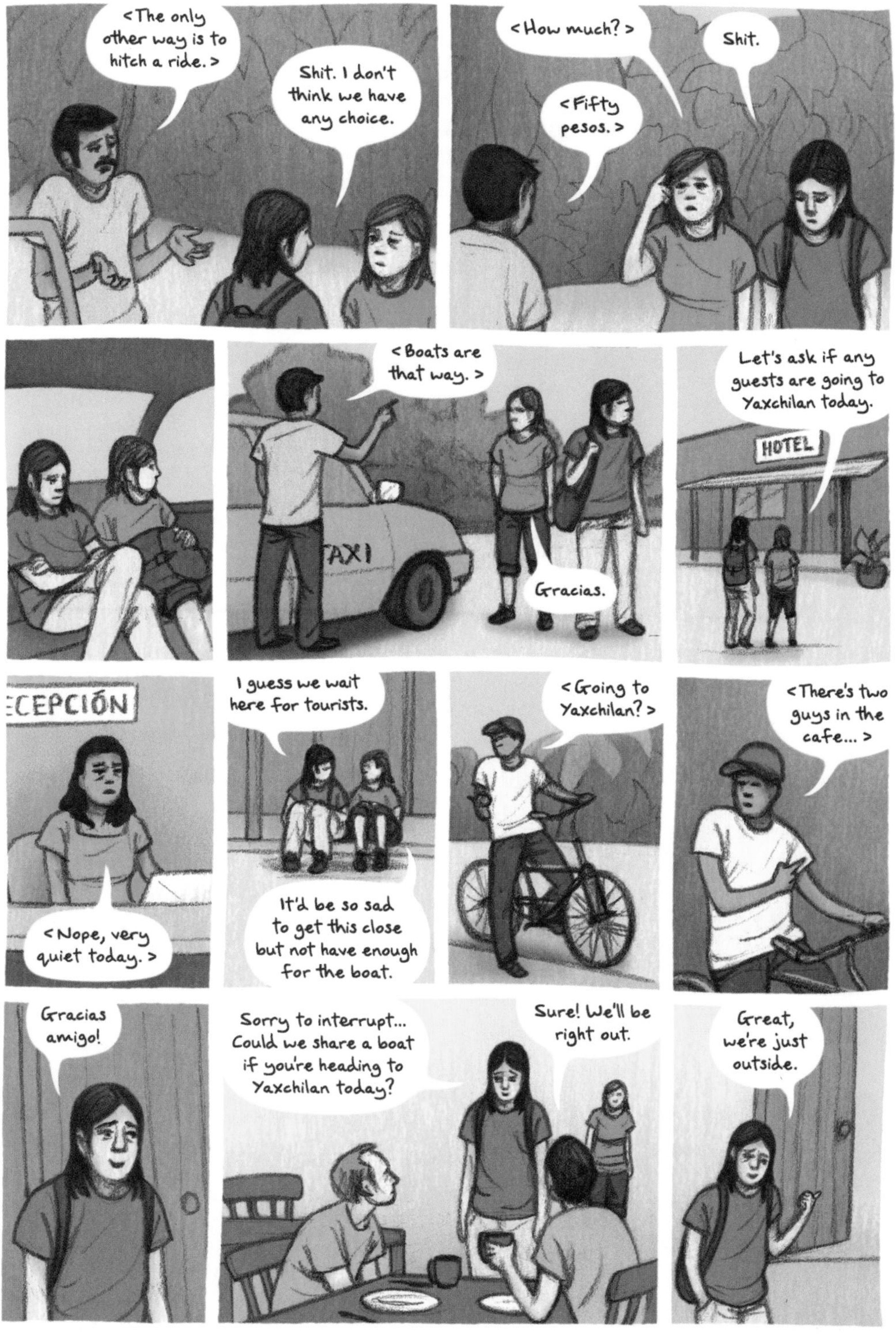
<The only other way is to hitch a ride.>
Shit. I don't think we have any choice.
<How much?>
<Fifty pesos.>
Shit.
<Boats are that way.>
TAXI
Gracias.
Let's ask if any guests are going to Yaxchilan today.
HOTEL
ECEPCIÓN
<Nope, very quiet today.>
I guess we wait here for tourists.
It'd be so sad to get this close but not have enough for the boat.
<Going to Yaxchilan?>
<There's two guys in the cafe...>
Gracias amigo!
Sorry to interrupt... Could we share a boat if you're heading to Yaxchilan today?
Sure! We'll be right out.
Great, we're just outside.

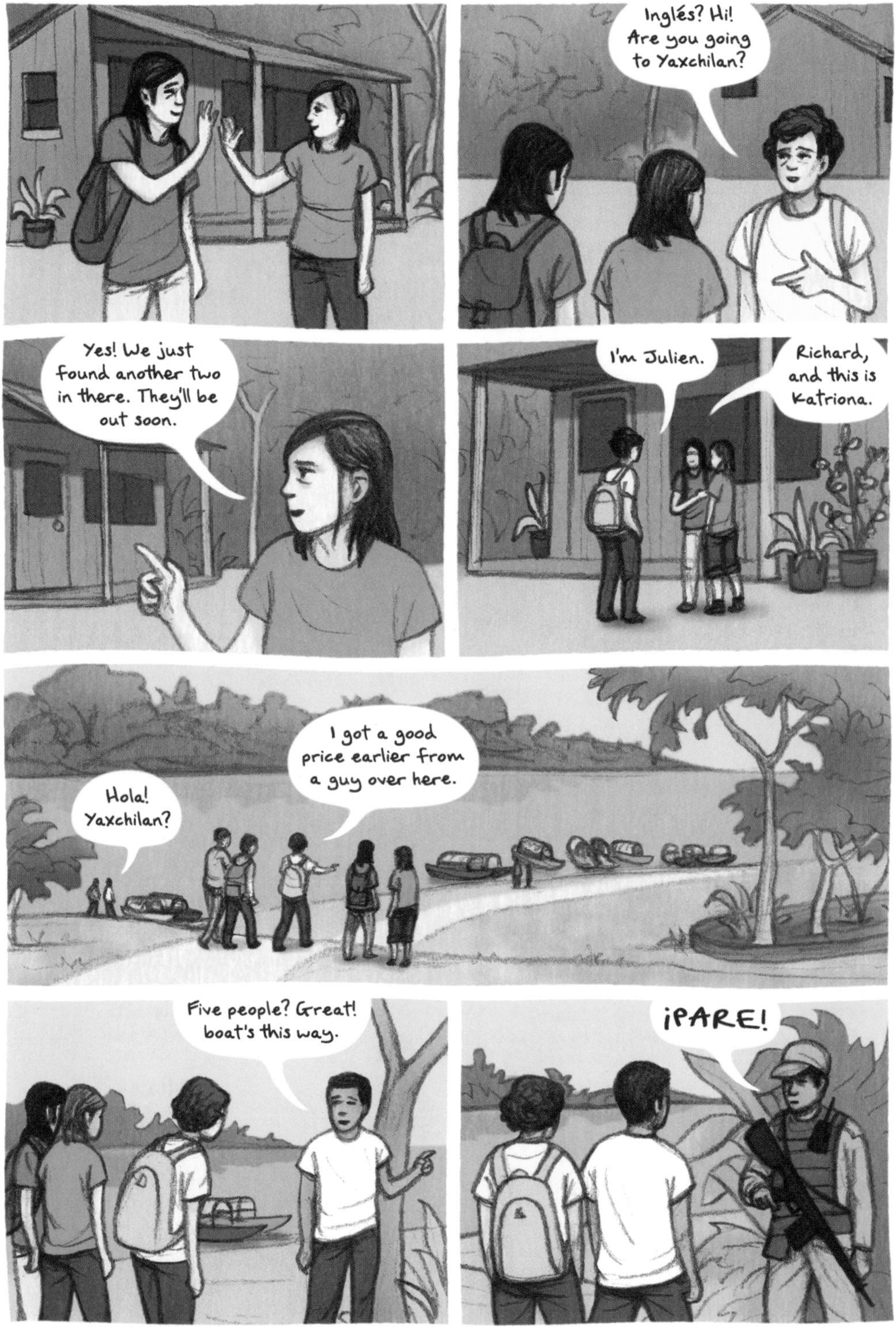

Inglés? Hi! Are you going to Yaxchilan?
Yes! We just found another two in there. They'll be out soon.
I'm Julien.
Richard, and this is Katriona.
Hola! Yaxchilan?
I got a good price earlier from a guy over here.
Five people? Great! boat's this way.
¡PARE!

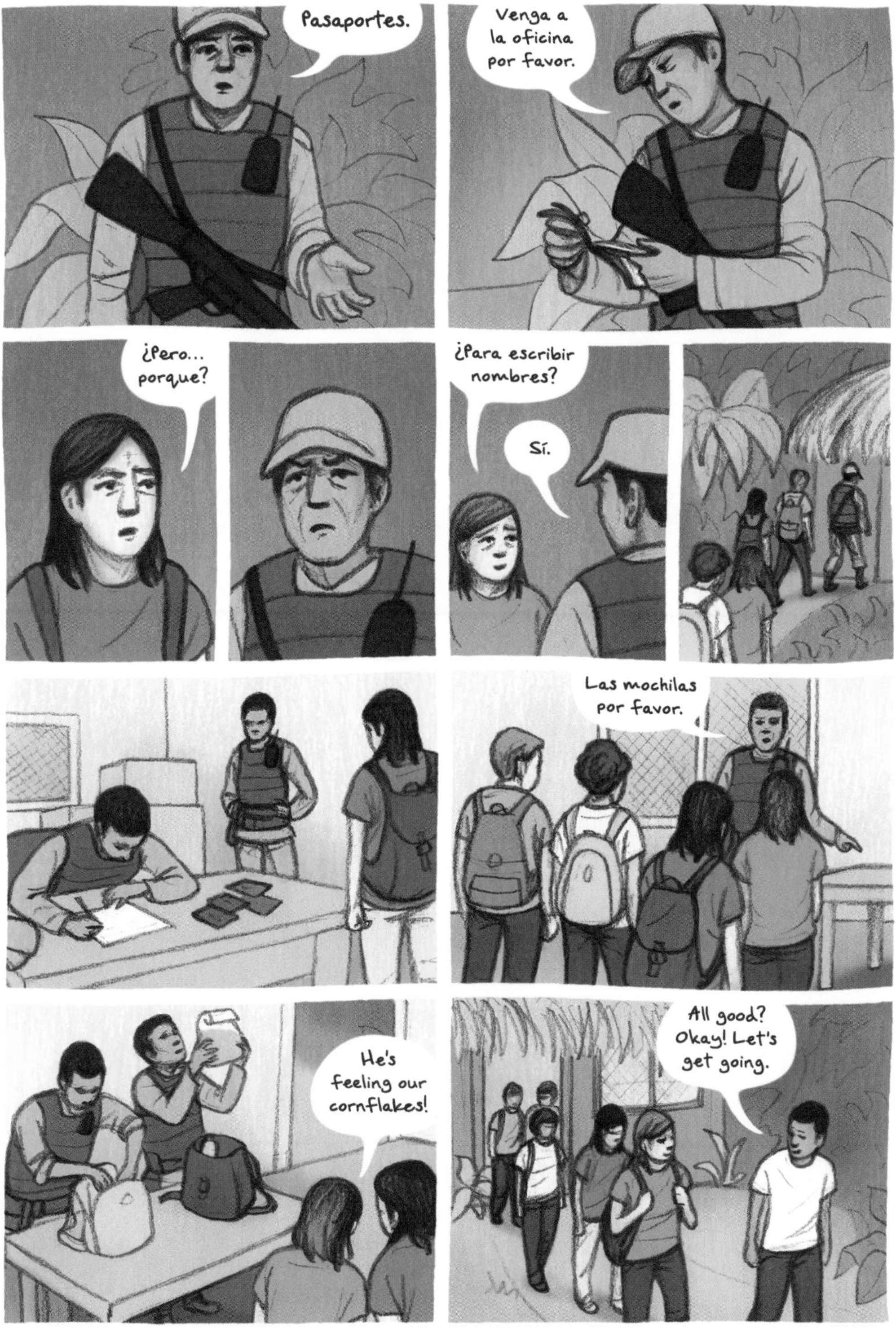
Pasaportes.
Venga a la oficina por favor.
¿Pero... porque?
¿Para escribir nombres?
Sí.
Las mochilas por favor.
He's feeling our cornflakes!
All good? Okay! Let's get going.

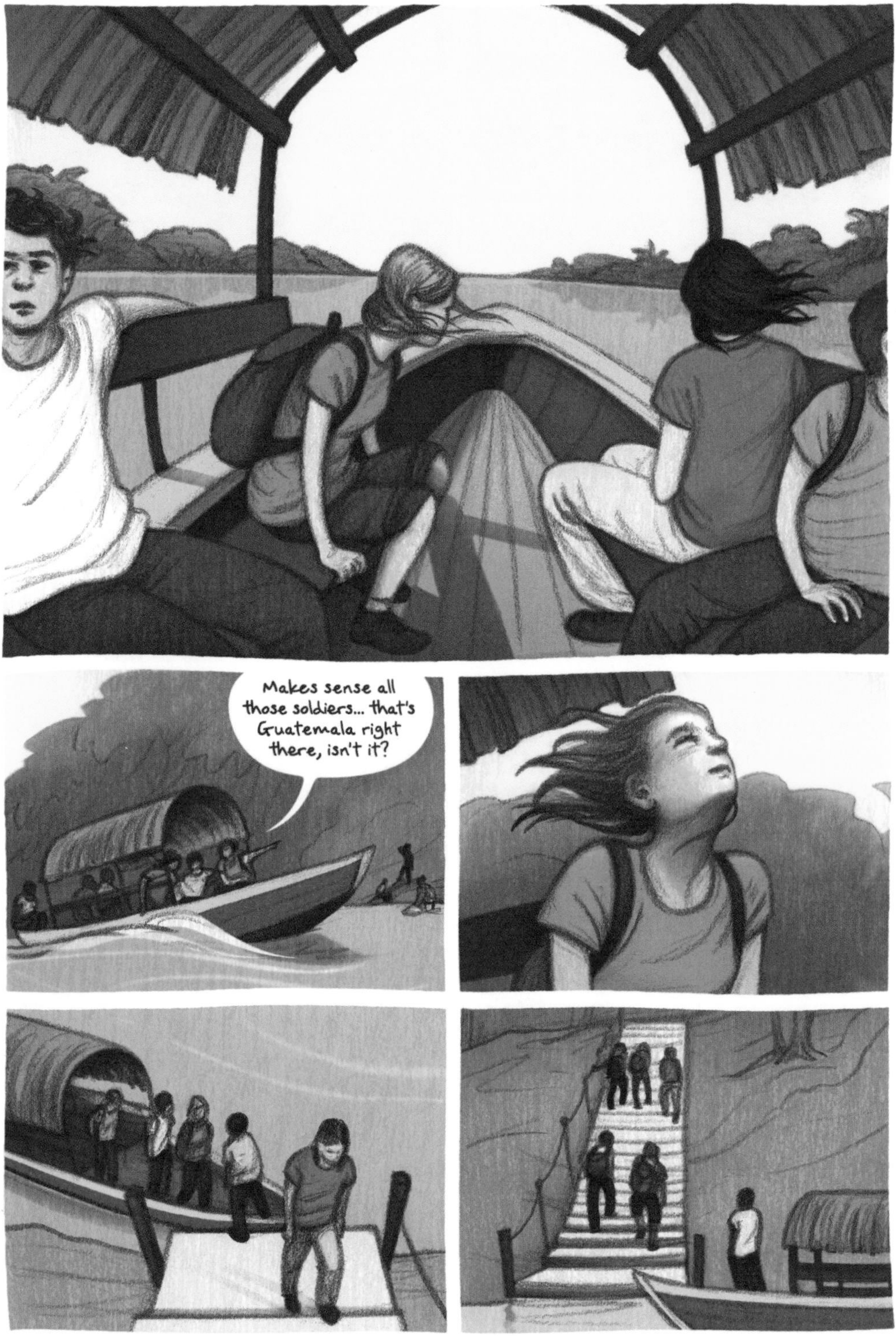
Makes sense all those soldiers... that's Guatemala right there, isn't it?

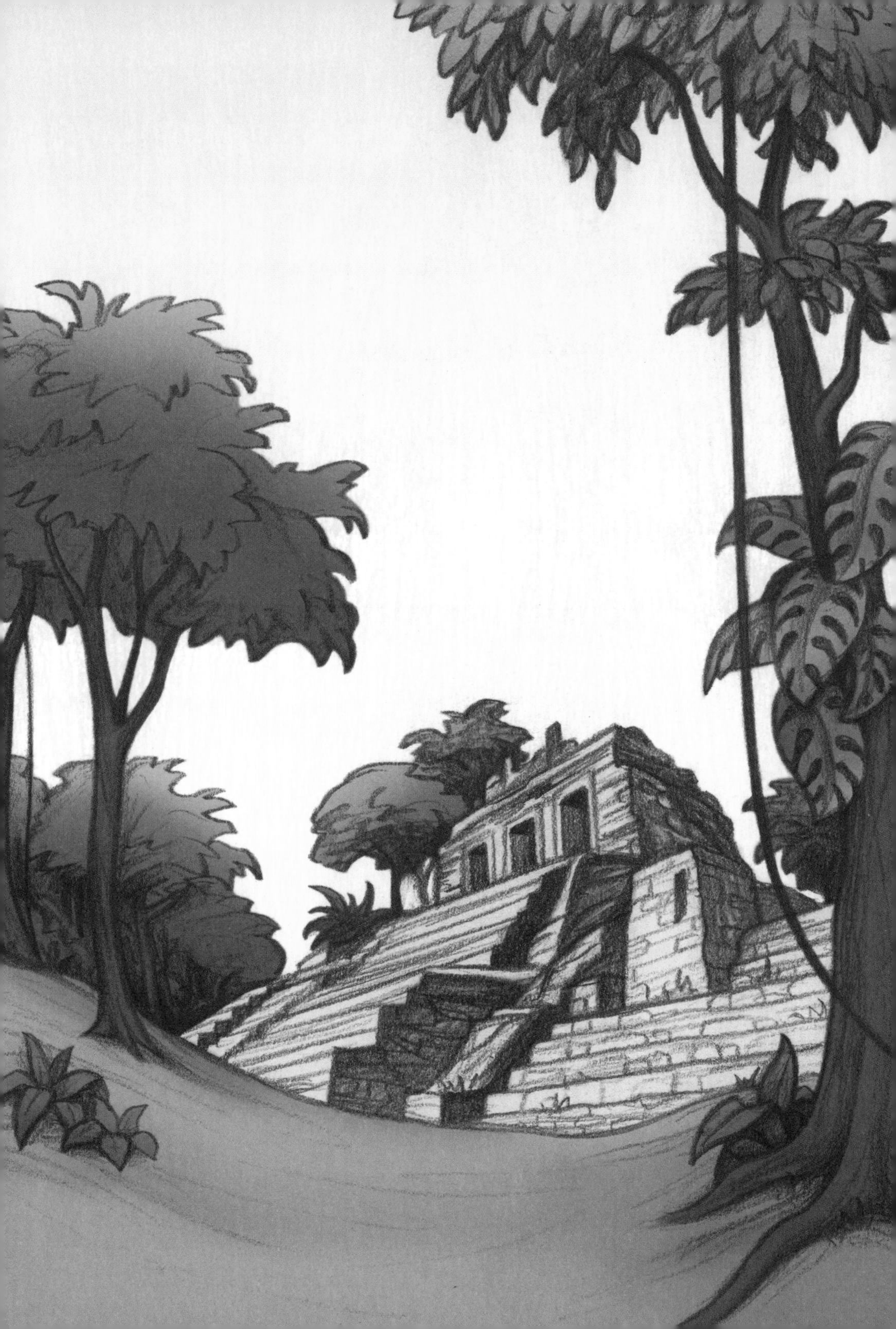

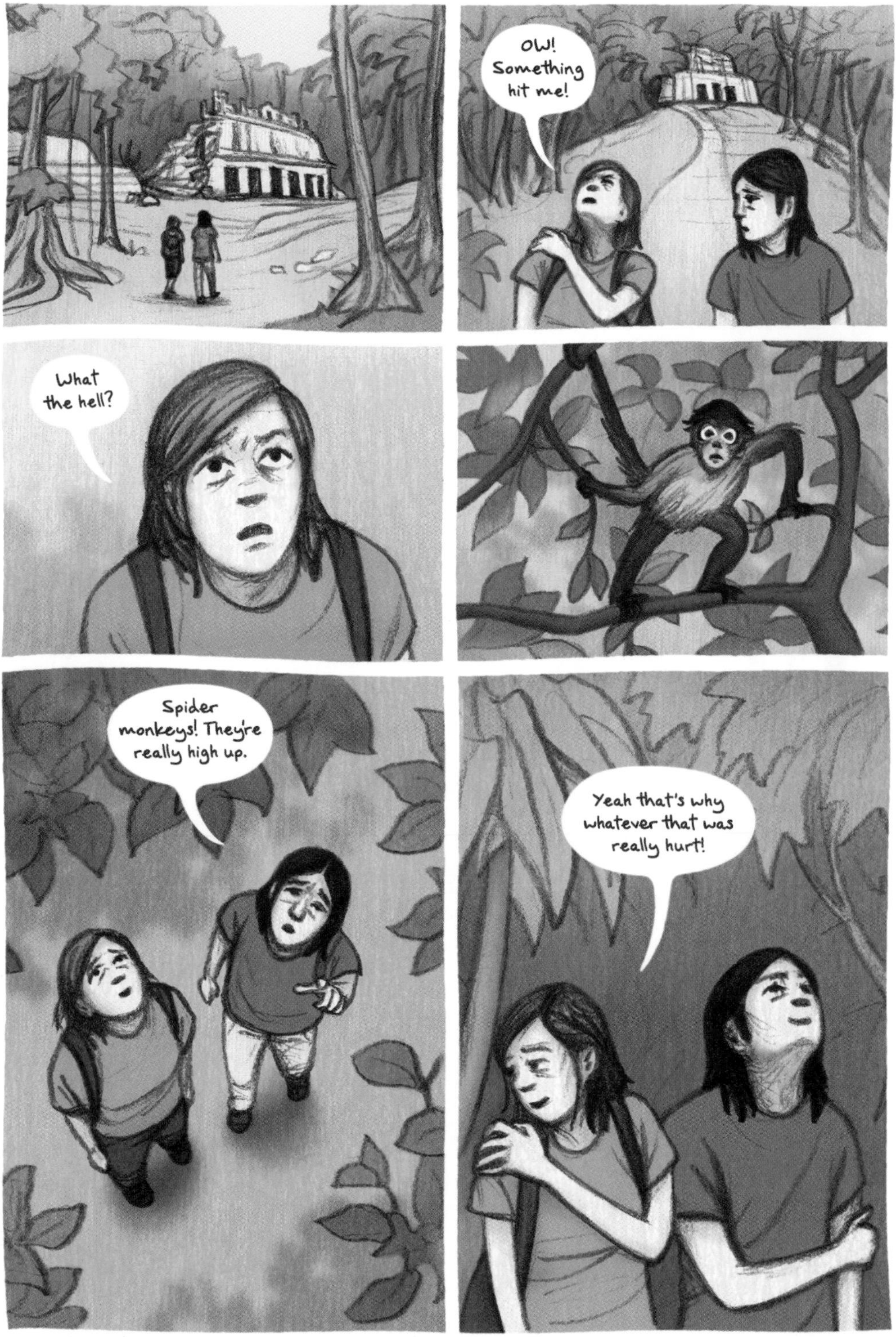
OW!
Something
hit me!
What
the hell?
Spider
monkeys! They're
really high up.
Yeah that's why
whatever that was
really hurt!

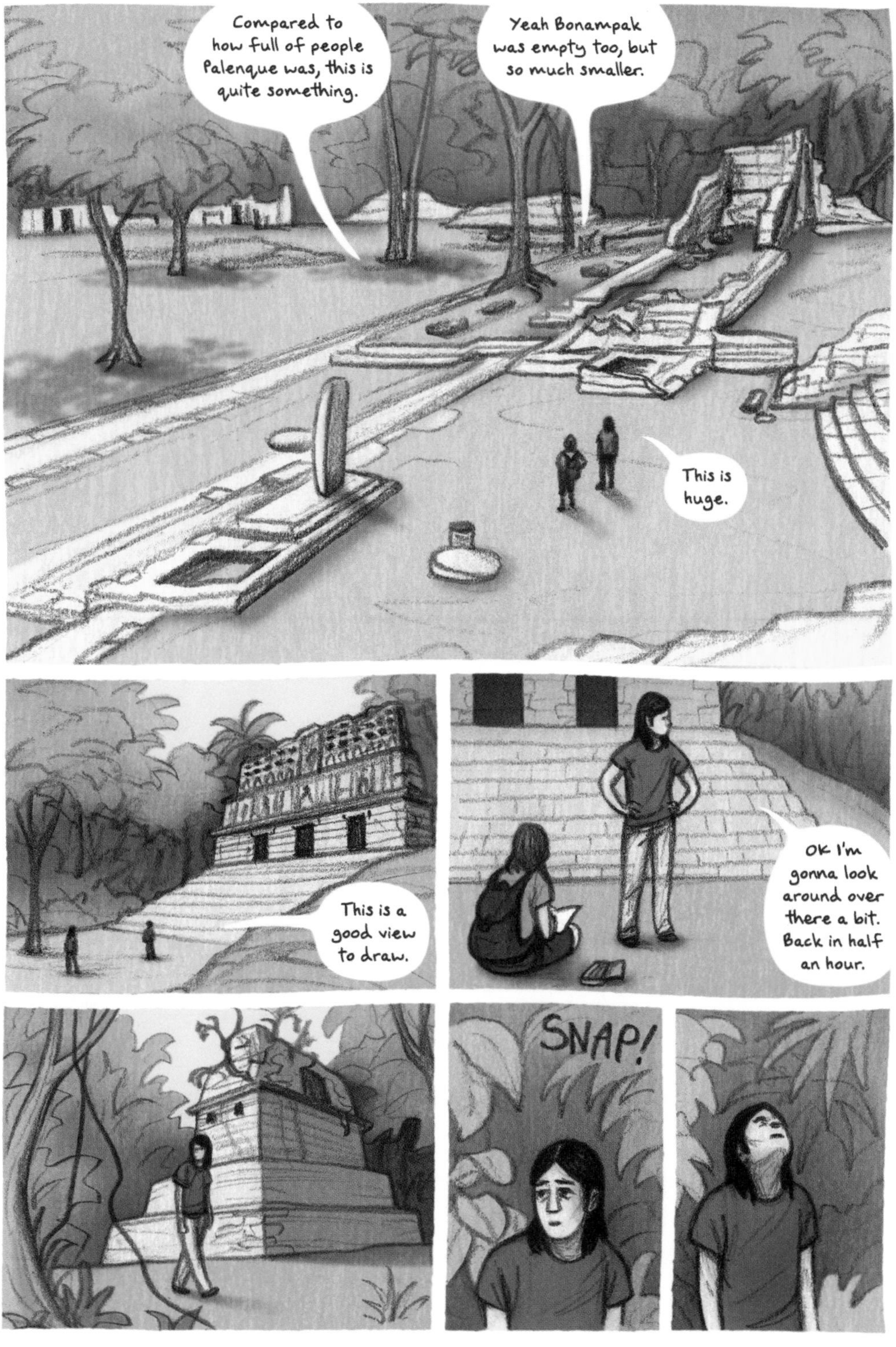
Compared to how full of people Palenque was, this is quite something.
Yeah Bonampak was empty too, but so much smaller.
This is huge.
This is a good view to draw.
OK I'm gonna look around over there a bit. Back in half an hour.
SNAP!

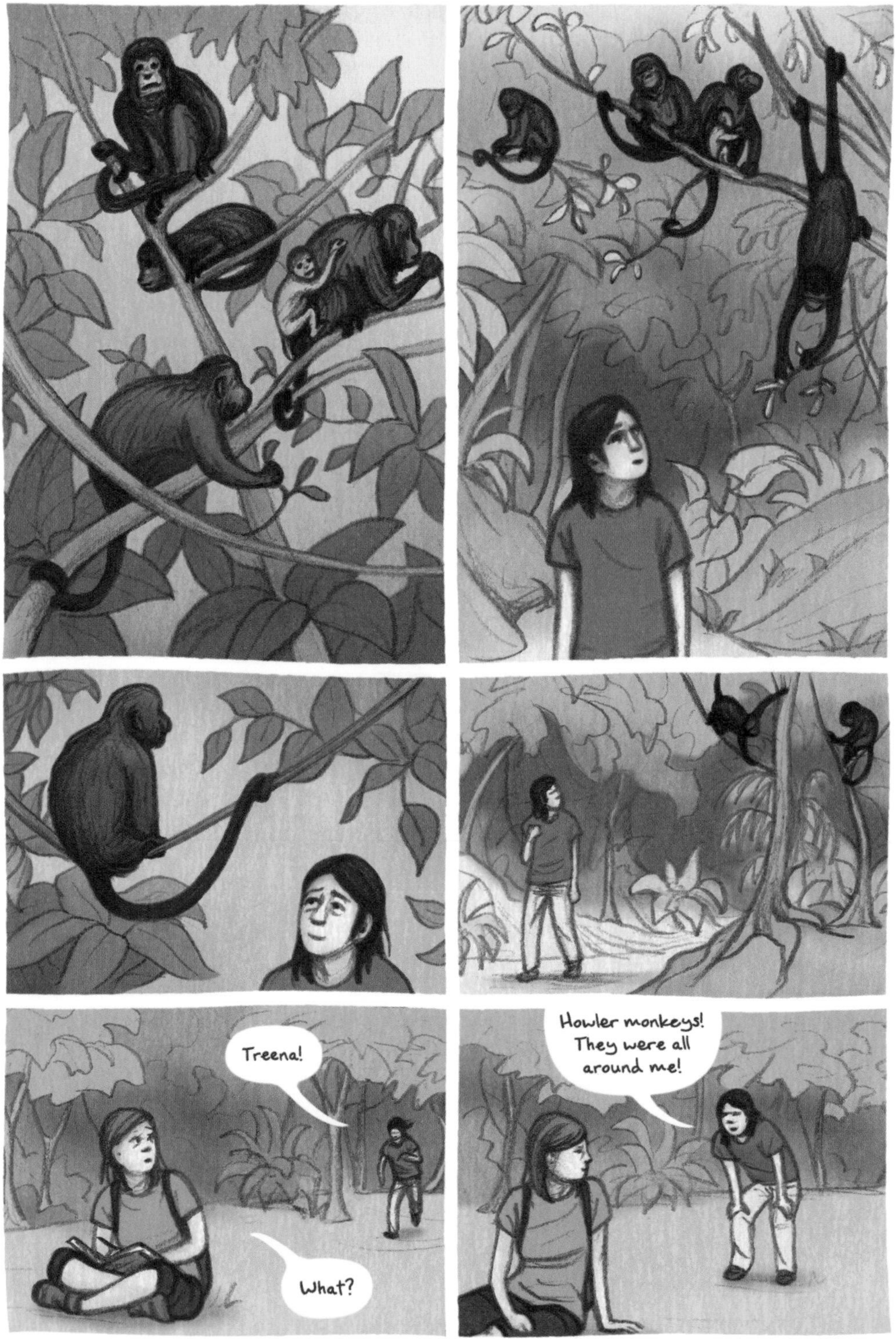
Treena!
What?
Howler monkeys! They were all around me!

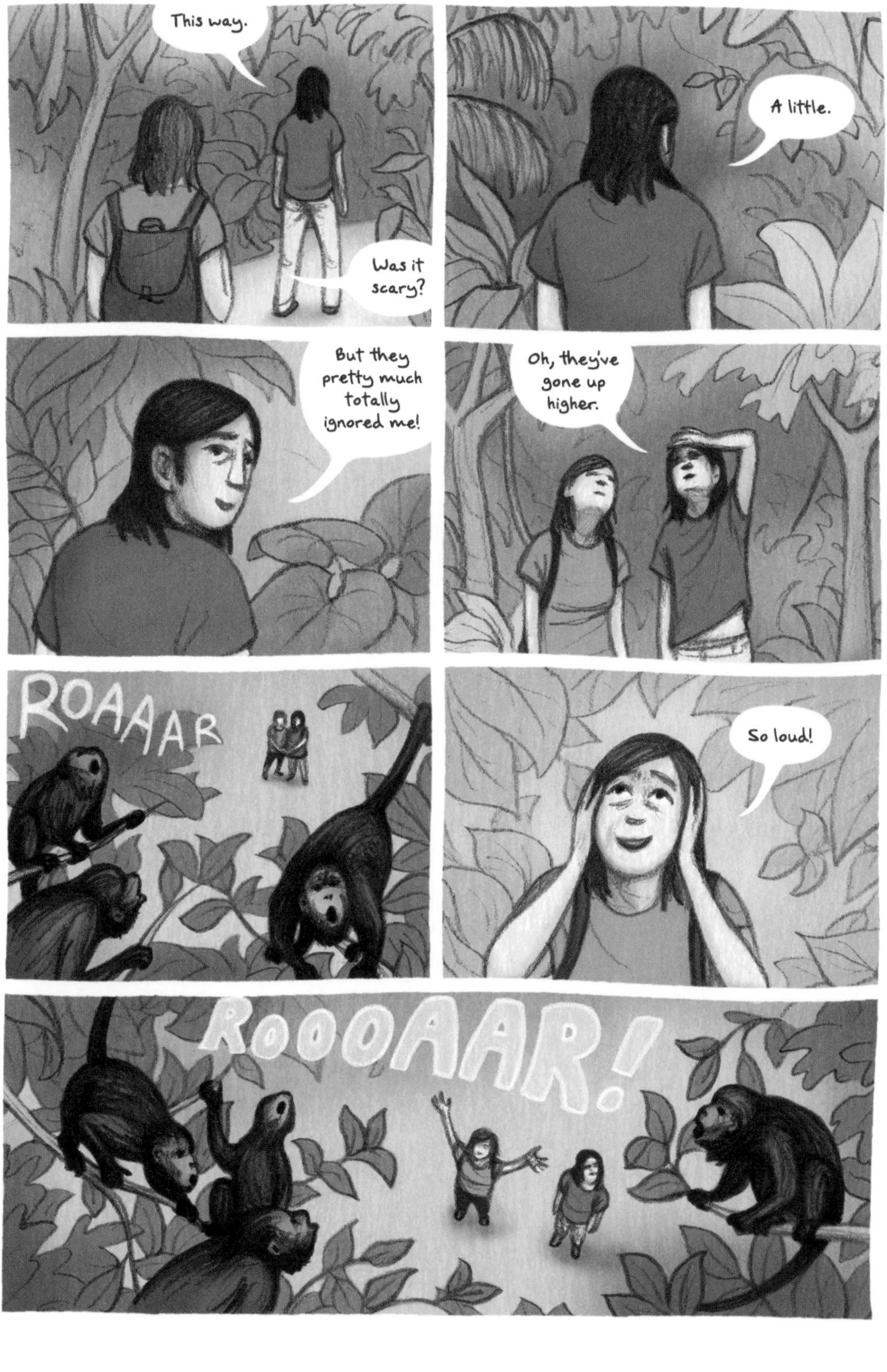
This way.
Was it scary?
A little.
But they pretty much totally ignored me!
Oh, they've gone up higher.
ROAAAR
So loud!
ROOOAAR!

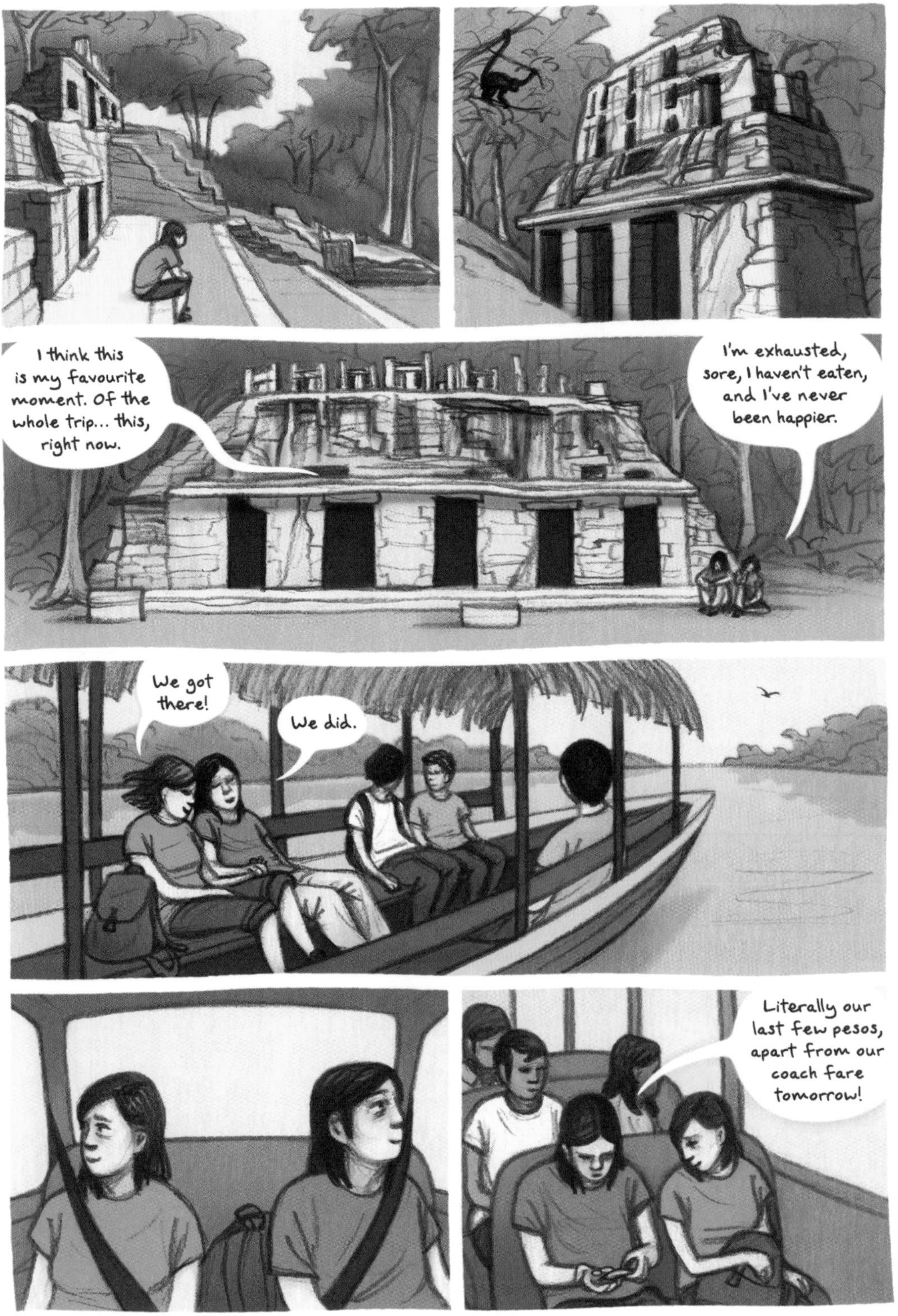
I think this is my favourite moment. Of the whole trip... this, right now.
I'm exhausted, sore, I haven't eaten, and I've never been happier.
We got there!
We did.
Literally our last few pesos, apart from our coach fare tomorrow!

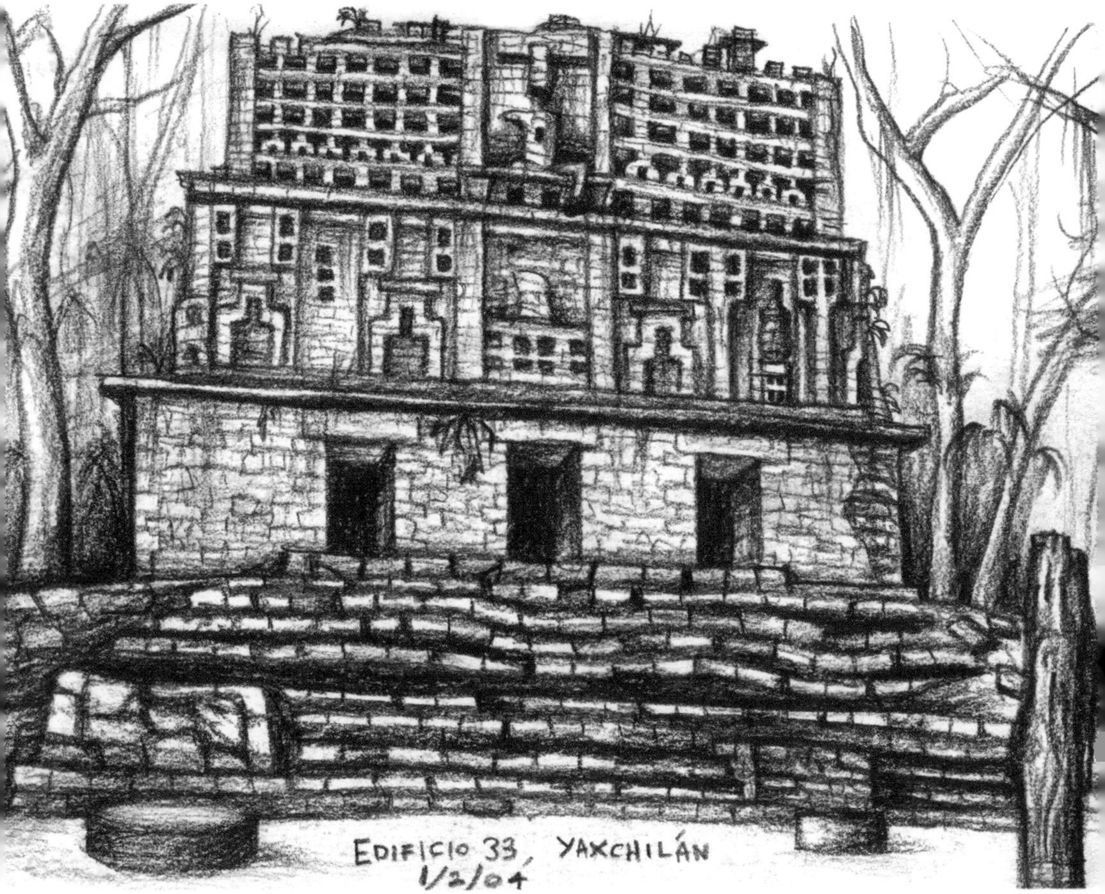
EDIFICIO 33, YAXCHILÁN
1/2/04

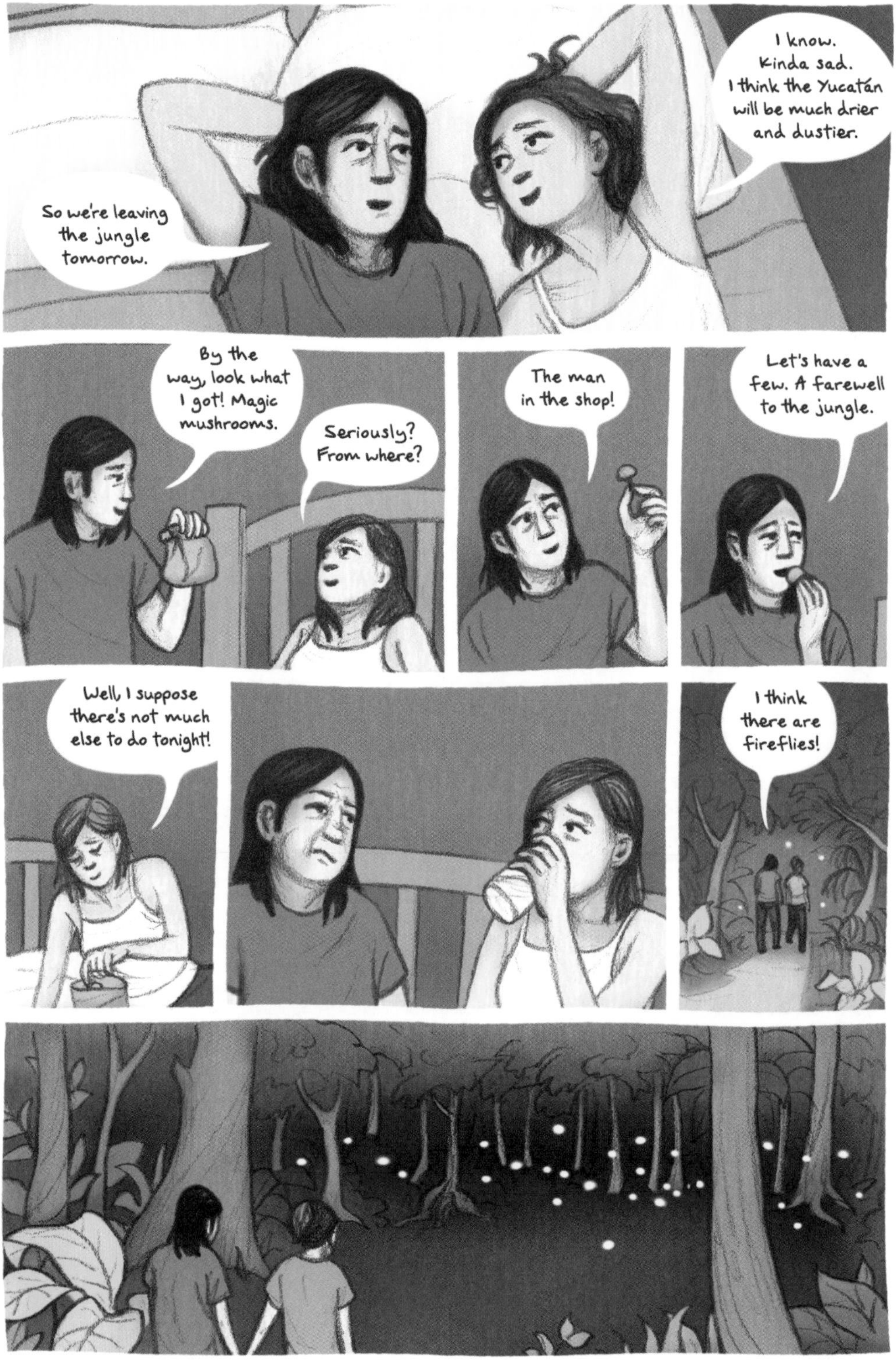
So we're leaving the jungle tomorrow.
I know. Kinda sad. I think the Yucatán will be much drier and dustier.
By the way, look what I got! Magic mushrooms.
Seriously? From where?
The man in the shop!
Let's have a few. A farewell to the jungle.
Well, I suppose there's not much else to do tonight!
I think there are fireflies!

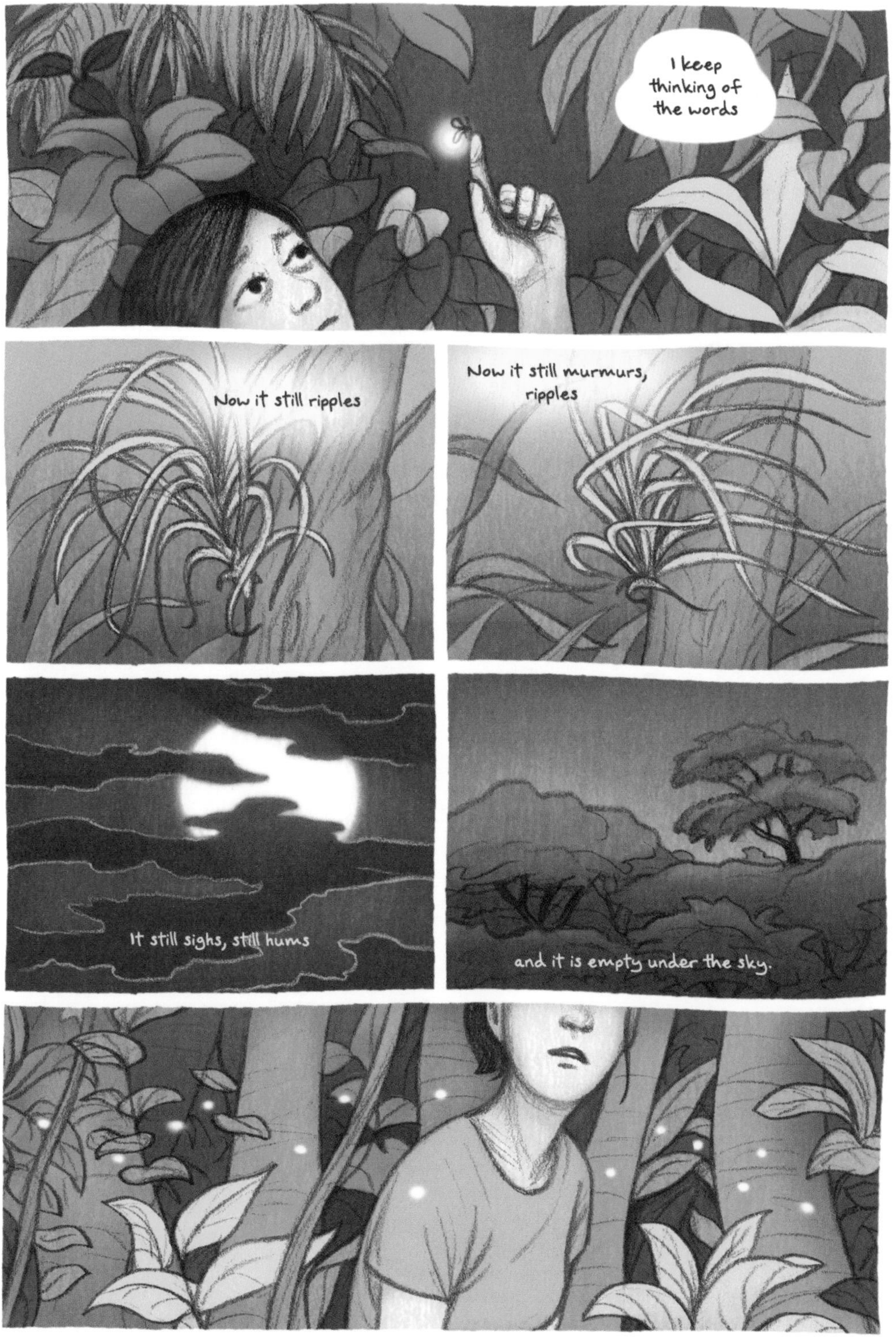
I keep thinking of the words
Now it still ripples
Now it still murmurs, ripples
It still sighs, still hums
and it is empty under the sky.

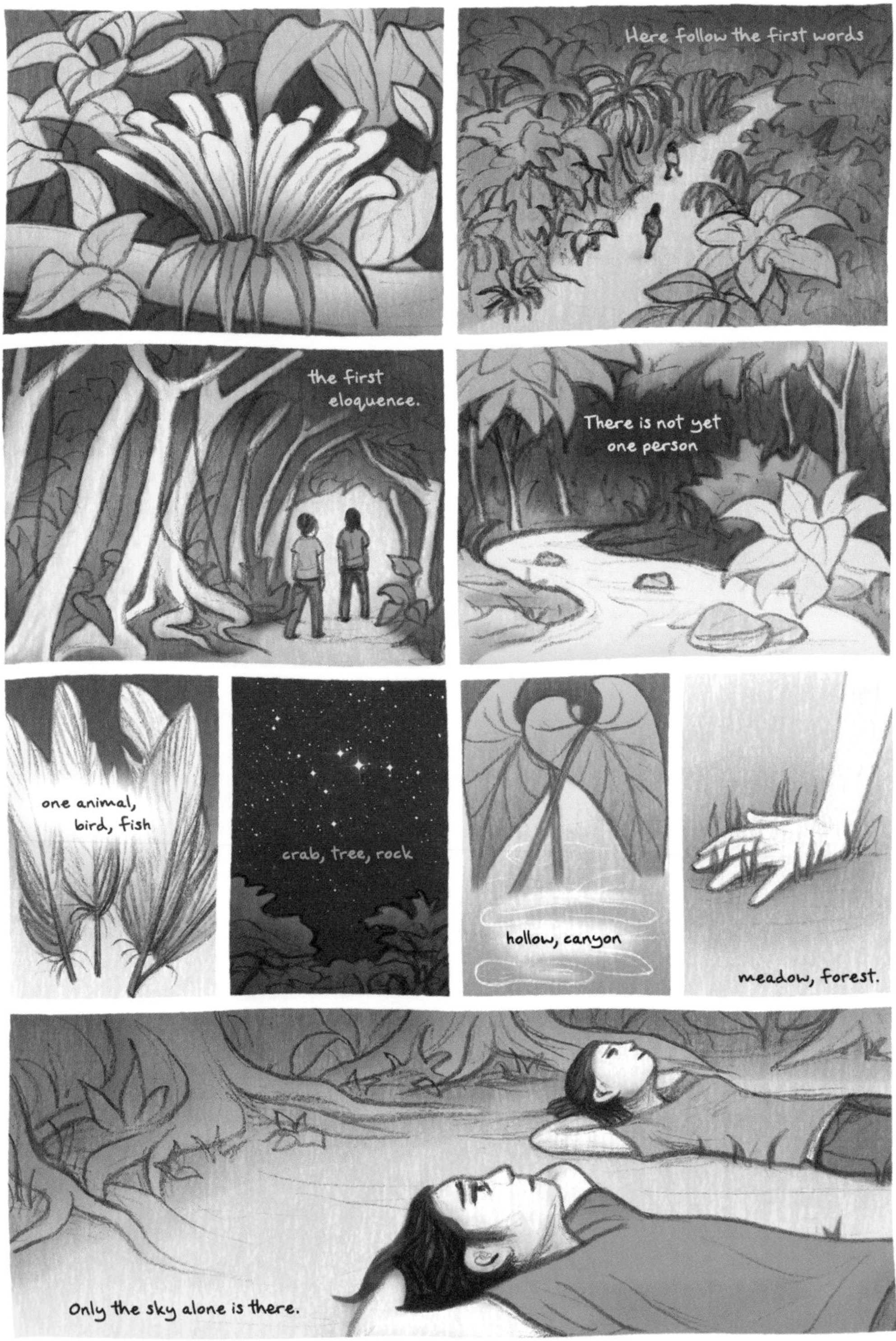
Here follow the first words
the first eloquence.
There is not yet one person
one animal, bird, fish
crab, tree, rock
hollow, canyon
meadow, forest.
Only the sky alone is there.

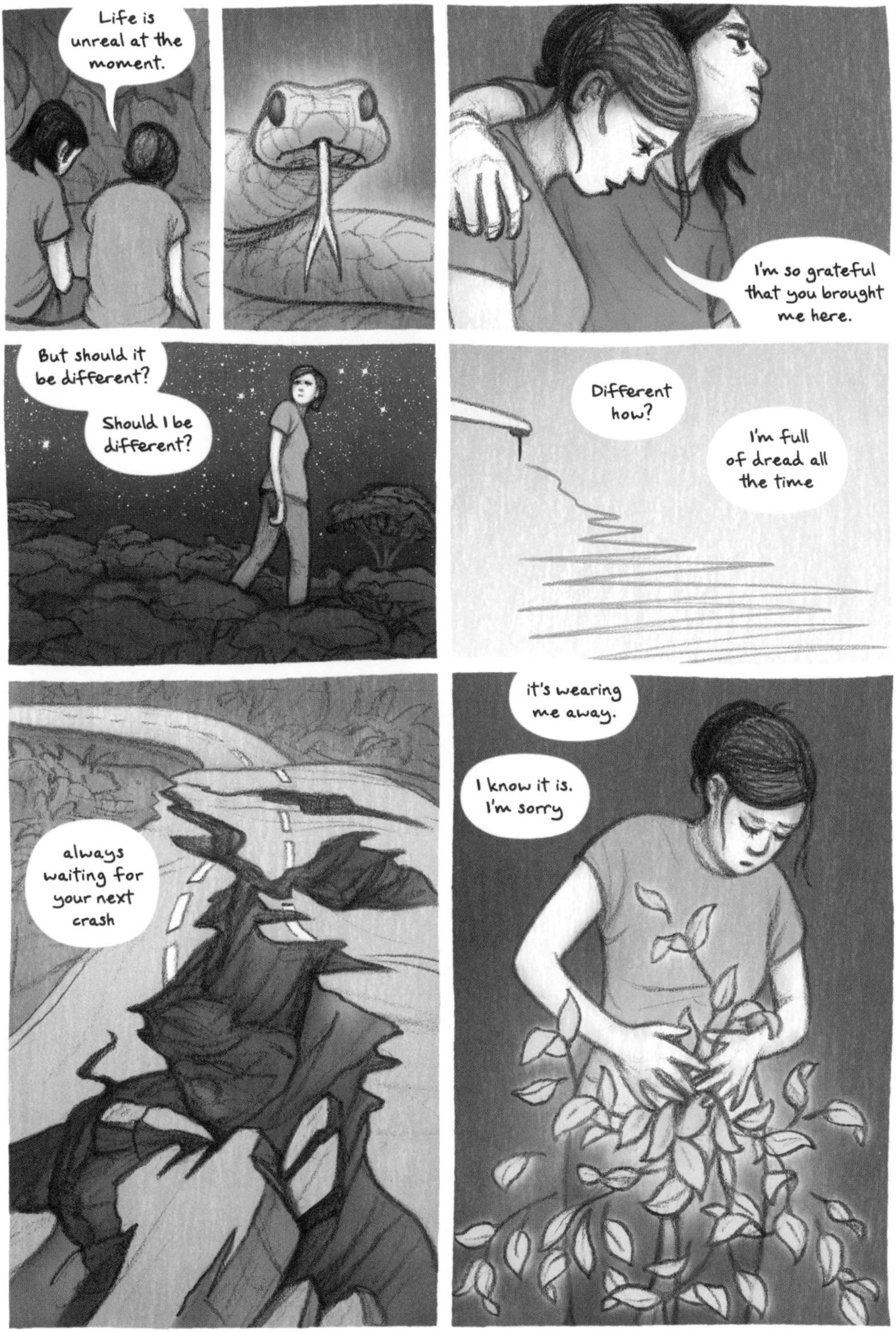
Life is unreal at the moment.
I'm so grateful that you brought me here.
But should it be different?
Should I be different?
Different how?
I'm full of dread all the time
always waiting for your next crash
it's wearing me away.
I know it is. I'm sorry

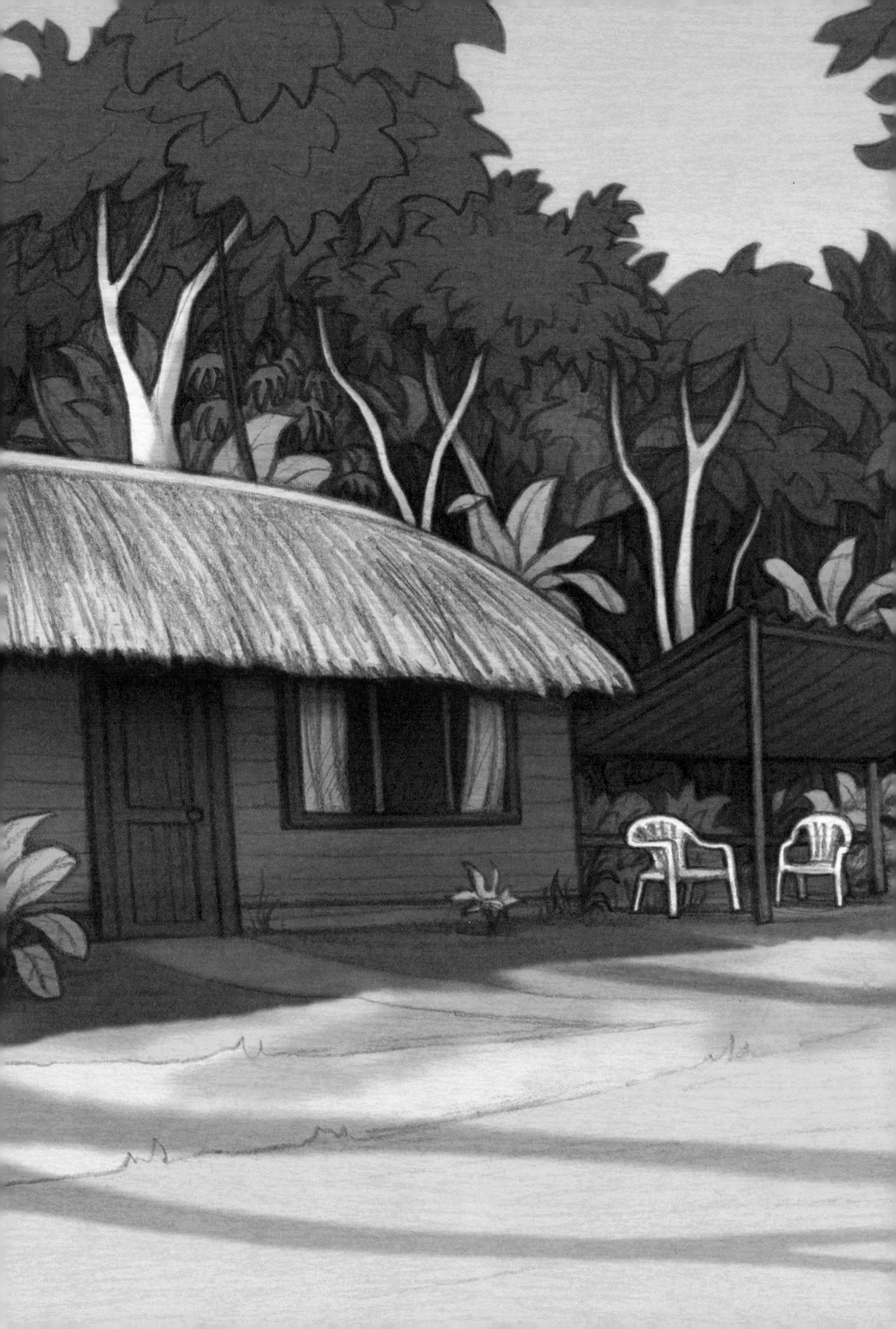

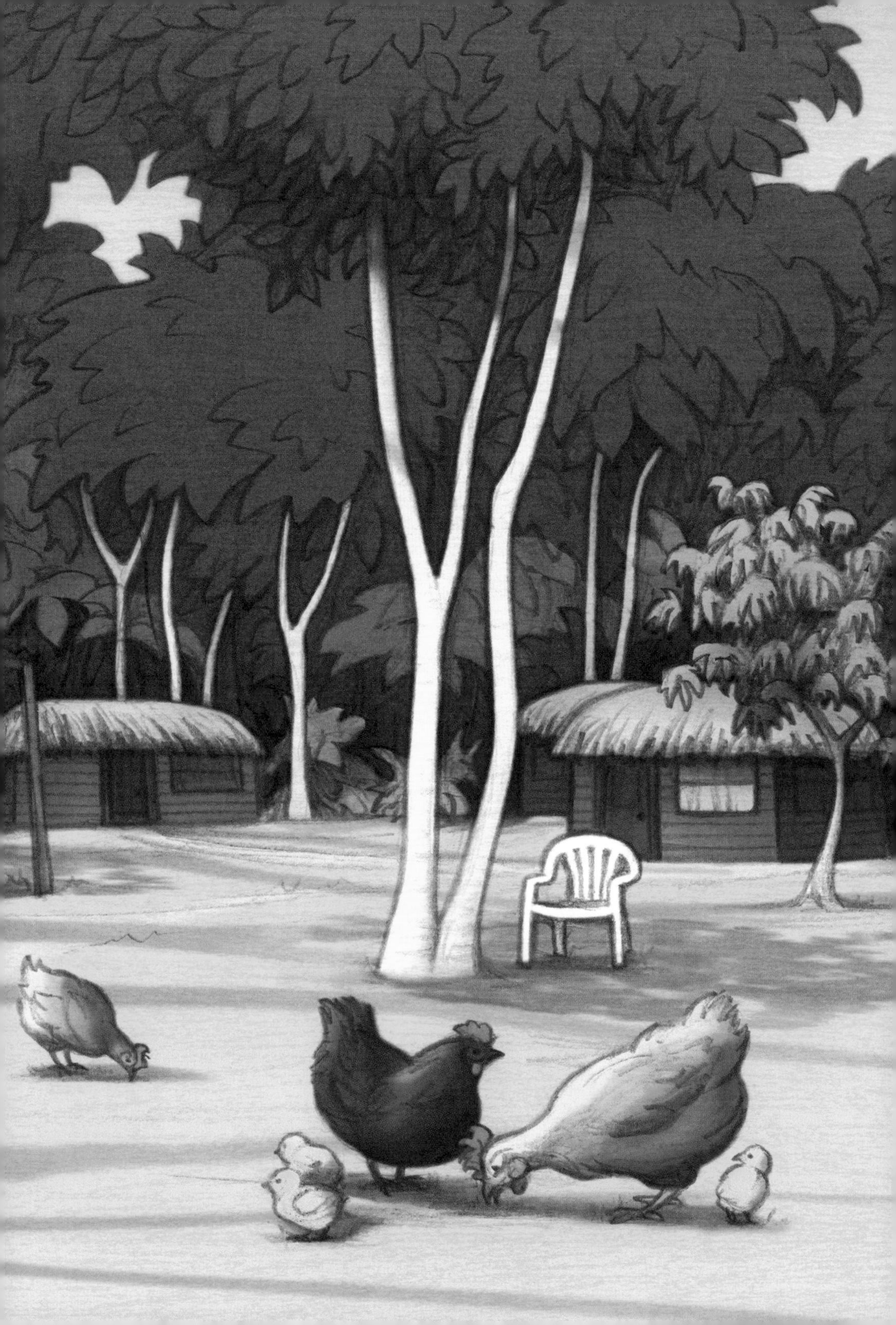

The Yucatán Peninsula

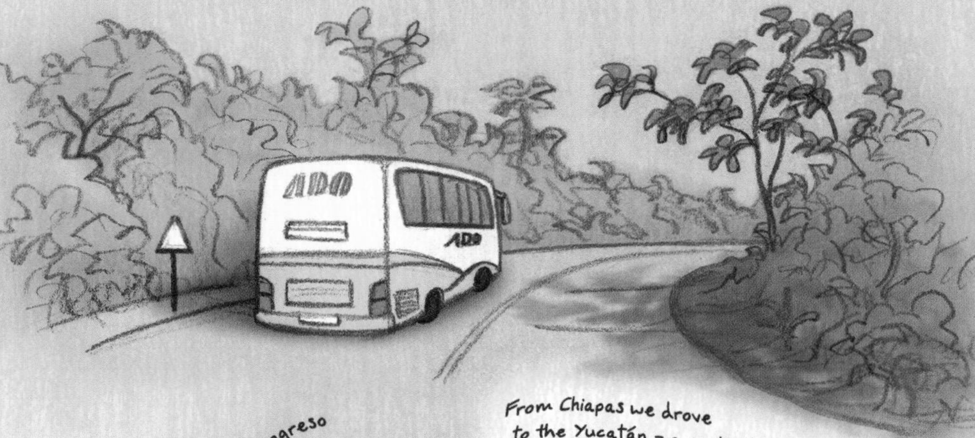
ADO
ADO
ADO

From Chiapas we drove to the Yucatán – a part of Mexico that at one time was an independent republic. It felt so different to what had come before, it was like we'd crossed a border to somewhere completely new.

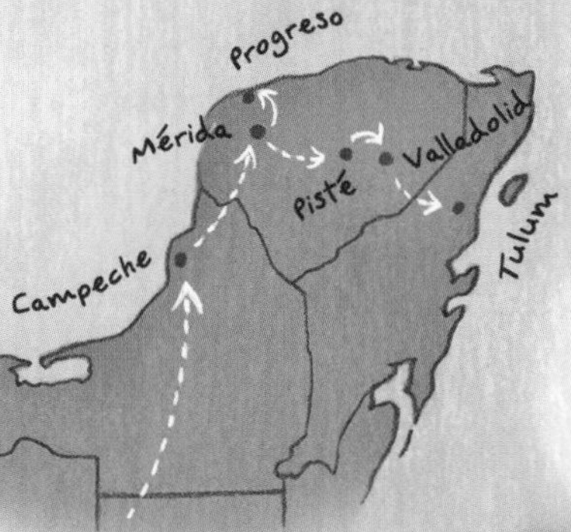
Progreso
Mérida
Valladolid
Pisté
Tulum
Campeche

The Yucatán peninsula is made up of three states – Yucatán, Campeche and Quintana Roo. It's a baking hot, flat limestone shelf with no surface water. A network of fissures and sink-holes drain rainwater into a vast underground network of caves and rivers.

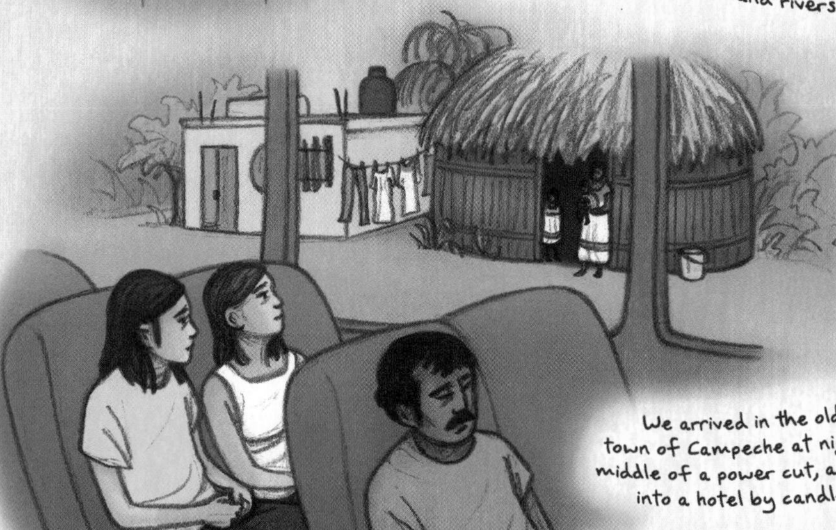

We arrived in the old port town of Campeche at night, in the middle of a power cut, and booked into a hotel by candle light.

After a few days there we headed to Mérida for Carnival.

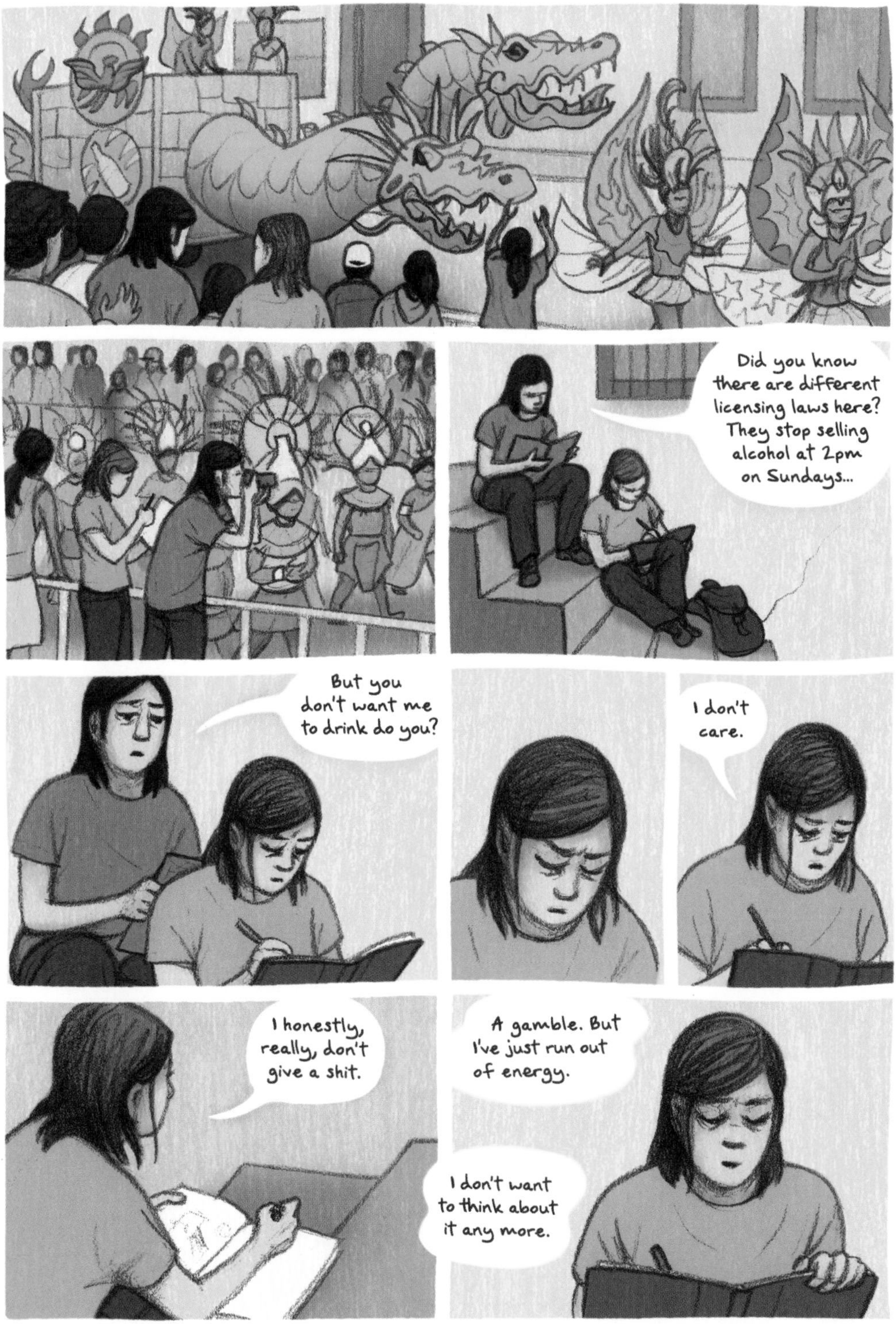
Did you know there are different licensing laws here? They stop selling alcohol at 2pm on Sundays...
But you don't want me to drink do you?
I don't care.
I honestly, really, don't give a shit.
A gamble. But I've just run out of energy.
I don't want to think about it any more.

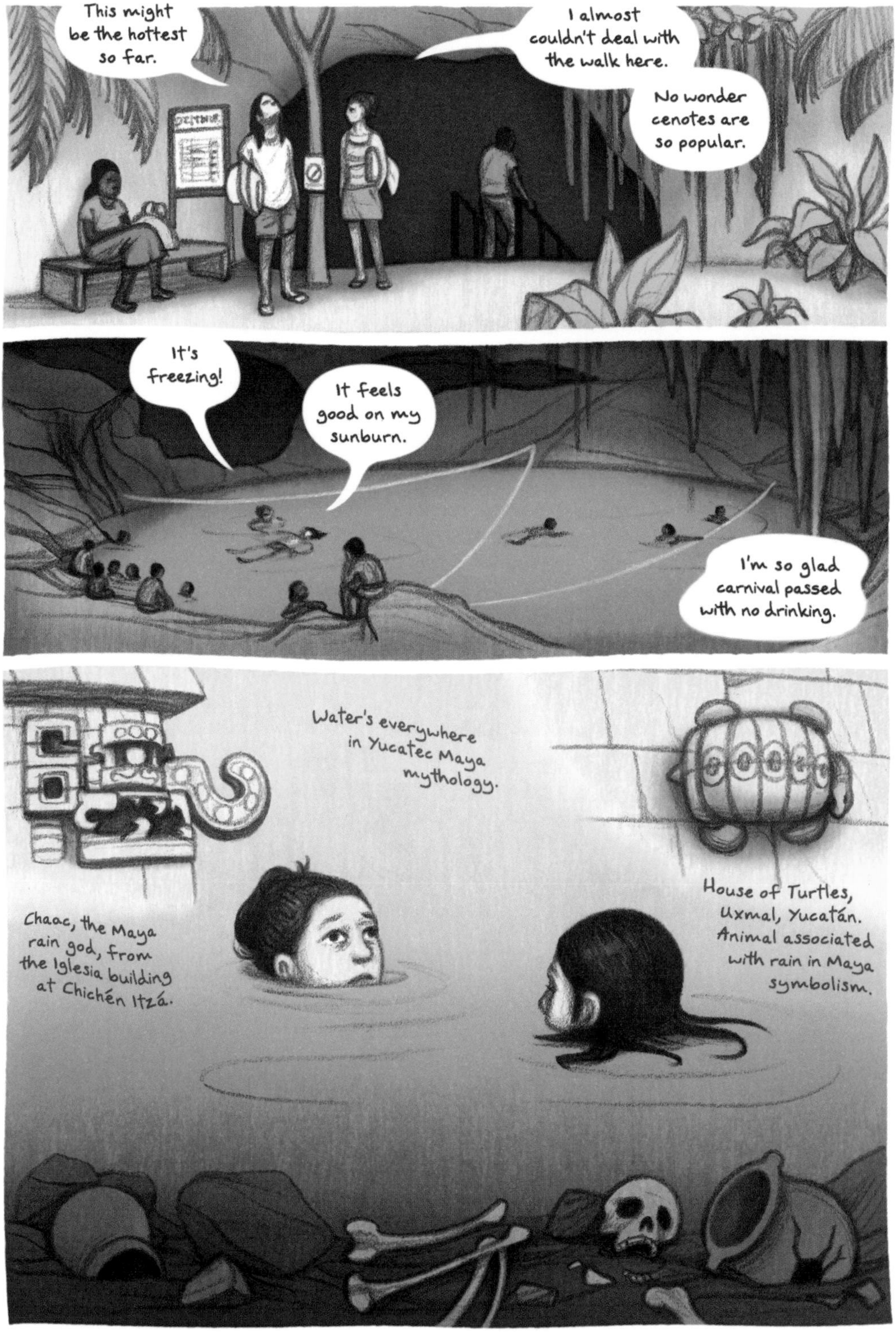
This might be the hottest so far.
I almost couldn't deal with the walk here.
No wonder cenotes are so popular.
It's freezing!
It feels good on my sunburn.
I'm so glad carnival passed with no drinking.
Water's everywhere in Yucatec Maya mythology.
Chaac, the Maya rain god, from the Iglesia building at Chichén Itzá.
House of Turtles, Uxmal, Yucatán. Animal associated with rain in Maya symbolism.

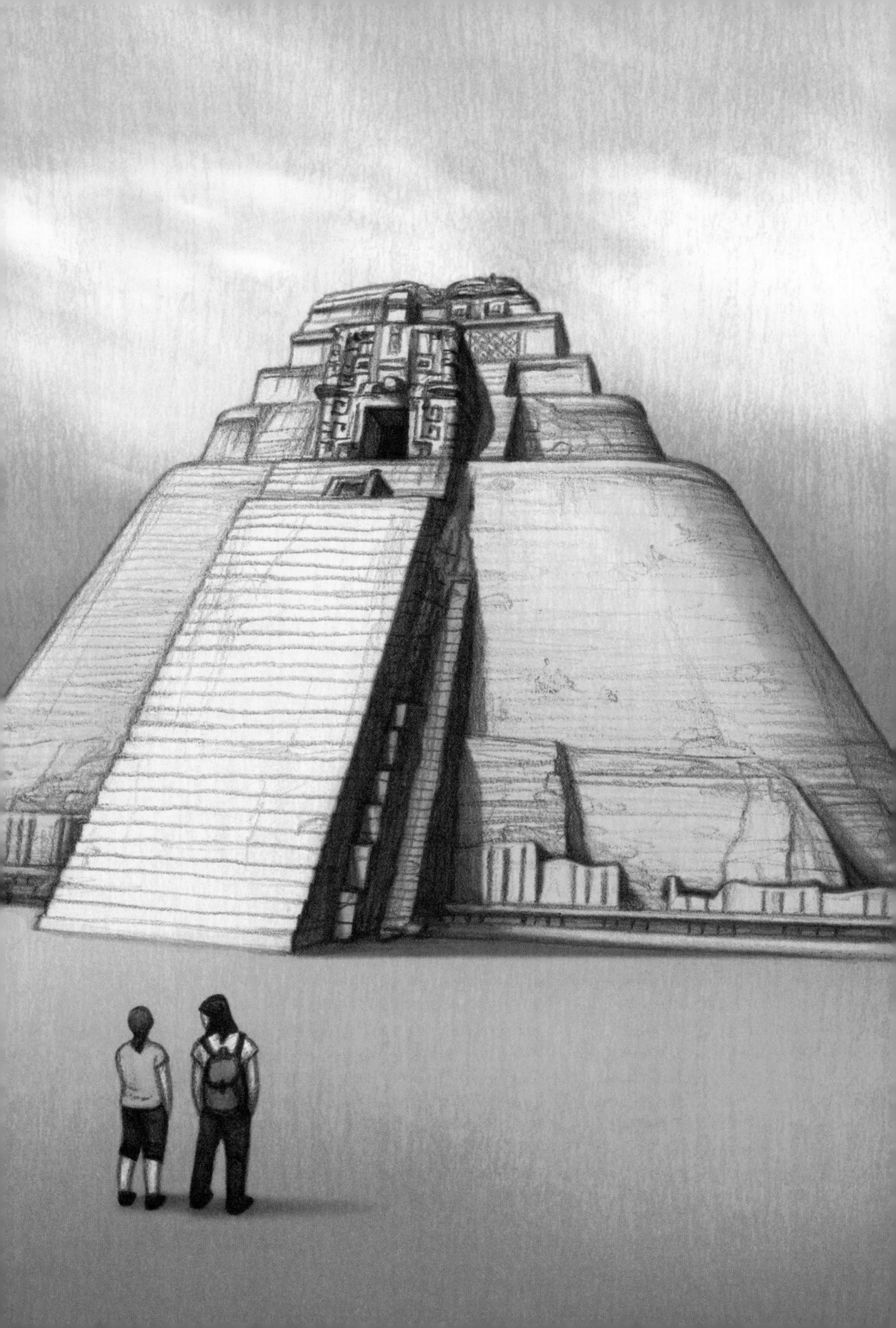

Yucatán

Chichén Itzá

Chichén Itzá is Mexico's most-visited archaeological sites, due to its proximity to the Caribbean coast beaches. It was one of the largest Maya cities and is very famous for the El Castillo building.

El Castillo

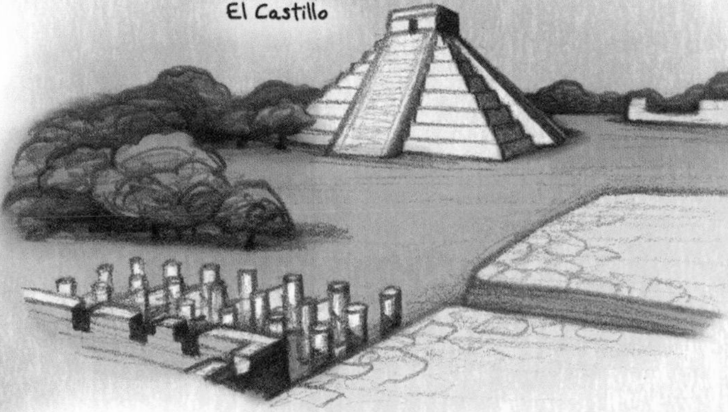

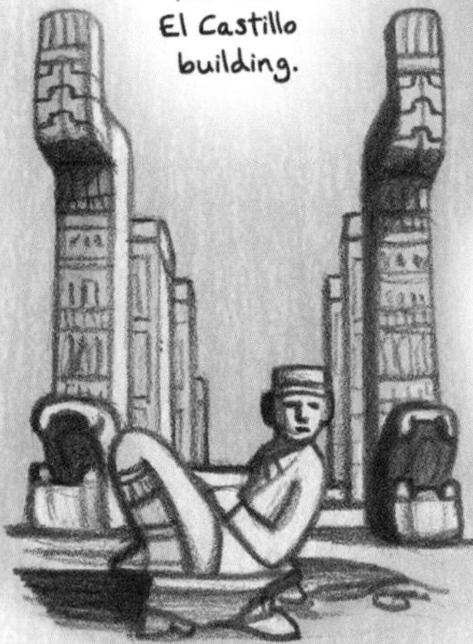

The Chacmool on top of the Temple of the Warriors. These sculptures have a bowl on their chest where ritual offerings are placed.

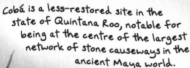

The observatory (or 'el caracol')

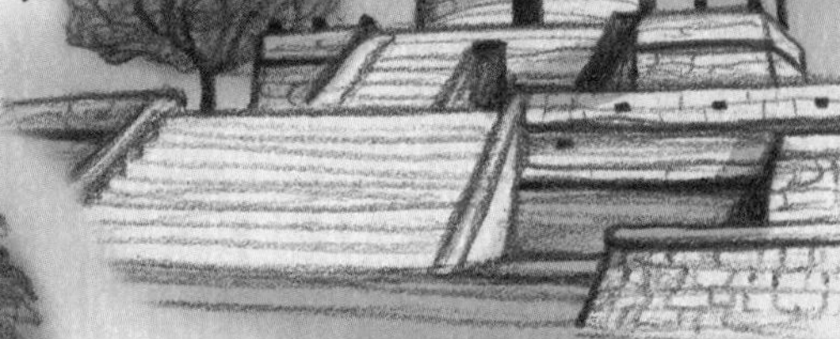

Cobá

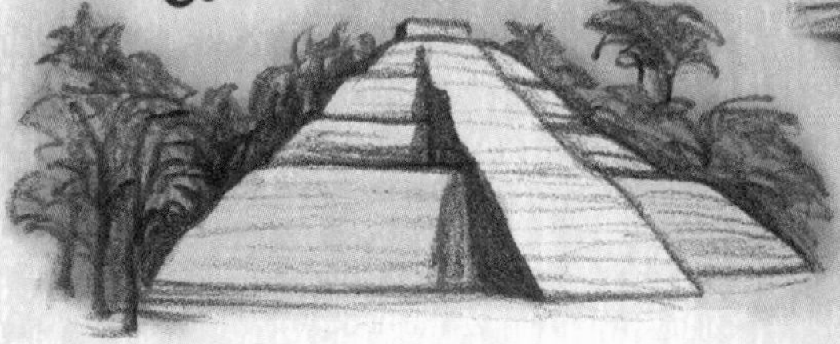

Cobá is a less-restored site in the state of Quintana Roo, notable for being at the centre of the largest network of stone causeways in the ancient Maya world.

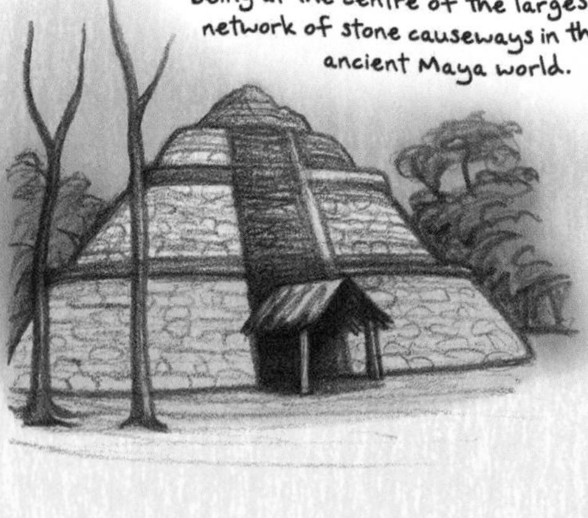

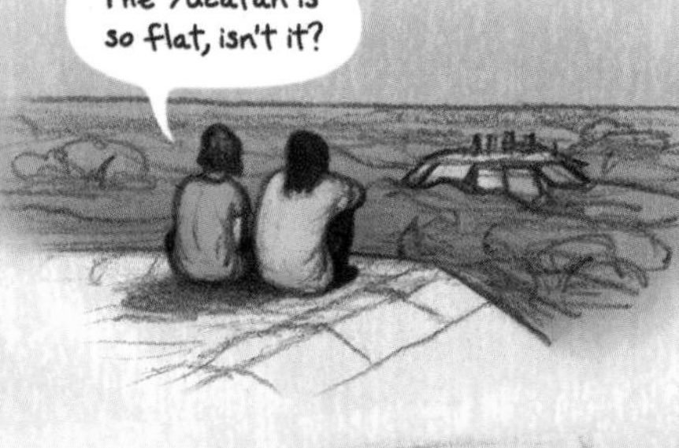
The Yucatán is so flat, isn't it?

Cobá like many of the Yucatán sites was filled with iguanas.

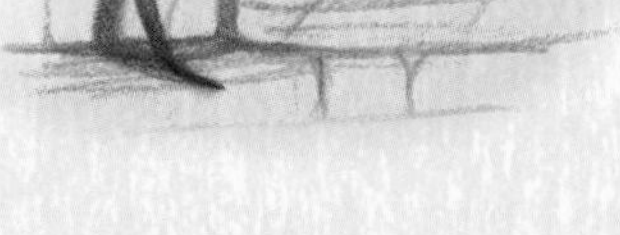

The Ruta Puuc

The Ruta Puuc is a network of roads in Yucatán state along which are located many important Maya sites in the Puuc style (characterised by the elaborate ornamentation of the facades of ceremonial buildings.)

We visited the sites Uxmal, Labná, Sayil and Kabah in a single day-trip from Mérida City. A bus dropped us off for a certain amount of time at each site and then ferried us to the next.

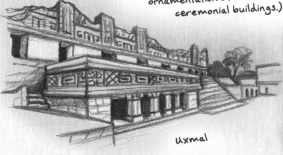

Uxmal

Labná

archeological sites

Sayil

Kabah

The architecture (particularly the use of columns) of the great palace at Sayil is quite distinctive and atypical.

'Codz poop' or the palace of the masks at Kabah. The facade is covered in repeated depictions of the long-nosed rain god Chaac.

Large-scale repetitions of the same motif are rare in Maya art which makes this building unusual too.

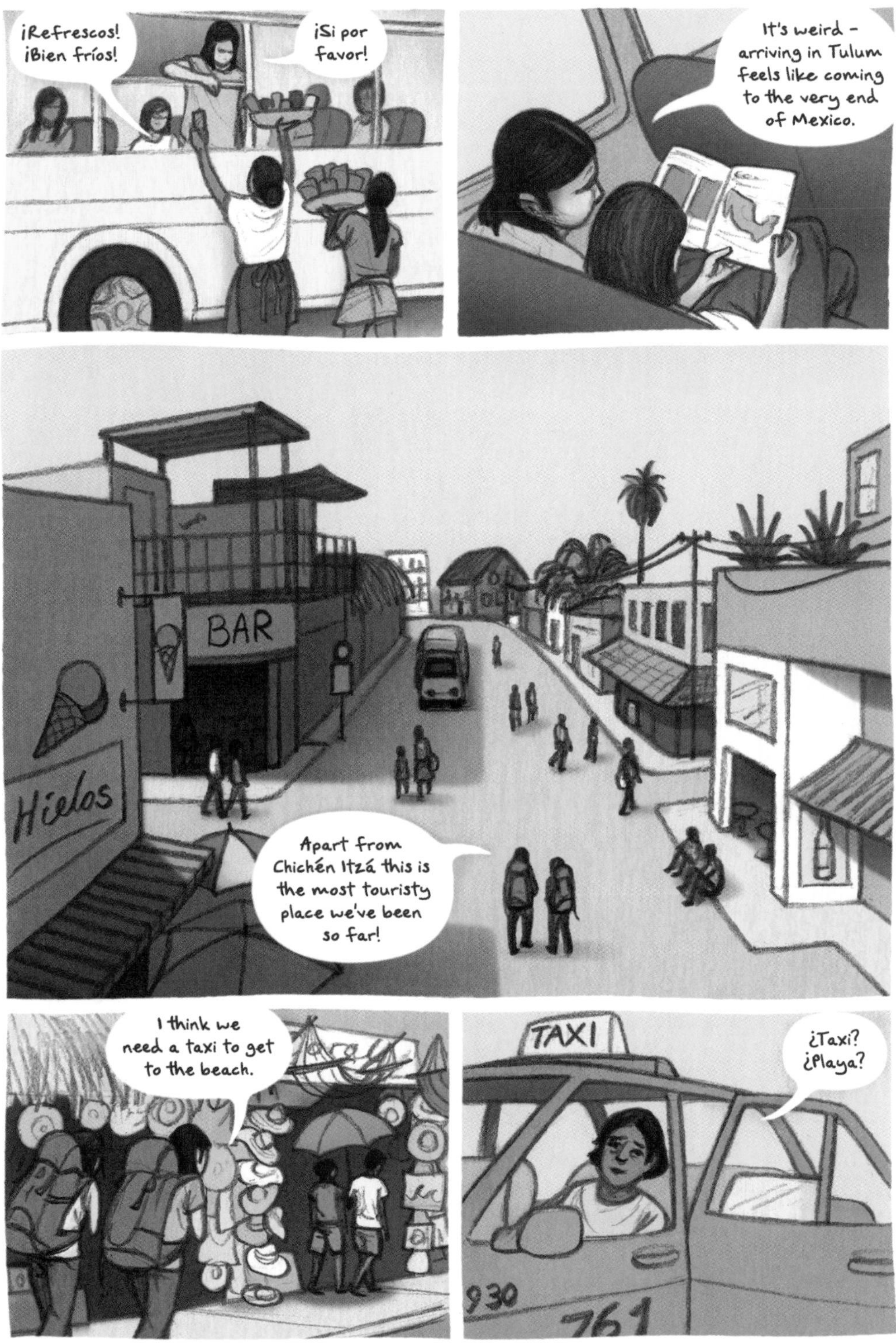
¡Refrescos! ¡Bien fríos!
¡Si por favor!
It's weird - arriving in Tulum feels like coming to the very end of Mexico.
BAR
Hielos
Apart from Chichén Itzá this is the most touristy place we've been so far!
I think we need a taxi to get to the beach.
TAXI
¿Taxi? ¿Playa?
930
761

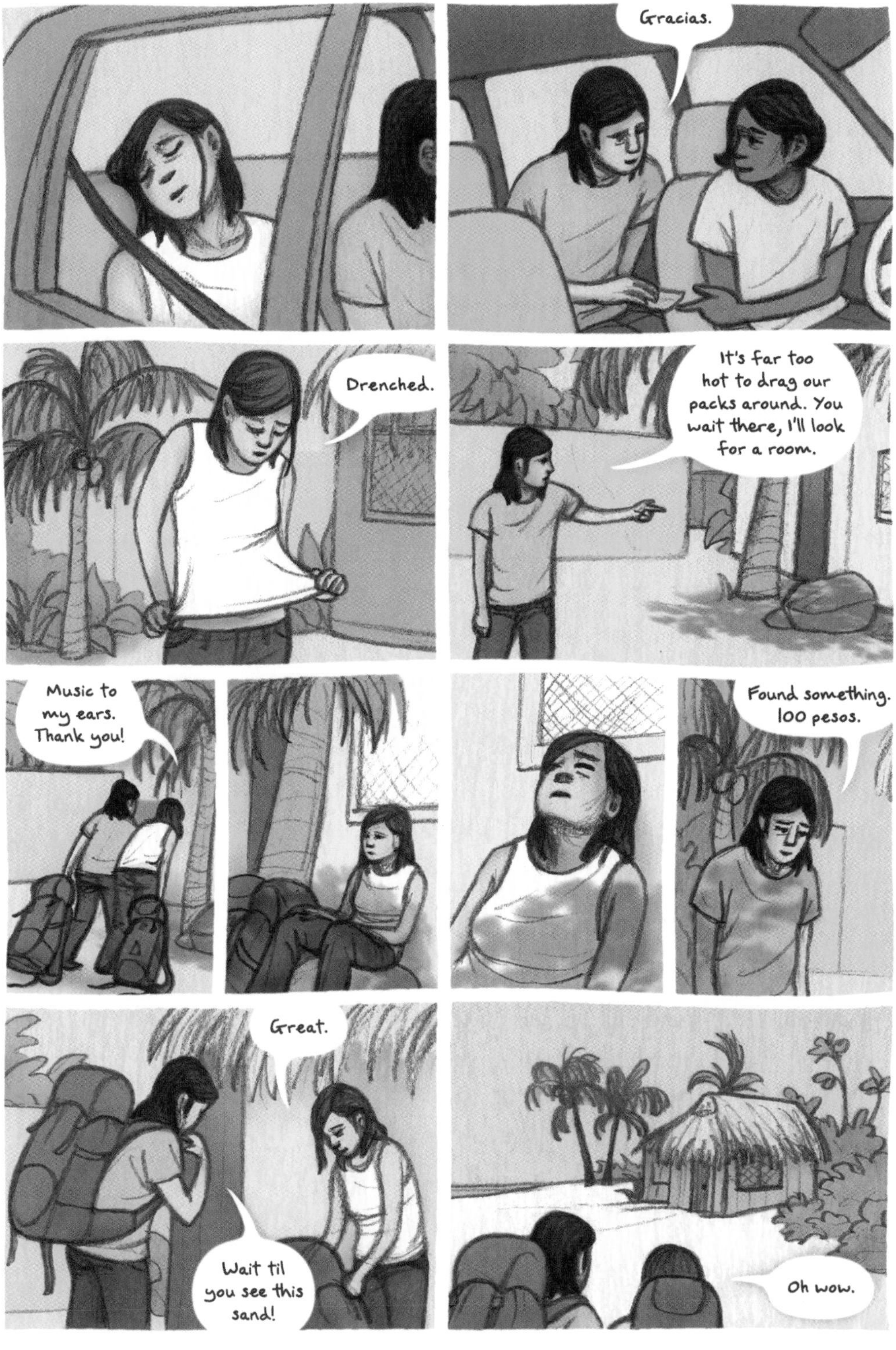
Gracias.
Drenched.
It's far too hot to drag our packs around. You wait there, I'll look for a room.
Music to my ears. Thank you!
Found something. 100 pesos.
Great.
Wait til you see this sand!
Oh wow.

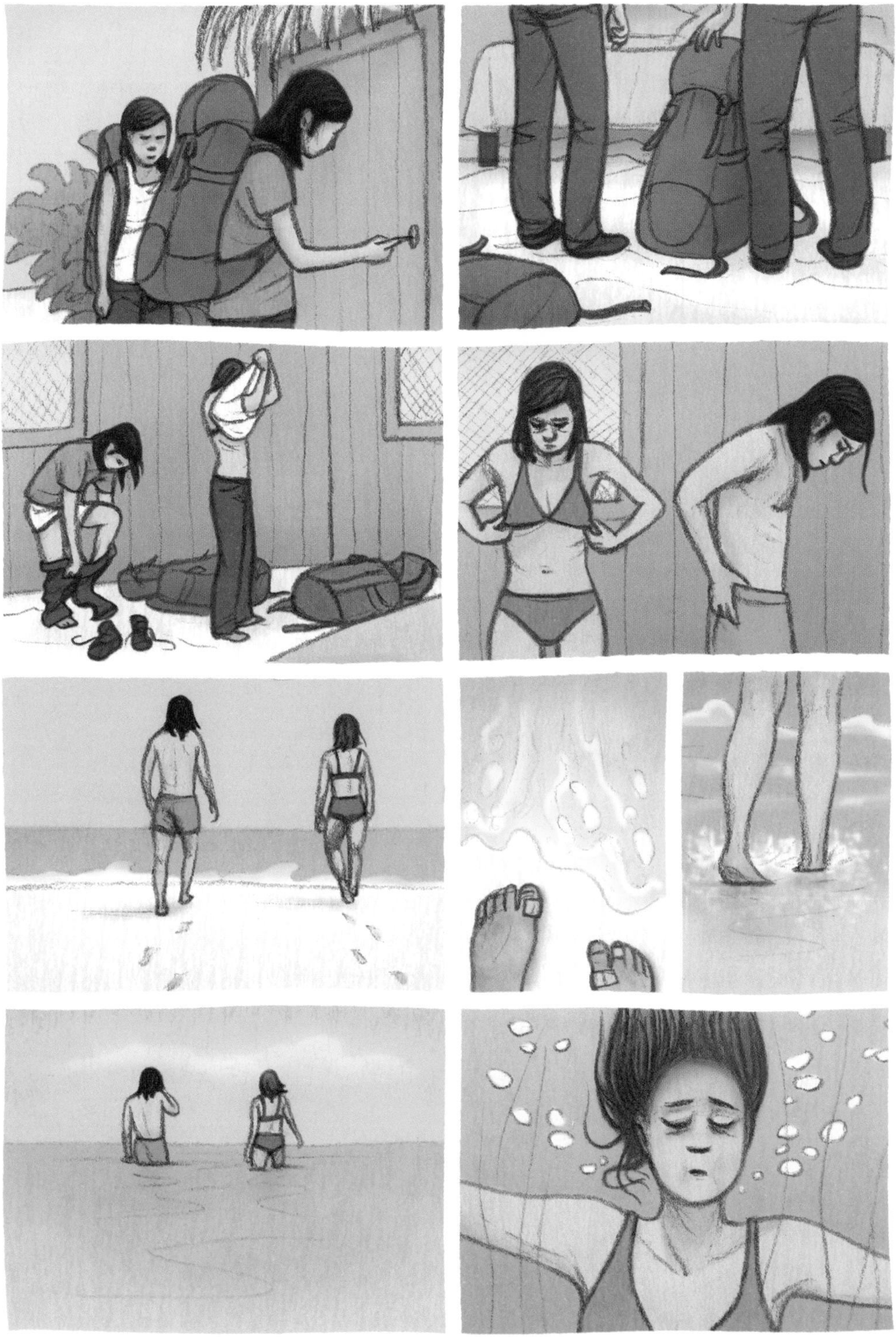

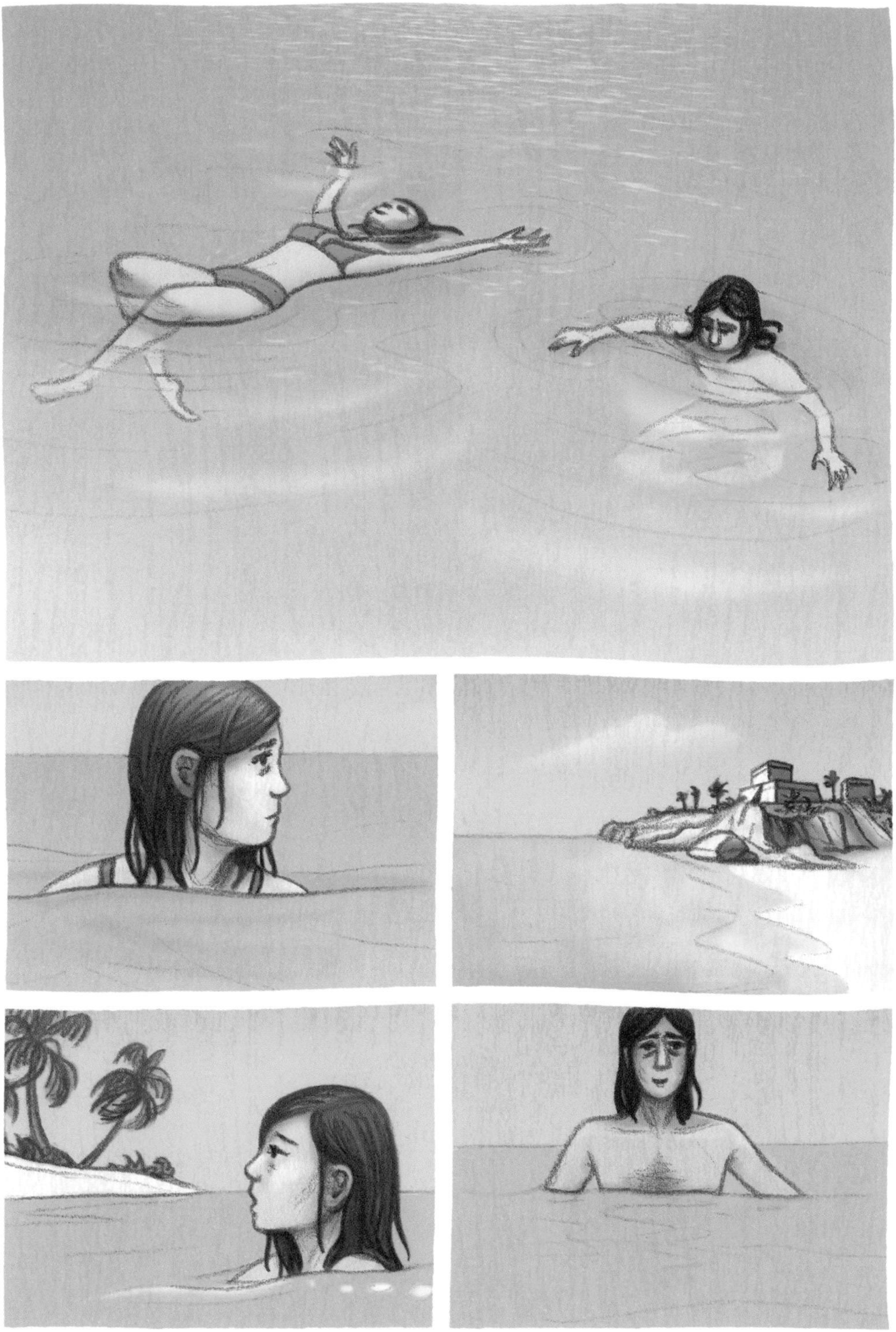

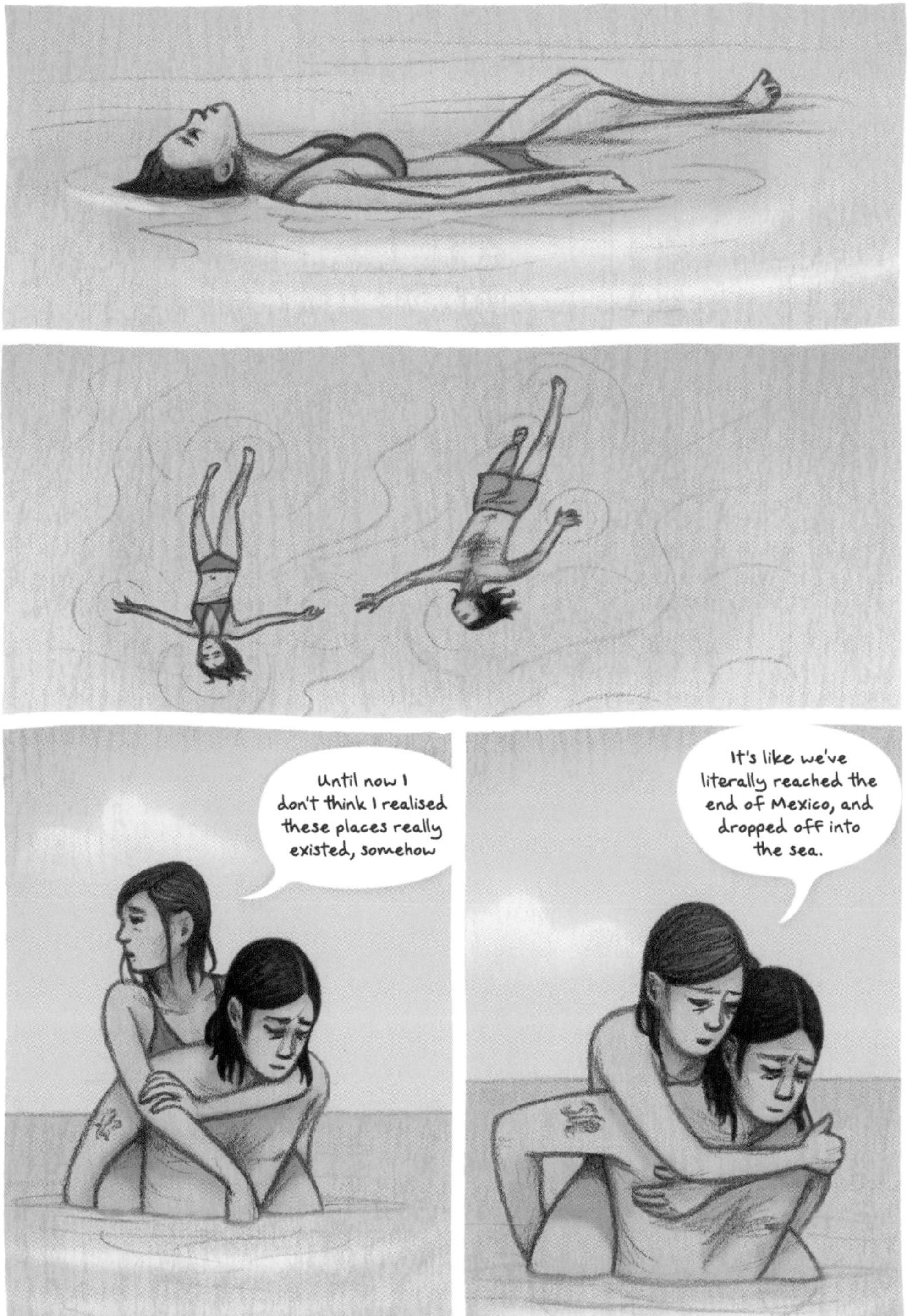
Until now I don't think I realised these places really existed, somehow
It's like we've literally reached the end of Mexico, and dropped off into the sea.

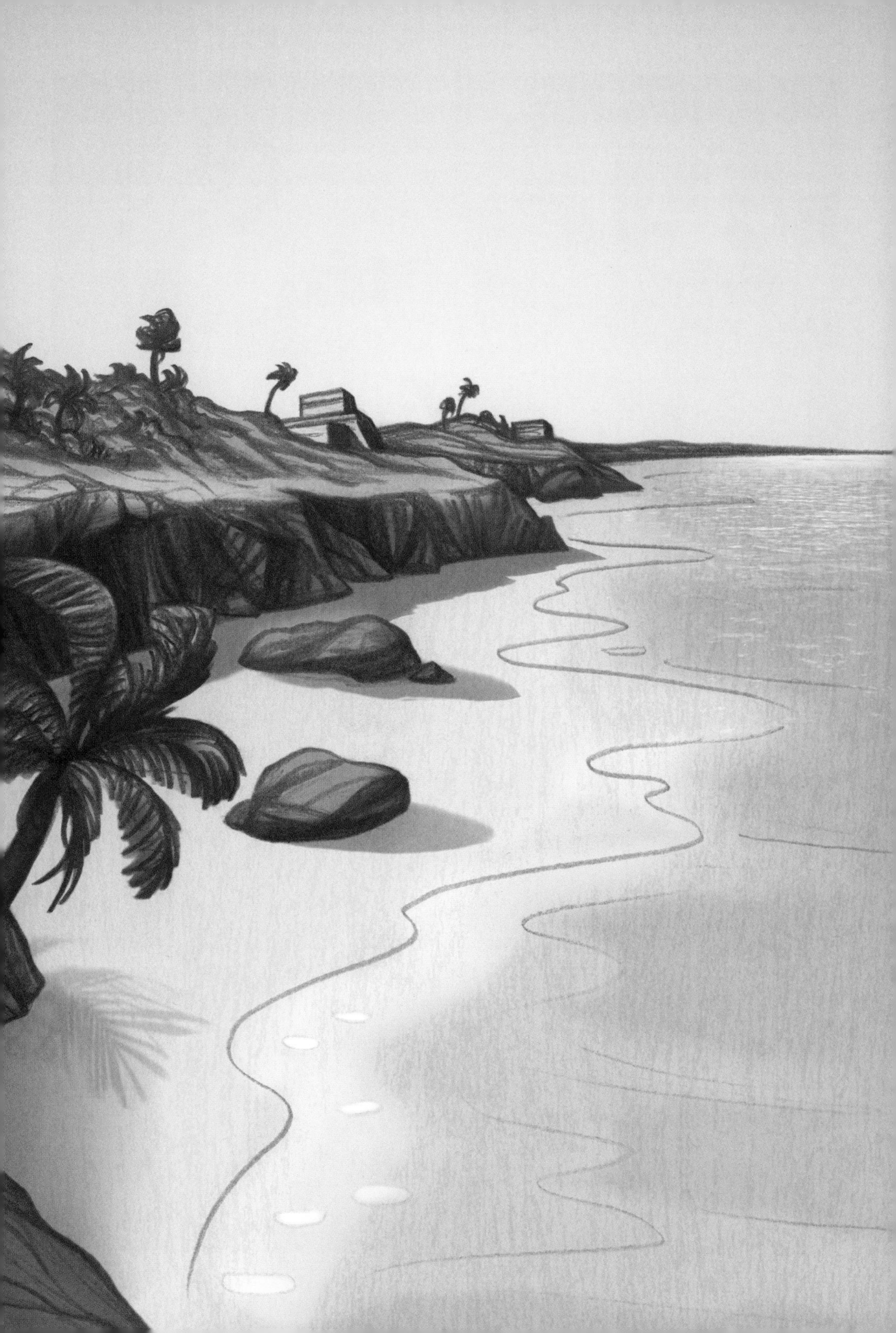

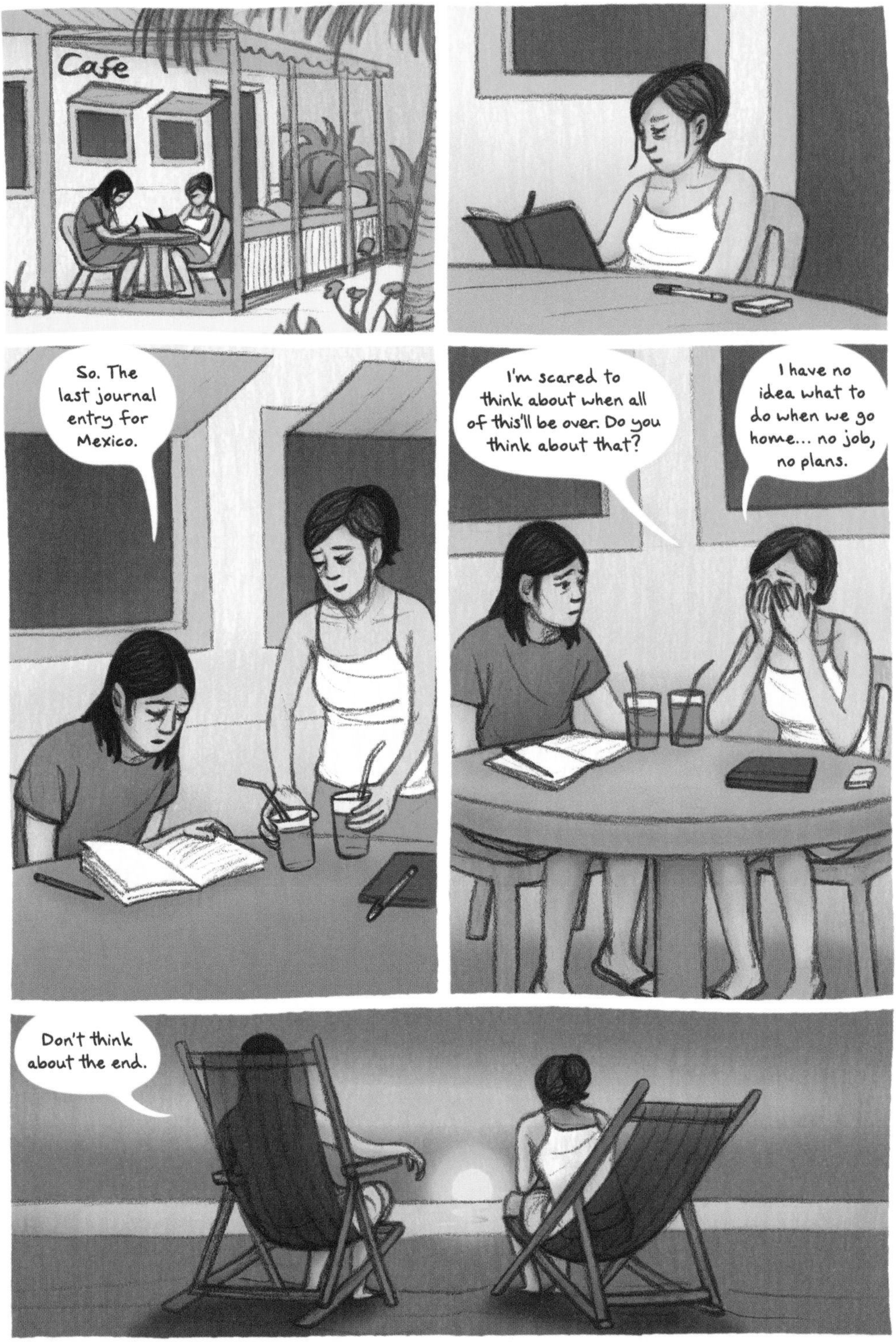
Cafe
So. The last journal entry for Mexico.
I'm scared to think about when all of this'll be over. Do you think about that?
I have no idea what to do when we go home... no job, no plans.
Don't think about the end.

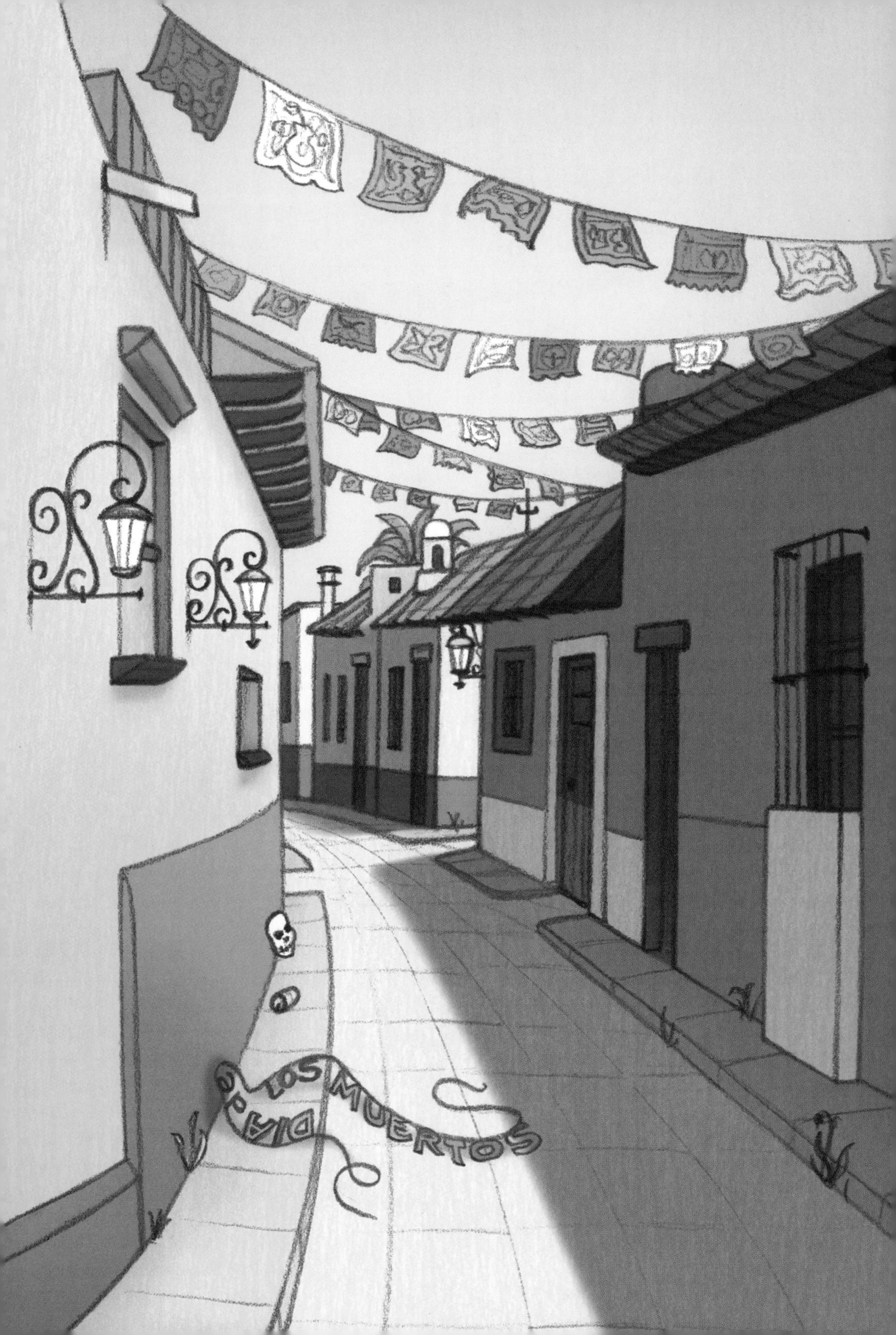
LOS MUERTOS

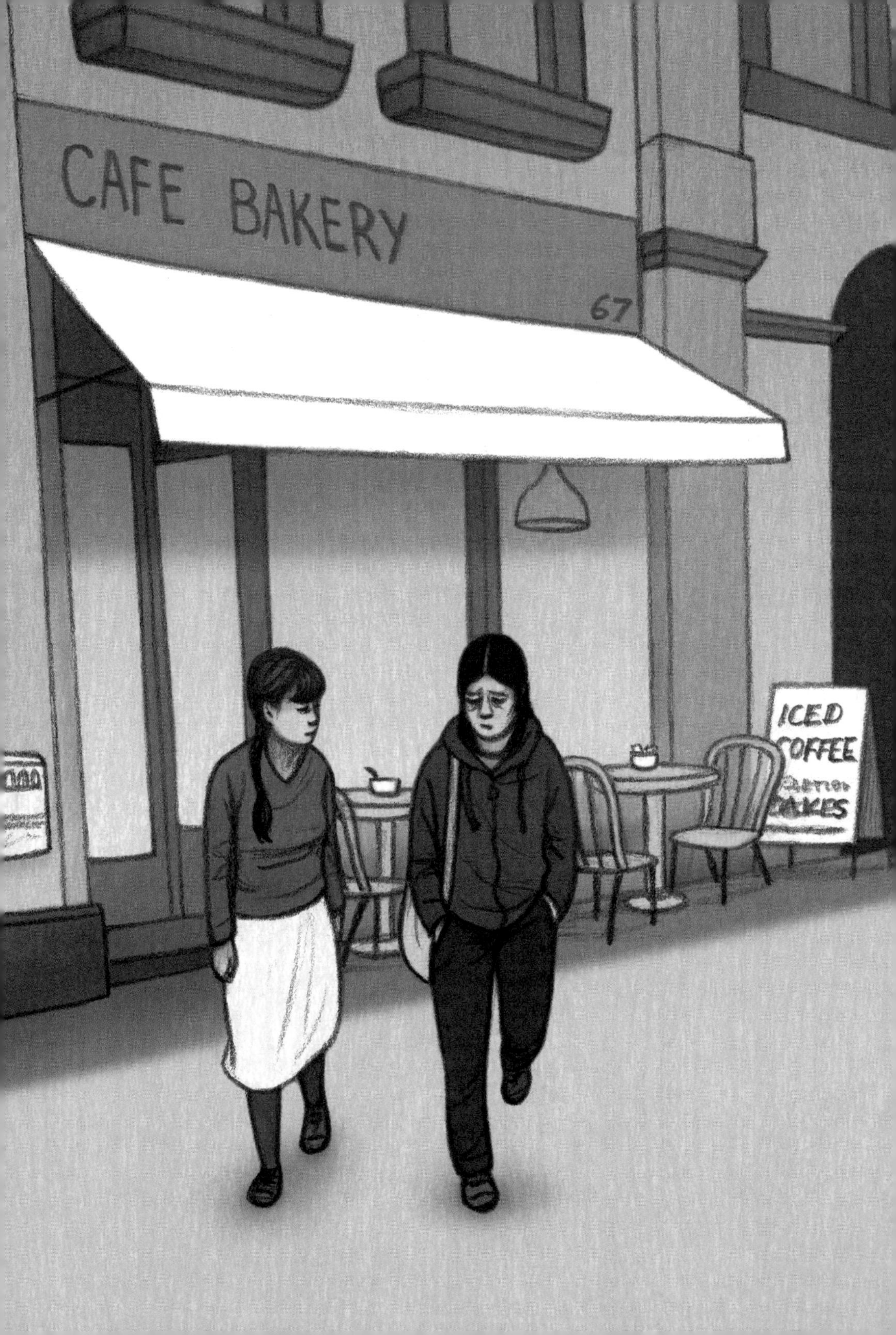
CAFE BAKERY
67
ICED
COFFEE

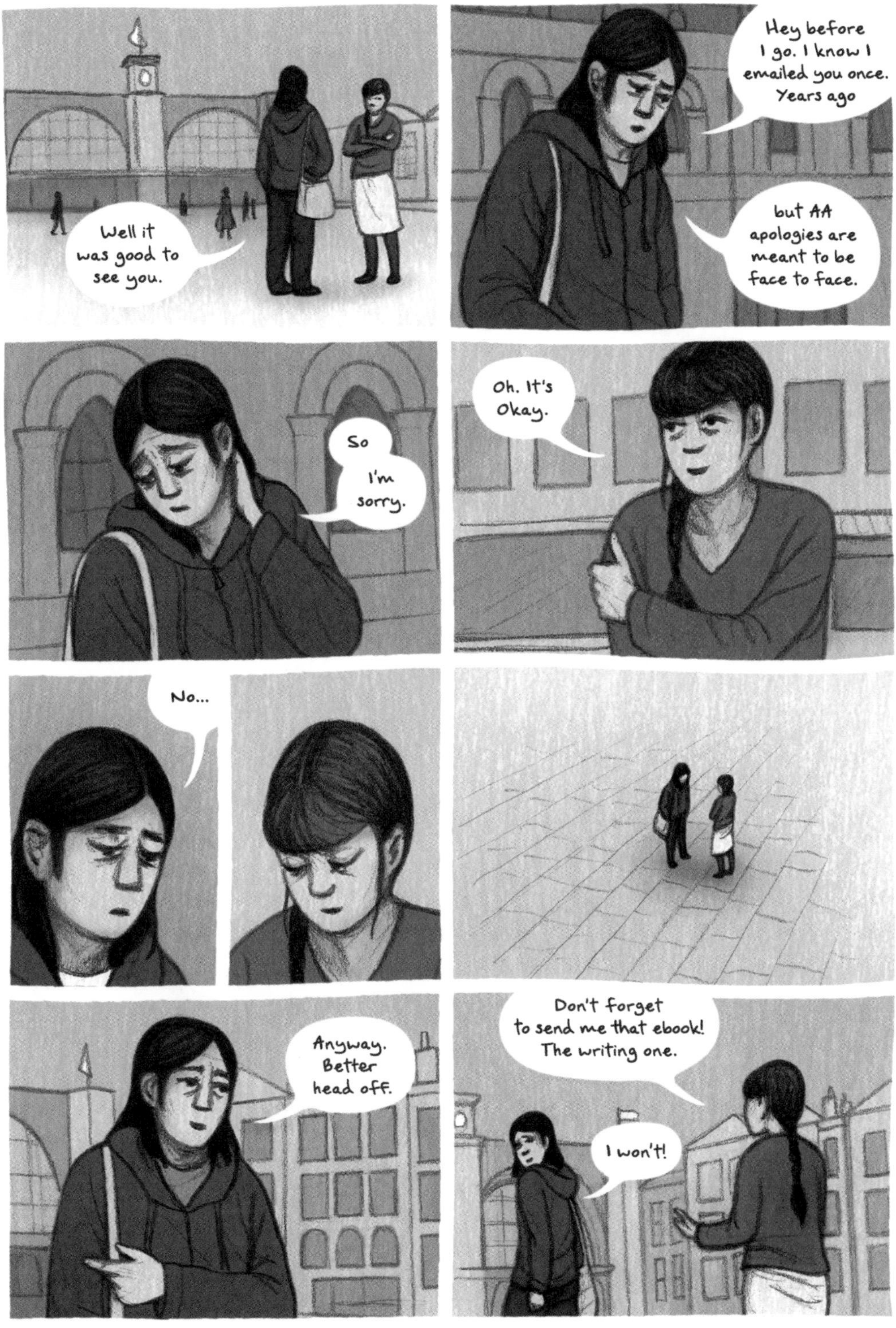

Well it was good to see you.
Hey before I go. I know I emailed you once. Years ago
but AA apologies are meant to be face to face.
So
I'm sorry.
Oh. It's Okay.
No...
Anyway. Better head off.
Don't forget to send me that ebook! The writing one.
I won't!

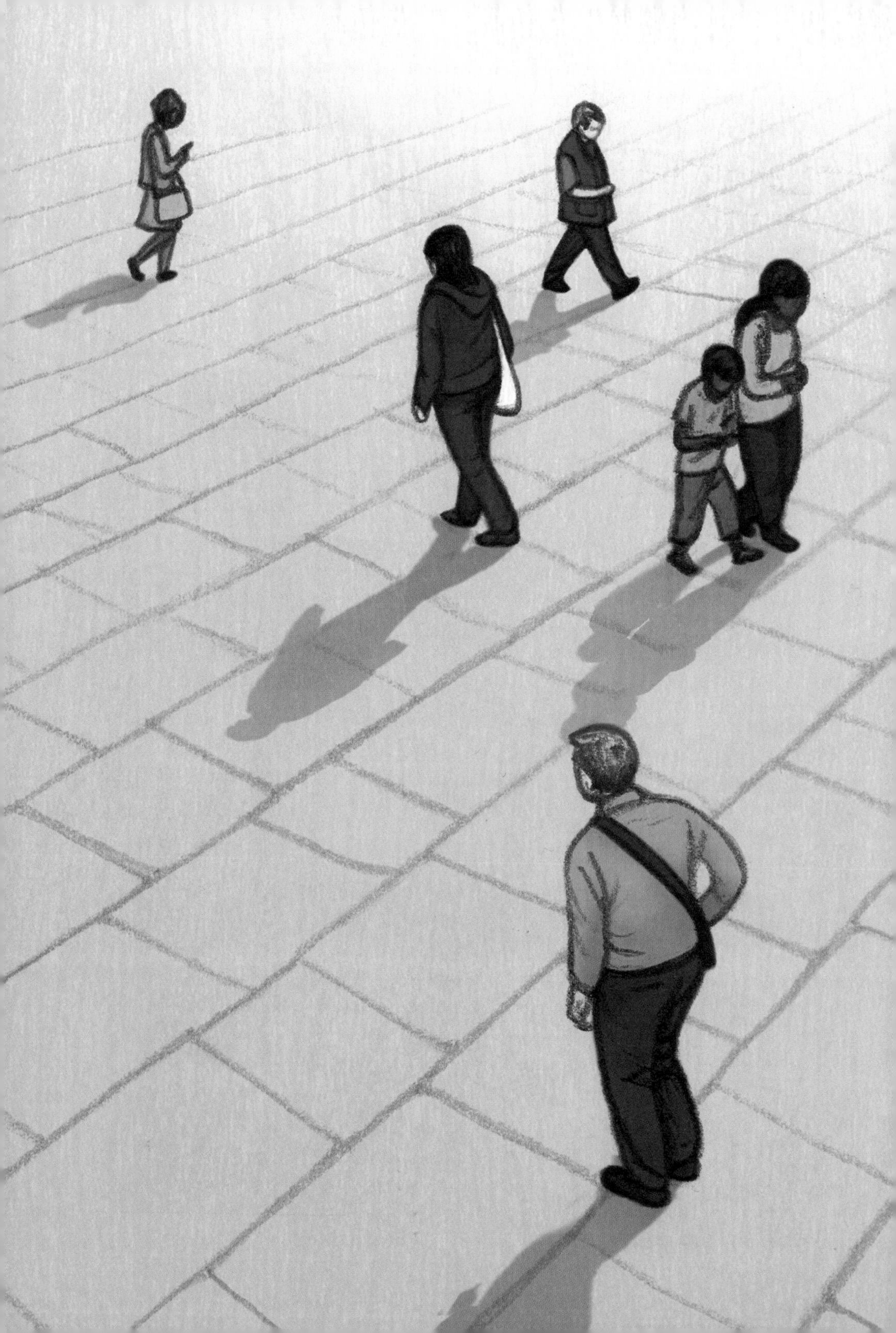

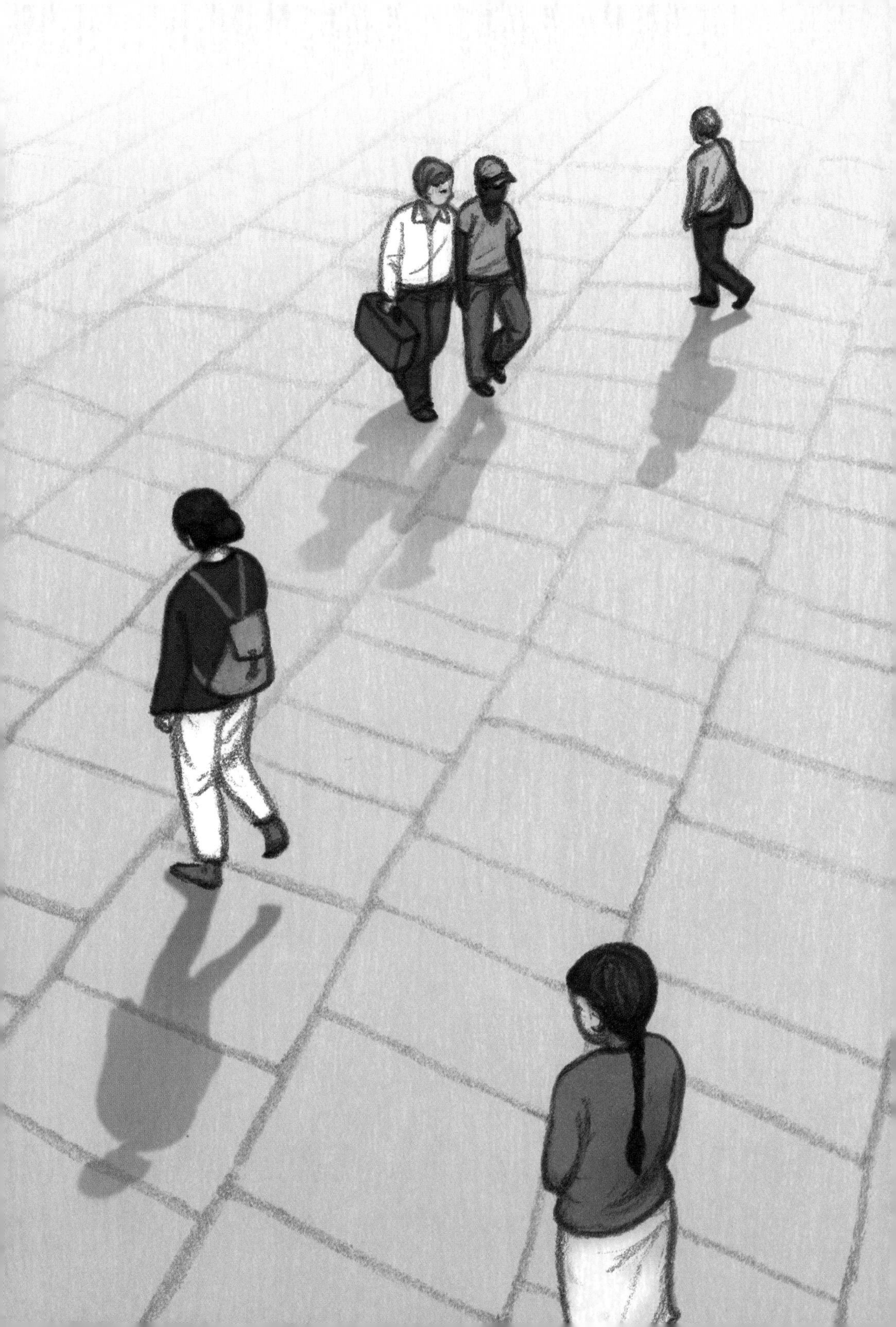

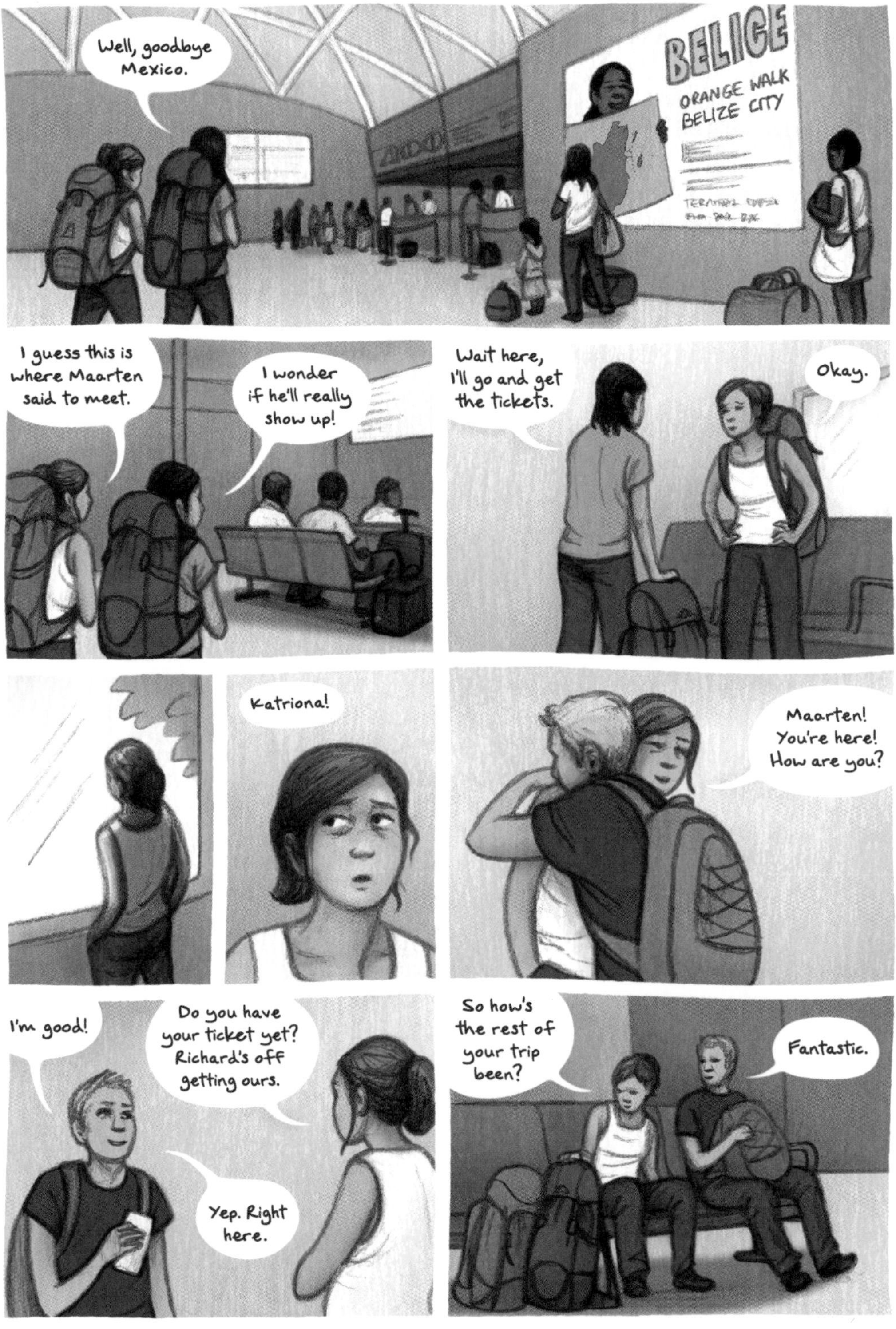
Well, goodbye Mexico.
BELICE
ORANGE WALK
BELIZE CITY
I guess this is where Maarten said to meet.
I wonder if he'll really show up!
Wait here, I'll go and get the tickets.
Okay.
Katriona!
Maarten! You're here! How are you?
I'm good!
Do you have your ticket yet? Richard's off getting ours.
Yep. Right here.
So how's the rest of your trip been?
Fantastic.

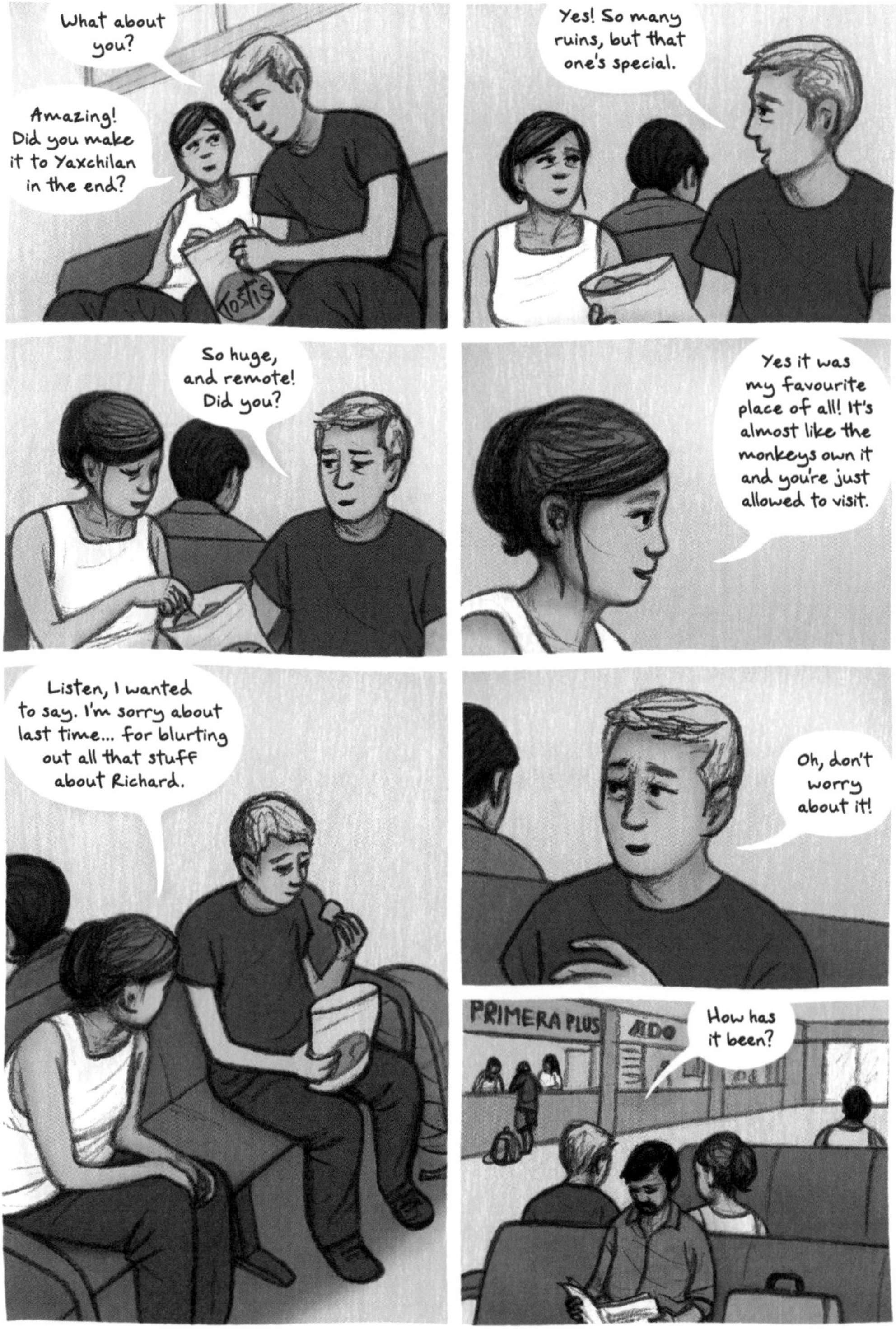
What about you?
Amazing! Did you make it to Yaxchilan in the end?
Tostis
Yes! So many ruins, but that one's special.
So huge, and remote! Did you?
Yes it was my favourite place of all! It's almost like the monkeys own it and you're just allowed to visit.
Listen, I wanted to say. I'm sorry about last time... for blurting out all that stuff about Richard.
Oh, don't worry about it!
PRIMERA PLUS
ADO
How has it been?

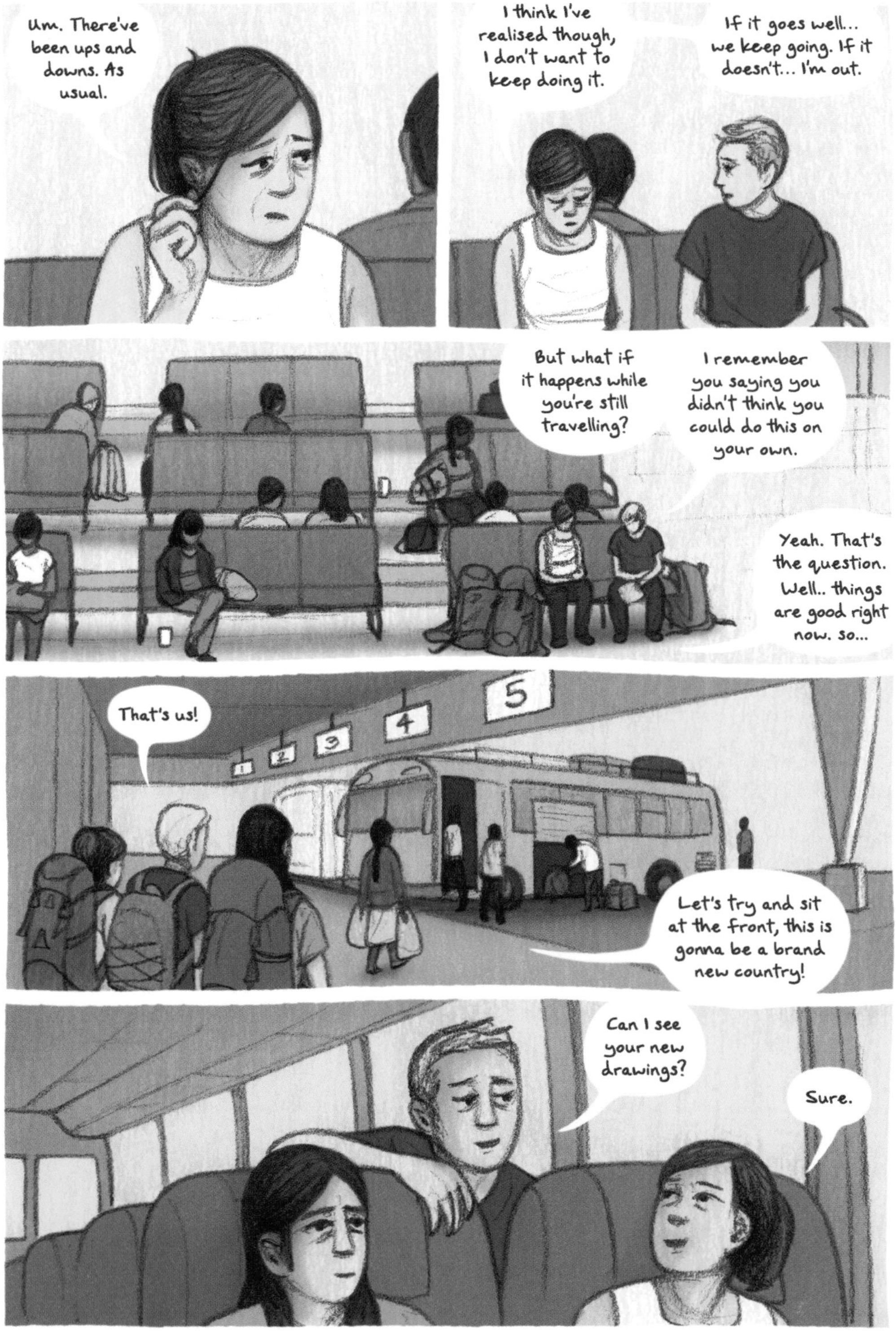
Um. There've been ups and downs. As usual.
I think I've realised though, I don't want to keep doing it.
If it goes well... we keep going. If it doesn't... I'm out.
But what if it happens while you're still travelling?
I remember you saying you didn't think you could do this on your own.
Yeah. That's the question. Well.. things are good right now. so...
That's us!
1
2
3
4
5
Let's try and sit at the front, this is gonna be a brand new country!
Can I see your new drawings?
Sure.

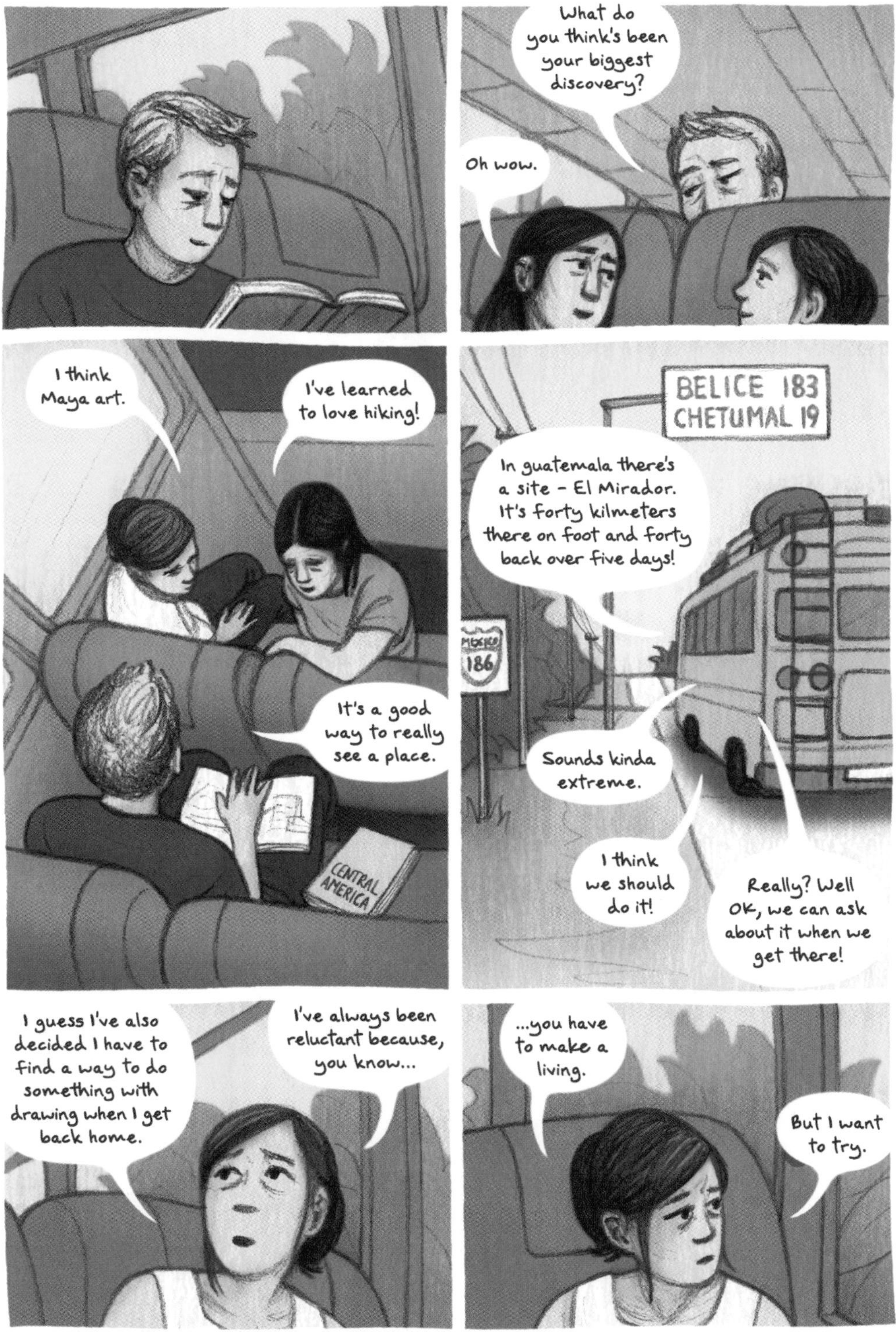
What do you think's been your biggest discovery?
Oh wow.
I think Maya art.
I've learned to love hiking!
It's a good way to really see a place.
CENTRAL AMERICA
BELICE 183
CHETUMAL 19
MEXICO
186
In guatemala there's a site - El Mirador. It's forty kilmeters there on foot and forty back over five days!
Sounds kinda extreme.
I think we should do it!
Really? Well OK, we can ask about it when we get there!
I guess I've also decided I have to find a way to do something with drawing when I get back home.
I've always been reluctant because, you know...
...you have to make a living.
But I want to try.

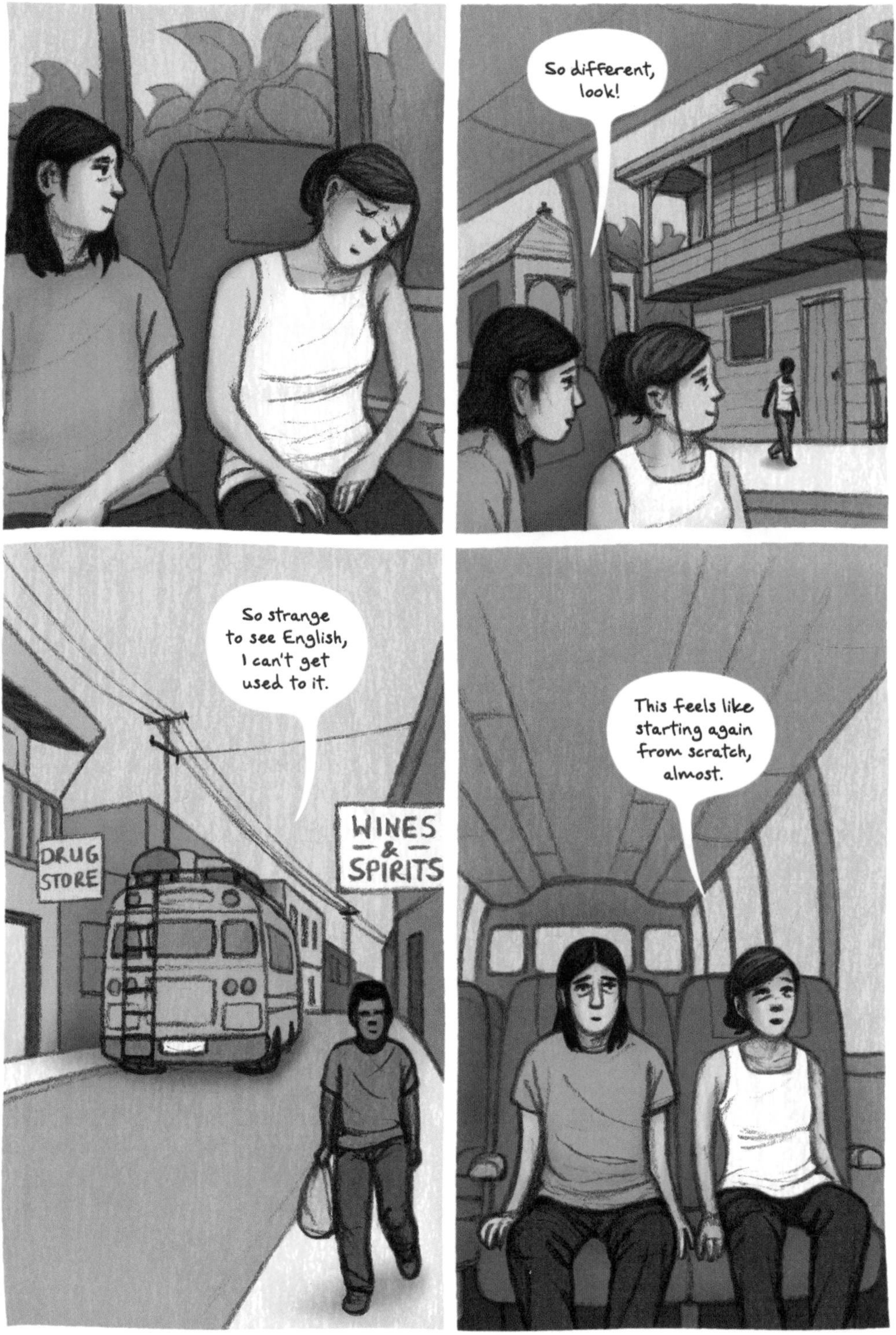
So different, look!
So strange to see English, I can't get used to it.
DRUG STORE
WINES & SPIRITS
This feels like starting again from scratch, almost.

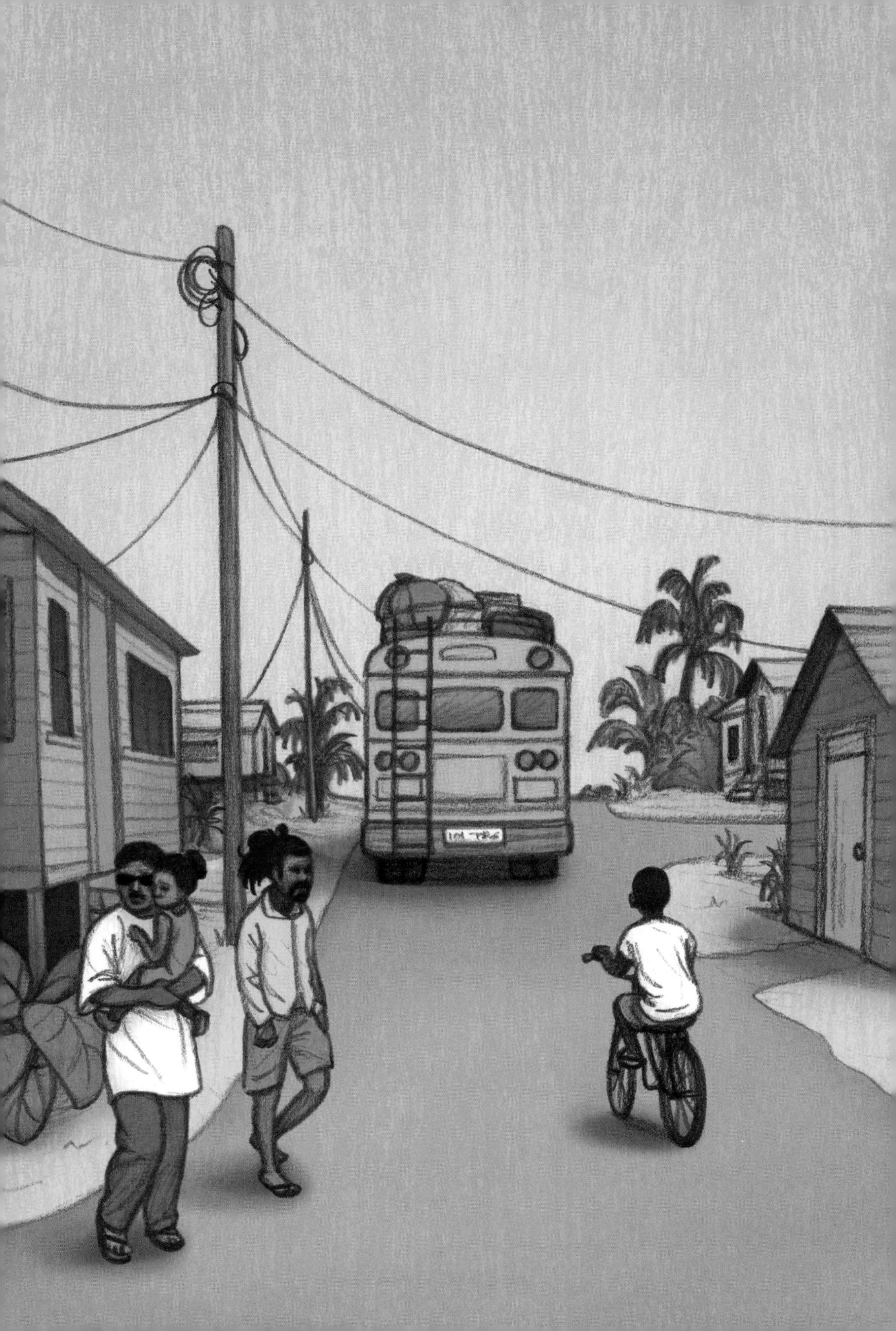

Published by Avery Hill Publishing, 2018

10 9 8 7 6 5 4 3 2 1

Copyright © Katriona Chapman, 2018

With thanks to Sergio Galaviz and Mona Robles

Katriona Chapman has asserted her right under the Copyright,
Designs and Patents Act 1988 to be identified as the author of this work.

First published in the UK in 2018 by

Avery Hill Publishing
Unit 8
5 Durham Yard
London
E2 6QF

A CIP record for this book is available from the British Library
ISBN: 978-1-910395-38-7

Katriona Chapman is a comic artist and illustrator based in London UK.
www.katrionachapman.com

Avery Hill Publishing
www.averyhillpublishing.com